Gothic incest

Gothic incest

GENDER, SEXUALITY AND TRANSGRESSION

Jenny DiPlacidi

MANCHESTER UNIVERSITY PRESS

Copyright © Jenny DiPlacidi 2018

The right of Jenny DiPlacidi to be identified as the author of this work has been asserted
by her in accordance with the Copyright, Designs and Patents Act 1988.

Published by Manchester University Press
Altrincham Street, Manchester M1 7JA, UK
www.manchesteruniversitypress.co.uk

British Library Cataloguing-in-Publication Data is available

An electronic version of this book is also available under a Creative Commons (CC-BY-NC-ND) licence, thanks to the support of Knowledge Unlatched, which permits non-commercial use, distribution and reproduction provided the author(s) and Manchester University Press are fully cited and no modifications or adaptations are made. Details of the licence can be viewed at https://creativecommons.org/licenses/by-nc-nd/4.0/

ISBN 978 1 7849 9306 1 hardback
ISBN 978 1 5261 4811 7 paperback
ISBN 978 1 5261 0755 8 open access

First published by Manchester University Press in hardback 2018

This edition published 2020

The publisher has no responsibility for the persistence or accuracy of URLs for any external or third-party internet websites referred to in this book, and does not guarantee that any content on such websites is, or will remain, accurate or appropriate.

Typeset by Out of House Publishing

Contents

Acknowledgements	*page* vii
Introduction: disrupting the critical genealogy of the Gothic	1
1 'Unimaginable sensations': father–daughter incest and the economics of exchange	34
2 'My more than sister': re-examining paradigms of sibling incest	85
3 Uncles and nieces: thefts, violence and sexual threats	139
4 More than just kissing: cousins and the changing status of family	190
5 Queer mothers: female sexual agency and male victims	246
Coda: incest and beyond	277
Bibliography	283
Index	300

Acknowledgements

The genealogy of this book is, like those of the books discussed in the pages that follow, an unruly one of overlapping origins and intersecting concerns. I am indebted to my father, whose passion for history insists on the relevance of the past to contemporary politics, laws and culture; to my mother, who taught me always to question established wisdom; and most of all to my brother, who long ago determined my focus on the marginalized. I would like to thank in particular Jennie Batchelor, in whom I have been lucky enough to find a colleague at once challenging, insightful, encouraging and inspirational and who unfailingly and generously gave (and continues to give) of her time and guidance. Without her invaluable and constant support and friendship this project would not have been possible.

I would like to thank Donna Landry for spurring me to new lines of enquiry in my research, providing many valuable conversations, being an ever-encouraging and astute critic and not least of all for reading and commenting upon the manuscript in various drafts. I am grateful to the many colleagues and friends whose insights and time have strengthened this book, particularly Vybarr Cregan-Reid, Marie Mulvey-Roberts, Karl Leydecker, Gillian Dow, Phil Stevenson, Sarah Horgan, Petr Barta, Monica Mattfeld, Steve Martin, Manushag Powell, Koenraad Claes, Peter Brown, Cathy Waters, Robert Maidens, Kat Peddie, Barbara Franchi and Declan Wiffen.

The wonderful staff at the University of Kent have been a constant source of help and I offer thanks to Megan Barrett, Gemma Vaughan, Faith Phoenix, Anna Redmond, Andrea Griffith, Claire Lyons, Helena Torres and Emma Bainbridge.

The institutional support that has been crucial to my research must be acknowledged; through the University of Kent I have received funding that has facilitated my research at various libraries and participation in academic conferences and the award of a Chawton House Library fellowship enabled my work on manuscripts and texts that have been vital to my research. I would like to thank the editorial team at Manchester University Press, and particularly Matthew Frost, who have provided guidance and help during the publication process.

Throughout the writing of this book I have been supported by the best of friends and colleagues, Kim Simpson and Victoria Bennett. Without their strength and insight that, to paraphrase Margaret Atwood, taught me to steer through darkness by no stars, I could not have written this book and it is to them that I dedicate this work.

Introduction: disrupting the critical genealogy of the Gothic

Dreadful was the whole! truly dreadful! A story of so much horror, from atrocious and voluntary guilt never did I hear! Mrs. Smelt and myself heartily regretted that it had come in our way, and mutually agreed that we felt ourselves ill-used in ever having heard it.

Frances Burney (1786)[1]

We do not pretend to give this novel as one of the first order, or even of the second; it has, however, sufficient interest to be read with pleasure. The terrible prevails, and the characters of the two heroes in crime, are *too* darkly tinctured ... There is no fine writing in these volumes ... but in point of moral tendency they are unexceptionable.

Review (1794) of Eliza Parsons, *Castle of Wolfenbach* (1793)[2]

Frances Burney's assessment of Horace Walpole's play *The Mysterious Mother* (1768) reflects a strong discomfort with its depiction of mother–son incest that offers revealing insights into the nature of the play's reception. Almost universally condemned or criticised, Walpole's play was unperformed in his lifetime and was read by a narrow audience as a consequence of its limited print run from Walpole's Strawberry Hill Press. Burney's own experience of the play was itself suggestive of the illicit atmosphere that surrounded the work. Though long eager to read Walpole's work, Burney found that the play's restricted availability made this impossible until she received a copy from the Queen. After Burney's friends learned that the play was in her possession, they requested a reading. However, 'the loan being private, and the book having been lent to her Majesty by Lord Harcourt' subject to 'restrictions' of which Burney was not fully aware, she requested permission from the Queen before reading it aloud with Mr and Mrs Smelt, Mr de Luc and the Rev. Charles de Guiffardière at a private gathering.[3] Burney's description of her reaction is characterised by horror, regret and ill-use at having been witness to, and participant in, the reading of the play. While Burney's belief that the play had forever prejudiced her against Walpole did not persist – on seeing him some months later she 'forget[s] the spleen I had conceived against him upon reading his tragedy' – her reaction illuminates the play's content as highly troubling.[4] Her pointing towards the 'voluntary' nature of maternal guilt alludes to the agency of the mother's instigation of incest by posing as a servant and having sex with her unwitting son. In the play the mother reveals her incestuous capacity to her son in a scene that disrupts the gender ideologies informing conventional representations of incest in which men are the active abusers of women. Burney's discomfort with the 'dreadful' and 'atrocious' work, typical of reactions to the play, indicates a sense of how deeply it troubles ideologies of gender and sexuality that implicitly inform readings of mother–son incest as the most disturbing of all incestuous relationships.

Samuel Taylor Coleridge was even more repulsed by the play than Frances Burney, calling it 'the most disgusting, vile, detestable composition that ever came from the hand of man. No one with a spark of true manliness, of which Horace Walpole had none, could have written it.'[5] Coleridge's detestation of the play and his sense that it was 'vile' inform his disparagement of the author's 'manliness'; he believed that only an aberrant man could have imagined scenes of a passive and victimised son. His assertion that a man could not have written the play underscores the extent to which Coleridge identified the victimisation and passivity of the son as the conception of a non-normative male author. Coleridge's disgust is explicated by George E. Haggerty, who argues that 'abject, passive masculinity challenges the status quo with the "disgusting" proposition that some men are victims too'.[6] And to an even greater extent than the passive masculinity that is repulsive to Coleridge, it is the simultaneous agency of the mother that so upsets the dominant ideologies.

Conversely, the anonymous reviewer of Eliza Parsons's *The Castle of Wolfenbach* (1793), a Gothic novel that, like Walpole's play, centres on incestuous desire, reads the work 'with pleasure'. This is quite a departure from Burney's and Coleridge's reactions to reading the incestuous plot in Walpole's play. In fact, although the villains in Parsons's novel are described as 'too darkly tinctured' and the quality of writing is not praised, the reviewer summarises the narrative as morally 'unexceptionable'. The difference between the responses to these Gothic works lies in the type of incestuous relationship depicted. Parsons's novel depicts the growing romantic love of an uncle, Mr Weimar, for his niece, Matilda, who recounts: '"[my uncle] was for ever seeking opportunities to caress me, his language was expressive of the utmost fondness, he praised my person in such glowing colours … I began to be extremely uneasy at freedoms I scare knew how to repulse."'[7] The uncle's incestuous designs turn violent and culminate with him stabbing Matilda, who survives. Parsons's novel is praised (though faintly) by the reviewer because the form of incest appears to conform to conventional sexual and gender ideologies. An uncle's sexually violent pursuit of his niece positions the female as passive victim to an aggressive male sexuality that, while condemned for its violation of the incest taboo, nonetheless adheres to a familiar structure of power and sexuality. The reactions to these different configurations of incest in *The Mysterious Mother* and *The Castle of Wolfenbach* reveal a marked discomfort with incestuous behaviour that subverts heteronormative ideologies of gender and sexuality.[8]

What becomes clear in these examples is that incest is employed by male and female authors of the Gothic in a variety of familial relationships that vary as much in their formulations as they do in their functions. In this book I intervene in the scholarly accounts of incest that, much like the Gothic's contemporary readings, rely on gendered divisions of the genre that, I will argue, limit ways of reading incestuous relationships. By questioning the gender logic according to which the genre has been read, I argue that it is possible to see how incest functions in a number of paradoxical ways, acting as a consequence of patriarchy's control of female bodies and property, as an escape from this patriarchal control and as an exposure of the inadequacy of heteronormative models of sexuality.[9] In so doing, I demonstrate that incest was representative of a range of interests crucial to writers of the Gothic – often women or homosexual men who adopted a critical stance in relation to the heteronormative patriarchal world. In repositioning the Gothic, representations of incest are revealed as synonymous with the Gothic as a whole: complex, multifaceted and consciously resistant to the dominant social and sexual hegemonies in their models of alternative agencies, sexualities, forms of desire and family structures.

Whether defined in anthropological, biosocial, or psychoanalytic terms the incest taboo is viewed generally as an essential prohibition without which society would not function. The prohibition of incest was defined by Claude Lévi-Strauss as 'the fundamental step' in forming society, the transgression of which causes atavistic endogamy.[10] Joseph Shepher located the incest taboo as being rooted in biology as well as social rules and customs and argued that violations against it are genetically and socially damaging.[11] The Freudian understanding of the incest taboo positions it as a necessary part of psychosexual development for adolescents that allows them to distance themselves from their sexual desires for their parents and form non-familial attachments.[12] In these understandings the incest taboo serves to prohibit sexual acts between biologically related family members, yet psychiatrist Judith Herman argues that incest should be viewed as a sexually motivated act that violates the relationship between a child and adult in a position of familial power, regardless of blood kinship.[13] In this book I widen Herman's definition to include any sexual behaviour (suggested or explicit) between people of any age involved in a familial relationship, regardless of a blood tie. My deployment of the term 'incest taboo' indicates established definitions of incest as a natural, universal proscription, a prohibition against violating positions of familial power and understandings of it as law instituted by society.

Incest, a sexual act associated with transgression, violations of power and violence, has readily been conflated with sexual violence in Gothic scholarship and consigned to one of two gendered plots. Anne K. Mellor, for example, argues that 'the Gothic novel written by men presents the father's incestuous rape of his daughter as the perverse desire of the older generation to usurp the sexual rights of the younger generation, while the Gothic novel written by women represents incest as a cultural taboo which functions to repress the sexual desires of women'.[14] Mellor's assessment represents what a large proportion of scholarship on the genre argues: that meanings of incest differ based on their presence in works designated as Male or Female Gothic. Such distinctions relegate individual depictions of incest into categories of overt masculine perversion or feminine sexual repression and entrench understandings of the Gothic novel as written by women as departures from or reactions to male-authored texts. This standard view is corroborated by David Punter and Glennis Byron: 'the male Gothic text, both in its subject matter and its narrative conventions, is usually considered to be particularly transgressive: violence, especially sexual violence, is dealt with openly and often in lingering detail ... In the female Gothic plot, the transgressive male becomes the primary threat to the female protagonist.'[15] While Mellor's argument pertains specifically to the author's sex and Punter and Byron focus on gendered plot conventions, both divide representations of sexuality into distinct male or female modes. Yet scholarly understandings of representations of incest in the Gothic as having distinct meanings determined by authorial gender overlook the variety of ways in which writers use incestuous relationships and neglect the complexity of their implications.

Eliza Parsons's and Horace Walpole's Gothic works, like many other Gothic texts, resist the models of incest discerned by modern scholarship. Parsons's novel uses incest to highlight the inequities of primogeniture and the links between financial, sexual and legal constraints and acts of violence against women. It would, however, be difficult to argue that Parsons's representation of incest positions Mr Weimar's violent and sexual attacks on his niece as a cultural taboo repressing her sexual desires. As subsequent chapters will explore, there are examples of Gothic novels written by women in which incest functions in this way. Eleanor Sleath's *The Orphan of the Rhine* (1798) is, I argue, critical of laws that deny or reject incestuous unions while novels by Ann Radcliffe that position the brother as an ideal but unavailable mate include *The Castles of Athlin and Dunbayne: A Highland Story* (1789) and *A Sicilian Romance* (1790). But to attempt to fit Parsons's novel to the theoretical framework advanced by Mellor would be to distort its purpose. Walpole's *The Mysterious Mother* equally defies such paradigms of male- or female-authored representations of incest. The mother's agency in the play reveals, not a desire to usurp her son's sexual rights, but to reassert her own via the closest physical substitute for her husband. The play presents laws repressing female sexual desire outside of wedlock as aberrant, a theme close to what Mellor identifies as presented by the Gothic as written by women. Similarly, Parsons's fictional uncle, in his violent pursuit of his niece, is aligned with Mellor's understanding of male-authored Gothic incest as a perverse desire unjustly to control the younger generation. Such disparities reveal that scholarly accounts of two mutually exclusive modes of Gothic incest ignore the interconnected nature of incestuous representations.

THE FORMATION OF MALE AND FEMALE PARADIGMS OF INCEST IN THE GOTHIC

Sexuality, questions of ownership, inheritance, women's subjugation to male authority, laws of coverture and primogeniture and issues concerning gender roles pervade Gothic works from the mid-eighteenth century on. Authors of the Gothic explore the non-normative and unconventional sexuality inherent in the genre to expose the limitations and dangers of conventional ideologies through incestuous configurations in importantly divergent ways. My use of the terms ideology and hegemony relies on Antonio Gramsci's deployment of them as well as later evaluations thereof by scholars such as Terry Eagleton and Raymond Williams. Gramsci understood hegemony as the consent of society to be dominated by force; a consent that is engendered partially through the use of ideology as 'an instrument of domination and social hegemony'.[16] Gramsci clarifies that ideologies operate as weapons wielded by the dominant social or political class in order to create a consensually subordinate society. He argues that 'the "normal" exercise of hegemony ... is characterized by a combination of force and consent which balance each other so that force ... appears to be backed by the consent of the majority, expressed by the so-called organs of public opinion'.[17] Gramsci's belief that the exercise of hegemony cannot rely entirely on the government's 'power and material force'[18] finds articulation in society through the function of ideology. This is expanded on in Eagleton's description of hegemony as 'the ways in which a governing power wins consent to its rule from those it subjugates'; that hegemony '*includes* ideology, but is not reducible to it'.[19] These understandings of hegemony and ideology contribute to my examination of the Gothic in part through the insights they make available regarding the genre's function and reception within its contemporary social hegemony; how representations of incest within the Gothic depart from or shore up various ideologies; and how scholarship has itself frequently adhered to such ideologies of gender and sexuality in its treatment of incest within the genre.

Heteronormative ideology ensures behaviour abides by seemingly 'natural' social rules and produces the heterosexual/queer binary that demonstrates hegemony's ability to allow for resistance.[20] In such a system apparently transgressive behaviour can be tolerated, even though it is ostensibly taboo, if it corresponds to the overriding power structure. This can be seen in the contemporaneous responses to Parsons's *Wolfenbach* and Walpole's *The Mysterious Mother* discussed earlier; Parsons's work was considered unobjectionable as the incest demonstrated a recognisable pattern of male-perpetrated sexual violence while Walpole's depictions of maternal incestuous desire exceeded the tolerated level of nonconformity in its simultaneous confrontations with sexual, gender and power norms. Walpole's work is no more radical than Parsons's; however, Parsons's challenges to inheritance and marriage laws were largely overlooked given their deployment alongside a representation of incest adherent to the gender and sexual ideologies. As the critical genealogy of the Gothic demonstrates, the genre's readings have often been informed by their participation in these ideologies and attempts either to locate Gothic incest within the dominant discourses or to reject them act as what Eagleton describes as a form of institutionalised social control.[21] Such functions of power are insidious: 'it is preferable … for power to remain conveniently invisible, disseminated throughout the texture of social life and thus "naturalized" as custom, habit, spontaneous practice'.[22] Eagleton's description of power disseminated as customs corresponds to Foucault's understanding of 'mechanisms of power … irreducible to the representation of the law'.[23] Readings of the genre can thus consent to and act as mechanisms of hegemonic power in their reproductions of 'natural' ideologies.[24] This book participates in the work being done by scholars who re-evaluate traditional accounts of the Gothic in order to argue that representations of incest frequently provide truly transgressive and counter-hegemonic models of desire, sexuality, gender and society.[25] These Gothic paradigms expose the dangers and effects of complicity to seemingly naturalised practices, rendering visible the invisible function of power to demonstrate that what society propagates as 'natural' practices are in fact highly unnatural constructs.[26]

The Gothic is still frequently understood, as it was by its contemporary readership, along apparently natural gender lines, in spite of its reclamation as a genre worthy of literary study in the 1970s by feminist scholars and later by queer theorists.[27] While Ellen Moers's first introduction of the term Female Gothic in the 1970s was not intended to position female-written novels as a deviation from a male originary genre, this was a consequence of its usage.[28] The term, though newly coined, echoed eighteenth- and nineteenth-century criticism in which female writers such as Ann Radcliffe and Eliza Parsons were set up as delicate and timid counters to the aggressive sexuality depicted in the works of male writers such as Matthew Lewis and William Beckford. As E. J.

Clery explains: 'Novels where spirits are not rationalised, the most famous example in the 1790s being *The Monk* ... are "real" Gothic, while the class of the "explained supernatural", largely authored by women, is a diminished, self-censoring version of the first.'[29] Sir Walter Scott certainly subscribed to such a view when he described Radcliffe's works as hesitant and tremulous in comparison to the bold and aggressive writings of Lewis early on in the Gothic's history by suggesting that Radcliffe's use of superstition was underpinned by 'anxiety' as opposed to Lewis's *The Monk* (1796), which was written 'as if he believed.'[30] Attempts to reposition the Female Gothic, such as Kate Ferguson Ellis's argument that the 'masculine Gothic' reacted to a female genus, risk reiterating a conformity to gendered ideologies that is, as I will argue, at odds with the content of the novels to be examined.[31]

The terms Male and Female Gothic are used in more recent scholarship as a means of describing narrative technique or of characterising the use of the supernatural and representations of violence. Diana Wallace and Andrew Smith identify the 1990s as a period in which 'critics came to distinguish between Female Gothic and Male Gothic, initially identified with the gender of the writer. The Female Gothic plot, exemplified by Radcliffe ... [and] the Male Gothic plot, exemplified by Matthew Lewis's *The Monk*.'[32] The distinction reproduces the gendered structure underlying critical accounts of the supernatural that Clery points to as a means by which critics could dismiss Gothic novels by women as less valid than their male-authored counterparts. A similar division emerges in discussions surrounding depictions of incest in the Gothic. With the exception of Mellor's conclusion that the functions of incest are determined by authorial gender, scholarly accounts of incest do not usually articulate an adherence to the earlier critical convention of gendering incest. However, readings of incest are invariably predetermined by this gendered framework. Violent, consummated, male-perpetrated acts of incest allow texts to be considered masculine or 'real' Gothic, while incest that is averted, non-violent or implied is considered part of the Female Gothic tradition. Such a view is apparent in James Watt's argument that Lewis's deployment of sexuality 'amplified the suggestion of impropriety that was only implicit in the work of a writer such as Ann Radcliffe.'[33] Similarly, Vartan P. Messier's description of Radcliffe's use of incest as 'restrained' in comparison to the 'truly transgressive' Lewis shows how conceptions of incest and sexuality continue to be read as part of a male or female tradition.[34]

In this book, I will employ the term Female Gothic as it applies to the extant scholarship and in my own analyses I will use the ungendered designation Gothic regardless of the supposedly gendered plot or author's gender. The term Male Gothic will be used in reference to scholarly examinations of texts typically referred to as Gothic and understood as part of the male tradition. With these terminological distinctions I hope to reveal the gendered division of the genre as a restrictive manoeuvre that has contributed to reductive gendered readings of incestuous relationships. My desire to trouble the ongoing use of the term Female Gothic is not without precedent. Recent scholarly works such as *The Female Gothic: New Directions* (2009) question the term, though the study ultimately argues for its continued use.[35] Subdividing the genre into families born of Radcliffean or Walpolian parents imposes boundaries within the Gothic's literary genealogy that is, like the families in the novels themselves, a large and unwieldy one that defies such neat categorisation. Though the clues may seem to point in one direction – a touch of the explained supernatural indicating 'Mother Radcliffe', much like Ellena's miniature necklace points to Schedoni as her father in *The Italian* (1797) – characteristics can betray the imprint of more than one parent.[36] Gothic novels do not belong to one of two distinct, gendered approaches, but to one genre that uses representations of incest to demonstrate a range of violent behaviour, unjust legal positions, ideal egalitarian relationships and the demands and dangers of the heteronormative culture from which they deviate.

MODES OF READING INCEST IN THE GOTHIC

If incest in the Gothic has been viewed by scholars through restrictive gendered lenses, modern literary analyses of the genre have equally been constrained by feminist perspectives on incest derived from sociological and psychological theories. The understanding of incest as a typically violent or non-consensual act reflective of male power is typified by psychologists and sociologists such as Lena Dominelli and Julie Brickman, who view incest almost exclusively as the rape of girls by older male family members.[37] That such formations of this incest paradigm coincided with feminist criticism's reclamation of the Female Gothic in the 1970s undoubtedly determined literary scholarship to read incest in the Gothic as representative of violent sexual aggression.[38]

Seminal works on the Female Gothic by scholars such as Ellen Moers's *Literary Women* and Sandra Gilbert and Susan Gubar's *The Madwoman in the Attic: The Woman Writer and the Nineteenth-Century Literary Imagination* (1979) were written alongside works such as Juliet Mitchell's influential *Psychoanalysis and Feminism* (1974) and Luce Irigaray's *This Sex Which is Not One* (1977). Mitchell retrieved Freudian theory from feminist abandonment to explain that the Oedipus complex 'is *not* about the nuclear family, but about the institution of culture within the kinship structure and the exchange relationship of exogamy ... It is specific to nothing but patriarchy.'[39] Mitchell's work examines how psychoanalysis can be used to understand patriarchal and capitalist adherence to the incest taboo while Irigaray's work troubles theories of the exchange of women as essential to the maintenance of patriarchal structures. The positions may seem diametrically opposed, but both Irigaray and Mitchell use Lévi-Strauss's argument that the incest taboo is essential to society to analyse what feminist scholar Gayle Rubin calls 'the traffic in women'.[40] In contrast, Dominelli and Brickman contended that the taboo is constantly violated by the very men who should desire to uphold it. However, all these feminist scholars expose patriarchy's control of female sexuality through abuses of power that are encoded within the social structure. In a sense, the exchange of women that demands the incest taboo concurrently creates a system of control over female bodies that lends itself to incestuous sexual abuse. These scholars have revealed through the intersections of psychoanalytic, cultural and sociological discourses on incest the ways coercive or forced incestuous assaults reflect the wider structures of patriarchy's control of women.

The sociological understanding of incest as a violent abuse of male power inherent in the family structure is relied upon by much modern scholarship on the Gothic that thus reads incest in the Female Gothic as a violent expression of the dangers of patriarchy. This understanding of incest has focused scholarship most intently on instances of father–daughter incest to the exclusion of other configurations of incestuous desire. As Fred Botting writes: 'Familial and sexual relations, power and suppression, turn on the roles and figures of father and daughter.'[41] Similarly, the reliance of Gothic scholarship on Freudian models of desire that require the child's sexual desire for and rejection of the parent has contributed to the emphasis on readings of incestuous fathers and daughters.[42] Robert Miles, for example, observes the Freudian model of desire at work in Radcliffe's novels, noting that: 'the daughter is frequently in flight from the "father", or his substitutes, often with incestuous entanglements and overtones'.⁴³ The sociologically informed mode of understanding incest also focuses on the social implications of patriarchy, and scholars of the Gothic who work within this framework often examine the legal implications of coverture, primogeniture, divorce and issues of gender, sexuality and family to demonstrate how incest is united with these themes under the rubric of abusive male power.⁴⁴

Perhaps best exemplified by Ellis's groundbreaking and influential *The Contested Castle* (1989), this important body of work exposes fundamental dangers in the assumed safe haven of the home, establishing the correlation between Gothic representations of the family, domesticity and terror.⁴⁵ Building on such work, Ruth Perry describes incest as 'the meaning of the gothic novel' that represents through its repeated depictions of 'a girl singled out, against her will, in her own domestic space, for the sexual attentions of a father, an uncle, or a brother' the dangers of male tyranny.⁴⁶ Underscoring connections between family and fear, sexuality and imprisonment, feminist scholars equate patriarchal institutions with violence and terror, locating incest as an extension of these dangers.⁴⁷ In this vein Angela Wright argues that: 'the Gothic genre's treatment of violence, murder and incest is linked symbiotically with issues of sexuality and gender within the fiction'.⁴⁸ Wright's partnering of incest with violence is connected to Perry's description of a girl singled out in what should be a safe space. Relating sexual violation within the home to male tyranny, this model shows that incest is understood as a culmination of public and private abuses.⁴⁹ When Maggie Kilgour argues that 'Incest ... suggests an abnormal and extreme desire (a violation of natural familial ties)', she similarly picks up on the notion of incest as an aberrant violation of the bonds of family.⁵⁰ In locating incest as an unwanted and forceful transgression of 'natural familial ties', these desires are identified as synonymous with the equally unnatural abuses of power committed by male family members.⁵¹

When Gothic scholars privilege Freudian over sociological understandings of incest in their readings, the father–daughter relationship – while still emphasised – is read not only as an abuse of male power, but also as a threat existing sometimes solely in the heroine's mind. Relying on Freud's psychoanalytic framework that female sexuality develops in response to the father before being transferred to another man causes literary scholarship to position the Gothic heroine in flight from threats that are more fantasy than fact. Such arguments underpin Diane Long Hoeveler's claim that Female Gothic heroines imagine incestuous threats because they have 'an infantile desire to remain in the paternal and protective domicile of childhood' and can only reconcile leaving this sphere to marry an outsider if they 'fancy' their fathers are evil.[52] In using psychoanalytic theory to examine the Female Gothic's subversive nature, scholars point to the heroine's fantasy of paternal threats as reflective of a passive resistance to patriarchy.[53] This assessment of the Female Gothic identifies a combination of personal, psychological, social and economic anxieties expressed through the heroines' fears of malevolent parents and locates these fears as the genre's 'originating fantasy'.[54] Scholars such as Eugenia C. DeLamotte and Ellis likewise read incest portrayals as representative of the distinctly unique experience of women and women writers in the long eighteenth century, serving to foreground their subjugation to patriarchal power, the trap of domesticity and anxieties relating to the changing structure of the family and their shifting role therein as daughter and/or wife.[55] Incest, in this body of scholarship, is viewed as imagined by heroines who are shaped by their desires for their fathers or as a hyperbolisation of their psychological anxieties and disempowered legal status and these scholars have offered nuanced and important insights into the genre.

Yet the sociological and psychological understandings of incest that influence modern scholarship on the Gothic contribute to overlapping paradigms of incest that are inadequate to account for incestuous configurations that do not posit real or imagined threats from a father or father figure. The view of incest in the Gothic that arises from Freudian understandings of incest asserts heroines must invent incestuous threats in order to flee from their fathers and form attachments to non-kin lovers who will replace their fathers as their protectors.[56] The second model relies on feminist sociologists' definition of incest as a violent literalisation of the unequal power relations in the patriarchal family. The psychological understanding of incest as integral to female development is, Haggerty reveals in his analysis of *The Italian*, also underpinned by the sociological understanding of the inherent violence in this incestuous configuration. Haggerty concludes: 'this midnight encounter of incestuous violation always already suggests the paternal … Paternal violence shapes the heroine just as the terms of her very existence seem to depend on his whim, or rather his pleasure.'[57] Haggerty's reading demonstrates that these two models are not oppositional accounts of incest, but provide in their intersections of violence, sexuality, power and family a means of theorising incest as a potential threat inherent within the power structures of male–female relationships.

It is easy to see why scholars of the Gothic often subscribe to psychological and sociological paradigms of incest that readily accord with the notion of the Gothic as a subversive genre, but they nonetheless restrict incest to a 'bad daddy' model that claims older men as father-substitutes and positions both fathers and father-substitutes as inhabiting the same paternal role. The limitations become clear when the instances of father–daughter incest arising as a natural consequence of sympathetic minds and physical attraction, as sought by the daughter, or as unknowingly committed or sought are analysed closely to reveal how they trouble notions of incest as imagined, violent or representative of male power.[58] Reading uncles as father-substitutes is typical of scholarship on Radcliffe's novels in which uncles in paternal roles are common; Hoeveler positions Schedoni in *The Italian* as Ellena's father rather than as her uncle, arguing that Ellena 'fancies that … her father has tried to kill her'.[59] Similarly, Frances A. Chiu refers to Schedoni as Ellena's 'nominal father and church father' and describes Emily's uncle-by-marriage in Radcliffe's *The Mysteries of Udolpho* (1794) as 'the father and his friends [who] are made to appear especially threatening to the child'.[60] However, as I argue in Chapter 3, that these men are not fathers but the heroines' uncles by blood or marriage is an important part of how Radcliffe models usurpations of power, property and bodies as caused by attempts to rearticulate the available power structure informed by laws of coverture and primogeniture.[61] In locating most older men as father-substitutes, the unique positions and important implications for non-paternal male relationships in which power and attraction are figured differently are overlooked. Accounts of the Gothic that suggest 'a father, an uncle, or a brother' represent the same types of abuses and threats are ultimately too narrow to encompass the various types and functions of incest in the genre.[62] Scholars have used non-paternal relationships to corroborate an understanding of father–daughter incest that is not as monolithic as those following the psychological and sociological lines make out. While such approaches are fruitful they fail to account for the profound differences between configurations of incest featuring older male figures.

DEFINING FAMILIAL RELATIONSHIPS IN THE EIGHTEENTH CENTURY AND THE GOTHIC

In my analyses of incestuous relationships in the Gothic I borrow the insights of social historians who have widened understandings of the family in the eighteenth century to include equally conjugal, affinal and consanguineal relations as kin. The changing structure and understanding of family and kinship in eighteenth-century England is the subject of important recent work by Naomi Tadmor and Joanne Bailey, each of whom examines the shifts in configurations of kinship, sexuality, marriage and laws.[63] Lawrence Stone's narrative of the family as evolving linearly with the economic move towards capitalism into nuclear families grounded in companionate marriage has been largely displaced by the work of these more recent social historians, particularly by Tadmor's *Family and Friends in Eighteenth-Century England* (2001) and Bailey's *Unquiet Lives: Marriage and Marriage Breakdown in England, 1660–1800* (2003).[64] Their accounts delineate the legal and social shifts in definitions of family to reveal that the historical narrative of family as moving away from an emphasis on consanguineal bonds to the conjugal tie is too simplistic. Rather, in the long eighteenth century, conjugal, affinal and consanguineal relatives were all considered kin and integral to the family structure, which was, Bailey argues, much more adaptable than traditional evolutionary models suggest.[65] The familial bond existed regardless of actual kinship status and allowed for broader definitions of family than traditional narratives previously asserted. Drawing on these multiple models of family for analyses of incest is particularly productive for reading the Gothic, wherein multiple representations of family comprised of non-blood individuals, foster, adopted and blood kin overlap and blur. Historical accounts of kinship provide a social context for the sometimes elusive nature of family bonds underpinning representations of incest and not only allow for a greater range of relationships to be understood as incestuous, but also reveal that the Gothic engaged with wider understandings of marriage and family than previously thought.

Scholarship on the Gothic that relies on Stone's teleological narrative of family rather than the new insights provided by more recent social historians locates increased representations of incestuous desires as occurring alongside the development of a nuclear family that had less consanguineal loyalty and thus abided less by the incest taboo. This contextualisation focuses scholarship on violent depictions of incest and leaves out the potential for female sexual desires and agency by positioning women as victims without offering an alternative narrative to their role within the family and home. In reading incestuous threats as created by a shift towards companionate marriage and a concurrent weakening of the incest taboo, Perry argues: 'both fathers and brothers began to see their female relatives … as possessions in their power and hence possible sex objects'.[66] In a similar vein, Margot Gayle Backus's account of the weakening of the incest taboo concludes that 'with the nuclearisation of the family, the incest taboo … came to depend on the contingent goodwill, integrity, value and self-discipline of individual fathers and brothers'.[67] These accounts of a new, eroticised nuclear family quite correctly focus on the restraint required by fathers and brothers and importantly illuminate the threat of masculine desire within the patriarchal family yet they also ignore female incestuous desires.[68] Perry maintains that the incest thematic in eighteenth-century literature, particularly the Gothic, is a consequence of the decreased emphasis on consanguineal bonds that enabled men 'to see their female relatives as sexual prey rather than co-inheritors of family traditions'.[69] Part of my investment in social historians' work on the family structure is that their insights into the coexisting nature of various family bonds open incest in the Gothic up to being read as not solely a threat to women in the nuclear family by their blood kin but as a form of desire existing within the multiple definitions of family.

The concept of non-kin becoming like kin is a common thread in the eighteenth-century novel, particularly in the Gothic, where non-kin are often co-reared. Sociologist Edward Westermarck argued that non-kin raised together during childhood form aversions to each other due to reverse sexual imprinting that makes marriages between non-blood-related siblings impractical and undesirable.[70] Such an effect is seen in novels like Sarah Sheriffe's *Correlia, or The Mystic Tomb* (1802), Sleath's *The Orphan of the Rhine* or the anonymously written *Adeline or The Orphan* (1790), where family groups are composed of a variety of members who may eventually be revealed as sharing consanguineal ties. The co-reared foster/adopted/blood siblings in these novels are assumed by their foster/adopted/blood parents to be capable of seeing each other only as siblings. However, this belief is frequently undermined by one or both offspring falling in love with their 'siblings'. It is not the specific kinship tie that is emphasised in these Gothic texts, but rather the coexistence of feelings that make it possible for some people to locate an individual as both family and erotic choice. That in novels like *Correlia* we see different characters subscribe to each of these models – Correlia's foster-brother loves her passionately and proposes marriage before discovering she is in fact his half-sister, while Correlia only ever loves him as a sibling – highlights the ambivalence with which incestuous desires are depicted. Representations of incestuous love occurring simultaneously with family feeling resist the theory that relaxed consanguineal bonds led to a heightening of male sexual threats and support the idea that multiple concepts of family coexisted in the long eighteenth century.[71] Alternatively, depictions of family members who meet and fall in love as adults before discovering a blood kinship and conforming to a familial relationship privilege the blood tie as fundamental to family and incest as antithetical to this structure.[72] Kinship can be consanguineal or created from a shared childhood and incestuous desires are capable of forming in both of these models of families, the recognition of which fact highlights the fluidity of conceptions of family, sexuality and desire. The feelings of those in the consanguineal family towards their non-kin relatives are crucial in establishing whether or not an individual is regarded as family and thus if erotic desires constitute incestuous desires.[73]

In the Gothic the incest taboo acts as a vehicle through which to literalise arbitrary laws and regulations as it is itself an arbitrary legal limitation on desire, behaviour and marriage that is flexible only insofar as it benefits the dominant hegemony's financial and political control.[74] The repeated use of incest and differing kinship bonds exposes the paradoxical crack in the social contract that forbade whilst encouraging incestuous relationships and behaviour, and thus created multiple demands and restrictions across a multitude of incestuous configurations. These contradictory requirements can be seen in Anna Maria Bennett's *Ellen, Countess of Castle Howel* (1794), in which the heroine is discouraged from a financially imprudent marriage with her co-reared (presumed) cousin but encouraged to marry her wealthy father-substitute. That the heroine's family views the threat of incest as an obstruction to the former marriage and not the latter focuses attention on the financial motive and reveals the hypocrisy of overlooking incest restrictions to benefit the patriarchal structure of the family.[75] Making use of the variety of conceptions of kinship established by social historians when analysing incest in the Gothic illuminates that Gothic authors' representations of different familial bonds as incestuous – or not – expose as arbitrary the laws governing desire and how readily they are transgressed.

As we saw in the previous section, incest is not always subsumed into a model of abusive patriarchal/familial threats and violence, but has frequently been described in terms of its transgressive and subversive nature. The incest thematic as employed by women writers in the early modern period is shown to be transgressively endogamic in Maureen Quilligan's excellent work on incest in Elizabethan England.[76] Pat Gill's study of

Restoration drama describes incest as 'a metaphor for a fundamental disorder in the condition of the state', pointing towards its use as a social critique of a lack of control or order.[77] Such interpretations of incest are readily applicable to the breadth of relationships and depictions of incest in the Gothic as well as the variety of earlier time periods used as Gothic settings.[78] As I will demonstrate in subsequent chapters, incest, an act that paradoxically demonstrates the control the law has over family and sexuality, can equally stand for the extreme imposition of the hypocritical upholders of the law, an active renunciation of these unfair laws, or the rejection of society and its laws.[79] Sought after or forced, idealised or horrifying, incestuous desires and acts emblematise the intersection of the individual with the controlling bodies of family and heteronormative society. Relocating and identifying family becomes a transformative act in which the legal and social constraints of society are avoided within a newly constructed and ideally egalitarian circle of kinship, as exemplified by the endings of *The Italian* and Emily Brontë's *Wuthering Heights* (1847).[80] Family – previously lost through acts of violence or usurpation required by a society with arbitrary laws governing inheritance and sexuality – is re-established as beyond the influence of such regulatory forces.

DISCIPLINARY APPROACHES TO INCEST IN THE GOTHIC

My use of a broad methodological framework within which to analyse representations of incest in literature has precedents in the work of scholars such as Ellen Pollak and Adam Kuper. Pollak's important and comprehensive *Incest and the English Novel, 1684–1814* (2003) troubles existing accounts of incest using a variety of historical, legal and anthropological approaches to contextualise her literary analyses.[81] Kuper similarly supports an anthropological approach with social history and literary analysis in *Incest and Influence* (2009).[82] Other scholars, such as Hoeveler and DeLamotte, combine psychoanalytic frameworks with literary analysis to interpret incest and the Gothic.[83] In addition to these approaches, a yet more inclusive methodology that incorporates modern sociological and scientific research can reveal the complexities of different incestuous configurations.[84] The various disciplinary approaches available for reading the Gothic provide important and useful accounts of incest that I have relied on, combined, and expanded on in my analyses, arguing that specific incestuous configurations lend themselves to different methodological approaches. A disciplinary flexibility is required in order to accommodate the various incestuous configurations within and beyond literature and fully to account for the complexity of these representations in the Gothic. By understanding incest in the Gothic using a broader methodology, the genre is revealed as even more politically charged than previously thought.

One of the frameworks that has dominated scholarly accounts of incest in the Gothic is the psychoanalytic approach, upon which I have already touched. Freudian theory underpins the works of Gilbert and Gubar, DeLamotte, Hoeveler, Eve Kosofsky Sedgwick, Michelle A. Masse and Pamela Kaufman.[85] Psychoanalysis is also the theoretical framework for Anne Williams's *Art of Darkness: A Poetics of Gothic* (1995), in which she argues that Male and Female Gothic narrative strategies are underpinned by different Greek mythologies.[86] Such strategies offer important readings of Gothic texts, but make it difficult to move away from a gender-divided model of the Gothic through the use of a psychoanalytic lens that is predicated on such differences. The limitations of Freudian analysis are evaluated by Nancy Chodorow, who argues that Freudian psychoanalysts 'in the case of rape and incest … have found it hard to give up the view that unconscious desires on the part of the female victim are involved'.[87] Such feminist critiques help to demonstrate that Freud's theories are grounded in a heteronormative ideology that positions women as victims with rape fantasies. Freudian analysis also risks relying on an ill-fitting model of desire as many representations of incest refuse classification within its requisite structure of an opposite sex-/dual-parent childhood to form incestuous desires. There is a further, important argument that Freudian theory itself stems from Gothic literature: 'Prefiguring Freud as much Gothic writing does, moreover, there is a case to be made for reversing the direction of influence so that psychoanalysis becomes an effect of 150 years of monster-making.'[88] Botting reveals a sense that the application of psychoanalysis to the genre that informed it is potentially anachronistic. In spite of the insights it has yielded to literary scholars of the Gothic, I argue that Freudian theories are of less use in understanding incestuous desires and models of sexuality than recent developments in the scientific and sociological fields.

Examinations of the development of the Gothic genre and its critical reception undertaken by scholars such as James Watt are particularly helpful to my argument that Gothic scholarship's ongoing adherence to gendered paradigms is grounded in its contemporary reception. Watt uses critical receptions of the Gothic and its changing conventions to argue that the genre is far from cohesive and displaces Walpole's *The Castle of Otranto* (1764) as 'an empowering fictional manifesto' that birthed Gothic spawn, examining the genre as 'an assimilative literary hybrid'.[89] Watt and I make related arguments that nevertheless diverge at a crucial point: Watt believes literary criticism understands the Gothic genre as homogeneous and argues that it requires a variety of labels including feminine (exemplified by Radcliffe) and canonical (as in Lewis's *The Monk*), while I argue that these labels rearticulate the same limited critical traditions.[90] However, Watt's methodology, with its incorporation of literary analysis and contemporary critical reception, is one that shows, in its displacement of *Otranto*, the potential for such analyses to yield new insights into longstanding scholarly understandings of the genre. I employ a similar methodology in my treatment of the critical reception of Radcliffe and Lewis to undo critical genealogies locating specific Gothic texts as male or female works that represent incest functioning in oppositional ways.

The legal lens is frequently taken up by Gothic scholars who locate within the texts criticisms and representations of specific laws and legal institutions. Historical legal contexts, such as that provided by William Blackstone's works, and current literary scholarship that uses legal frameworks with which to discuss the Gothic are integral to readings of incest. Some of the scholars whose works have provided essential analyses of the Gothic and law upon which I draw include Sue Chaplin, Ruth Bienstock Anolik, Leslie J. Moran, Pollak, Punter and Wallace.[91] Moran writes that 'the Gothic and law are intimately connected institutions', viewing the genre as a philosophy rich in meaning used in legal scholarship.[92] The legal framework can at times limit literary analysis: Chiu's use of legal history to analyse the father figure is built on her assumption that authors such as Radcliffe used 'wildly tyrannical' and 'indistinguishable' fathers, causing her to struggle to make her literary examples conform to the historical models she provides.[93] But other scholarly works – such as Punter's book, which argues that the intersections between the Gothic and law are productive of transgression – show just how profitable the legal lens can be.[94] In taking up Blackstone's legal descriptions of civilly dead women in marriage, Wallace reveals how these metaphors haunt Gothic writing and inform feminist criticism on it.[95] Anolik examines the laws of coverture and primogeniture to argue that the effacement of the mother in Gothic works is a literalisation of her legal status, an argument that informs my chapter on mothers.[96] Pollak's account of the changes in law under Henry

VIII that allowed cousin marriage and altered the criteria for a relationship to be declared incestuous is particularly insightful.[97] Her discussion provides important background for my chapter on cousins, just as laws of inheritance and primogeniture underpin my arguments on younger brothers and sexual violence in my chapter on uncles.[98] By focusing on legal and ecclesiastical laws as well as their intersections with philosophical understandings of natural law in eighteenth-century debates, Pollak provides context for her discussion of incest's potential for transgression in the literature of this time and demonstrates the advantages of combining disciplinary methodologies.

The history of sexuality is also essential to my analyses of Gothic texts: Michel Foucault's and Leo Bersani's understandings of power and sexuality inform my discussion of incest as politically conservative or radical.[99] Bersani's argument that reproductions of power are non-disruptive of the status quo if they simply reverse power structures provokes a re-evaluation of the understanding of incest as inherently disruptive.[100] As such, instances of incestuous desires where power structures are reversed or rearticulated without being disrupted, questioned or redefined are not necessarily subversive of heteronormative ideologies or patriarchal structures. Thus, rather than locating incest as always radical, what Foucault describes as an 'object of obsession and attraction' may at times be presented as a rather prosaic marriage option.[101] Novels such as Elizabeth Thomas's *Purity of Heart, or The Ancient Costume* (1816) and Regina Maria Roche's *Clermont* (1798), both of which conclude with incestuous unions, are not necessarily subversive.[102] The representation of incest as a normative choice in Thomas's portrayal of cousin marriage is revealed as an unexpectedly conservative marriage option that shores up patriarchal structures. Novels in which incestuous relationships are rejected in favour of exogamy are not necessarily conservative, as in the case of Charlotte Brontë's *Jane Eyre* (1847).[103] Bersani's argument that representations of non-normative sexuality are not guaranteed to be subversive requires representations of incest to be analysed within their literary and historical contexts and within the larger framework of desire, power and sexuality. Foucault's understandings of sexuality place sexual desires within a socio-historical framework of power relations and Bersani's theories require each act to be scrutinised in terms of adherence to the power structures that inform potentially subversive acts.

Anthropological insights into the incest taboo are equally vital to my approach here. I argue that twentieth-century theories on incest aversion can be seen in readings of eighteenth-century Gothic works, demonstrating that modern understandings of incest have long been part of the cultural discourse of desire. The Westermarck effect, as already outlined, though not taken up until the twentieth century, can nonetheless be identified as present in eighteenth-century depictions of those raised as siblings resisting or forming erotic desires for one another. Similarly, theories of women as gifts and objects of exchange advanced by Marcel Mauss and Lévi-Strauss are anticipated in eighteenth-century understandings of marriage, society and incest.[104] Recent scholarship on gift exchange by scholars such as Cynthia Klekar and Linda Zionkowski demonstrates the relevance of these theories to the literature of the eighteenth century.[105] Ideas of gifts, exchange and endogamy permeate *The Sons of the Viscount and the Daughters of the Earl*, in which an uncle's incestuous desire for his niece is portrayed as greed to keep beauty and wealth within the closed circuit of the family, thus illustrating authorial awareness of the balance between exchange and the incest taboo.[106] Representations of incest in the eighteenth-century Gothic are rooted in shifting economic and social systems and weighted with differing consanguineal, conjugal and affinal notions of kinship.[107] These representations demonstrate Gothic authors were alert to the inconsistent and coexisting ideas of kinship, exogamy and endogamy, although they use a different vocabulary with which to discuss these tensions.

This different vocabulary is perhaps most readily apparent when we turn to the framework of genetics and attraction, which sheds further light on how and why incestuous desires are represented in such seemingly inconsistent ways in the Gothic. Advances in research pointing towards the influence of shared genetic material, which causes attraction between family members, give us a modern, scientifically based lexicon through which to discuss the mechanics of incest.[108] Borrowing this vocabulary to explore the implications of incest representations enables us to see how Gothic writers expanded on or departed from eighteenth-century understandings of blood recognition. The scientific lens allows for some of the physiological and biological aspects of incestuous desires to be presented in the language that these writers were unable to access but nonetheless understood as the pull of blood. Maurice Greenberg (a psychotherapist), David Livingstone Smith (a cognitive psychologist) and Lynn Åkesson (an ethnologist) are researchers who investigate the relationships between shared genetic material, attraction and the social consequences thereof. Smith writes: '[Genetic Sexual Attraction] suggests that inhibitions against incest must operate against an especially potent prior attraction: sexual feelings experienced by reunited relatives are often especially intense'.[109] Greenberg's, Smith's and Åkesson's theories beg us to reconsider the notion of narcissism that so dominates discussions of sibling incest as more than a literary convention and to understand it as a biological phenomenon.[110] Using scientific examinations of this 'especially potent' attraction reveals how Gothic writers explained the allure of incest and how their representations differ from other non-Gothic depictions in ways often overlooked.[111] While there is a tradition of viewing Gothic incest as encompassing 'less ideal themes of violence, incest, passion and agony' than are figured in the canonical texts of Romanticism, I argue that Gothic sibling incest prefigures narcissistic Romantic sibling attraction as a mutually sought and ideal relationship.[112] Gothic writers frequently used the language of desire, attraction, recognition and kinship to explain what scientists now understand as genetic sexual attraction.

The following five chapters address representations of incest within different family relationships, each exploring the underlying social, sexual and legal anxieties the texts articulate through a variety of analytic lenses suited to the specific kinship bond. My chronology 1764–1847 encompasses the works of Walpole through those of the Brontës, and covers this wide span in order to engage with the ongoing developments in representations of incest from the emergence of the Gothic genre in the mid-eighteenth century through what I will argue is the culmination of the genre's representations of incest within the Brontë's complex depictions of endogamic conjugality.[113] My range of texts is similar to that specified by Rictor Norton in *Gothic Readings: The First Wave, 1764–1840* (2000), to which I add the Brontës as an essential component given their distinctive treatments of the incest thematic.[114] I analyse this wide range of texts to point towards how early forms of the novel, for example, the sentimental and the romance, helped to shape the Gothic, which then influenced movements such as Romanticism, that, in turn, had distinct effects on late Gothic representations of incest. My selections, in this sense, owe a debt to the work of those scholars whom Michael Gamer describes as having 'banished the traditional Walpole-to-Maturin, 1764–1820 account of the gothic, with its well-demarcated origins and endings'.[115] I argue that extending the traditional endpoint of the Gothic makes it possible to understand the full range of familial, legal, marital, sexual and class implications associated with the genre's deployment of incest that, in later interventions in the Gothic, take on more weight and are made possible due to their engagement with the conventions established through Romantic representations of incest.[116]

Gothic authors deploy the generic convention of incest to reveal as inadequate heteronormative ideologies of sexuality and desire in the patriarchal social structure that render its laws and requirements arbitrary. I examine the various familial ties and incestuous relationships in the Gothic to show how they depict and disrupt contemporary definitions of gender, family and desire. Many of the methodologies adopted in Gothic scholarship and analyses of incest reveal ongoing continuities between their assumptions and those of the very ideologies Gothic authors strove to disrupt through their use of the incest trope. Methodologies such as Freudian psychoanalysis, as Botting argues, can be positioned as a product of Gothic monster-making, showing the effect of Gothic conventions on psychoanalytic theories that are still in wide use today.[117] Similarly, Wallace's and Fitzgerald's points about the Gothic's ongoing influence on literary criticism and feminist metaphors usefully signal the reproduction of Gothic plots in the same scholarly accounts that seek to explain them.[118] Not only does modern literary scholarship often replicate the eighteenth-century understandings of incest in the Gothic and its division on gendered lines, as I have argued, but modern scholarship across a multitude of disciplines also reveals a similar adherence to heteronormative ideologies pertaining to incest that can be located in the original critical accounts of incest in the Gothic.

An adherence to eighteenth-century understandings of incest is discernible in current laws on incest and marriage and it is particularly dangerous when its complicity with the normative models of sexuality, desire and marriage is overlooked. When Mary Jean Corbett deploys the nineteenth-century debates over the illegality of marrying a dead wife's sister to argue that '[w]e are far removed from a time when some relations by marriage … did figure by orthodox standards as … those "consanguines" related to us by blood whom we cannot legally marry', she asserts that there are fundamental differences between the definition of family then and now.[119] Corbett's conclusion ignores modern laws on incest that equally limit marriage to affinal relations. In fact, although it has been legal since the 1907 Deceased Wife's Sister's Marriage Act to marry a sister- or brother-in-law, it remains illegal to marry a mother- or father-in-law unless all the original spouses are dead or to marry a step-sibling with whom one lived before the age of eighteen or by whose parents one was raised.[120] Such laws indicate a continued uneasiness over notions of family and potential incest and are part of an ongoing debate over which relatives by marriage and with which individuals we were raised we may marry.

The conviction that there is a gap between how the family was perceived during the long eighteenth century and current perspectives on family and incest fails to hold up under scrutiny. Modern legal, sociological and scientific analyses help to shed light on the structures of law and ideologies of sexuality that attempted to name and regulate incestuous behaviour in the long eighteenth century and that remain in place in modern society. Using the most current research on incest across the disciplines demonstrates that the works of the Gothic writers are not part of a long-dead past, but are still of significance in today's society, which continues to restrict certain desires while demanding others. These ongoing restrictions of desire and marriage, based partly in shifting definitions of kinship, reveal that we share many similarities with the Gothic world of draconian laws. In disrupting the gendered division of the Gothic and revealing the heteronormative ideologies underpinning scholarly discussions of incest, we can see the Gothic as a genre that operates against these ideologies. Through its representations of incest the Gothic genre offers a non-heteronormative understanding of social and sexual relations, making available alternative models of family, desire and sexuality.

NOTES

1 Frances Burney, *Diary and Letters of Madame D'Arblay, Author of "Evelina," "Cecilia," &c. Edited by Her Niece*, ed. Charlotte Barrett, 7 vols (London: Henry Colburn, 1842), diary entry for 28 November 1786, III, p. 235.
2 *The Critical Review, or, Annals of Literature*, 10 (1794), 50.
3 Burney, pp. 234–6.
4 Burney, diary entry for June 1787, p. 371.
5 Samuel Taylor Coleridge, 20 March 1834. *Specimens of the Table Talk of Samuel Taylor Coleridge*, ed. Henry N. Coleridge, 2nd edn (London: John Murray, 1836), p. 293.
6 George E. Haggerty, 'Psychodrama: hypertheatricality and sexual excess on the Gothic stage', *Theatre Research International*, 28:1 (2003), 32. Haggerty argues that Coleridge's reaction reveals a sense that 'unmanliness is revealed by means of sexual excess' (21).
7 Eliza Parsons, *The Castle of Wolfenbach*, ed. Devendra P. Varma (London: The Folio Press, 1968), pp. 11–12.

8 Michael Warner defines heteronormativity as 'basic conceptualisations [that] ... presuppose and reinforce a paradigmatically male position' and describes 'the depth of the culture's assurance (read: insistence) that humanity and heterosexuality are synonymous'. See his 'Introduction', *Fear of a Queer Planet: Queer Politics and Social Theory*, ed. Michael Warner (Minneapolis: University of Minnesota Press, 1993), p. xxiii.

9 For example, I argue that in configurations of incest between uncles and nieces such as in *Wolfenbach* incest often represents a combination of male abuses and control of women and their property while incestuous relationships such as that of the siblings in Eleanor Sleath's *The Orphan of the Rhine* (1798) represent the imposition and arbitrary nature of cultural rules and laws regarding desire and marriage. These regulations are escaped through the recognition of incestuous desires and a retreat from society in novels such as Mary Shelley's *Matilda* (completed in 1820; published in 1959).

10 Claude Lévi-Strauss, *The Elementary Structures of Kinship* (London: Taylor & Francis, 1969), p. 24.

11 Joseph Shepher, *Incest: A Biosocial View* (New York: Academic Press, 1983), p. 97.

12 Sigmund Freud, *Three Essays on the Theory of Sexuality*, ed. and trans. James Strachey [1953] (New York: Basic Books, 2000), p. 91.

13 Judith Lewis Herman with Lisa Hirschman, *Father–Daughter Incest* (Cambridge, MA: Harvard University Press, 1981), p. 27.

14 Anne K. Mellor, *Mary Shelley: Her Life, Her Fiction, Her Monsters* (London: Routledge, 1989), pp. 197–8.

15 David Punter and Glennis Byron, *The Gothic* (Oxford: Blackwell Publishing, 2004), pp. 278–9.

16 Antonio Gramsci, *The Prison Notebooks*, vol. III, ed. and trans. Joseph A. Buttigieg (New York: Columbia University Press, 2010), pp. 213; 299.

17 Antonio Gramsci, *The Prison Notebooks*, vol. I, ed. and trans. Joseph A. Buttigieg (New York: Columbia University Press, 1992), pp. 156–7.

18 Gramsci, I, p. 137.

19 Terry Eagleton, *Ideology: An Introduction* (London: Verso, 1991), p. 112. See also Raymond Williams, *The Long Revolution* (Peterborough, Ontario: Broadview, 2001), in which Williams argues that society's complex social relations, 'the social character – a valued system of behaviour and attitudes – is taught formally and informally' (p. 63).

20 See Warner's examination of 'culture's assurance ... that humanity and heterosexuality are synonymous', p. xxiii.

21 Eagleton, p. 116. See also Foucault's analysis of discourse and power in *Power/Knowledge: Selected Interviews and Other Writings 1972–1977*, ed. Colin Gordon, trans. Colin Gordon *et al.* (Brighton: Harvester Press, 1980), pp. 93–4.

22 Eagleton, p. 116.
23 Michel Foucault, *The History of Sexuality Volume I: An Introduction*, trans. R. Hurley [1979] (Harmondsworth: Penguin, repr. 1981), p. 89. Examinations of social customs that act as substitutes for the law are essential in analysing Gothic writers like Eleanor Sleath, who describes female behaviour and desire as regulated by 'the laws of delicacy, which are sometimes severe and arbitrary', in *The Orphan of the Rhine* (London: The Folio Press, 1968), p. 127.
24 Scholarly accounts grounded in heteronormativity may inscribe these ideologies onto the texts; see particularly Diane Long Hoeveler's arguments, influenced by psychoanalysis, that Gothic writers advocated victim feminism in *Gothic Feminism: The Professionalization of Gender from Charlotte Smith to the Brontës* (Liverpool: Liverpool University Press, 1998), pp. x–xvi.
25 For analyses of the Gothic that work against traditional accounts see Ellen Malenas Ledoux's 'Defiant damsels: Gothic space and female agency in *Emmeline*, *The Mysteries of Udolpho* and *Secresy*', *Women's Writing*, 18:3 (2011), 331–47; Maria Purves's *The Gothic and Catholicism: Religion, Cultural Exchange and the Popular Novel, 1785–1829* (Cardiff: University of Wales Press, 2009); and Lauren Fitzgerald's 'Female Gothic and the Institutionalization of Gothic Studies', in Diana Wallace and Andrew Smith (eds), *The Female Gothic: New Directions* (Basingstoke: Palgrave Macmillan, 2009), pp. 13–25.
26 By its effects I mean not only the perpetuation of submission and dominance within these relationships but also the reinforcement of the structures of law and inheritance that maintain social hegemony.
27 Works by scholars who began to interrogate the traditional marginalisation of the genre include Juliann Fleenor's *The Female Gothic* (Montreal: Eden Press, 1983), Eve Kosofsky Sedgwick's *The Coherence of Gothic Conventions* (New York: Arno Press, 1980) and Ellen Moers's *Literary Women: The Great Writers* [1976] (Oxford: Oxford University Press, repr. 1985).
28 Moers, p. 90.
29 E. J. Clery, *The Rise of Supernatural Fiction* (Cambridge: Cambridge University Press, 1995), p. 110. Similarly, Robert Miles argues that the critical distinctions made between the Female Gothic and the German schauerroman (shudder novel) and works like it – traditionally positioned as Male Gothic – are based on false perceptions of difference in depictions of violence and the supernatural in *Ann Radcliffe: The Great Enchantress* (Manchester: Manchester University Press, 1995), p. 44.
30 Walter Scott and J. W. Lake, *The Poetical Works of Sir Walter Scott, With a Sketch of His Life* (Philadelphia: J. Crissy and Thomas, Cowperthwait & Co., 1838), p. xxii.
31 Kate Ferguson Ellis, *The Contested Castle: Gothic Novels and the Subversion of Domestic Ideology* (Urbana: University of Illinois Press, 1989), p. xiii.

32 Diana Wallace and Andrew Smith, 'Introduction', Wallace and Smith, *The Female Gothic: New Directions*, p. 3.
33 James Watt, *Contesting the Gothic* (Cambridge: Cambridge University Press, 1999), p. 8.
34 Vartan P. Messier, 'The conservative, the transgressive, and the reactionary: Ann Radcliffe's *The Italian* as a response to Matthew Lewis' *The Monk*', *Atenea*, 25:2 (2005), 39.
35 Wallace and Smith, 'Introduction', p. 11. See also Lauren Fitzgerald's 'Female Gothic and the Institutionalization of Gothic Studies'. Fitzgerald points to feminist critical accounts of the Gothic that adhere to its ongoing gendered division as consequently reproducing the plots of the Female Gothic in an attempt to reclaim the genre for women.
36 John Keats to George and Georgiana Keats, 24 February 1819. *The Complete Works of John Keats*, vol. V, *Letters, 1819–1820*, ed. H. Buxton Forman (New York: Thomas Y. Crowell & Co., 1901), p. 25. In this letter Keats refers to Ann Radcliffe as 'Mother Radcliffe'.
37 See Julie Brickman, 'Female Lives, Feminist Deaths: The Relationship of the Montreal Massacre to Dissociation, Incest and Violence against Women', in Renée R. Curry (ed.), *States of Rage: Emotional Eruption, Violence and Social Change* (New York: New York University Press, 1996), pp. 15–34; and 'Feminist, nonsexist, and traditional models of therapy: implications for working with incest', *Women and Therapy*, 3:1 (1984), 49–68; Lena Dominelli, 'Betrayal of trust: a feminist analysis of power relationships in incest abuse and its relevance for social work practice', *British Journal of Social Work*, 19:1 (1989), 291–308 and 'Father–daughter incest: patriarchy's shameful secret', *Critical Social Policy: Special Feminist Issue*, 6:16 (1986), 8–22; Juliet Mitchell, *Psychoanalysis and Feminism: Freud, Reich, Laing and Women* [1974] (repr. as *Psychoanalysis and Feminism: A Radical Reassessment of Freudian Psychoanalysis*, New York: Basic Books, 2000), pp. 370–8.
38 Punter and Byron summarise the rise of feminism in the 1960s and 1970s as coinciding with and influencing the ways in which the Female Gothic was read in *The Gothic*, pp. 278–81.
39 Mitchell, pp. 370–8.
40 Gayle Rubin, 'The Traffic in Women: Notes on the "Political Economy" of Sex', in Rayna R. Reiter (ed.), *Toward an Anthropology of Women* (New York: Monthly Review Press, 1975), pp. 157–210.
41 Fred Botting, *Gothic: The New Critical Idiom* (London: Routledge, 1996), p. 20.
42 Freud, *Three Essays on the Theory of Sexuality*, p. 91; and *The Interpretation of Dreams*, ed. and trans. James Strachey [1953] (New York: Avon, 1980), p. 256.
43 Miles, p. 106.
44 See also: Ruth Perry, *Novel Relations: The Transformation of Kinship in English Literature and Culture 1748–1818* (Cambridge: Cambridge University

Press, 2004); and Ruth Bienstock Anolik, 'The missing mother: the meanings of maternal absence in the Gothic mode', *Modern Language Studies*, 33:1/2 (2003), 25–43.

45 Ellis, pp. 37–45.
46 Perry, pp. 388–90.
47 Betty Rizzo identifies the Gothic as a genre in which 'the usurping patriarch' abuses power inherent in the patriarchal structure of the conjugal family in 'Renegotiating the Gothic', in Paula Backscheider (ed.), *Revising Women: Eighteenth-Century "Women's Fiction" and Social Engagement* (Baltimore: Johns Hopkins University Press, 2000), p. 61.
48 Angela Wright, *Gothic Fiction: A Reader's Guide to Essential Criticism* (Basingstoke: Palgrave Macmillan, 2007), p. 147.
49 Rizzo, p. 63.
50 Maggie Kilgour, *The Rise of the Gothic Novel* (London: Routledge, 1995), p. 12.
51 Recent work on the Gothic has opposed readings of the genre as always representative of patriarchal dangers. See, for example, Ledoux's excellent 'Defiant damsels', in which she challenges 'the domestic-imprisonment' understanding of the Gothic advanced by scholars such as Ellis, arguing instead that through their navigations of Gothic space heroines demonstrate agency and empowerment (333).
52 Hoeveler, p. 56.
53 Punter and Byron, p. 280.
54 Hoeveler, pp. 56–7.
55 See Eugenia C. DeLamotte, *Perils of the Night: A Feminist Study of Nineteenth-Century Gothic* (Oxford: Oxford University Press, 1990) and Ellis, p. 118.
56 Hoeveler, pp. 34–5.
57 George E. Haggerty, *Queer Gothic* (Urbana: University of Illinois Press, 2006), p. 31.
58 Shelley's *Matilda* represents female-sought father–daughter incest between a like-minded father and daughter, while Anne Ker's *The Mysterious Count; or, Montville Castle* (1803) shows a father's incestuous pursuit of a beautiful young woman who is, unbeknownst to him, also his long-lost daughter. Once this becomes known (via the plot device of a last-minute discovery of matching daggers) he ceases his pursuit and attempts to act in a strictly paternal role.
59 Hoeveler, p. 57.
60 Frances A. Chiu, 'From nobodadies to noble daddies: writing political and paternal authority in English fiction of the 1780s and 1790s', *Eighteenth-Century Life*, 26:2 (2002), 9, 13.
61 See Chapter 3 for a detailed examination of uncle–niece incest in the Gothic.
62 Perry, p. 290.
63 Joanne Bailey's *Unquiet Lives: Marriage and Marriage Breakdown in England, 1660–1800* (Cambridge: Cambridge University Press, 2003) and Naomi

Tadmor's *Family and Friends in Eighteenth-Century England* (Cambridge: Cambridge University Press, 2001) are particularly useful studies of family and marriage in the long eighteenth century.
64 I refer particularly to the narrative advanced in Stone's *The Family, Sex and Marriage in England, 1500–1800* (London: Weidenfeld & Nicolson, 1977).
65 Joanne Bailey, 'Review of Perry, Ruth, *Novel Relations: The Transformation of Kinship in English Literature and Culture 1748–1818* by', H-Albion, H-Net Reviews (June 2006), www.h-net.org/reviews/showrev.php?id=11824 [accessed 30 March 2011].
66 Perry, p. 377.
67 Margot Gayle Backus, *The Gothic Family Romance: Heterosexuality, Child Sacrifice, and the Anglo-Irish Colonial Order* (Durham, NC: Duke University Press, 1999), p. 43.
68 Perry, pp. 375–6. Novels that undermine Perry's claim about brothers viewing sisters as possessions or sex objects include *The Castles of Athlin and Dunbayne* and *A Sicilian Romance*, both featuring protective and loving brothers who represent an ideal partner, as well as *Adeline or the Orphan* (1790), an anonymous novel in which the heroine forms a deep and lasting platonic love with her adopted brother.
69 Perry, p. 376. Perry also describes the Gothic as offering 'the terms to critique a kinship system that invested a sinister degree of power in individual men over their immediate conjugal families' (p. 396).
70 Edward Westermarck, *A Short History of Human Marriage* (London: Macmillan, 1926), p. 80.
71 Bailey, 'Review of Perry'.
72 Novels like *Correlia, The Mysterious Count* and Selina Davenport's *The Sons of the Viscount and the Daughters of the Earl* (1813) depict the tensions in negotiating the demands of desires and consanguineal loyalties.
73 In novels like *Adeline or the Orphan* where the heroine is raised in a foster family whose biological son is encouraged by his parents to view and treat her as blood kin, Adeline and her adopted brother only ever see each other as kin in spite of their knowledge that there is no blood bond between them. In contrast, in Sleath's *The Orphan of the Rhine*, Laurette's presumed status as Enrico's illegitimate half-sister is no hindrance to their romantic love.
74 Adam Kuper, 'Changing the subject – about cousin marriage, among other things', *Journal of the Royal Anthropological Institute (NS)*, 14:4 (2008), 727. Kuper argues that greed causes the incest taboo to become flexible when financially beneficial.
75 Ellen's marriage to the wealthy Lord Howel allows her family to keep their ancestral estate, a fact that reinforces the benefits of flexible incest regulations that are, in this instance, tied up with symbols of aristocratic and patriarchal institutions.

76 Maureen Quilligan, *Incest and Agency in Elizabeth's England* (Philadelphia: University of Pennsylvania Press, 2005), pp. 1–32.
77 Pat Gill, 'Pathetic passions: incestuous desire in the plays of Otway and Lee', *The Eighteenth Century: Theory and Interpretation*, 30:3 (1998), 206.
78 In *Gothic: The New Critical Idiom*, Botting refers to the use of historical settings as 'the continued fascination with the architecture, customs and values of the Middles Ages' (p. 5).
79 For example, in Radcliffe's *The Mysteries of Udolpho* (1794) Emily is held against her will by her uncle through marriage, who uses legal rhetoric and illegal sexual threats in his attempts to steal her property; in *The Orphan of the Rhine* the co-reared foster-siblings declare their love for each other in spite of their mother's fears regarding the illegality of their union; and in *Matilda* the eponymous heroine flees from the society that has caused her father's suicide through its prohibition of incest.
80 In *The Italian* Ellena and Vivaldi marry at a new, idyllic estate in a celebration with individuals of all social ranks, while in *Wuthering Heights* Cathy and Hareton's union binds individuals of very different social backgrounds into a family circle comprising only themselves and a servant.
81 Ellen Pollak, *Incest and the English Novel, 1684–1814* (Baltimore: Johns Hopkins University Press, 2003). Pollak's analyses of incest disrupt understandings of it as an inherently transgressive act, while revealing this potential in its literary representations.
82 Adam Kuper, *Incest and Influence* (Cambridge, MA: Harvard University Press, 2009). Kuper illuminates the role of incest in the private and public spheres of eighteenth- and nineteenth-century England to shed light on the overlapping kinship networks created by (primarily) cousin and uncle–niece marriages that allowed families such as the Rothschilds to gain financial and political power.
83 See DeLamotte; and Hoeveler.
84 Research on genetics and attraction such as that undertaken by Maurice Greenberg and Roland Littlewood is presented in Littlewood's *Pathologies of the West: An Anthropology of Mental Illness in Europe and America* (London: Continuum, 2002). Lynn Åkesson's 'Bound by Blood? New Meanings of Kinship and Individuality in Discourses of Genetic Counseling', in Linda Stone (ed.), *New Directions in Anthropological Kinship* (Oxford: Rowman & Littlefield, 2001), pp. 125–36, reveals the influence of modern scientific advances on understanding incestuous relationships and configurations of kinship. Susan McKinnon's 'American Kinship/American Incest: Asymmetries in a Scientific Discourse', in Sylvia Yanagisako and Carol Delaney (eds), *Naturalizing Power: Essays in Feminist Cultural Analysis* (New York: Routledge, 1995), pp. 25–46, examines the role of gender ideologies underlying scholarly and cultural understandings of incest.

85 See Sandra M. Gilbert and Susan Gubar, *The Madwoman in the Attic: The Woman Writer and the Nineteenth-Century Literary Imagination* (New Haven, CT: Yale University Press, 1984); DeLamotte; Eve Kosofsky Sedgwick, 'Toward the Gothic: Terrorism and Homosexual Panic', in *Between Men: English Literature and Male Homosexual Desire* (New York: Columbia University Press, 1985), pp. 83–96; Michelle A. Masse, *In the Name of Love: Women, Masochism and the Gothic* (Ithaca, NY: Cornell University Press, 1992); and Pamela Kaufman, 'Burke, Freud and the Gothic', *Studies in Burke and His Time*, 13:3 (1972), 2179–92, in which Kaufman identifies the Gothic with a 'deliberate masochistic reveling in terror' in her Freudian reading of the genre (2179).

86 Anne Williams, *Art of Darkness: A Poetics of Gothic* (Chicago: University of Chicago Press, 1995).

87 Nancy Chodorow, *Feminism and Psychoanalytic Theory* [1989] (New Haven, CT: Yale University Press, repr. 1991), pp. 195–6. See also Samuel Slipp's exploration of the patriarchal and phallocentric premises that render Freudian analysis inadequate in *The Freudian Mystique: Freud, Women, and Feminism* (New York: New York University Press, 1993), pp. 13–19 and 188–202.

88 Fred Botting, 'Introduction', Fred Botting (ed.), *The Gothic: Essays and Studies* (Cambridge: D. S. Brewer, 2001), pp. 4–5.

89 Watt, p. 3.

90 Watt, p. 4.

91 See Sue Chaplin, *The Gothic and the Rule of Law, 1764–1820* (Basingstoke and London: Palgrave Macmillan, 2007); Leslie J. Moran's 'Law and the Gothic Imagination', in Botting, *The Gothic: Essays and Studies*, pp. 87–109; David Punter's *Gothic Pathologies: The Text, the Body and the Law* (Basingstoke: Macmillan Press, 1998); and Anolik.

92 Moran, p. 91.

93 Chiu, 1–2.

94 Punter, *Gothic Pathologies*.

95 Diana Wallace, '"The Haunting Idea": Female Gothic Metaphors and Feminist Theory', in Wallace and Smith, *The Female Gothic: New Directions*, pp. 26–41.

96 Anolik, 26. Similarly, Chiu picks up on this when she argues: 'Primogeniture was increasingly viewed as a means more destructive of than conducive to domestic harmony' (13).

97 Pollak, pp. 30–51.

98 Pollak, pp. 30–8.

99 See Foucault, *History of Sexuality*.

100 Leo Bersani, 'Foucault, Freud, fantasy, and power', *GLQ: A Journal of Lesbian and Gay Studies*, 2:1/2 (1995), 18.

101 Foucault, *History of Sexuality*, p. 109.
102 *Clermont* is not a wholly conservative or radical Gothic novel, but in its representation of cousin marriage demonstrates the subversive potential of incest and the conflicts of individual desires and familial duty.
103 Davenport's *The Sons of the Viscount and the Daughters of the Earl* depicts exogamy as subversive of normative models of desire in a portrayal of an uncle's desire to keep his niece within the family as caused by his privileged social status that creates a sense of entitlement to whichever female body he desires.
104 See Marcel Mauss, *The Gift: The Form and Reason for Exchange in Archaic Societies* [1925], trans. W. D. Halls (London: Routledge, 1990); Lévi-Strauss; and Margaret Mead, *Male and Female* [1949] (New York: HarperCollins, 2001) for anthropological investigations of culture, the exchange of women and the effect of culture on gender formation.
105 Cynthia Klekar and Linda Zionkowski (eds), *The Culture of the Gift in Eighteenth-Century England* (Basingstoke: Palgrave Macmillan, 2009).
106 Klekar and Zionowski's arguments about gift exchange and notions of obligation provide important context for reading *Correlia*, in which the heroine's foster-father (who is later revealed to be her blood father) uses the language of obligation in attempting to solicit her love.
107 See Mitchell, p. 380 for an analysis of incest as decreasingly taboo in capitalist society.
108 Littlewood's *Pathologies of the West* examines genetic attraction and incest; David Haig (in 'Asymmetric relations: internal conflicts and the horror of incest', *Evolution and Human Behaviour*, 20:2 (1999), 83–98) views incest's potential to create genetically healthy offspring. Justin H. Park's article, 'Is aversion to incest psychologically privileged? When sex and sociosexuality do not predict sexual willingness', *Personality and Individual Differences*, 45:7 (2008), 661–5, contains an extremely useful review of anthropological, genetic, biological and sociological understandings of incest avoidance.
109 David Livingstone Smith, 'Beyond Westermarck: can shared mothering or maternal phenotype matching account for incest avoidance?', *Evolutionary Psychology*, 5:1 (2007), 206.
110 Narcissism and incest are discussed most often in relation to sibling incest in Romantic works, but the frequent absorption of the Gothic into this period has allowed scholars to look at these sibling relationships as narcissistic or an inversion thereof. See Alan Richardson, 'Rethinking Romantic incest: human universals, literary representations, and the biology of mind', *New Literary History*, 31:3 (2000), 553–72.
111 Romantic works of sibling incest, such as Lord Byron's *Manfred* (1817) or Shelley's *Frankenstein* (1818), often end in death for one or both siblings, while this is much less common in the Gothic. See also Gail Finney,

'Self-reflexive siblings: incest as narcissism in Tieck, Wagner, and Thomas Mann', *German Quarterly*, 56:2 (1983), 243–56.

112 Botting in *Gothic: The New Critical Idiom*, pp. 10–18 identifies the scholarly history of viewing the Gothic as broadly Romantic in nature while simultaneously positioning its themes as oppositional to many of the Romantic ideals, locating this tradition in Mario Praz's *The Romantic Agony* (1933) and Eino Railo's *The Haunted Castle: A Study of the Elements of English Romanticism* (1927).

113 I am not attempting to argue that the Gothic would have been recognisable to its contemporary readership as a distinct genre by the mid-eighteenth century, but that, as Michael Gamer argues, the conventions, aesthetics and aims that are associated with the Gothic, as well as the term, appeared consistently in texts from this time. See Michael Gamer, *Romanticism and the Gothic: Genre, Reception, and Canon Formation* (Cambridge: Cambridge University Press, 2000), p. 49.

114 Rictor Norton, *Gothic Readings: The First Wave, 1764–1840* (London: Leicester University Press, 2000).

115 Gamer, p. 28.

116 In this sense I take up the developments that Gamer finds have been made available by those scholars who 'have been arguing for a more intimate and active relation between romantic and gothic writers' (p. 28), pointing to the conventions of Romantic narcissistic incest or the Romantic siblings-as-soulmates configurations (see Finney) within later Gothic works.

117 Botting, 'Introduction', pp. 4–5.

118 Fitzgerald, pp. 13–25; Wallace, pp. 26–41.

119 Mary Jean Corbett, *Family Likeness: Sex, Marriage and Incest from Jane Austen to Virginia Woolf* (Ithaca, NY: Cornell University Press, 2008), p. 59.

120 'Prohibited marriages: forbidden degrees of relationship', www.weddingguideuk.com/articles/legal/prohibited.asp [accessed 24 June 2010].

I
'Unimaginable sensations': father–daughter incest and the economics of exchange

> Let a veil be drawn over the unimaginable sensations of a guilty father.
> Mary Shelley, *Matilda* (1959)[1]

There are several problems that usually emerge in scholarship examining representations of father–daughter incest in the Gothic, even in works by scholars whose goal is to lay bare the feminist themes that are central to the genre. Principal among these is that representations of father–daughter incest often cause works to be placed in the gendered subgenre of Female Gothic and to be viewed through a lens predicated on this generic division. What frequently stems from this homogenising gesture is a misinterpretation or misrepresentation of the ambition of the Gothic as displaying what E. J. Clery refers to as an 'intrinsic "femaleness"'.[2] This leads to texts being viewed as part of a Male or Female Gothic form and their representations of father–daughter incest to be understood through these gendered divisions. As I suggested in the Introduction, the application of Freudian theory, sociological approaches to incest and structural anthropological discussions of the incest taboo contribute to reading father–daughter incest within a gendered framework that tends to view this incestuous relationship as alternately imagined or abusive. Freudian approaches are often applied in conjunction with anthropological understandings of incest such as those advanced by Claude Lévi-Strauss, who theorised that: 'the prohibition of incest is ... the fundamental step ... in which the transition from nature to culture is accomplished'.[3] The Freudian psychoanalytic preoccupations that underpin much scholarship on the Gothic similarly identify the prohibition of incest as fundamental to the formation of culture, as incest allows adolescents to move from the family into exogamic relationships that complete the transition into culture. Sociological approaches that are informed by the equation of father–daughter incest with abuses of power contribute to readings of these relationships as reflective of the abuses inherent in the emerging nuclear family and domestic spaces.[4] These understandings have focused scholarly readings of father–daughter incest in the Gothic on locating the perceived or real threats against the heroine within the home or castle. I argue that in moving away from these approaches to rely instead upon feminist theories on the traffic in women, representations of father–daughter incest can be understood as engaging with and troubling notions of the exchange of women deemed necessary to culture.

The Freudian mode of viewing incest is, inconveniently for those who use it to lend credence to their arguments regarding incest in the Female Gothic, predicated on the notion of children desiring the opposite-sex parent who raises them and seeing the same-sex parent as a rival. Sigmund Freud argued that 'the simplest course for the child would be to choose as his sexual objects the same person whom, since his childhood, he has loved with what may be described as a damped-down libido'.[5] Freud believed that incestuous desires rearoused at puberty must be fought against in order for adolescents to distance themselves from their parents and therefore the incest barrier is 'a cultural demand made by society'.[6] In *The Interpretation of Dreams* (1900) Freud's statement that 'boys regarded their fathers and girls their mothers as rivals in love, whose elimination could not fail but to be to their advantage', was founded on his belief that the first sexual desire of children is towards their mothers, an argument explored further in *Totem and Taboo* (1912).[7] This theory, which stipulates that female desire and sexuality are developed in response to the father figure, allows first for a pre-Oedipal stage in which the daughter loves and bonds with the mother before turning to her desire and love for the father, a stage that engenders rivalry with the mother. The incestuous desire is resolved later when the daughter is able to transfer her incestuous desires to another male. The Oedipal phase has two periods, between ages three to five, after which there is a waning consequent upon repression, and then it is reactivated in puberty, when puberty makes possible the transference of incestuous desires.[8]

Freudian theories of incest have become increasingly discredited in the psychological community, in part due to the work of modern psychologists who argue that Freud discounted the actual experiences of his female patients' sexual abuse and that his theories have limited applicability to female sexuality and desire.[9] Psychologist Anne Cossins describes Freud's work on incest as 'discredited due to the circumstances surrounding his initial revelations of incest in patients he was treating and his subsequent repudiations of those claims [as fantasies]'.[10] Similarly, psychiatrist Peter D. Kramer calls Freud modern history's 'most debunked doctor', whose work 'doesn't hold up very well at all … every particular is wrong: the universality of the Oedipus complex, penis envy, infantile sexuality'.[11] In an article that describes the displacement of Freud's incest theories, Bruce Bower states: 'one current school of psychoanalytic thought rejects Freud's assertion that the Oedipus complex occurs universally, arguing instead that psychologically disturbed parents sometimes stir up incestuous and intensely competitive feelings in their children'.[12] Though this theory fails to account for incestuous feelings and desires exhibited by parents or children not raised by the relations they desire, it is more closely linked to the types of incest uncovered in the Gothic than a purely Freudian interpretation. The sexism underlying Freudian theory is pointed out by feminist scholar Gayle Rubin, who finds it challenging to use Freud and Lévi-Strauss to account for the incest taboo as '[they] write within an intellectual tradition produced by a culture in which women are oppressed … the sexism in the tradition of which they are a part tends to be dragged in with each borrowing'.[13] In spite of what Rubin describes as the misogynistic tradition underlying these modes of analysis that has led to a feminist re-evaluation of Freudian psychoanalysis and Lévi-Strauss's structural anthropology, these are still privileged approaches in analyses of female sexuality and incest that find their way into literary scholarship on the Gothic.[14]

Even scholars who seek to displace Freudian models of sexual desire sometimes return to the Freudian paradigms that are so entrenched in literary analyses of incest and sexuality more generally.[15] Julie Shaffer, for example, argues first that 'by situating explicit incestuous lust in the father's desire, such desire need not be projected onto the daughter in the way Freud does'.[16] However, Shaffer subsequently gives credence to Freudian theory when she argues: 'Arraigning patriarchal power in the form of the father figure … situates that power in the home, site of the construction of the female character's sexuality where it develops ostensibly in response to the father.'[17] In a similar way, Tania Modleski argues that Ann Radcliffe's plot 'became popular at a time when the nuclear family was being consolidated. ... It spoke powerfully to the young girl struggling to achieve psychological autonomy in a home where the remote, but all-powerful, father ruled over an utterly dependent wife.'[18] These readings rely on both the psychological and sociological models of incest and although they provide important insights into viewing incestuous threats as linked to the domestic structure they focus exclusively on the father as a threat within the nuclear family.[19] Part of the problem in deploying this Freudian model to explain incest and female sexuality in the Gothic is that it requires father–daughter incest to be read as a product of a familial dynamic seldom present within the texts.[20] Freudian theory that claims girls develop incestuous desires for the fathers who raise them is not applicable to the many Gothic novels in which girls are not raised by their fathers. Its application can thus lead to misreadings that diminish the importance of incest to the narrative and position heroines as victims of fantasies rather than threats. For incest to be a result of children desiring the opposite-sex parent who raises them in infancy and toddler-hood, there clearly needs to *be* an opposite-sex parent present during these developmental periods, which is not the case in many Gothic works. In addition to the lack of the appropriate family structure, authors did not often depict daughters who desire their fathers, but when/if they do, it rarely correlates to a synonymous hatred of the mother figure, who in these instances is most often absent.[21] The Freudian paradigm is therefore irrelevant to analyses of novels where the narrative and/or familial structure prohibit conformity to it.

Applying Freudian theory to analyses of heroines can trivialise incestuous threats by framing them as fantasies. Hoeveler, for example, asserts that Gothic heroines seek or fear incest because they have 'an infantile desire to remain in the paternal and protective domicile of childhood'.[22] Recognising that she must leave home to marry, the heroine attempts to make her father appear evil as she

> does not want to leave her father and marry another ... Therefore, she fancies that her father has attempted to rape her (*The Romance of the Forest*) or her father is an adulterer (*Mysteries of Udolpho*) or her father has tried to kill her (*The Italian*). Only if she can convince herself that she exists in such a super-charged moral universe ... can she agree to separate from the paternal abode.[23]

Uniting incest with the Gothic tropes of murder, adultery and hidden secrets seems to corroborate Freudian theory on incest as fantasy or seduction, but when the novels used to support this point are closely examined some disturbing discrepancies emerge. If the heroine of Radcliffe's *The Italian* (1797), Ellena di Rosalba, encounters an internal struggle between remaining within the protective paternal home or marrying an interloper, she would necessarily have experienced such a patriarchal home. However, Ellena, raised by her aunt since the age of two in an exclusively female society, has no memory of a patriarchal house. As such, a Freudian analysis of Ellena's desires and motivations becomes impossible to reconcile with her upbringing. The second point, that because of Ellena's desire to remain in the paternal abode she imagines an attempted murder by her father, misidentifies both the violent encounter and the familial relationship between Schedoni and his brother's daughter, Ellena. Schedoni enters his niece's room, intent on killing her as she sleeps, but is stopped by the sight of a miniature she wears that he believes is his likeness. The attempted murder is real and, therefore, the use of the term 'fancies' with its implicit denotation of belief without fact or foundation is inaccurate. Aligning Ellena's murder fantasy with other Radcliffean heroines' imagined fears seeks to legitimise the use of Freudian theories yet also conflates the Gothic tropes of terror, incest and hidden secrets. This diminishes the relevance of individual conventions – particularly incest and its various configurations – to the subversive agenda of the Gothic.

Rather than apply a Freudian methodology that is often combined with structural anthropological and feminist sociological approaches, I argue that feminist theory on the exchange of women and recent advances in scientific and anthropological theory better serve analyses of representations of incest in the Gothic. Opponents of Freud's incest ideas include psychiatrist Mark T. Erickson, anthropologists Arthur P. Wolf and William Durham and feminist theorist Florence Rush, all of whom argue that rather than desiring those by whom one is surrounded in infancy and adolescence, humans tend sexually to reject those by and with whom they are raised.[24] This theory, put forth by sociologist Edward Westermarck and known as the Westermarck effect, can be summarised as 'an innate aversion to sexual intercourse between persons living very closely together from early youth'.[25] An intriguing aspect of the Westermarck effect is the notion that although brothers and sisters (and indeed, any non-related children) who are raised together will tend to be sexually averse to one another, if there is a separation at birth and siblings are not raised together they are likely to be highly sexually attracted to one another in adulthood.[26] Foreshadowing recent anthropological and scientific research, there are many instances in Gothic texts of fathers and daughters and other blood relations who sexually desire or who are highly attracted to one another after a period of separation. Such texts deploy contemporary understandings of the pull of blood to trouble available models of female desire and the paternal exchanges of daughters.

In analysing representations of father–daughter incest in the Gothic it is necessary to move away from Freudian approaches and examine more closely the attention paid in these depictions to issues of marriage, the exchange of women and female agency. The legal reality of women's experience of marriage was famously described by eighteenth-century legal scholar William Blackstone as a civil death.[27] Gothic scholars such as Ruth Bienstock Anolik and Diana Wallace have taken up Blackstone's description of women after marriage to argue that conventions such as the imprisonment, starvation, haunting and disappearance of wives at the hands of violent husbands or brothers-in-law reflect this legal non-existence. The twin threats of patriarchy and domesticity to women are also manifest, as Ruth Perry and Kate Ferguson Ellis have argued, in the oft-employed Gothic trope of incestuous desires and relationships.[28] Gothic representations of the constraints and dangers experienced by women after marriage are, I argue, not only literalisations of their legal status and entrapment in domesticity, but are also the consequence of the economics of exchange that positions women as objects transferred and – as Anolik points out – 'possessed' by the husband in marriage.[29] In order more fully to explore the implications of these repeated concerns alongside father–daughter incest I look to the works of Luce Irigaray and Gayle Rubin, who question Lévi-Strauss's widely accepted assumptions about the exchange of women as fundamental to society.

Irigaray and Rubin articulate different understandings of the development of a (patriarchal) culture that demands the incest prohibition in order to facilitate the building of alliances through the exchange of women. Irigaray disrupts traditional thinking that the exchange of women as commodities is necessary to patriarchal society in *This Sex Which is Not One* (1977), in which she examines Lévi-Strauss's premise regarding the incest taboo and the construction of culture through such exchanges. Irigaray argues that 'women are "products" used and exchanged by men. Their status is that of merchandise, "commodities" …

The use, consumption, and circulation of their sexualised bodies underwrite the organisation and the reproductions of the social order, in which they have never taken part as "subjects".[30] Gayle Rubin similarly questions Lévi-Strauss's assertion that culture would not exist without the incest taboo and exchange of women, elaborating that culture is inventive and 'kinship systems do not merely exchange women. They exchange sexual access, genealogical statuses, lineage, names and ancestors, rights and people – men, women, and children – in concrete systems of social relationships'.[31] Rubin resists Lévi-Strauss's structural anthropological understanding of the incest taboo as the basis of culture because 'there is an economics and a politics to sex/gender systems which is obscured by the concept of "exchange of women".[32] I use these approaches to position the exchange of women as a necessary though not natural demand of patriarchy, arguing that in specific incestuous configurations women are removed from their position in the market economy as a method of exchange and wealth accumulation, causing a fracture in society that allows for the development of alternative models of female agency and desire.

In light of these insights, this chapter will set out to examine the incestuous relationships between fathers and daughters in Horace Walpole's *The Castle of Otranto* (1764), Radcliffe's *The Romance of the Forest* (1791) and Mary Shelley's *Matilda* (1959) and the texts' attendant scholarship. These three works have been selected in order to compare the way that incest is rendered in a representative chronology of Gothic texts beginning with what has been traditionally defined as the original Gothic novel. Incestuous desire is characterised in Walpole's work as a threatening, male-situated passion; it is also one of the novel's means of political parody. This contrasts with representations of father–daughter incest in Radcliffe's novel, in which such relationships are the underlying narrative force spurred by an at times reciprocal, though unrealised, desire. This incestuous relationship is reworked into a mutual desire that is presented as capable of being actualised in Shelley's text, which, like Radcliffe's, uses father–daughter desires to structure the novel. These three novels offer fertile ground on which to examine the effect of the depictions of incest in both male- and female-authored novels and over a half-century of changing social values, laws and traditions. The representations of father–daughter incest and female exchange are essential to the social structure in Walpole's political/Gothic text, while in the Gothic novels of Radcliffe and Shelley these representations allow escapes from and destructions of culture. Irigaray's point that 'the economy of desire – of exchange – is man's business' is prefigured by Gothic writers and, through the configuration of father–daughter incest sought by the daughter, Shelley offers a model of female desire that moves beyond the exchange of female bodies.[33] By positioning these works in terms of anthropological and feminist insights into sexuality I argue that father–daughter incest in the Gothic reveals the status of women as commodities and through incestuous sexual agency affords women a means to remove themselves from the marriage market. The result of father–daughter incest is often the destruction of the patriarchal family followed by the formation of alternative structures of family, female agency and desire.

RETURNING TO THE CASTLE: INCEST RESTORES THE RIGHTFUL HEIR IN *THE CASTLE OF OTRANTO*

Literary scholars have long positioned *The Castle of Otranto* as the first Gothic novel and credited Horace Walpole as the genre's originator. Even feminist scholars who are invested in divulging the female roots of the genre silently assent to the critical myth of Walpole as 'the father of the Gothic'. Subsequent attempts to re-evaluate Walpole's role as Gothic progenitor have struggled to work against this long-standing tradition. Ellis, for example, argues that 'it was women writers in the late eighteenth century who took up [Walpole's] literary curiosity and transformed it into a vehicle capable of didacticism as well as entertainment'.[34] That re-evaluations of the genre's origins are beginning to take hold is evidenced by Michael Gamer's criticism that Rictor Norton's *Gothic Readings: The First Wave, 1764–1840* (2000) is not disruptive enough to the status quo of Gothic paternity and chronology, stating that 'here, Walpole is still the first Gothicist, and the proliferating categories … are left intact and unquestioned' and that Norton's account of the Gothic is 'old-fashioned in its treatment of genre and literary periods'.[35]

The language that informs the scholarly placement of Walpole as the 'father of the Gothic' is haunted by the preoccupation with establishing paternity and genealogies that is present in Walpole's first introduction to *Otranto*. Walpole's assertion that he is the progenitor of the Gothic is compromised by the location of this self-conscious declaration within the framework of a text comprising true and false fathers. By describing himself as the discoverer of the manuscript and then revising this statement within subsequent introductions, Walpole establishes himself as a claimant to a title who, much like Manfred himself, is relying on a false – or self-asserted – basis for his declaration. Walpole's position as a pretender to the throne of the Gothic thus parodies the claims of Manfred and the old and young pretenders to the English throne, James Francis Edward Stuart and his son and Charles Edward Stuart, and potentially also George III, given that Walpole 'composed the novella during a fit of intense disillusionment with what he perceived to be George III's excessive use of the royal prerogative'.[36] His declared role as the originator of the Gothic draws attention to the falsity of such claims and ridicules pretend progenitors rather than being a serious statement of paternity. Benjamin Bird argues that Walpole's fiction was 'a safe outlet for … his frustration with the monarchial system of government' and notes that Walpole used the Gothic to 'parody the very notion of hereditary succession' in his later *Hieroglyphic Tales* (1785).[37] Along these lines, James Watt argues that '*Otranto*'s position within any larger cultural movement needs to be qualified, since it seems to construct the Gothic as a source of the ridiculous as much as the sublime.'[38] Walpole's use of parody criticises notions of kingship, inheritance and paternity, deliberately troubling his claim to be the father of the Gothic.

Under the fiction that he translated the text from an ancient manuscript, Walpole wrote about the imagined author: 'I could wish he had grounded his plan on a more useful moral than this; that *the sins of fathers are visited on their children to the third and fourth generation*.'[39] That Walpole singled this out as the overriding moral of the piece locates the text's meaning in the language of paternity, a move that is underscored by the weight scholarship attributes to *Otranto*'s influence on subsequent Gothic generations. In the second introduction, though abandoning the fiction regarding the text's origins, Walpole lays further claim to his literary fatherhood as the genre's originator, stating that the novel was 'an attempt to blend the two kinds of romance, the ancient and the modern' (p. 9), concluding: 'I might have pleaded that having created a new species of romance, I was at liberty to lay down what rules I thought fit for the conduct of it' (p. 14).[40] However, rather than being a wholly new creation, Walpole's work was shaped by contemporary novels and political allegories of which he would certainly have been aware.[41] Walpole described his writing of *Otranto* as a type of therapy 'during a particularly bad year in parliament', which evidences his recognition of the tale's function as a political parody. Sue Chaplin examines 'the fictions of origin Walpole himself generated in respect of this aberrant text', pointing towards it as 'a manifestation of ... political anxieties'.[42] She argues that 'the giant hand of Walpole's dream-text represents the remnants of an aristocratic power that still had sufficient presence in the mid-eighteenth century to challenge the Whig conceptualisation of liberty purportedly embodied in the 1688 settlement'.[43] Accordingly, to read *Otranto* only as a precursor of later Gothic works can lead to a misunderstanding of Walpole's text and the literary tradition of the Gothic.[44] Chaplin's argument that Manfred is an imposter who 'seeks to establish himself as the founding father of a new order of lineage', particularly her point that Manfred 'posits himself as the originating "name of the father" in respect of a political order that has not yet been properly legitimated', applies readily to Walpole and the Gothic genre.[45] Examining the novella's heir who ascends a throne 'only his by virtue of a convoluted, *matrilineal* genealogy', Chaplin asserts that 'the power of the maternal as an originating principle in *Otranto* is denied within an economy that posits paternal lineage as the only source of legitimate authority'.[46] Such points evoke comparisons to Walpole's reign as the father of the genre supported by a tradition in viewing him as such that is centuries old. Walpole's forged and fake paternity is sanctioned as legitimate, while the maternal contribution to the Gothic has been long denied its status as real progenitor. Genres, like people, must have fathers, regardless of women's formative role in their creation. Thus, Walpole, by way of his parodic self-assertion in *Otranto*, is perceived as the paterfamilias of the Gothic, a genre in actuality born of many mothers.[47]

Displacing *Otranto* is a necessary disruption of the traditional genealogy which maintains that Walpole's work established Gothic tropes – such as incest – and their meanings to be taken up by subsequent writers.[48] In relocating *Otranto* as a hybrid of political parody and Gothic romance by a creator self-consciously playing with the notion of real progenitors, I argue that later works by Radcliffe can be understood as creating, rather than reacting to, configurations of father–daughter incest that function very differently from Walpole's representation of violent incest.[49] While Walpole's novel influenced the works of authors such as Clara Reeve, Radcliffe, Charlotte Smith and the Brontës, so too did the emerging sentimental novel, from which Walpole and the later Gothic writers borrowed images and conventions such as those of the imperilled heroine and threats of incest.[50] In Walpole's deployment of incest, father–daughter desires are depicted as a consequence of patriarchy – in many ways, similar to the feminist sociological understandings of incest as an abuse of male power – and as a threat to women and the stability of society, as in Lévi-Strauss's understanding.[51] Incest functions as one convention of many with which Walpole criticises the political structure in general and the aristocracy in particular as invested in controlling the younger generations. Later Gothic novels use representations of father–daughter incest – which Walpole endowed with political significance to expose Parliamentary and governmental flaws – quite differently: in order to offer alternative social models to a society structured around the exchange of women.

Walpole's novel is unique in its sheer silliness. The humour of the servants and the confusion over birth, inheritance and identity are taken to extremes, as is the utter implausibility of the circumstances that bring the characters together at the castle. The manner in which the loose ends are tied together by disclosures from the key characters is comedic in its improbability. Furthermore, the initial murder/destruction of Conrad, the son of the household, is never explained, by means wholly supernatural or other. Walpole describes Manfred, Conrad's father and the head of the castle and family, as: 'not one of those savage tyrants who wanton in cruelty unprovoked … his virtues were always ready to operate, when his passion did not obscure his reason' (p. 33). As passion always obscures Manfred's reason, the ironic description is one of many humorous instances in the text. Although Walpole's iconic scenes of ghosts and subterranean flights are reproduced in countless Gothic novels that followed, that few of them maintain the parodic humour of his tale supports a repositioning of Walpole's novel as a political parody veiled within a Gothic framework. In this respect *Otranto* is more a precursor to George Orwell's *Animal Farm* (1945) than the first example of the Gothic genre.[52] While sentimental, Romantic and other Gothic novels use the convention of coincidence that stretches believability to breaking point, Walpole's integration of humour alongside this convention reveals his text as a work of parody rather than horror. Along these lines, Clery states: '[*Otranto*] seems at first glance to offer the basic stock of Gothic character-types, but closer attention suggests an ambivalence in each of them that verges on irony'; the novel's imagery, including the giant armoured hand, 'provides the opportunity for a humorous subversion of authority'.[53] The size of the hand to which Clery refers links the enormity of the title, land and obligations of men to estate and nobility, subverting authority through the use of ironic and parodic hyperbolic metaphor that is not often encountered in Gothic novels.[54]

Otranto draws attention to size twice within the opening pages: first in reference to the size of the rightful owner of the castle and lordship of Otranto and then to the helmet that kills the presumed heir of Otranto. The hasty, intended marriage of Manfred's only son, Conrad, to Isabella introduces the reader to the ancient prophecy that 'the castle and lordship of Otranto should pass from the present family whenever the real owner should be grown too large to inhabit it' (p. 17). Almost immediately, Conrad dies: 'dashed to pieces, and almost buried under an enormous helmet' (p. 19). When Father Jerome asks an unknown herald whence he comes, the herald replies: '"from the knight of the gigantic sabre"' (p. 60). Walpole's phallic symbol represents the true heir to the castle of Otranto. This size motif is repeated throughout the novel, becoming synonymous with the bloated aristocracy and inheritance structure of the wealthy, property-owning, titled elite.

The sins of the father to which Walpole directs attention in his first preface govern the plot of his novel that focuses on inheritances as a metaphor for the state, and thus provide further evidence for a reading of the text as a contemporary political criticism. Clery points to Walpole's depiction of 'the nightmarish collapse of a system of power that contains the seeds of its own destruction'.[55] In Walpole's tale order is restored when the rightful male heir is placed in his kingdom, while in later Gothics it is the heroine who reclaims her usurped property, wealth and lineage. The issues with which Walpole's novel is concerned – unmanageable and dominating government, laws disregarded or distorted for personal gain, inheritance and social order – are similar preoccupations for subsequent Gothic writers who depict these issues as a consequence of heteronormative and gender ideologies rather than a specific political machine. Walpole shows the omnipresence of the political institutions as contrary to human felicity, while later Gothic novels present their underlying ideologies (and most of the arbitrary laws and regulations of the patriarchy) as fundamentally opposed to female agency and desire, suggesting these rights are obtainable only once the old order is broken down.

If Walpole's novel established the tropes that later became standard to the Gothic, then it is important to look closely at his treatment of female characters who supposedly provide the foundation for the Gothic heroines to follow. That the differences between Walpole's female characters and those who come after are glaring speaks to just how sharply the genre was defined by its later writers. The central female characters in *Otranto* are kind, dutiful, patient and chaste. Stripped of voices with which to protest at anything but incestuous threats to their chastity, heroines are frequently silent or deaf even to these threats and fail to voice their own desires. Though Hippolita, as a mother, is not a virgin, her piety and obedience towards her husband lend her a nun-like demeanour.[56] This otherworldly saintliness extends to Matilda, Hippolita's daughter, and Isabella, who would have been her daughter-in-law, both of whom view the convent and life as a nun as an appealing option. The servant Bianca is the only character to protest against the idea of life-long celibacy, saying to Matilda: '"I do not wish to see you moped in a convent, as you would be if you had your will, and if my lady your mother, who knows that a bad husband is better than no husband at all, did not hinder you"' (p. 40). Bianca's class enables her to voice the presence of 'masculine' passions, freeing her from the silence that Hippolita, Matilda and Isabella must maintain regarding sexual desire.[57] When Hippolita is anxious to see her husband, 'Matilda made signs to Isabella to prevent Hippolita's rising; and both these lovely young women were using their gentle violence to stop and calm the princess' (p. 33). Matilda does not speak; she makes 'signs' and the beautiful heroines exert a peculiarly feminine 'gentle violence'. Women are shown to be complicit in keeping other women from taking action; it is no coincidence that Matilda and Isabella prevent Hippolita from the traditionally male act of 'rising'. Walpole's female characters are entrenched in heteronormative ideologies of maternity and female sexuality. Though they are often viewed as stock figures of the Gothic, Walpole's depictions of women and incest differ from later Gothic novels in which heroines under similar threats effect escapes through their own voice and agency.

The representation of father–daughter incest, a means by which the older generation seeks to extend the lifeline of patriarchal and aristocratic family structures, serves as a further disparagement of the state, but it does so by effectively suppressing women and replacing incestuous exchanges with ones only technically non-incestuous. Irigaray questions the status of women as commodities or merchandise: 'How can such objects of use and transaction claim the right to speak and to participate in exchange in general? Commodities, as we all know, do not take themselves to market on their own.'[58] Irigaray's point is provocatively demonstrated in the effective muting of Isabella when she attempts to control her own exchange by refusing to be Manfred's commodity. When Manfred proposes to Isabella, his deceased son's intended bride – and his daughter's contemporary in age and friend – she shrieks, objects and is pursued by Manfred. Repeatedly imploring Isabella to be quiet when she protests that he is still married to Hippolita, Manfred says: '"I desired you once before not to name that woman"' (p. 25). Isabella's ability to participate in exchange by rejecting Manfred as a marriage choice is denied as Manfred understands her only as an object he has inherited from his son. She is allowed voice only to protest against the proposed incestuous union (incestuous as although Isabella and Manfred are not blood-related, they were almost affinal kin and now share a ward–guardian bond) and even this speech is stifled.

Hippolita is not only mute, but also metaphorically blind. She refuses to see the incestuous desires Manfred has for Isabella, and her blindness leads her to offer up her own daughter, Matilda, as a bride to Isabella's father, Frederic. She believes that this will avert the destruction of her family by unifying it with Frederic's, who will become the lord of Otranto. Hippolita's blindness, deafness and muteness render her complicit in the incestuous urges of Manfred and Frederic. Isabella cries out that Hippolita will cause their downfall by refusing to listen to the truth regarding Manfred's incestuous desire, saying: '"The purity of your own heart prevents you from seeing the depravity of others. Manfred, your lord, that impious man—'" (p. 89). Hippolita communicates only to defend Manfred and is dutiful beyond comprehension. When Father Jerome speaks pointedly about Isabella remaining in the convent for safety, Hippolita says: '"it is my duty to hear nothing that it pleases not my lord I should hear"' (p. 50). Her reward is lifelong celibacy in a nearby convent. That she happily exchanges her position as a wife for a non-sexualised existence and accomplishes this through her silent accession to violent incestuous male desires against other women affords Hippolita an agency through passivity. While I argue that the model of passive feminism fails largely to account for the agency and sexual desires of Gothic heroines, Hippolita in fact fits this model closely.[59] Her actions and their consequences contrast with the punishments suffered by female characters who are silent and complicit with unwanted or violent male incestuous desires in later Gothic works.[60] Walpole's passive and collusive mother is frequently rejected by subsequent Gothic writers in favour of the missing and reclaimed mother who provides support and assistance to the heroine.[61]

Manfred's designs on Isabella conform, in part, to a father–daughter configuration of incest, although the violent and undesired nature of his desires share similarities with the model of uncle–niece incest.[62] While sociological explanations of incest as an abuse of male power located in the nuclear family structure are inadequate to account for most father–daughter incest in the Gothic, this approach is a profitable one in terms of Walpole's work, in which Manfred's desires for Isabella exemplify the threat of male familial power. That *Otranto* fits this framework – as Hippolita fits that of passive feminism – furthers my argument that this work should be displaced as the originary Gothic text, in part because subsequent Gothic novels elude strict adherence to either psychological or sociological models of incest. Isabella is positioned as a daughter figure to Manfred as the intended daughter-in-law now under his paternal protection. Manfred's proposal to Isabella adheres to the incest laws of his and Walpole's time: no marriage between Isabella and Conrad took place and so if Manfred can obtain a divorce from Hippolita, there is no legal obstacle to their union. Isabella's disgust at the proposed union between herself and Manfred is thus not based on legal apprehension but on the familial ties by which she understands she is bound to Manfred. Fleeing from Manfred, Isabella decides, 'if no other means of deliverance offered, to shut herself up for ever among the holy virgins' (p. 27). Isabella's iconic flight through the subterranean passage to the neighbouring convent is reproduced repeatedly, with subtle variations, in many Gothic novels.[63] The crucial distinction between Isabella's flight, initiated by paternal incestuous threats, and those that follow is that her destination – a convent offering lifelong celibacy – is the only alternative model of sexuality available if she refuses a paternal cycle of exchange.

Incest functions as an extension of the male desire that prizes Isabella's physical beauty and her biological ability to produce another heir for Manfred – to 'preserve his race' as Manfred phrases it. Irigaray points to this when she asks: 'why are men not objects of exchange among women? It is because women's bodies – through their use, consumptions, and circulation – provide for the condition making social life and culture possible.'[64] Walpole depicts incestuous desires as the natural consequence of the supposedly legitimate need to produce heirs. In seeming contradiction to Lévi-Strauss's theories on the incest taboo as the requirement that allowed civilisation to develop, Walpole presents incest as a culturally mandated male desire that is not at all at odds with reproduction and culture. The apparent paradox is resolved when it is understood that Isabella, not Manfred, defines the desires as incestuous – a rejection that is meaningless if the male does not also so locate the desires. That these desires are unfulfilled confirms Walpole's novel to be deeply critical of the institutions of government and law that place such power to determine what constitutes incest in the paternal body of the monarch (here: Manfred).[65] Isabella is unable to remain in the convent but is forced back into circulation; the commodity has no say in whether or not it will be exchanged.

Walpole demonstrates the fluidity of conceptions of incest and the arbitrary nature of the law through comic irony. The novel's dual condemnation of the hypocrisy of the law and definitions of family is manifest in the depiction of Manfred as so blinded by lust and his desire to produce another heir that he pleads incest laws as an excuse to leave his marriage to Hippolita in order to commit incest with Isabella. Incest is first named by Father Jerome, who uses the term to draw attention to Manfred's proposed marriage with Isabella as the incestuous relationship, saying to Manfred: '"by me thou art warned not to pursue the incestuous design on thy contracted daughter"' (p. 50). Manfred's desires correspond to Ruth Perry's understanding of incest as a Gothic convention that depicts 'a girl singled out, against her will, in her own domestic space, for the sexual attentions of a father, an uncle, or a brother'.[66] Walpole's deployment of the incest trope, however, seems less to point towards the threats of domesticity and the nuclear family than to demonstrate the potential danger of adhering to archaic laws. In the same conversation Manfred cites the illegality of incest in an effort to free himself from his marriage vows to Hippolita: '"It is some time that I have had scruples on the legality of our union: Hippolita is related to me in the fourth degree … Ease my conscience of this burden; dissolve our marriage"' (p. 50). Father Jerome sees through Manfred's transparent ploys to end his legally binding union to Hippolita, locating as incestuous the relationship that involves, not distant blood ties, but the abuse of paternal power from a guardian figure over his ward.

The union Manfred contemplates with his son's fiancée is more appalling to Father Jerome than Manfred's marriage to Hippolita because the affinal father–daughter bond he almost shared with Isabella is understood as a stronger kinship tie than that of blood four times removed. Thus, the repugnance at the idea of a father–daughter union, in spite of no actual blood tie, is stronger than the revulsion towards an actual – though diluted – blood tie. This understanding parallels Father Jerome's objection to incest with the understanding of seventeenth-century English theologian and clergyman Jeremy Taylor, who believed that marriages between parents and children or children-in-law overturned 'the proper order of familial authority'.[67] Manfred's proposed marriage to Isabella would violate the authority of the (patriarchal) family and so Walpole's priest is ironically positioned as objecting to the union with Isabella as incestuous on grounds as irrational as those on which Manfred proposes to divorce his wife. The consanguineal tie is not presented as an obstacle to marriage or an object of disgust as long as the blood is diluted enough the make the transfer of property and wealth (and therefore accumulation) a viable option within the context of a consanguineal union.[68] Adam Kuper discusses this flexible nature of the incest taboo, arguing that the prohibition can be transgressed when so doing benefits members of the dominant group (read: men).[69] The paradoxical and arbitrary nature of the incest taboo is underscored by Manfred, who bases the dissolution of his union with Hippolita on the grounds that they are '"related within the forbidden degrees"' (p. 69), while simultaneously declaring his wish to marry Isabella, who is as '"dear to me as my own blood"' (p. 69). Manfred uses the language of consanguineal incest to reject his wife (who is no longer of child-bearing years) as he attempts to unite with Isabella, whom he locates as having an equal, though non-consanguineal, claim of kinship.

The incestuous lust that Manfred feels for Isabella is mirrored in her father, Frederic, who has incestuous father–daughter desires for Matilda, Manfred's daughter. Manfred, bent on fulfilling his desire to sire a son with Isabella, is happy to sacrifice his own daughter to Frederic: 'Manfred … proposed the double marriage. That weak prince, who had been struck with the charms of Matilda, listened but too eagerly to the offer' (p. 96). Frederic readily consents to his daughter's marriage to her contracted father-in-law because it enables him to realise his desires for Matilda. The fathers agree to trade ownership of their daughters between themselves to have sex with their daughters' substitutes. Irigaray suggests that 'the law that orders our society is the exclusive valorisation of men's needs/desires, of exchanges among men … wives, daughters, and sisters have value only in that they serve as the possibility of, and potential benefit in, relations among men. The use of and traffic in women subtend and uphold the reign of masculine hom(m)o-sexuality.'[70] The fathers embody Irigaray's claims about the exchanges of women that uphold patriarchal society and sexuality. The mutual lust that Frederic and Manfred feel for each other's daughters suggests such desires substitute that which they feel for their own daughters. The proposed trade exposes that the girls are commodities and points to the interchangeable, deindividuated nature of female bodies: 'That prince [Frederic] had discovered so much passion for Matilda that Manfred hoped to obtain all he wished by holding out or withdrawing his daughter's charms' (p. 100). Matilda and Isabella are bargaining chips in the game of their fathers' lust.

Lévi-Strauss's description of the structure of marriage as an 'exchange … between two groups of men' is borne out in the reciprocal trade in which Manfred and Frederic participate and that elides any remaining distinction between Matilda and Isabella.[71] While the exchange has an incestuous father–daughter configuration, that there is no affinal or consanguineal tie allows for its occurrence without a legal violation of the incest taboo – though it clearly encroaches on the taboo as defined by theologians, sociologists and psychiatrists in that it violates a position of familial authority or power.[72] Manfred has ownership of Matilda's 'charms' – her beauty and virginity – and offers them to Frederic in exchange for Isabella's beauty, virginity and presumed fertility. Frederic and Manfred exchange the virginity of one daughter for the virginity of the other. Indeed, the interchangeability of the girls that emphasises their fathers' incestuous desires is brought to a head when Matilda is killed mistakenly by her father. Matilda's desire for Theodore prompts her to free her lover in an act that she states is unwomanly as it disregards her filial duty to her father. The disruption of paternal authority in favour of female desire does not go long unpunished. Manfred slays his daughter – believing she is Isabella – by plunging his dagger into her bosom in an act symbolic of incestuous rape.[73] The interchangeability of Matilda and Isabella is reinforced further when Theodore later marries Isabella; Matilda's dead body is replaced with Isabella's living one. Though the girls have managed to escape the incestuous designs of their fathers, they have done so through no direct action of their own – Matilda escapes through death and Isabella becomes a replacement commodity to fill the gap Matilda has left in the market. Isabella avoided replacing Hippolita only to perform a near identical replacement of a body no longer capable of reproduction when she takes Matilda's place as Theodore's wife.

Representations of incest in *Otranto* operate as hyperbolisations of antiquated social systems and laws that lend themselves to abuses of male power and desire, functioning to reinforce patriarchal dominance through the culturally demanded exchange of women as commodities. The insights of Lévi-Strauss and Irigaray allow Walpole's representations to be placed within the anthropological understanding of the exchange of women as necessary to culture and feminist challenges to this theory. Such understandings demonstrate that although Walpole's often subversive parody plays with disrupting the notion that the incest taboo creates culture, the novel ultimately reinforces the position of women as commodities whose exchange is a social necessity. In recognising these representations of father–daughter incest as aligned with the sociological model of incest as abuses of power encoded within the family and social structures, incest is revealed as a consequence of these structures of power. Walpole's work presents father–daughter incest as scholarship commonly perceives the function of incest in the Gothic: as an abuse against unwilling young women that is the effect of archaic institutions of power, law, family and marriage. But as we will see, this understanding of father–daughter incest is largely questioned and overturned in later Gothic novels, in which it provides additional models of female desire and agency, affording an escape from the economics of female exchange as necessary to culture.

ESCAPING FROM THE CASTLE: INCEST AND HEROINIC ACTION IN *THE ROMANCE OF THE FOREST*

The striking similarities between many of the incestuous situations, characters' personalities and even names in Radcliffe's *The Romance of the Forest* and Walpole's *Otranto* beg a comparison between the two works that provides an important means of repositioning Radcliffe's novel – and many that follow – as part of a Gothic tradition distinct from that represented by Walpole's parodic and satirical work. The contrast between the depictions of incest, sexuality and female agency in *The Romance of the Forest* and *Otranto* are marked in that Radcliffe's representations of father–daughter incest allow the heroine access to desire, voice and action. Radcliffe reworks many of the conventions used in *Otranto* to model alternatives to the exchange of women that remains, in Walpole's work, the only means of theorising culture. In reimagining the heroine as having sexual desires presented as naturally occurring, as capable of manipulating the father–daughter incestuous desires encoded within the ward–guardian power relation and as able effectively to flee from incestuous threats and rescue wounded heroes, Radcliffe establishes the heroine, Adeline, as an active agent who removes herself from the traffic in women. In analysing this work, I continue to rely on the theories of Irigaray and Rubin concerning the economy of female bodies and employ insights on representations of consanguineal bonds in eighteenth-century narratives from scholars such as Perry. Scholarship that relies on Freudian incest theory and approaches Radcliffe's novel as belonging exclusively to a Female Gothic tradition overlooks female agency and desire by focusing on the heroine as a manipulator of male desires. I argue that Radcliffe explodes the understood – though in her time as yet widely unchallenged – commodification of women by using father–daughter incest as a means of troubling notions of the family, driving female action and depicting female desire as natural.

The novel opens with a description of Pierre de La Motte (one of Adeline's father figures), who, like Walpole's Manfred, lacks sufficient self-control to overcome his passions and desires: 'with strength of mind sufficient to have withstood temptation, he would have been a good man; as it was, he was always a weak, and sometimes a vicious member of society'.[74] La Motte and Manfred are both of good character if not confronted with temptation and passion, which corrupts and dominates them. Radcliffe's young, virtuous and beautiful heroine is, superficially, similar to Walpole's Isabella. However, a significant difference in their characters and behaviour emerges when comparing their actions and reactions towards father–daughter incest. This uncanny doubling of characters is repeated by the echoing of names from earlier works – a common occurrence throughout the generations of Gothic texts – as Walpole's imprisoned young lover, Theodore, is refashioned in Radcliffe's imprisoned young lover, Theodore. That the very names, experiences and personalities of characters are reused reinforces the closed-in and repetitious nature of the Gothic world.[75] The effect of the duplications not only creates a claustrophobic environment, but also gives a greater sense of freedom when the characters, previously viewed as synonymous with their literary predecessors, are able to break the mould of repetition and with it, the cyclical nature of the patriarchal power structure that previously contained them.

Incest, depicted in Walpole's novel as a male-desired and male-sought threatening horror to be fled from to the safety of a convent, is portrayed in Radcliffe's novel as a masculine weakness that allows the heroine the opportunity to save herself and her lover. While in Walpole's work incestuous desires reinforced the interchangeability of women and their place as marketable goods, the incestuous passions in Radcliffe's Gothic are manipulated and destroyed by the heroine and allow her to exhibit action, female desire and self-sufficiency. Adeline's agency is evinced through her ability to feel desire for and attraction to several of the male characters – who are often a blend of good and evil – and in her power successfully to flee from the danger they present. The effect of this at times perversely presented attraction is described by Perry as mirrored in the reactions of the readers of the Gothic: 'the confusion of good and evil projected by the attractive male villain produces in its readers a perverse attraction to threatening force, a hankering after unnatural domination'.[76] I argue that this attraction is found in Adeline, who is initially drawn to the Marquis de Montalt, who becomes the greatest threat to her virtue and freedom. The irrational attraction signifies a consanguineal relationship that is currently unknown to the heroine, exposing a desire that becomes dangerous.[77] Radcliffe reconfigures incest from its representation as a male-wielded weapon of female subjugation to a weakness the heroine exploits to her own advantage. Father–daughter incest thus becomes a transgressive force that enables the heroine to reject patriarchy's notions of female sexuality, save her lover and fight free of the crumbling castles and convents of archaic domination.

Gothic heroines must frequently rescue themselves from the incestuous designs of an older male relative, guardian or father figure because there is no male hero or protector on whom they can rely, although this agency is often disregarded. The understanding of Gothic feminism as a 'pretended weakness, a pose of innocent victim, a masquerade of asexual passivity' overlooks the contrasting depictions of heroines and their male counterparts in situations of imprisonment, threats and violence.[78] I refer to 'Gothic feminism' as 'passive feminism' so as not to confuse 'victim feminism' with the feminist themes found throughout the Gothic that are characterised by action and response rather than pose and passivity. Scholars such as David Durrant corroborate this understanding of passive feminism; Durrant asserts that the Radcliffean heroine ultimately 'ignore[s] the real world, and live[s] docilely as a child for all of her life. But it is worth it, the outside world is too fraught with perils to be endured.'[79] These readings tend to minimise the heroine's triumphs over dangers and obstacles – an oversight necessary to maintain a notion of passive feminism. If the Gothic heroine's manipulation of the father's incestuous desires provided the only escape from danger, such a passive reading might be possible, but this is only one aspect of the heroine's actions that culminate with flights from patriarchal figures and institutions.

The argument for passive feminism rests partly on Hoeveler's claim that: 'to the female gothic consciousness, the patriarchy … exists as a huge protection racket … Gothic heroines, if they were to survive, were then forced to seek protection from any surrogate protection agency …

a means of protection that they did not possess in their own right.'[80] Identifying the Female Gothic heroine as one who sells herself to the 'most controllable' bidder to better manipulate her putative protector, this line of scholarship views the lover's wounding or imprisonment as a symbolic castration that relegates him to a position of eternal subordination or feminisation.[81] Thus, the true Gothic heroine chooses the most easily controlled husband (protection system) so that she may reclaim the title, wealth and property usurped from her.[82] Gothic heroes are frequently subjected to woundings, but if this does metaphorically castrate them for part of the novel, they generally make full recoveries and thus regain their masculinity by the novels' endings.[83] The shift that Perry notes from paternal to spousal patriarchy that positioned first fathers and then husbands as protectors and keepers of women occurred alongside the rise of Gothic fiction that, as she convincingly demonstrates, contended with the change through portrayals of dangerous and incestuous father figures.[84] Yet scholarship that understands protection as located exclusively in either the husband or the father overlooks the ways many Gothic heroines triumph with little real male protection.[85] It is crucial to distinguish between the conclusion that heroines turn to marriages that 'are quiet acceptances of their new keepers' to ensure a male guardian and how such engagements and marriages are presented in the Gothic novels themselves.[86] The convention of the wounded male lover, rather than creating a malleable protector, forces the heroine into successful self-reliance, reclaiming her name, property and family before marrying. The threat of father–daughter incest works similarly to the wounded hero convention: it does not offer the heroine a permanent protector; rather, it propels the heroine's escape from the very society that requires such defences. In its father–daughter configuration, incest is a pivotal part of uncovering the Gothic's rejection of patriarchal culture and passive feminism because it demonstrates that the patriarchal protection system is one that cannot be trusted, no matter how disposed it is to manipulation. In contrast to the notion that Gothic heroines sell themselves to a controllable guardian, these women rather learn that there is no such male defender capable of being influenced permanently; that even fathers and guardians cannot be trusted, that to be safeguarded they must remove themselves from the patriarchal protection system that, in fact, offers them no material security at all.[87]

Patriarchy's inability to imagine or allow for female desire, a method of controlling female behaviour, is rejected through the representation of desire that allows Adeline to refuse a celibate life.[88] Radcliffe combines the convention of the convent with the threats of the father to reveal the sexual tyranny over women that fathers attempt to maintain, here using Catholicism and later incestuous threats to enforce female celibacy. Adeline's repudiation of coercion into celibacy is a drastic revision of Walpole's female characters' choices. Adeline describes her removal to a convent at the age of seven and her years of withstanding the efforts of her (believed) father, Louis St Pierre, and the abbess to persuade her to take the veil.[89] Adeline refers to '"the wretchedness of my situation, condemned to perpetual imprisonment, and imprisonment of the most dreadful kind, or to the vengeance of a father, from whom I had no appeal"' (I, p. 55). In contrast to Walpole's characters who view the convent as a sanctuary, Adeline – like many Gothic heroines after her who are thrust into cloisters and forced, coerced or threatened into taking vows – identifies celibacy as 'perpetual imprisonment'.[90] Convent life is viewed as a non-life: 'the horrors of the monastic life rose fully to my view ... excluded from the cheerful intercourse of society ... condemned to silence – rigid formality – abstinence and penance – condemned to forego the delights of a world' (I, p. 67). Radcliffe uses the word 'abstinence' rather than 'celibacy' to leave the meaning open to being read as abstaining from vices or indulgences, although the sexual connotation was the most common contemporary understanding of the term.[91] That Adeline unites the words 'horror' and 'abstinence' makes explicit that her dread of the nunnery lies in the prospect of life without sexual (as well as social) intercourse, while offering an alternative meaning for a censorious readership that fears the expression and existence of female sexuality.[92] The convent, the physical manifestation of superstition and repression identified with Catholicism, is loaded with additional terrors through the heroine's fear of a permanent removal from a sexual existence.[93] Catholicism in the Gothic novel, described as exemplifying 'tyranny in all its forms: political, intellectual, and sexual', is tied here to the figure of the father and his demands.[94] In refusing the celibate life of the convent and her father's demand that she take the veil, Adeline rejects both institutionalised and familial attempts to curtail her sexual choices.

Not only does Adeline reject St Pierre's demand for her to become a nun, but she also uses it as reason to dissolve their father–daughter relationship: '"Since he can forget ... the affection of a parent, and condemn his child without remorse to wretchedness and despair – the bond of filial and paternal duty no longer subsists – he has himself dissolved it"' (I,

p. 55). Adeline, far from the fearful justifications of Walpole's Matilda, succinctly justifies irrevocably severing the bond of paternal duty to her father.[95] Shortly thereafter, her father retrieves her from the convent, bringing Adeline to the house from which La Motte takes her. That night she dreams of her father:

> I thought that I was in a lonely forest with my father; his looks were severe, and his gestures menacing: he upbraided me for leaving the convent, and while he spoke, drew from his pocket a mirror, which he held before my face; I looked in it and saw (my blood now thrills as I repeat it) I saw myself wounded, and bleeding profusely. Then I thought myself in the house again; and suddenly heard ... 'Depart this house, destruction hovers here.' (I, pp. 61–2)

The sexual imagery in the dream hints at incestuous passions that 'thrill her blood' – a far cry from the horror she felt at the prospect of an abstinent life. That she is upbraided and wounded after leaving the convent furthers the conclusion that Adeline eschews chastity in favour of sexual intercourse. Her father's anger at her for leaving the religious house warns her of a sexual danger. The dreamed encounter and its violent, destructive consequences embody the 'perverse attraction' towards danger that Perry describes in relation to readers' reactions to attractive villains. Adeline's agency and thrill at the sexual wounding experienced with (if not by) her father is a radical departure from the terror of male desire exhibited by Isabella in Walpole's novel. Radcliffe turns what was in Walpole's work female victimisation by the father figure (made not only possible, but also mandatory by the absence of female desire) into a dream of incestuous desires that provokes Adeline's flight from the father who would control her sexuality.

There is a marked relationship between women, property and exchange in eighteenth-century literature. This connection is assessed by Pollak, who argues that 'as reproducers women alone made possible the orderly transmission of property and patronym from father to son. As objects of exchange in an exogamous kinship system, they were the conduits through which heirs were produced and fraternal bonds between men were established and strengthened.'[96] Such exchanges, which occur in *Otranto*, are rejected in Radcliffe's novel. The Gothic convention of the father or father figure who attempts to sell the virginal heroine to a wealthy, older man presents the guardian figure as one who protects the heroine only to maintain her chastity as a valuable commodity.[97] An exchange in marriage results in a shift from being the property of the father or father figure to being the object of another older man.[98] The heroine has a limited number of options by which to remove herself from this economy of exchange. She can elope with her lover and lose the appearance, if not fact, of her chastity and thus her value in the economy. Alternatively, she can join a convent and remove herself from threats to her chastity (a possibility in Walpole's work, but not an option for Radcliffe's heroine). Finally, she can manipulate the father figure into serving her needs, which is often presented at some point in the narrative as the most viable option that allows the heroine to act from within her position as a commodity. This is what Adeline accomplishes. Her escape strips her of the protection of one father to deliver her into the arms of a father substitute: La Motte. Adeline controls this ward–guardian relationship and the quasi-incestuous desire it entails before she flees it as well. In relation to the cycle of consumption, Irigaray argues that 'the economy ... that is in place in our societies thus requires that women lend themselves to alienation in consumption, and to exchanges in which they do not participate'.[99] However, in many of the Gothic representations of father–daughter incest, it is precisely from this place of alienated exchange that heroines first assert their agency, rejecting the dual threats of celibacy or exchange and escaping to an alternative model of economy and sexuality with the lover of their choice.

This renunciation of exchange is exemplified in multiple interactions between La Motte and Adeline in which she demonstrates her value within the endogamic family unit by exploiting her sexual commodification before abandoning the economy that makes such demands. Adeline's temporary manipulation of the culture of exchange belies the assertion that Gothic heroines assume a mask of femininity to gain a permanent and malleable male protector. Such a 'gain' is at odds with Irigaray's analysis of woman as performing a 'masquerade of femininity' on the exchange market for which she goes uncompensated 'unless her pleasure comes simply from being chosen as an object of consumption or of desire by masculine "subjects"'.[100] Adeline's temporary masquerade is not performed for pleasure or to gain a lasting protector, but is a calculated strike at the system that aids her escape from culture.[101] When La Motte, his wife and Adeline enter an abandoned monastery Madame de la Motte voices the most fear, yet it is Adeline who clings to La Motte. In a description charged with sexual undertones, Adeline 'uttered an exclamation of mingled admiration and fear. A kind of pleasing dread filled her bosom, and filled all her soul. Tears started into her eyes: – she wished, yet feared, to go on; – she hung upon the arm of La Motte, and looked at him with a sort of hesitating interrogation' (II, p. 26). Adeline is ostensibly fearful of entering the passageway and the scene functions as a one of sexual transgression or loss of virginity. Adeline, with her new father figure and guardian, is both scared and desirous, fearing and wishing to proceed, and supplants Madame de La Motte's position by clinging to her husband's arm in the older woman's place. Adeline is here a willing usurper of Madame de La Motte, using her youth and beauty to influence La Motte. In unequivocal contrast to the understanding of Gothic heroines as passive and docile, Adeline engages in both physical and emotional agency to gain control and receives the desired response from La Motte. The father–daughter-type relationship, with its incestuous air, grants Adeline power over her new father figure and his wife, whose pleas he ignores to prove his bravery to Adeline. It is important that Adeline is both fearful and desirous – the dread she feels is 'pleasing' and though she looks at La Motte with a 'hesitating interrogation' she directs this scene; rather than being persuaded to go on against her wishes, she desires La Motte to continue. Radcliffe's heroine effectively manipulates the father figure into incestuous longings that keep her out of the convent and unexchanged.

In another scene, Adeline pleads with her guardian for protection from the Marquis de Montalt, who has both homicidal and incestuous designs upon her. La Motte, who enters Adeline's room at the Marquis's murderous bidding, gazes upon her beautiful form and listens to her sing in her sleep. When Adeline wakes she fears La Motte will hand her over to the Marquis. She throws herself on La Motte's mercy: '"You once saved me from destruction … O save me now! Have pity upon me – I have no protector but you"' (II, p. 186). Adeline's plea appears spontaneous but it is unlikely she was singing in her sleep. She exploits her innocence, beauty and youth, successfully locating herself as the object of her guardian's gaze. La Motte, overcome by her appearance, allows her to flee from the castle and Adeline undertakes a long, dangerous and ultimately triumphant journey to escape from the Marquis. The Gothic heroine uses her sexuality in an incestuous explosion of traditional patriarchal values, figuratively lying down with the father to get to the hero, and thus breaking down the exchange of female bodies by men to gain freedom and choice. Accessing their own sexuality allows heroines to control the desires of men and the course of their futures, disrupting the incest taboo and its simultaneous traffic in women.

Many Gothic novels, following Radcliffe, rework the eighteenth-century literary convention of instinctual kinship recognition and the corresponding disinclination to mate with unknown relatives into an immediate attraction or desire. Perry describes the repugnance characters often display towards members of their families who are hitherto unknown: 'instinctual disgust warned the sister and brother, although ignorant of their consanguineal connection, that their mating was somehow beyond the pale'.[102] Missing family members are often hinted at by being presented as sexually unpalatable to the hero or heroine by a sort of sixth sense. In the Gothic, rather than the unknown relations feeling disgust, there is often an instant recognition or attraction that helps the long-lost relative to discern his or her missing kin. The heroine feels this attraction towards unknown relatives and to the man (kin or non-kin) she eventually marries. In this sense, the Gothic identifies kin both as those with whom we are related by blood and those we marry.[103] Adeline shows this instant recognition or preference for the Marquis, though the attraction is emphasised on his side. When the Marquis first sees Adeline after she faints, he attempts to lift her:

> Upon Adeline, who was yet insensible, he gazed with an eager admiration, which seemed to absorb all the faculties of his mind … Her beauty, touched with the languid delicacy of illness, gained from sentiment what it lost in bloom. The negligence of her dress, loosened for the purposes of freer respiration, discovered those glowing charms, that her auburn tresses, which fell in profusion over her bosom, shaded, but could not conceal. (I, p. 131)

Perry's arguments about the repugnance that signifies previously unknown family members would imply this older, handsome soldier is certainly not related to Adeline. But the Marquis de Montalt is in fact Adeline's paternal uncle. The initial mutual attraction that is sexual rather than familial in nature troubles contemporary understandings of attraction and kinship. The existing normative accounts of instinctual recognition/disgust that Perry points to as operating in literature as warnings that a potential mating is incestuous are subverted when female desire is depicted as an instinctive attraction towards the incestuous relationship.

The passivity often attributed to Gothic heroines is challenged by a comparison of their actions to those of the male characters who Radcliffe and other Gothic writers frequently depict as imprisoned, terrified and in search of sanctuary.[104] Adeline's lover, Theodore, is removed from the novel's action after being arrested by the King's Guard; Radcliffe incarcerates the male who would otherwise be the heroine's saviour. La Motte is similarly imprisoned at the novel's opening: 'Alone, unarmed – beyond the chance of assistance … he endeavoured to await the event with fortitude; but La Motte could boast of no such virtue' (I, p. 4). La Motte's confinement, though brief, shows his lack of courage and inability to affect an escape; a lack accentuated by Adeline's unaided flights from danger. Adeline, whilst held captive by her uncle at his chateau, refuses to be either his mistress or wife, unwilling to sell herself to him honourably or dishonourably and thus re-enter the market of exchange.[105] The threat of incest underlies Adeline's multiple escapes that cause her to develop the self-reliance that later enables her to exonerate Theodore from the false charges levelled against him, rescuing him from an unjust imprisonment. The heroinic action breaks down gendered ideologies of masculinity and femininity by requiring that the hero be saved by the heroine.[106]

When the Marquis leaves Adeline for the night she searches for a means of egress. Seeing a window: 'she sprang forward and alighted safely in an extensive garden. … Thence she had little doubt of escaping, either by some broke fence, or low part of the wall' (II, p. 250). It is only after Adeline frees herself from her uncle's harem-like imprisonment that Theodore 'rescues' her in an attempt that goes woefully awry. The Marquis discovers Theodore and Adeline in a small town, where Theodore is dangerously wounded in a fight with the Marquis and arrested. Adeline again relies on herself – this time, not only to save herself, but Theodore as well. The use of incestuous threats to drive action comes full circle when the Marquis is brought up on charges regarding the murder of his brother, Adeline's father. The judge requires Adeline give evidence to save La Motte's and Theodore's lives (both of whom are awaiting execution) by incriminating the Marquis in the murderous plot against herself. Adeline reflects on the Marquis, who she now (falsely) supposes is her father: 'her horror of the Marquis, whom she could not bear to consider as her father … redoubled, and she became impatient to give the testimony' (II, p. 239). Adeline is given voice to make public the incestuous crimes and condemn her pursuer: she 'gave her little narrative with clearness and precision' (II, p. 240). Afterwards, Adeline reflects on the circumstances of her birth: 'From an orphan, subsisting on the bounty of others, without family, with few friends, and pursued by a cruel and powerful enemy, she saw herself suddenly transformed to the daughter of an illustrious house, and the heiress of immense wealth' (II, p. 249).

This transformation has been orchestrated by Adeline; she has refused a life in a convent, fled from the incestuous and murderous uncle, prepared to testify in a public court, caused Theodore to be freed from prison and a sentence of execution and learned the truth about her parents and birthright. When Gothic heroines such as Adeline are described as 'a professional girl-woman, a … creation of the fertile but bored brain of Ann Radcliffe, bourgeois wife of a man who stayed late at the office almost every evening … one bored and neglected housewife [who] decided to translate her personal and social anxieties into words that could be read by other presumably bored housewives', both Adeline's power and agency and the talent and motivations of Radcliffe are marginalised.[107] Adeline is far from the 'wily little woman [who] would triumph through her skilful use of femininity as manipulation and guile' and hardly supports the notion that 'Gothic feminism taught women that pretended weakness was strength, and that the pose, the masquerade of innocent victim, would lead ultimately to possessing the master's goods and property. Gothic feminists believed … women's best defenses were a beguiling demeanor and a sweet smile.'[108]

The most pressing danger in this understanding of Gothic feminism is that it become the standard definition, casting the work of Gothic writers as a female anxiety release that taught women to become professional victims. Such a conclusion overlooks the physical threats and dangers, flights, difficult journeys, recourses to the legal system, use of voice, reliance on mothers and mother figures, pursuit of truth and the intelligence that contribute in large part to the ability of the heroines to destroy the patriarchal system that forced them to perform masquerades. While *Otranto* parodies the structure of exchange at play in society, Walpole is unable to reimagine a world in which women do not function as objects of exchange and thereby foreshadows Lévi-Strauss's view that an escape from the exchange is impossible. In contrast, Radcliffe depicts the destruction of exchange, completing 'the revolution in kinship' that Rubin theorises as taking place 'if the sexual property system were reorganized in such a way that men did not have overriding rights in women (if there was no exchange of women) and if there were no gender'.[109] Adeline successfully dissolves paternal ties and gender ideologies in her escape from the castle, driven by the Gothic incest thematic to forever break from the bonds of patriarchal power.

BREAKING DOWN THE CASTLE: INCEST DESTROYS
PATRIARCHAL SOCIETY IN *MATILDA*

Shelley's *Matilda*, written between 1819 and 1820, is an erotic Gothic work that focuses on the incestuous love between the sixteen-year-old heroine Matilda and her unnamed father. Although the incest within the novel is never actualised it is made overt through the father's verbal declaration and written confession and Matilda's later revelation of her own incestuous longings. That Matilda and her father's incestuous relationship is never consummated with sexual intercourse is a crucial point, as, despite the scholarly preoccupation with father–daughter incest, heroines rarely engage in forced or sought sexual intercourse with their fathers.[110] Shelley sent the manuscript to her father, William Godwin, who found the theme of father–daughter incest 'disgusting' and the novel subsequently remained unpublished until 1959.[111] Shelley's biography has thus been used frequently a basis for critical interpretation of the novel and its incest plot by scholars such as Terence Harpold, who argues *Matilda* depends on the details of Shelley's life and her relationships with her parents.[112] Hoeveler is just as keen to treat the novel as autobiographical, arguing it 'reads … as an embarrassingly personal fantasy'.[113] Harpold's reading, like the majority of psychobiographical analyses of *Matilda*, relies heavily upon the Freudian paradigm that attempts to situate desire and sexuality as responses to a nuclear family structure that does not exist in the novel. Shelley's *Matilda*, I argue by contrast, deploys father–daughter incest to refute definitions of women as exchangeable goods and dissolve the market economy of women in favour of an endogamic society.

Psychobiographical readings of Shelley's novel often inappropriately position Matilda as a passive spectator of surrounding events and fail to differentiate between Shelley's and Matilda's upbringings. The use of psychobiographical approaches is complicated by applying to Matilda the conclusions drawn (based on the Freudian theory of female psychological and sexual development) regarding Shelley's development in the absence of her mother, Mary Wollstonecraft. Although aspects of the novel and Shelley's life are similar – Matilda's mother dies in childbirth – they also diverge in important ways: Matilda's father leaves the infant Matilda to be reared by her aunt, whereas Shelley was raised by her father. Whatever the effects of Wollstonecraft's death on Shelley's relationship with Godwin, reading Matilda's mother's absence as causing the perpetual victimisation of the daughter to her father's desires, given that Matilda does not meet her father until age sixteen, interprets Matilda in a way the structure of the novel does not allow. These analyses tend to identify Matilda as passive; Hoeveler, for example, argues that 'Matilda's passivity or rather her ostensible lack of control ... suggests the nature of trauma, as well as the posture or pose of gothic feminism. The daughter effectively destroys both her parents simply by being; her very ontology is fatal.'[114] Harpold asserts that Matilda is a product of Shelley's psychosexual development: 'Mary's capacity for "pre"-oedipal identification with the mother ... would have been sharply restricted, in effect, already oedipalized, irreducibly subject to the imperatives of the father's desire. This is what happens in *Mathilda*.'[115] Both Freudian-based analyses suggest Shelley is psychologically incapable of the pre-oedipal state of loving her mother and will thus always and only be subject to the father's desires. Tilottama Rajan notes the limitations of these approaches, arguing that 'we cannot read incest in biographical terms, and what is at issue here is not so much Mary's desire for Godwin enacted in the substitutive medium of fiction, as a form of desire whose textual transmission ... recognizes is figural structure'.[116] Readings of Shelley's work that displace it from the literary realm to the autobiographical by applying Freudian theories of female desire and sexual development to an amalgam of Shelley and her character seem doomed to fail.

Far from being passive or ruled by her father, Matilda's intense love for him enables her active transgression of the social prohibitions of incest and female desire and her escape from the traffic in women. Matilda's sexual love for her father is revealed in her self-descriptions as a passionate individual who finds only one release for her love: 'the idea of my unhappy, wandering father was the idol of my imagination. I bestowed on him all my affections; there was a miniature of him that I gazed on continually ... his first words [in my fantasies] were always "My daughter, I love thee"! What ecstatic moments were passed in these dreams!' (p. 157). Raised from infancy by an affectionless aunt, Matilda fixates on the image of her father. Reminisces of her early teen years offer no mention of young love or sexual awakening: all her fantasies and hopes of future happiness are settled on the reunion with her father. The language used is essential to understanding the sexual rather than filial nature of Matilda's love. She passes 'ecstatic moments' in dreams with a man she has never met but on whose picture she gazes continually, making her father the object of her female gaze in a fixation of desire that functions in two important ways. First, it exemplifies what Judith Butler describes as the failure of the incest taboo, the existence of which: 'appears to suggest that desires, actions, indeed, pervasive social practices of incest are generated precisely in virtue of the eroticization of that taboo'.[117] Secondly, it defies the system of exchange that requires woman to be the object and demands 'that she herself never have access to desire', a condition that 'has as its founding operation the appropriation of woman's body by the father or his substitutes'.[118] Matilda challenges the requirements of this system by locating her father as the object of her desire in a reversal of the normative. As Irigaray points out, 'where pleasure is concerned … to reverse the relation, especially in the economy of sexuality, does not seem a desirable objective'.[119] Matilda's objectification of her father via her gaze is a reversal with fatal consequences.

Matilda's reunion with her father is an eroticised and romanticised moment that establishes the incestuous nature of their attachment: 'I approached the shore, my father held the boat, and in a moment I was in his arms. And now I began to live. All around me was changed from a dull uniformity to the brightest scene of joy and delight' (p. 161). This reunion is Matilda's rebirth; she begins to live only in her father's embrace, which is equally her awakening and arousal and the description of their reunion has orgasmic qualities. Matilda is jealous of her time with her father and her descriptions of the 'paradisiacal' time with him read like the musings of a lover: 'it was a subject of regret to me whenever we were joined by a third person, yet if I turned with a disturbed look towards my father, his eyes fixed on me and beaming with tenderness instantly restored my joy to my heart. O, hours of intense delight!' (p. 163). Any outsider is looked upon as an intruder, potentially a usurper of affection and a cause of distress. The father is hardly immune to Matilda as he returns her looks, making her the focus of his masculine gaze. When her father suddenly turns cold without explanation Matilda weeps, worries, is miserable and incapable of eating. Her reaction is not that of a daughter, but a lover abandoned by her beloved; the language Shelley uses to describe Matilda's emotions is the lexicon of romantic attachment rather than that of filial devotion.

The father's incestuous desires are exposed partially through a depiction of his anxiety regarding a suitor interested in Matilda, an anxiety that Matilda manipulates to demonstrate to him her value on the market of exchange so he will remove her from it. The suitor's presence creates tensions between Matilda and her father that reveal his emotions as too excessively jealous to be purely the product of paternal love. Matilda is aware of her father's unease, though she claims to be ignorant of its cause: 'I now remember that my father was restless and uneasy whenever this person visited us, and when we talked together watched us with the greatest apparent anxiety' (p. 164). Matilda's claim that she recognises her father's discomfort only in hindsight is dubious given that she uses the suitor to exhibit her sexuality – her desirability – to elicit a response from her father.[120] Matilda's value as a commodity is not shown in reference to another woman, which Irigaray argues is requisite: 'in order to have a relative value, a commodity has to be confronted with another commodity that serves as its equivalent. Its value is never found to lie within itself.'[121] Matilda establishes her own worth in a way that Irigaray posits she cannot: she manipulates the system of exchange to position herself as valuable in relation to another 'buyer' on the market. Elaborating on Lévi-Strauss's theories, Irigaray acknowledges the position of women as commodities but questions the assumption that society could not exist without such exchanges: 'the exchanges upon which patriarchal societies are based take place exclusively among men. Women, signs, commodities, currency all pass from one man to another; if it were otherwise, we are told, the social order would fall back upon incestuous and exclusively endogamous ties that would paralyze all commerce.'[122] Shelley's representation of Matilda's value and removal from commerce demonstrates the validity of both Lévi-Strauss's and Irigaray's theories. When Matilda is removed from the marriage market there is a paralysis of commerce, as Lévi-Strauss assumed, but the endogamous incestuous ties that are meant to be a consequence of the lack of exchange are instead the cause of it. This paralysis of commerce – resulting from incestuous desires – enables the formation of a wholly new social order rather than the end of culture that Irigaray argues is an insurmountable flaw in Lévi-Strauss's theory. That Matilda's father is incapable of offering his daughter as an object of exchange to the suitor begins the breakdown of the traffic in women that is completed when Matilda forces his incestuous declaration.

Matilda receives a letter from her father that expresses his incestuous longings, though its lack of details and fluctuating tone create a sense of hesitancy fully to disclose his desires and accept blame that refuses moral condemnation. The father claims he limits descriptions of his desires to keep vulgarity out of the letter: 'let a veil be drawn over the unimaginable sensations of a guilty father; the secrets of so agonized a heart may not be made vulgar' (p. 179). However, by veiling the 'unimaginable sensations' one is compelled to imagine them. Shelley thus allows the reader to judge the father's culpability and leaves open the possibility of a reconciliation between him and Matilda. The metaphoric veil operates here in a more complicated manner than its typical use – concealing sexual activity or violence – becoming a tool of morality that enables the father to be both innocent and guilty and that permits the reader to condemn or to condone his desires. Even the clearest language that the father uses does not explicate the true nature of his love: 'if I enjoyed from your looks, and words, and most innocent caresses a rapture usually excluded from the feelings of a parent towards his child, yet no uneasiness, no wish, no casual idea awoke me to a sense of guilt' (p. 179). The confession does not explain if the 'rapture' was a purely emotional response or a physical reaction to his daughter's caresses. While he clarifies that his feelings are excluded from the emotional range of other fathers, he immediately denies they caused him a sense of guilt. The language obfuscates his awareness of his loving Matilda incestuously. The word 'rapture' seems to indicate a strictly psychological state – that of ecstasy or bliss – but the fact that it is paired with 'innocent caresses' points to sexual ecstasy. Shelley's blending of the psychological and sexual, paternal and incestuous alongside the use of the veil creates a fluctuating sense of guilt and morality and depicts incestuous desires as an unintentional emotional and physical response the father struggles against acknowledging or indulging.

A refusal to condemn incestuous desires is present from the moment of reunion between Matilda and her father, during which Shelley plays with the Gothic conventions of recognition, genealogy and Orientalism to render the father's incestuous love possible. Matilda's resemblance to her mother, Diana, plays a part in his love, as does his belief that Matilda is an angelic soul in a human body and/or the reincarnation of Diana's soul. This belief makes the idea of incest with his daughter less horrifying as her body is a shell housing his deceased wife's spirit. That the father's admission is contextualised within his earlier discussion of his sixteen years in the East lends credence to reading his desires as incestuous without inspiring guilt: 'The burning sun of India, and the freedom from all restraint had rather encreased the energy of his character ... He had seen so many customs and witnessed so great a variety of moral creeds that he had been obliged to form an independent one for himself which had no relation to the peculiar notions of any one country' (p. 161). Matilda's father may be more inclined to understand or act on his desires without guilt because of the variety of moral codes he has witnessed. The belief that incest in India was prevalent is noted by psychohistorian Lloyd DeMause, who describes its occurrence as 'as far [back] as records exist'.[123] The Orientalism that often implies exotic sexualities, the setting of India and a variety of ethical creeds position the father as altered in principles by years of exposure to incestuous customs.[124] The father thus eludes the moral condemnation not permitted to a man with a wholly English experience of life.[125] This cultural dissonance is pointed to in William D. Brewer's examination of Shelley's 'unnationalizing' of male characters who 'find reassimilation into their native cultures difficult if not impossible'.[126] If Matilda's father feels guiltless rapture at his daughter's touch, the 'independent' ethical system he has formed suggests that incest is an inherently natural desire restrained by society, rather than morality. In opposition to Lévi-Strauss's understanding of the prohibition of incest as creating culture, Matilda's father suggests that it is only the creation of (Western) culture that demands the incest taboo.[127]

Matilda claims repeatedly that the bliss of her and her father's reunion is ruined by no fault of her own, yet her part in pressing her father to confess his love is a calculated move that renders her self-absolution false. Her claim of innocence is contradicted both by her actions and Shelley's biblical allusions: 'I lament now, I must ever lament, those few short months of Paradisiacal bliss; I disobeyed no command, I ate no apple, and yet I was ruthlessly driven from it. Alas! My companion did, and I was precipitated in his fall' (p. 162). When Matilda begs her father to speak, he confesses his 'unnatural passion' and concludes: '"my daughter, I love you"' (p. 173). With these words Matilda sinks to the ground, 'covering [her] face and almost dead with excess of sickness and fear' (p. 173). The reaction is seemingly at odds with his revelation; after all, Matilda has not, like her father, had a sixteen-year exposure to the 'freedom from all restraint' that would allow her to identify incestuous desires; her sixteen years have been ones of innocence and emotional desolation. Yet Shelley implies that these years of intense longing for her father have similarly prepared Matilda to understand incestuous desires. Matilda's reaction to her father's declaration is only appropriate if she reciprocates this passion, otherwise the words 'I love you' would surely not have filled her – who has so frequently spoken of her love for him – with fear. Hoeveler regards this scene as 'a cover for Mary's own ambivalence towards Godwin … The real passion motivating the relationship between father and daughter is hate'.[128] This autobiographical reading interprets Matilda's hatred as a 'negative Oedipus complex' that causes her to 'long to escape with an idealized and phantom mother'.[129] Nevertheless, it is not her mother to whom Matilda longs to escape, but with the father whom she loves and drives to confess his love to her.

Passive before his arrival, the incestuous desires her father inspires turn Matilda into an active, aggressive agent who incites him to declare his love. Reminiscing about the day she entreats her father to speak, Matilda blames their ruin on herself, in contrast to her earlier self-absolution: 'had not I, foolish and presumptuous wretch! hurried him on until there was no recall, no hope … I! I alone was the cause of his defeat' (p. 169). Matilda takes responsibility for her demands that precipitated her father's admission, reflecting that: 'it was May, four years ago, that I first saw my beloved father; it was in May, three years ago that my folly destroyed that only thing I was doomed to love' (p. 209). Her love for her father precludes Matilda from loving any other individual or participating in any of life's pleasures and the loss of his esteem renders her desolate. After her father's confession Matilda resolves never to see him again; however, almost immediately she devises ways to reunite with him. She believes that if her father wanders for another sixteen years his passion will fade as he ages, enabling him to love her paternally, desiring that he: 'go, and return pure to thy child, who will never love aught but thee' (p. 175). Her resolution to end the relationship with her father is not sincere; it is an attempt to absolve herself from the guilt of sexual desire. It is only by metaphorically castrating her father with age that Matilda can reconcile being with him again – not because she wants him to be rendered impotent but because it is the only way she can conceive of in which they can be together without consummating physically their love. Her father's inability to so delude himself contributes to his suicide: an act of ultimate self-castration engendered by his fear at the power Matilda's reciprocal incestuous passion gives her over him.[130]

Matilda refuses to re-enter the economy of exchange demanded by society. After her father's suicide relatives force her to move to London and oppress her with demands to seek an appropriate suitor, but the confined and suffocating world of patriarchal control impel Matilda to fake her own suicide and flee. Her apparent inaction in the cottage on the heath is a deliberate rejection of the cultural demands of exchange, a choice to leave civilisation and live in solitude wearing a 'fanciful nunlike dress' (p. 187). The purity of the garb is off-putting to men, rather like widow's weeds but here denoting virginity. Matilda dresses as a bride of Christ who is allowed to remain untouched.[131] She describes herself in her new life as 'a selfish solitary creature, ever pondering on my regrets and faded hopes' (p. 189). As she declares, Matilda does not ever love again. Woodville, a friend who intrudes on her self-imposed solitude, demonstrates how fully she has cut herself off from the possibility of any love other than her father. Woodville is brilliant, beautiful and kind but Matilda views him as a platonic friend. If writers of the Female Gothic wound the hero to render him a safe, feminised mate for the heroine, Woodville seems the perfect choice for Matilda. But this solution is never realised; Matilda does not desire a wounded and feminised hero/lover with whom she can share an asexual relationship any more than she truly desired her father to be rendered impotent with age, except as a psychological absolution of the guilt she feels for her incestuous desires.[132] Matilda is aware that her love for her father is the real reason she cannot accept a suitor or remain with her relations who demand that she marry and this spurs her to dress in the nun-like habit far from the culture that traffics in women.

Matilda describes her emotional state after her father's suicide: 'infamy and guilt was mingled with my portion [of misery]; unlawful and detestable passion had poured its poison into my ears and changed all my blood ... [to] a cold fountain of bitterness, corrupted in its very source' (p. 196). The description comingles her wish to return to her father with language that evinces hostility, yet the tones of anger, hate and guilt do not reconcile themselves with her desire to reunite with her father, and it is her expression of faded hopes and sorrow that seem more honest. She uses the language of anger and guilt to justify her indulgent grief and need for solitude, pretending to be tainted by her father's incestuous desires while consistently revealing that she longs to return to him. Matilda seeks solitude until her eventual reunion in death with her father and only refrains from suicide on religious grounds: 'With all the energy of desperate grief I told him [Woodville] how I had fallen at once from bliss to misery; how for me there was no joy, no hope; that death however bitter would be the welcome seal to all my pangs; death the skeleton was to be as beautiful as love' (p. 198). Death will be as beautiful as love because it is in death that she will be reunited with her love.

Matilda employs images of death united with the language of natural and unnatural emotions to trouble the surface narrative of pollution she associates with incestuous desires and reveal her understanding of her equally incestuous desires for her father.

> I was doomed while in life to grieve, and to the natural sorrow of my father's death and its most terrific cause, imagination had added a tenfold weight of

woe. I believed myself to be polluted by the unnatural love I had inspired, and that I was a creature cursed and set apart by nature ... I was impressed more strongly with the withering fear that I was in truth a marked creature, a pariah, only fit for death. (pp. 203–4)

The 'unnatural love' Matilda inspired in her father is akin to the mark of Cain; she feels set apart from the outside world, separated by her father's love and the knowledge that she incited it. Matilda later uses the word 'unnatural' to describe her childhood pleasures: 'I enjoyed what I may almost call unnatural pleasures, for they were dreams and not realities' (p. 208). That the pleasures are 'unnatural' and the adjective is linked to her affectionless childhood and dreams that focused on her father's miniature image unites her father's incestuous love and the 'unnatural' pleasures of her youth.

In so doing Matilda represents her and her father's desires paradoxically as culturally unnatural yet naturally occurring. Matilda believes it is 'imagination' that causes the idea of being 'polluted' as opposed to the 'natural' sorrow she feels at her father's death. The use of the word 'imagines' in relation to her idea that she has been violated, her purity stolen by her father, is tied to the descriptions of her childhood in which the word 'imagination' is so important. It was, after all, her childhood practice to envision her father's return to her and it was on his idea and image that her imagination dwelled: 'the idea of my unhappy, wandering father was the idol of my imagination' (p. 157). In a sense, Matilda blames herself for causing her father's love and his declaration of it, using the same language that characterised her childhood fixation on her father in her descriptions of the love that she incited him to verbalise. Yet her feelings of guilt and pollution are bound up in her blissful love for her father. Therefore, she emphasises her 'mark' as being caused by 'imagination'; that she 'believes' herself polluted, that the idea she is a pariah is 'impressed' upon her clarifies that the pollution is not so much physical but emotional, caused by her recognition that her childhood imaginings make her as complicit in incestuous love as her father. What is explicit and 'natural' is her grief at being parted from her father through the realisation of the love that she had for so many years fixated on.

The most concrete language Shelley uses in her depiction of incestuous love presents Matilda jeopardising her health in order to bring about her death and reunion with her father.[133] Once aware of her impending death, Matilda states: 'I shall be with my father ... In truth I am in love with death; no maiden ever took more pleasure in the contemplation of her bridal attire than I in fancying my limbs already enwrapped in their shroud: is it not my marriage dress? Alone it will unite me to my father when in an eternal mental union we shall never part' (p. 208). Matilda's death will precede and effect her marriage yet she hastens to add that this will enable an eternal 'mental' bond. Her shroud – here doubling as her wedding dress – seems to literalise Blackstone's understanding of wives as civilly dead after marriage. Shelley presents Matilda's union with her father as offering the eternal experience of life after death and 'after marriage', eliciting a comparison between this marriage and the Gothic wife's civil death explored by scholars such as Anolik and Wallace. Matilda's death and union challenge the scholarly understandings of marriage as resulting in the death of the narrative and the wife by requiring the heroine's death – and thus the death of the narrator and narrative – before the incestuous union can take place. Incestuous love here removes the female body from the marriage market but requires the ultimate erasure of self from culture before the father–daughter union can be consummated.

It is towards the end of her life and her disclosure of her life's events that she has abandoned bitterness and sorrow in favour of hope and yearning; Hoeveler notes that Matilda shifts from hatred and guilt until it is 'the dead father who is the love object, the ultimate goal at the end of the daughter's quest'.[134] Matilda's parting words reinforce her belief that her future and hopes lie in the grave: 'Farewell, Woodville, the turf will soon be green on my grave; and the violets will bloom on it. There is my hope and my expectations; yours are in this world; may they be fulfilled' (p. 210). Matilda's desires cause her to leave her patrimony, her estates, her name – the very things that Gothic heroines often fight so hard to recover – effectively destroying the patriarchal world of exchange that prohibits incest as a threat to its existence. She does not attempt to escape her female body by denying her desire or sexuality, but embraces it – dressing it with care in the death shroud/wedding dress in which she will meet her father.[135] Matilda's incestuous desires for her father are the effect of sixteen years of longing for and imagining a reunion that will eventually take place in another world, one beyond the rejected system of exchange that would relegate Matilda to the status of object/commodity.

Incest, whether sought by the father, father figure or the heroine, cannot be dismissed as a mere Gothic convention or as a simple metaphor for the dangers of patriarchy or domesticity. Incest is almost always the subtle means of destroying the patriarchal world that imprisons the

Gothic heroine, acting as a multifaceted construction encompassing the ambivalence of father–daughter relationships, differing configurations of desire, the potential for liberation in transgressive choices and the dangers of unchecked passions. The heroines' responses to incest – whether they fight, manipulate, flee from, take part in, desire or initiate it – show their ability to act, to choose and to escape. Through the father–daughter incestuous configuration the ideas of Irigaray, Butler and Lévi-Strauss regarding the exchange of women between paternal figures of control are most clearly visible and underscore how dissolutions of paternal ties through incestuous desires break down the exogamic exchanges on which patriarchal society is based. In moving away from Freudian concepts that lead scholars to argue that 'phobias and persecution fears ... are crucially bound up with "normal" feminine psychological development' it becomes possible to see that the fears and phobias are in fact tangible threats that women face in a culture that deals in the traffic of women.[136] The experiences of Gothic heroines cannot be reduced to an explanation of mere poses of weakness and victimisation without adopting the language of patriarchal power that ignores the abuses perpetrated against women. The Gothic heroine does not pretend to be a victim but overcomes the real dangers endemic to the heteronormative world that demands the objectification and exchange of women. Father–daughter incest has a transgressive power to break apart the familial and kinship ties necessary to the patriarchal society of oppression and exchange, causing a rupture in the efficacy of patriarchy to make available an alternative model of female agency that reconfigures society without the exchange of female bodies.

NOTES

1 Mary Shelley, *Matilda*, ed. Janet Todd (Harmondsworth: Penguin, 1992), p. 179. Subsequent references will be given in the text.
2 E. J. Clery, 'Ann Radcliffe and D. A. F. de Sade: thoughts on heroinism', *Women's Writing*, 1:2 (1994), 203.
3 Claude Lévi-Strauss, *The Elementary Structures of Kinship* (London: Taylor & Francis, 1969), p. 25.
4 Julie Brickman, 'Female Lives, Feminist Deaths: The Relationship of the Montreal Massacre to Dissociation, Incest, and Violence against Women', in Renée R. Curry (ed.), *States of Rage: Emotional Eruption, Violence and Social Change* (New York: New York University Press, 1996), pp. 15–34. See also: Lena Dominelli, 'Betrayal of trust: a feminist analysis of power

relationships in incest abuse and its relevance for social work practice', *British Journal of Social Work*, 19:1 (1989), 291–308 and 'Father–daughter incest: patriarchy's shameful secret', *Critical Social Policy: Special Feminist Issue*, 6:16 (1986), 8–22.

5 Sigmund Freud, *Three Essays on the Theory of Sexuality*, ed. and trans. James Strachey [1953] (New York: Basic Books, 2000), p. 91.
6 Freud, *Three Essays on the Theory of Sexuality*, p. 91.
7 Sigmund Freud, *The Interpretation of Dreams*, ed. and trans. James Strachey [1953] (New York: Avon, 1980), p. 256.
8 Freud, *The Interpretation of Dreams*, p. 256.
9 See Bruce Bower, 'Oedipus wrecked: Freud's theory of frustrated incest goes on the defensive', *Science News*, 140:16 (1991), 248–51; and Nancy Chodorow, *Feminism and Psychoanalytic Theory* [1989] (New Haven, CT: Yale University Press, repr. 1991), pp. 195–6 for evaluations of how Freudian psychoanalysts tend to view female victims of sexual abuse as having underlying rape fantasies.
10 Anne Cossins, *Masculinities, Sexualities, and Child Sexual Abuse* (New York: Springer, 2000), p. 35. Cossins points to an 1897 letter to William Fleiss in which Freud discounts his patients' claims of incestuous abuse as fantasy.
11 Jerry Adler, Anne Underwood and Marc Bain, 'Freud in our midst', *Newsweek* 147:13 (27 March 2006). http://search.ebscohost.com/login.aspx?direct=true &db=a9h&AN=20199528&site=ehost-live [accessed 20 May 2009].
12 Bower, 251.
13 Gayle Rubin, 'The Traffic in Women: Notes on the "Political Economy" of Sex', in Rayna R. Reiter (ed.), *Toward an Anthropology of Women* (New York: Monthly Review Press, 1975), p. 200. See also Jane Gallop, *The Daughter's Seduction: Feminism and Psychoanalysis* (Ithaca, NY: Cornell University Press, 1982) for an examination of how women reject the father's law by refusing to submit to either his desire or his prohibition of her desire, thus destabilising the categories of male/female through a challenge to language and law.
14 For critiques of Freudian incest theory and its applicability to female psychology see Bower, 251; and Samuel Slipp, *The Freudian Mystique: Freud, Women, and Feminism* (New York: New York University Press, 1993), pp. 13–19 and pp. 188–202. For Gothic analyses based in Freudian theory see Diane Long Hoeveler, *Gothic Feminism: The Professionalization of Gender from Charlotte Smith to the Brontës* (Liverpool: Liverpool University Press, 1998); Terry Castle, *The Female Thermometer: Eighteenth-Century Culture and the Invention of the Uncanny* (Oxford: Oxford University Press, 1995); Kate Ferguson Ellis, *The Contested Castle: Gothic Novels and the Subversion of Domestic Ideology* (Urbana: University of Illinois Press: 1989); and Eugenia

C. DeLamotte, *Perils of the Night: A Feminist Study of Nineteenth-Century Gothic* (Oxford: Oxford University Press, 1990).

15 Rita Felski, *Literature after Feminism* (Chicago: University of Chicago Press, 2003), pp. 153–5. Felski argues that feminist scholarship has allowed the Gothic to be revisited as a genre and explores how Freudian psychology has become intertwined with scholarly readings of the Gothic.

16 Julie Shaffer, 'Familial love, incest, and female desire in late eighteenth- and early nineteenth-century British women's novels', *Criticism: A Quarterly for Literature and the Arts*, 41:1 (1999), 78.

17 Shaffer, 75.

18 Tania Modleski, *Loving with a Vengeance: Mass-Produced Fantasies for Women* [1982] (New York: Routledge, repr. 2008), p. 11.

19 As I argued in the Introduction, Lawrence Stone's model of the emergent nuclear family in the long eighteenth century in *The Family, Sex and Marriage in England, 1500–1800* (London: Weidenfeld & Nicolson, 1977) contributes to reading the father as a sexually dangerous threat within the domestic space.

20 For an overview of the feminist rejection of Freudian theories and the difficulty in using them in feminist analyses of literature, see Fiona Tolan, 'Feminisms', in Patricia Waugh (ed.), *Literary Theory and Criticism: An Oxford Guide* (Oxford: Oxford University Press, 2006), pp. 319–39.

21 As Shelley's *Matilda* meets her father as a teenager after being raised by an aunt, the depiction does not fit Freud's parameters for the formation of incestuous desires.

22 Hoeveler, p. 56.

23 Hoeveler, p. 57.

24 For analyses of the validity of the Westermarck effect over Freudian paradigms of incestuous behaviour see Mark T. Erickson, 'Evolutionary Thought and the Current Clinical Understanding of Incest', in Arthur P. Wolf and William H. Durham (eds), *Inbreeding, Incest and the Incest Taboo: The State of Knowledge at the Turn of the Century* (Stanford: Stanford University Press, 2004), pp. 161–89; and Arthur P. Wolf, 'Westermarck redivivus', *Annual Review of Anthropology*, 22 (1993), 157–75. See also Florence Rush, *The Best Kept Secret: The Sexual Abuse of Children* (Englewood Cliffs, NJ: Prentice Hall, 1980). Rush argues that Freud's portrayal of children as seducing parents contributes to the psychological oppression of women.

25 Edward Westermarck, *The History of Human Marriage* (London: Macmillan and Co., 1903), p. 320.

26 See Tamaz Bereczkei, Petra Gyuris and Glenn E Weisfeld, 'Sexual imprinting in human mate choice', *Proceedings of the Royal Society B: Biological Sciences*, 271 (2004), 1129–34; and Alix Kirsta, 'Genetic sexual attraction', *Guardian*, 17 May 2003, www.guardian.co.uk/theguardian/2003/may/17/weekend7.weekend2 [accessed 15 December 2008], in which Kirsta describes the nature

of incest and attraction and how GSA (Genetic Sexual Attraction) first came into public discussion.

27 William Blackstone wrote: 'by marriage, the husband and wife are one person in law: that is, the very being or legal existence of the woman is suspended during the marriage, or at least is incorporated and consolidated into that of the husband'. *Commentaries on the laws of England. Book the first. By William Blackstone, Esq. vinerian professor of law, and solicitor general to her majesty*, 4 vols (Oxford: Clarendon Press, 1765), I, p. 430.

28 See Ellis, p. x; and Ruth Perry, *Novel Relations: The Transformation of Kinship in English Literature and Culture 1748-1818* (Cambridge: Cambridge University Press, 2004), pp. 388-98.

29 Ruth Bienstock Anolik, 'The missing mother: the meanings of maternal absence in the Gothic mode', *Modern Language Studies*, 33:1/2 (2003), 27.

30 Luce Irigaray, *This Sex Which is Not One* [1977], trans. Catherine Porter and Carolyn Burke (Ithaca, NY: Cornell University Press, 1985), p. 84. Irigaray takes issue with Lévi-Strauss's acceptance of the exchange of women as a natural requirement in the creation of culture, questioning why it is women rather than men who are the objects of exchange (p. 171).

31 Rubin, p. 93.

32 Rubin, p. 101.

33 Irigaray, p. 189.

34 Ellis, p. 52.

35 Michael Gamer, 'Gothic origins: new primary scholarship', *Eighteenth-Century Fiction*, 14:2 (2002), 217. In his work *Romanticism and the Gothic: Genre, Reception, and Canon Formation* (Cambridge: Cambridge University Press, 2000), Gamer argues for an earlier Gothic origin than 1764, stating that: 'with Ian Duncan, Robert Miles, and Edward Jacobs, then, I read the emergence of gothic fiction between 1760 and 1790 as a response *to* the novel', pointing to John Home's *Douglas* (1757) and Thomas LeLand's *Longsword, Earl of Salisbury* (1762) as, along with *Otranto*, 'the texts most often involved in literary histories of early gothic fiction and drama' (p. 57).

36 Benjamin Bird, 'Treason and imagination: the anxiety of legitimacy in the subject of the 1760s', *Romanticism*, 12:3 (2006), 192-3. Bird argues that what 'particularly aroused Walpole's wrath was a case of seditious libel brought by the crown against forty-nine employees of the dissident journal "North Briton"' and cites his votes in two parliamentary debates in 1763 in opposition to King George III's administration that made use of 'general warrants' which Walpole considered 'illegal and an abuse of the royal prerogative' (193).

37 Bird, 193-4.

38 James Watt, 'Gothic', in Thomas Keymer and Jon Mee (eds), *The Cambridge Companion to English Literature, 1740-1830* (Cambridge: Cambridge University Press, 2004), p. 120.

39 Horace Walpole, *The Castle of Otranto*, ed. E. J. Clery and W. S. Walpole (Oxford: Oxford University Press, 1998), p. 7. Subsequent references will be given in the text.
40 Frederick S. Frank argues that Walpole 'counterfeited his authorship' in claiming the book was an Italian manuscript translated by William Marshal and notes that Walpole's use of the term Gothic in the second preface recalls Bishop Hurd's 'earlier use of the phrase "Gothic romance"' in his 'Introduction', Horace Walpole, *The Castle of Otranto and The Mysterious Mother* (Peterborough, Ontario: Broadview, 2003), p. 16.
41 Walpole would have been familiar with Henry Fielding's play *The Welsh Opera* (1731), a political allegory that satirised the government of his father, Robert Walpole, and which is examined in this context in Albert Rivero's *The Plays of Henry Fielding: A Critical Study of His Dramatic Career* (Charlottesville, VA: University of Virginia Press, 1989), pp. 91–2.
42 Sue Chaplin, 'Spectres of law in *The Castle of Otranto*', *Romanticism*, 12:3 (2006), 177–8.
43 Chaplin, 178.
44 Michael Gamer, 'Introduction', Horace Walpole, *The Castle of Otranto* (Harmondsworth: Penguin, 2002), p. xxviii.
45 Chaplin, 182–3.
46 Chaplin, 185–6.
47 Watt points to the parodic nature of *Otranto* when he notes its 'playfulness' in *Contesting the Gothic* (Cambridge: Cambridge University Press, 1999), pp. 120–1.
48 Watt argues that 'Walpole helped to establish a vocabulary of themes and tropes that was later resorted to across the genres' ('Gothic', p. 121).
49 In contrast to most critics, Watt displaces *Otranto* as the first Gothic novel (*Contesting the Gothic*, p. 3).
50 Modleski notes the conventions that Gothic novels and sentimental and domestic novels share, such as paranoia, persecution and threatened domestic spaces (pp. 10–22). Examples of the sentimental novel include Samuel Richardson's *Pamela, or Virtue Rewarded* (1740), Henry Mackenzie's *The Man of Feeling* (1771) and Frances Burney's *Evelina* (1778).
51 In 'Betrayal of trust' Dominelli argues that 'like Freud, experts drawing on psychoanalytical approaches ignore the significance of gender in incestuous relationships, the power emanating from the subordination of women to men (McLeod and Saraga, 1988) and the impact of the power relations inherent in adult-child relationships' (292–3).
52 Cynthia Wall's essay on Walpole's resentment of political authority and use of subterranean images in his correspondence and fiction argues that Walpole deploys the blending of genres found in Shakespeare to construct 'a nonspecific political satire against typical patriarchal assumptions' in '*The*

Castle of Otranto: A Shakespearo-Political Satire?', in Lorna Clymer and Robert Mayer (eds), *Historical Boundaries, Narrative Forms: Essays on British Literature in the Long Eighteenth Century in Honor of Everett Zimmerman* (Newark: University of Delaware Press, 2007), p. 195. Wall argues that *Otranto* 'as gothic parent is only partly satisfactory' but if viewed as 'political and generic satire ... just might work' (p. 196).
53 E. J. Clery, 'Introduction', Horace Walpole, *The Castle of Otranto* (Oxford: Oxford University Press, 1998), p. xviii.
54 Anolik's 'The missing mother' examines how Gothic writers literalise women's disempowered status in society through their textual erasure, a technique similar to (though reversed in) Walpole's exaggeration of the physical symbols of the aristocracy to create political metaphors.
55 Clery, 'Introduction', p. xxii.
56 For a comprehensive treatment of the maternal and sexuality in eighteenth-century literature, see Felicity A. Nussbaum, *Torrid Zones: Maternity, Sexuality, and Empire in Eighteenth-Century English Narratives* (Baltimore: Johns Hopkins University Press, 1995), pp. 22–46.
57 Nussbaum points to this association of the domestic female servant with sexuality (pp. 25–6).
58 Irigaray, p. 84.
59 Hoeveler, p. 246.
60 Unlike Hippolita, who is rewarded for her complicity with male-based incestuous desires, female characters who endanger heroines in other Gothic works are punished severely. In Radcliffe's *The Mysteries of Udolpho* (1794) Madame Montoni allows the heroine to be offered to the richest suitor and is imprisoned by her husband and dies; in *The Italian* (1797) the Marchesa dies of guilt after plotting the heroine's murder. In Charlotte Smith's *Emmeline* (1788) Lady Montreville dies after attempting to coerce the heroine into undesired marriages.
61 See Anolik, 25–43. Examples of this type of mother or mother-substitute include Radcliffe's characters of Olivia in *The Italian* (1797) and the Marchioness Mazzini in *A Sicilian Romance* (1790); the Countess of Wolfenbach in Eliza Parsons's *The Castle of Wolfenbach* (1793); and Correlia in Sarah Sheriffe's *Correlia, or The Mystic Tomb* (1802). An alternative maternal model is the sexually aggressive mother, such as Walpole's Countess in *The Mysterious Mother* (1768), analysed in Chapter 5.
62 See Chapter 3 for an examination of violent uncle–niece incest as representative of male usurpations of property and female bodies.
63 This trope recurs in novels such as Smith's *Emmeline*, Radcliffe's *The Romance of the Forest* (1791) and *The Italian*, Parsons's *Wolfenbach*, Matthew Lewis's *The Monk* (1796), Eleanor Sleath's *The Orphan of the Rhine* (1798) and Charles Maturin's *Melmoth the Wanderer* (1820), among others.

64 Irigaray, p. 171.
65 This is similarly an implicit criticism of the changes in law regarding marriage under Henry VIII that allowed him to marry Anne Boleyn, who was technically within the forbidden degrees of affinal connection to him, given her consanguineal relationship to his first wife, only to later charge her with incest (among other crimes) in order to have her executed so he could marry Jane Seymour. For an in-depth treatment of the historical and political allusions in Walpole's novel, see, for example, Carol M. Dole's article 'Three tyrants in *The Castle of Otranto*', *English Language Notes*, 26:1 (1988), 26–3.
66 Perry, pp. 388–90.
67 Ellen Pollak, *Incest and the English Novel, 1684–1814* (Baltimore: Johns Hopkins University Press, 2003), p. 37.
68 This is why in *Emmeline* Smith's heroine is not considered a viable marriage option for her cousin. Although the blood ties are far enough removed to allow property and wealth movement, because her uncle misappropriated her father's property, the wealth is already reallocated to her cousin's family. Emmeline's aunt and uncle do not object to the union on consanguineal grounds but because their son does not need to marry Emmeline to gain access to her property. An incest taboo is necessary to patriarchy's maintenance of exogamic exchange; it can only be overcome if the exchange of wealth or power coincides with the incestuous union.
69 Adam Kuper, 'Changing the subject – about cousin marriage, among other things', *Journal of the Royal Anthropological Institute (NS)*, 14:4 (2008), 727.
70 Irigaray, pp. 170–1.
71 Lévi-Strauss, p. 115. Lévi-Strauss's theories regarding women as objects of exchange are predicated on understanding the incest taboo as essential to exogamy, and thus culture. Without the ban on incestuous relationships, men would marry within their families and social structures and alliances would not be built.
72 See previously cited models of incest as an abuse of power or violation of familial authority as analysed by Dominelli, Brickman and Taylor.
73 This is like the scenes of incestuous stabbings (or near-stabbings) in novels including Radcliffe's *The Italian*, Parsons's *Wolfenbach* and Anne Ker's *The Mysterious Count; or, Montville Castle* (1803).
74 Ann Radcliffe, *The Romance of the Forest*, ed. Chloe Chard (Oxford: Oxford University Press, 1986), p. 2. Subsequent references will be given in the text.
75 Modleski points to 'enforced confinement' as underlying the paranoia of Gothic heroines (p. 11). Modleski's treatment of claustrophobic domestic spaces yields important analyses of repeated Gothic conventions.
76 Perry, p. 389.
77 Perry describes the phenomena of feelings of kinship or attraction to those who turn out to be related as the '*cri du sang* or the call of blood [that]

signified a fictional instinct whose popularity apparently reassured society that consanguinity was still powerful' (p. 95).

78 Hoeveler offers this label in the preface to *Gothic Feminism*, stating that it is a tactic found in most Gothic heroines who 'cannot bare their teeth in anything other than a smile', taking what had previously been called 'victim feminism' in application to the Female Gothic and terming it 'gothic feminism' (p. 246).

79 David Durrant, 'Ann Radcliffe and the conservative Gothic', *Studies in English Literature, 1500–1900*, 22:3 (1982), 528.

80 Hoeveler, pp. 34–5.

81 Hoeveler, p. 36.

82 Hoeveler, pp. 36–50.

83 See Chapter 4's analysis of Rochester in Charlotte Brontë's *Jane Eyre* (1847), who is an exception to the recovery from wounding, although his injury neither castrates nor feminises him.

84 Perry argues that consanguineal ties were loosening while the marriage bond and affinal relatives were of increasing importance in society, a shift in the family structure that produced anxiety evidenced through representations of kinship in the eighteenth-century novel, particularly in the Gothic, which hyperbolised the threats implicit in the new nuclear family (pp. 388–90).

85 See Perry, pp. 86–8.

86 Hoeveler, p. 36.

87 See Hoeveler, p. 36.

88 See E. J. Clery, 'Horace Walpole's *The Mysterious Mother* and the Impossibility of Female Desire', in Fred Botting (ed.), *The Gothic: Essays and Studies* (Cambridge: D. S. Brewer, 2001), pp. 23–46.

89 See Claudia L. Johnson's excellent analysis of Adeline's rejection of the convent in *Equivocal Beings: Politics, Gender, and Sentimentality in the 1790s* (Chicago: University of Chicago Press, 1995), pp. 78–80.

90 Female characters are imprisoned in convents and threatened with perpetual celibacy following attempts to compel them into taking the vows of a nun in many Gothic texts, including George Moore's *Grasville Abbey* (1793), Radcliffe's *The Italian*, Lewis's *The Monk*, Sleath's *The Orphan of the Rhine* and George Barrington's *Eliza, or The Unhappy Nun* (1803). My argument here contrasts with that of Maria Purves in *The Gothic and Catholicism: Religion, Cultural Exchange and the Popular Novel, 1785–1829* (Cardiff: University of Wales Press, 2009). Purves argues that Gothic novels, while generally understood by scholarship as presenting anti-Catholic and anti-monastic views, actually depict the convent as a space of safety to heroines, an alternative to the outside world and its threats, as opposed to being conceived as a threat to female liberty.

91 Since the mid-fourteenth century 'abstinence' has been used to refer particularly to sexual appetites. http://dictionary.reference.com/etymology/abstinence [accessed 17 July 2009].

92 Leaving available a substitute meaning would have been a real concern for Radcliffe, who needed to maintain an image as a respectable woman writer in a genre frequently condemned for its promotion of individual desires. See Fred Botting, *Gothic: The New Critical Idiom* (London: Routledge, 1996), in which Botting describes the understanding of the genre as 'giving free rein to … sexual desires' (p. 4).

93 Hoeveler succinctly explains Gothic representations of Catholicism as: 'a sort of leitmotif throughout the gothic novel, reifying British and Enlightenment dread of medievalism, superstition, and uninformed prejudice' (p. 52).

94 Perry, p. 390.

95 Walpole's Matilda is barely able to overcome filial ties to save a man's life while Adeline dissolves them when her sexual freedom is threatened. The contractual nature of her obligation to her father is voided by his refusal to grant her rights – see the analysis in Chapter 4 of obligation and individual rights in relation to incestuous relationships.

96 Pollak, p. 47.

97 See, in addition to *Otranto* and *The Romance of the Forest*, Radcliffe's *A Sicilian Romance*, in which the heroine's father tries to exchange her in marriage to his wealthy and powerful friend, Anna Maria Bennett's *Ellen, Countess of Castle Howel* (1794), in which the heroine is given to a wealthy older man in marriage in exchange for him saving their family estate and Selina Davenport's *The Sons of the Viscount and the Daughters of the Earl* (1813), wherein the beauty of the heroine's sister renders her a marketable commodity protected by the family patriarch (an uncle).

98 Irigaray points to this circulation among men thus: 'the production of women, signs, and commodities is always referred back to men (when a man buys a girl, he "pays" the father or the brother, not the mother …), and they always pass from one man to another, from one group of men to the other. The work force is thus always assumed to be masculine, and "products" are objects to be used, objects of transaction among men alone' (p. 171).

99 Irigaray, p. 172.

100 Irigaray, p. 84.

101 Joan Riviere argued that 'womanliness therefore could be assumed and worn as a mask, both to hide the possession of masculinity and to avert the reprisals expected if she was found to possess it' in 'Womanliness as masquerade', *International Journal of Psychoanalysis*, 10 (1929), 306.

102 Perry, p. 397.

103 See Joanne Bailey, *Unquiet Lives: Marriage and Marriage Breakdown in England, 1660–1800* (Cambridge: Cambridge University Press, 2003) and Naomi Tadmor, *Family and Friends in Eighteenth-Century England* (Cambridge: Cambridge University Press, 2001) for comprehensive treatments of family, kinship and marriage in eighteenth-century England and

the divergent yet coterminous emphases on affinal, consanguineal and conjugal relations.

104 Imprisoned male characters include Vivaldi and Schedoni in *The Italian*, Valancourt and Du Pont in *Udolpho*, Hippolitus de Vereza in *A Sicilian Romance* and Albert in Anne Ker's *The Mysterious Count; or, Montville Castle* (1803), amongst others.

105 The figure of the uncle who offers either a role as sex-slave or wife to his niece is similarly presented in Parsons's *Wolfenbach*, in which the heroine rejects both options, locating them as objectionable and synonymous.

106 I borrow terms such as 'heroinism' and 'heroinic' used by Rachel M. Brownstein in *Becoming a Heroine: Reading About Women in Novels* (New York: Columbia University Press, 1994) and Ellen Moers in *Literary Women: The Great Writers* [1976] (Oxford: Oxford University Press, repr. 1985) to describe the action of the heroines.

107 Hoeveler, pp. 54–5.

108 Hoeveler, p. 246.

109 Rubin, p. 199.

110 Gothic heroines, in this sense, complete the disintegration of male/female distinctions and paternal authority suggested by Gallop without necessarily physically completing the incestuous sex act – their refusal to obey the father's law is almost always enough to cause the destruction of the patriarchal structure.

111 Frederick L. Jones, ed., *Maria Gisborne and Edward E. Williams, Shelley's Friends, Their Journals and Letters* (Norman: University of Oklahoma Press, 1951), p. 44. See Janet Todd's introduction to *Matilda* for further background and analysis of the novel, pp. vii–xxviii.

112 Terence Harpold, '"Did you get Mathilda from Papa?" Seduction fantasy and the circulation of Mary Shelley's *Mathilda*', *Studies in Romanticism*, 28:1 (1989), 50–6.

113 Hoeveler, p. 166.

114 Hoeveler, p. 162.

115 Harpold, 53.

116 Tilottama Rajan, 'Mary Shelley's *Mathilda*: melancholy and the political economy of Romanticism', *Studies in the Novel*, 26:2 (Summer 1994), 43–68. This analysis offers fascinating insights into the intertextualities and ambiguities in Shelley's novel produced by rewritings of her parents' works and focuses on the themes of trauma, affect and abjection.

117 Judith Butler, *Gender Trouble: Feminism and the Subversion of Identity* (London: Routledge, 1990), p. 54.

118 Irigaray, p. 189.

119 Irigaray concludes that 'even supposing this to be possible, history would repeat itself in the long run, would revert to sameness' (pp. 32–3). See

also: Leo Bersani, 'Foucault, Freud, fantasy, and power', *GLQ: A Journal of Lesbian and Gay Studies*, 2 (1995), 18.
120 Like the earlier analysis of Adeline's self-sexualising, Gothic heroines develop their sexuality before selecting a spouse.
121 Irigaray, p. 176.
122 Irigaray, p. 192.
123 Lloyd DeMause, 'The universality of incest', *Journal of Psychohistory*, 19:2 (1991), 123–64. DeMause cites the observations of scholars such as Catherine Mayo and Verrier Elwin and an old Indian proverb: 'for a girl to be a virgin at ten years old, she must have neither brother nor cousins nor father' (125). Such long-standing Western conceptions of Eastern attitudes towards incest support reading Shelley's representations of the father as having an altered moral code regarding incest based on his time in India.
124 This depiction of the East as having a more lax and passion-centred nexus of morality than that of Western societies echoes a monologue of the Marquis in *The Romance of the Forest* when, attempting to persuade La Motte to murder Adeline, the Marquis insists that it is a sign of superiority to lay aside the prejudices of education and country and embrace one's nature as those from the East do. The Marquis manipulates a perception of Eastern culture to introduce a more fluid morality to La Motte. See Ros Ballaster's excellent treatment of eighteenth-century literature and Orientalism in *Fabulous Orients: Fictions of the East in England 1662–1785* (Oxford: Oxford University Press, 2007).
125 Hoeveler points to this passage as allowing the father to 'rationalize incest in the extremely suspect regions of the Orient', concluding that Shelley does this to reveal 'another way that the middle-class domestic abode can be seen as a haven for fostering perverse and perverting love' (p. 167).
126 William D. Brewer, 'Unnationalized Englishmen in Mary Shelley's Fiction', *Romanticism on the Net*, 11 (1998), http://users.ox.ac.uk/~scat0385/mws-fiction.html [accessed 12 May 2009]. Brewer calls this 'unnationalized' man one who follows the 'Byronic pattern of transgressive action and self-banishment', arguing that Shelley's fiction relies heavily on her personal experiences with her husband, Lord Byron, and the effects of their time abroad.
127 Lévi-Strauss, p. 25.
128 Hoeveler, p. 172.
129 Hoeveler, pp. 172–3.
130 As Gallop argues throughout *The Daughter's Seduction*, the daughter's 'seduction' of the father – her refusal to be seduced by him or be submissive to the incest taboo – breaks down male/female hierarchies of law and desire, deconstructing rather than simply reversing them. Matilda's 'seduction' of her father so dismantles the hierarchies that she becomes his pursuer,

driving him to suicide, until the law of father, or patriarchal law, which demands that 'the daughter submits to the father's rule, which prohibits the father's desire' (p. 70), is not only inverted but destroyed.

131 Hoeveler likewise argues that Matilda rearranges her nun-like garb to become her father's bride (p. 180).
132 Hoeveler writes that Woodville's 'sufferings have effectively castrated him' but that despite this he is unsuitable for Matilda because she cannot 'find love or happiness with any living man, particularly one whose philosophical opinions bear such an uncanny resemblance to Percy Shelley's own ideas' (p. 179).
133 See Jacques Lacan, *Écrits* [1977] (London: Routledge, repr. 2001), in which Lacan describes 'the armature of the Freudian edifice, namely: the equivalence maintained by Freud of the imaginary function of the phallus in both sexes ... the castration complex found as a normative phase of the assumption by the subject of his own sex, the myth of the murder of the father rendered necessary by the Oedipus complex' (p. 144). Matilda's assumption of the seducer's role positions her as the male subject, both castrating and killing the Father and his law.
134 Hoeveler, p. 180.
135 Hoeveler argues that Matilda seeks death to 'escape the corrupted body' as Shelley viewed 'all women as diseased, aberrant, and freakish composites of the hopes and dreams of other people ... She inhabited a female body; she bled and caused bleeding in others, and those unfortunate facts defined for her and her fiction the gothic feminist nightmare in its starkest terms' (pp. 182–3).
136 Modleski uses these Freudian insights to locate the Gothic as 'the paranoid text' (p. 23).

2

'My more than sister':
re-examining paradigms of sibling incest

> [T]he blush that suffused her cheeks ... declared how tenderly she was interested in his concerns, and breathed more than sisterly affection.
>
> Eleanor Sleath, *The Orphan of the Rhine* (1798)[1]

In the first chapter relationships between fathers and daughters were examined; in particular, how the transgressive nature of father–daughter incest can cause a breakdown of patriarchal society that is more complex than the conventional positioning of paternal incest as representative solely of a threat to the heroine. Incest in the Gothic does not, however, exist exclusively between heroines and their fathers and/or father figures. The relationships between female characters and their brothers or brother-substitutes are often fraught with underlying incestuous desires that are expressed as hidden subtext or explicit incestuous love. In contrast to the potential for abuses of power with which father–daughter relationships are endowed by the nature of the familial bond, the relationships between siblings are grounded in a more even distribution of power.[2] Ruth Perry locates the brother as equally as dangerous to the heroine as the father or uncle, arguing that: 'both fathers and brothers began to see their female relatives ... as possessions in their power and hence possible sex objects'.[3] However, in the Gothic novel the brother rarely presents a threat to the heroine, instead functioning more commonly as an equal sufferer under patriarchal power. It is, I argue, the potential for equality – akin to what Caroline Rooney calls 'a feeling of universal sympathy associated with the sister' – that underpins the relationships between brothers and sisters and makes the bonds between siblings so dangerous and potentially destructive to patriarchal society.[4] This potential for unravelling society (in a way that renders father figures both obsolete and unnecessary) causes sibling desire to be treated as, perhaps, the most dangerous and complicated of all the incestuous relationships represented in the Gothic. The destruction of patriarchal society is effected through the dissolution of social growth into a condition of familial stasis that, unlike father–daughter incest, excludes any paternal or head of family position.

The anthropological understanding of the incest taboo as necessary to culture advanced by Claude Lévi-Strauss is similarly argued for by Leslie White, who describes the taboo's sociological impact as overcoming the human inclination to mate with intimate associates. While White, like Lévi-Strauss, views this taboo as necessary to ensure the growth of communities and the formation of social ties, his analysis points to a human tendency towards incest.[5] This qualification is essential to an examination of sibling incest in the Gothic, which scholarship has often viewed as an extension of the paternal incest threat, as many of these depictions are in fact bound up in the language of natural tendencies and desires.[6] Such representations frequently position brother–sister erotic love and familial love as equally instinctive emotions that grow alongside one another. For example, Leopold in Sarah Sheriffe's *Correlia* (1802) develops an incestuous love for his sister that is analogous to his brotherly love for her: 'he had imperceptibly, and without any sensible change from fraternal affection to one of a more tender nature, conceived a warm and lively passion for the humble companion of his infancy'.[7] White argues that the inclination towards incest would bar the alliance-building necessary to society and so 'a way must be found to overcome this centripetal tendency with a centrifugal force. This way was found in the definition and prohibition of incest.'[8] In other words, though we may instinctively sexually desire those with and by whom we are raised, society prohibits this inclination in order to promote group or social growth.

Feminist criticism has remained largely silent on the instances of brother–sister desire, which far from seeming threatening, in many cases exemplify an ideal relationship. In addition to the paternal threat model, the understanding of representations of sibling incest as a form of Romantic narcissism has been taken up by scholars to argue that sibling incest in the Gothic inverts Romantic paradigms.[9] However, both of these accounts fail fully to explore the complexities of the incestuous sibling relationships within the Gothic, on the one hand applying a model of incest that is predicated on a domestic and/or power threat and on the other employing retrospectively (and somewhat reductively) a paradigm of incestuous inversion. Rather than rely on these established modes of viewing sibling incest in the Gothic it is necessary to analyse the representations of brother–sister romantic love through a broader lens. In addition to relying on White's definition of incest as a basis of exploration, this chapter views sibling incest in the context of a wider anthropological and sociological understanding of the incest taboo. From this position analyses of sibling desire in the Gothic are revealed as being engaged not only with these understandings of the taboo but also with the corresponding concerns of the nature of family and attraction that prefigure the wider current scientific discourse on genetics and attraction.[10] The desires that underlie sibling relationships in the Gothic provide eighteenth-century accounts of the pull of blood that, when examined through a modern scientific lens, illuminate the ongoing relevance of kinship to attraction. Genetics, though not labelled as such at the time, of course, is always at play within the Gothic. The bloodlines that are so integral to the novels' plots, convoluted and complex as they often are, are essential to both the incest thematic and to understanding the uniquely erotic and egalitarian nature of the brother–sister bond. This shift in disciplinary approaches is necessary given the many representations of sibling incest that resist dominant understandings of incest as a threat or inversion, which do not account for the ways these relationships are tied to questions of equality, natural desires, the bonds of blood and the law.

Those accounts of sibling incest that do exist are incomplete in part due to their reliance on Romantic and sentimental modes of understanding such relationships in the Gothic.[11] Romantic models of narcissistic love presume a heightened self-love often not present in Gothic heroines, while sentimental models of incest rely frequently on a post-coital discovery of kinship or an implicit didacticism that is rarely present in the genre. The idea of blood telling, that blood will out, that nobility of birth shines through impoverished or hidden circumstances, is an oft-used trope within the eighteenth-century novel.[12] The widespread use of this convention created a context for readers of the Gothic; spontaneous attraction culminating in the discovery of blood kin would have been familiar to the eighteenth-century reader. However, the way in which Gothic writers subvert this device by both building on and altering it until blood and attraction become integral to their narratives emphasises the focus on incest and kinship in the genre. Nowhere are the ties of blood more important than within the Gothic, where hidden, missing and unknown relatives are often linked by familial blood as well as bound by sexual desires.

E. J. Clery refers to the Gothic combination of sexual, familial and economic restrictions that creates a constrained environment and forces the heroine to recognise 'the inescapable bonds of kinship'.[13] The hidden identities of characters and these 'inescapable bonds of kinship' that are linked to sexuality are revealed by endowing kin with either strikingly similar or opposite traits. Relatives are presented as either alike to the point of being interchangeable in looks, name and nature or as stark opposites.[14] In this respect, Gothic writers foreshadow many of the theories of geneticists regarding attraction and kinship recognition before their advancement. What seems scientific precognition on the part of eighteenth-century writers is rather the articulation of their understandings that bad and good blood is passed down through the generations and that nurture does not eradicate those bloodlines that will frequently inspire attraction. The nature versus nurture question that continues to be debated underlies Gothic representations of kinship and sibling incest that are now being increasingly substantiated by modern scientists.[15] Genetics – or blood – will tell, familial traits will be passed down and the power of attraction between two like beings is seen nowhere more strongly than between siblings.

Geneticists call it GSA (genetic sexual attraction) and it is a seemingly simple term for the complex realm of familial desires and the underlying factors that inspire incestuous attraction. The blood tie – or the genetic similarities – between two people often results in likenesses in looks, intellect, speech patterns, handwriting, even in the way people move and the gestures they make.[16] These similarities are the often unconsciously desired qualities we search for in a mate. A 2004 study on sexual imprinting argues that regarding mates or long-term partners: 'positive correlations have been found between their socioeconomic status, age, intellectual ability, education, personality variables, physical attractiveness, vocational interests and anthropometric measures … One possible explanation is genetic-similarity theory'.[17] Like Narcissus, who fell in love with his own reflection, so too do many people fall in love with the familiar or recognisable. Scientists focusing on mate selection contend that at the heart of desire is the pull of the similarities often found in shared genetic material. The concept of GSA is based on these notions and research suggests that sexual attraction between consanguineal relatives exists at unexpected rates.[18] Maurice Greenberg, who studies the prevalence of GSA between family members reunited after life-long separations, describes the attraction as both a form of mirroring that occurs most often between siblings who look similar and a normal reaction to reunification with a blood relative.[19] In fact, GSA is thought to occur in 50 per cent of reunions between long-lost relatives.[20]

What renders GSA particularly relevant to examining brother–sister attraction in the Gothic novel is its core premise that the familiar and the similar cause an intense desire. Catherine's declaration ' "Heathcliff is me!" ' in Emily Brontë's *Wuthering Heights* (1847) is in essence true: if Heathcliff is indeed her bastard half-brother, he is her; her blood, her genes, her double.[21] Desire, attraction, love, here, stem from the premise of sameness and are equally sought by the brother or the sister. The foundation of equality is consanguineally rather than socially formed; the siblings are born with a biologically based parity of genetics that causes similarities which effect desire, although society ultimately refuses the potential for equality to exist between male/female siblings. In addition, the location of the brother as the other half – the sibling as a double of the self – contributes to an understanding of the brother as a self-reflexive equal. The brother as other is the most dangerously seductive figure within the Gothic, presenting at once a mirror image and an escape from the patriarchal exchange of women, similar to that effected through father–daughter incest. As White clarifies, 'the desire to form sexual unions with an intimate associate is both powerful and widespread' and it is society and culture rather than instinct that create the taboo to prevent these unions.[22] The potential equality that siblings were born with was qualified by the laws of inheritance, such as primogeniture, as well as the social and cultural ideologies that enforced female subordination within and without the family. To achieve the potential equality, the siblings must remove themselves from the society that forbids its realisation. The Gothic deconstructs the family and social structures that prohibit incest in order to further exogamy, thus allowing the siblings to achieve endogamy.

The pathological exploration of kin and desire in the Gothic is at its pinnacle in the representations of sibling incest that are almost always shown to be ideal, positive, possible or limited only by the bounds of the arbitrarily created incest taboo. Sibling blood ties are presented as the cause of attraction rather than a hindrance to love and desire in a number of important Gothic texts. I will examine these bonds and the concurrent destruction and formation of familial and social structures to argue that a compelling model of Gothic sibling incest was established by Ann Radcliffe and taken up by subsequent writers in important ways, ending with the culmination of sibling ties and desires in Brontë's *Wuthering Heights*. Beginning with Radcliffe's *The Castles of Athlin and Dunbayne* (1789), an overlooked work that centres on a brother–sister relationship, and tracing the development of these themes in *A Sicilian Romance* (1790), I argue that Radcliffe's first two novels establish a paradigm of the brother as hero which, given the immense popularity of her novels, provided a model to which subsequent Gothic writers adhered or from which they departed. The inclusion of Matthew Lewis's *The Monk* (1796) is essential to disrupt the Gothic genealogy that so frequently reads Radcliffe's *The Italian* (1797) as a reaction to Lewis's novel without first examining *The Monk* as a response to and radical departure from the Radcliffean model of sibling incest. Eleanor Sleath's *The Orphan of the Rhine* (1798), a Gothic novel that lacks detailed scholarly analysis, provides a fascinating and unique account of brother–sister desire intertwined with criticisms of the law. Sleath's novel adheres to the Radcliffean sibling incest model while inverting the incest plot of the sentimental novel by revealing the siblings to be non-kin after they fall in love. I conclude my analysis with an examination of Brontë's *Wuthering Heights* that follows a gap of some forty-seven years that often causes it to be read within a well-established tradition of Romanticism and narcissistic incest. By repositioning Brontë's novel away from the texts it is normally read alongside, I find that a wider range of interpretative possibilities of the incest thematic becomes available: Heathcliff follows a Radcliffean sibling-hero model before evolving into the Radcliffean uncle-villain while encompassing aspects of the Romantic narcissistic incest model.[23] Disrupting the established genealogy of reading these texts is essential to breaking away from limiting models of incest and to place their subversive ambitions within a broader framework of incestuous desires, attraction, legal and familial structures and understandings of kinship.

In making this claim, this chapter does not suggest that all Gothic texts are necessarily intentionally subversive; neither does it intend to conflate the texts themselves by setting out deliberately to unify them under one thematic intent. The goal of examining the role that incest plays within the texts is not to reach an overarching conclusion about brother–sister relationships, but to understand several crucial things about the treatment of sibling love and how scholarship has traditionally treated it. Since the reclamation of the Female Gothic by feminist critics in the 1970s the genre has been delineated as articulating fears of domestic entrapment and patriarchal power. The incest thematic has primarily been theorised in such scholarship as a means of underscoring these fears as opposed to a means of resisting the forces of violence.[24] But as demonstrated in Chapter 1 this assumption is destabilised upon closer examination of specific incestuous configurations and the narratives that shape them. Sibling love is similarly represented in a number of texts as being incompatible with the view of the Female Gothic as subversive and feminist through this particular type of attack on the patriarchy. While the genre functions as a space in which writers articulated these views it does so as part of the wider Gothic genre rather than from within a Female Gothic tradition that questions patriarchy by presenting incest as a sexualised abuse of the power imbalance inherent in the familial and social structures. When Fred Botting and Dale Townshend state that 'incest in the Gothic novel is the visible or secret or absent centre of forbidden desire to which terror, always, ultimately, returns' they suggest that incest should be read ultimately as a terror convention.[25] However, as I will argue throughout my examinations of the aforementioned texts, depictions of brother–sister incest trouble the heteronormative ideology of culture by presenting the relationship's potential for equality rather than through uniting sibling desires with terror. Representations of this egalitarian potential alongside rejections of paternal authority and the natural development of sibling desires that are frequently couched in legal language cause such relationships to resist placement within the traditional scholarly models of incest in the Gothic. Sibling bonds constitute a radical mode of destabilising contemporary understandings of desire, laws and kinship.

THE MISPLACEMENT OF *THE MONK*

A great deal of scholarly attention on incest in the Gothic has focused on Lewis's representation of sibling rape in *The Monk*, which is taken to be paradigmatic of sibling relationships in the genre. This understanding of Lewis's text as establishing a model of violent brother–sister sexuality has distorted readings of Radcliffe's sibling relationships and those that follow her example. This is in part because of the way *The Italian* has been read as a response to *The Monk* without first addressing Lewis's novel as a counter to Radcliffe's already well-established Gothic tradition. As Kate Ferguson Ellis has observed: 'the earliest male Gothicists undertook to wrest the form from the female hands in which they saw it too firmly grasped ... [Lewis] liken[ed] himself to the "Villain" of *Udolpho* in a letter that acknowledges his debt to Radcliffe.'[26] Although Ellis points to Lewis's self-conscious use of Radcliffean elements, Lewis's novel is still frequently considered as offering the originary text of sibling incest. This understanding has limited readings of Gothic sibling incest to what is described as Lewis's perversion of the idealised sibling incest found in the works of the Romantics. The model of Gothic sibling incest as a distortion of Romantic narcissistic incest is exemplified by scholars such as Alan Richardson, who argues it is 'a perversion or accidental inversion of the normal sibling relation' that is intensified and idealised in Romantic works.[27] While scholarship has begun to restore Radcliffe's body of work as a precursor of Lewis's, an adherence to the model of incest that arose from the misplacement continues to limit treatments of sibling incest.[28]

Locating Gothic incest as 'a perversion or accidental inversion' of the sibling bond rather than a Romantic intensification of it risks reducing the thematic to a generic convention employed to produce disgust and terror. The conflation of the incest device with other Gothic tropes has supported scholarly readings of the brother–sister relationship as one fraught with violence and abuses of power. Similarly, the sibling relationship's alignment with the father–daughter and uncle–niece configurations of dangerous incest assists in this reductive understanding. Lewis's representation of a brother who rapes his younger sister is not the standard brother–sister Gothic relationship; rather it represents a deviation from the tradition that Radcliffe established. This misidentification has caused Lewis to be perceived as the subversive writer to whom the conservative Radcliffe reacted and offered correction.[29] However, Lewis's depiction of a rape committed at the urging of a demonic woman presents sibling desires as far less transgressive of the unequal and gendered power structures than Radcliffe's representations of egalitarian incest.[30] It is Radcliffe who influentially placed the brother as the sibling-lover in the Gothic and removed this incestuous configuration from its location as a social taboo.

E. Baker's 1906 introduction to *The Monk* claims that Lewis's novel achieves the genre's promise of unrestrained terror in contrast to the inadequacies of Radcliffe's novels as Gothic fiction which lack the appropriate masculine confidence:

> Instead of the mild titillation of the nerves produced by Mrs. Radcliffe's timid trifling with the world of phantoms and nameless terrors, [*The Monk*] threw away all restraint. There is nothing supernatural in Mrs. Radcliffe's novels; her ghosts are all make-believe, and the reader's alarm is carefully soothed before it exceeds the point of pleasant excitation ... [Lewis] outdid Mrs. Radcliffe, and in the same way he outdid every other writer from whom he borrowed.[31]

Baker represents the belief echoed in more recent criticism that Radcliffe's novels embody a delicacy that Lewis 'threw away' and implicitly correlates his gender with his rejection of Radcliffe's supposed timidity. The conclusion is clear: Radcliffe's femininity precluded her from depicting the masculine displays of violence that Lewis revelled in and that, although failing in producing true 'terror' in the reader, succeed in producing 'horror'.[32] While Radcliffe's atmospheres, Baker concedes, 'have not been without their influence on later literature', he simultaneously consigned her novels to the dustbin of feminine failure – narratives of terror bound by timidity from being transgressive.[33] Baker's introduction, albeit dated, continues to represent the assumption that male-written Gothics employ a 'masculine' ability to depict violence in ways that women cannot accomplish successfully.

As Clery notes, 'literary history provided a neat exemplification of the binary liberated/repressed ... by the couple Lewis/Radcliffe. The analogy was strengthened by speculation that *The Italian* had been written as a moralising corrective to *The Monk*.'[34] This idea is furthered by Fitzgerald's summary of scholarship that positions Radcliffe as writing a 'point-by-point' response to *The Monk*:

> According to Syndy Conger, *The Italian* is 'a sustained counterstatement' to and a 'near point-by-point refutation of' *The Monk*. And for many critics, Ross reports, 'Radcliffe had the last word in this "debate"'. Emily is finally able to reclaim her Gothic territory from Montoni; likewise, 'Radcliffe succeeded in claiming Gothic as "female"', Susan Wolstenholme argues, and in 'reclaiming a certain textual space' from male writers of the Gothic, particularly Lewis.[35]

The traditional scholarly understanding of Radcliffe as countering Lewis, while it may be appropriate in terms of *The Italian*, which chronologically follows Lewis's novel, ignores what Ellen Moers calls 'Matthew Lewis' avowed imitation of [Radcliffe's] work in his shocking novel'.[36] Much like the establishment of the binary to which Clery points, male-written Gothics are often viewed as creating and establishing models for incest that are used to shore up the bifurcation of the genre into the Male Gothic and a Female Gothic counter.

It is essential to recognise that *The Monk* was written within the context of Radcliffe's established oeuvre in order to examine how Lewis's aggressive and violent portrayal of sibling rape reinforces patriarchal power and values and has come to be understood as paradigmatic of Gothic sibling incest.[37] The horror and disgust evoked by Lewis's deployment of the incest trope are viewed by scholarship as characteristic of Gothic sibling incest: representations and perverted inversions of Romantic sibling relationships. Claudia L. Johnson offers the compelling argument that:

> In a fairly transparent opposition to Lewis's gothic, which inflates Ambrosio by its own hyperbole and thus both enjoys and colludes in the Promethean grossness of his crimes, Radcliffe's more muted representation of atrocious power – so often dismissed as emerging from bourgeois prudishness about sex – precludes such proto-Byronic reading by banalizing power, exposing the meretriciousness of its motives, and diminishing its sway by refusing its mystique.[38]

Johnson offers an important mode of retheorising Radcliffe's treatment of sex. Along these lines, I suggest that Radcliffe's novels' lack of horror and disgust in association with sibling incest does not demonstrate a repressed, timid femininity that shies away from such representations, but rather undermines the very notion of incest as taboo. Contrary to the scholarly model of incest based upon Lewis, it is Radcliffe who imagines truly unrestrained sibling incest. I argue that the normalising of incest that occurs from Radcliffe's conflation of sibling and hero is a radical disavowal of incest as perverted or disgusting and affirms the potential for an ideal, incestuous relationship.

THE COMPARISON OF BROTHER AND HERO: CONFUSING LOVERS AND SIBLINGS

The Castles of Athlin and Dunbayne (1789) is Radcliffe's first, and most overlooked, Gothic novel. Johnson describes this work and Radcliffe's subsequent *A Sicilian Romance* (1790) as 'fascinating ... in the sheer accretion of their conventionality'.[39] While the overwhelming body of scholarship on Radcliffe regards her first novels as conventional and focuses instead on her later novels, this tendency overlooks Radcliffe's innovations, which only later become conventions of the genre and which were established in these early works. Part of the focus on her last three novels may also be because of the progression of these works that critics can easily – though perhaps mistakenly – identify as improving successively.[40] To analyse incest within Radcliffe's works it is essential to examine closely the first two novels in which the heroines interact with siblings. That this kinship bond is not present in her following novels is further significant.[41] While scholarship has noted this later absence it has never been satisfactorily accounted for. I argue that Radcliffe eventually abandons the use of sibling relationships as the brother and the hero/lover are first made synonymous and then integrated in *The Castles of Athlin and Dunbayne* and *A Sicilian Romance* in a conflation of the familial and romantic that leads to the erasure of the brother's role in subsequent novels.

The Castles of Athlin and Dunbayne centres on two families connected through their sufferings at the hands of the proud and jealous Baron Malcolm. Malcolm murdered the late Earl of Athlin, who was survived by his widow, the Countess Matilda, and children, Osbert and Mary, who reside in the castle of Athlin. Malcolm lives in the nearby castle of Dunbayne, where he has imprisoned his brother's widow – his sister-in-law the Baroness Louisa – and her daughter Laura. The families are also connected through the peasant Alleyn, who loves Mary and is eventually revealed as the long-presumed dead son of the Baroness. Alleyn was given as an infant to a peasant couple by Malcolm, who reported him dead to the Baroness in order to inherit his brother's title and land in lieu of a male heir. They are further linked through Osbert, who, while imprisoned by Malcolm, meets and falls in love with the captive Laura, who strikingly resembles his sister Mary. The relationships between Laura, Alleyn, Osbert and Mary are not explicitly incestuous but the similarities between and interchangeability of the siblings render their eventual marriages substitutions for incestuous sibling desires. Osbert and Mary's bond acts as an idealised model for male–female partnerships and marriages, grounded in a basis of equality and similarity of age, class, education and resources and based in respect, mutual love and reason. Each of these factors is demonstrated within the text to be fundamental to happiness, yet Radcliffe indicates that such egalitarian unions are unattainable in a society in which incestuous relationships, threatening to the patriarchal order, are forbidden. The only option for an ideal relationship is to remain in a sexless, unwed partnership with one's brother – the closest alternative is to marry a sibling-substitute – thus, Osbert and Mary essentially marry mirror images of one another.

Much like the novel's double sibling wedding, depictions of families bound by consanguineal and conjugal ties and its various imprisonments, the plot points upon which the work progresses are claustrophobically parallel representations of passions, violence and sexual desire. Osbert's desire for revenge on his father's murderer leads to his imprisonment by the Baron that in turn forces Malcolm to choose between his warring passions for Mary and his desire to kill her brother. Radcliffe places Mary as the object of Malcolm's masculine gaze: 'An accidental view he once obtained of her, raised a passion in his soul, which the turbulence of his character would not suffer to be extinguished ... [H]e resolved to obtain Mary, as the future ransom of her brother.'[42] While the situation is not unique – Gothic heroines are frequently subjected to sexual or romantic advances after being viewed without their knowledge – what is unusual here is the ransom of a brother as a bargaining chip to gain the heroine.[43] Malcolm requires that Mary choose to sacrifice herself in marriage to her father's murderer or allow Osbert to be executed, forcing her compliance without resorting to threats of physical violence or rape. Mary is never in immediate bodily danger; rather, it is an emotional threat that compels her to choose to trade her freedom and virginity for Osbert's life. Malcolm's wish to kill Osbert that cedes to his desire to wed Mary is ironically summarised as 'revenge, at length, yielded to love' (p. 84). Malcolm's proposed exchange of Osbert's life for the body of the beautiful, virginal teenager exposes the asymmetrical gender and sexual politics of the exchange of women.

The wounded and imprisoned hero, a frequently addressed element of Radcliffe's later works, is one of the crucial points in identifying the fusion of the brother with the lover because in this first novel it is Osbert, the brother – not the hero – who is held captive and wounded.[44] During her brother's imprisonment Mary's lover Alleyn assists her and offers emotional support. In Radcliffe's second novel, *A Sicilian Romance*, the roles shift so that the brother supports his sister while the hero is wounded and imprisoned. The plot lines of these texts and Radcliffe's third novel, *The Romance of the Forest* (1791), in which the heroine is held hostage by an older man who wounds and imprisons her lover, are strikingly similar. However, by the third novel the figure of the brother has disappeared. Instead, in *The Romance of the Forest* and *The Mysteries of*

Udolpho (1794), Radcliffe introduces an obliging, noble friend (respectively, the young De la Motte and the Chevalier Du Pont) who loves the heroine but whom she views platonically. The substitution of this character for the brother appears unnecessary as both figures appear to fulfil the same position. However, the inclusion of the non-kin figure becomes imperative when it is understood as functioning not as a replacement of the brother, but of the lover as represented in the first novel. The brother is reimagined in Radcliffe's later novels as the lover whom the heroine eventually marries. The merging of the lover and the brother that occurs in the second novel is realised fully in *The Romance of the Forest*, wherein the newly introduced figure of the platonic friend performs the actions of the first lover, Alleyn, while the role of the lover corresponds to that of the original brother, Osbert. The lover is replaced with the friend and the brother is replaced with the lover. In Radcliffe's novels the brother, lover and friend are virtually interchangeable, being similar in looks, characteristics, education, class and desires; the difference between them lies not with the individual but with the heroine's identification of them as kin or non-kin, marrying only him who is most like a brother.

The interchangeability of the brother and lover is underscored when Mary is confronted with the possibility of endangering Alleyn to save Osbert. In contemplating the two men Mary conflates the presumed peasant with her noble-born brother, assigning equally to Alleyn the personal qualities of nobility, bravery and virtue associated with the aristocratic Osbert. When Matilda requests that Alleyn lead the rescue attempt, Mary

> glowed with the hope of clasping once more to her bosom her long lost brother; but the suspicions of hope were soon chaced by the chilly touch of fear, for it was Alleyn who was to lead the enterprise ... adorned with those brave and manly virtues which had so eminently distinguished his conduct: the insignificance of the peasant was lost in the nobility of the character. (pp. 73–4)

Alleyn, the long-lost son of Malcolm's imprisoned sister-in-law, is of noble blood, but Mary is unaware of this. It is not proof of his bloodline but her thought processes that link Alleyn's demonstrated virtues to a wider network of aristocratic qualities, producing his conflation with Osbert. Mary's hopes for a physical reunion with her brother are followed by her fear for Alleyn and his elevation to the same social status as her brother. Alleyn's virtue and class are merged with Osbert's in Mary's mind; contemplation of her brother has allowed the peasant to be raised to noble status.[45]

Though Radcliffe's social criticisms are often overlooked by scholars who view her as a conservative bourgeois writer, her representation of aristocratic pride as a source of incestuous desires renders her Gothics socially subversive.[46] Osbert's rejection of Alleyn as Mary's suitor is based on familial pride and social status, informed by his desire that his sister marry someone like himself. When Alleyn expresses his love for Mary, 'the Earl listened to him with a mixture of concern and pity; but hereditary pride chilled the warm feelings of friendship and gratitude' (p. 195). Osbert's pride precludes him from contemplating his sister wed a peasant. The importance placed on heredity and the ensuing sense of male ownership over female bodies cause Osbert to revolt at the idea of unlike blood joining. Osbert's honour extends from the past into the future: Mary's womb and potential children fall equally under the domain of his pride. While in Mary's mind Alleyn's conduct elevates him to her class, Osbert's need to maintain control over Mary's (and his) noble bloodline creates an incestuous jealousy. This is the cornerstone of the novel's criticism of a social system that creates incestuous possessiveness that renders integrity irrelevant in the face of blood.[47] David Durrant claims that Radcliffe's novels begin and end in 'the pastoral Eden of safe family life' and suggest that 'the only solution to the problems of adult existence lies in returning to traditional, conservative values'.[48] But this assessment overlooks the atmosphere of grief, anger and vengeance that fills the castles of Athlin and Dunbayne as well as the potential threat of incest caused by familial pride.[49] Radcliffe's novels do not depict the heroine's return to the archaic model of the family that privileges noble hubris, but instead portray her abandonment of this flawed structure in favour of a new composition of kinship. Misreading these plot developments leads to critical misunderstandings of the representation of family, desire, incest and thus Radcliffe's criticisms of society, class structures, the family and women's roles therein.

These arguments are furthered by the double sibling wedding that fuses two sets of siblings into two couples and that relies partly on Osbert's amalgamation of his sibling and his lover. The description of Laura, the 'beautiful luxuriance of her auburn hair, which curling round her face, descended in tresses to her bosom' (p. 125), is uncannily similar to that of Mary. Just as Mary flushes when she sees Alleyn, so too does Laura blush faintly when she perceives Osbert. Both women are 'of the middle stature' and 'extremely delicate and elegantly formed' and Laura, like Mary, has 'the bloom of her youth … shaded by a soft and pensive melancholy' (pp. 124–5). Osbert falls in love with the doppelganger of his sexually inaccessible sister. In fact, Mary and Laura are so similar that Osbert, feverish after his near death wounding, mistakes his sister for Laura: 'Seizing one day the hand of Mary, who sat mournfully by his bed-side, and looking for some time pensively into her face, "weep not, my Laura," said he, "Malcolm, nor all the powers on earth shall tear you from me"' (pp. 244–5). Once Osbert mistakes one girl for the other their melding is complete and Osbert can marry Laura, who is now interchangeable with Mary. Osbert gives away his sister (and her reproductive capabilities) only once he has secured her replacement. Biologically, Osbert and Mary's unconsummated incestuous desires subscribe both to the theory of GSA and to Westermarck's theory of sexual aversion. Mary and Osbert would have a natural repugnance towards each other because they were raised together as children; however, the siblings are also inherently attracted to those who look, act, speak and think similarly to themselves. That Radcliffe highlights familial and amatory ties in this way underscores her recognition that consanguineal ties are enmeshed in a complicated nexus of kinship, desire and ownership that can only be uneasily resolved through a conflation of sibling and lover.

It is no coincidence that Radcliffe's novel, in which overt sexual incestuous desire plays little part, concludes with the brother giving away the sister as a gift in order to unite two households and fortunes. The marriages fix together the sets of siblings in what Robert Miles describes as a double union 'which not only restores order, but which binds together the formerly antagonistic houses with indissoluble ties of kinship and property'.[50] Radcliffe reveals that a society governed by patriarchal and aristocratic notions of kinship that in turns incites, idealises and ultimately forbids incestuous desire serves to strengthen the unjust system of inheritance and wealth.[51] The ideal relationship exemplified by Mary and Osbert cannot be realised in the castles of Athlin and Dunbayne and so substitutive marriages that can only mimic this relationship while perpetuating an antiquated familial and social structure take place. Unlike her novels in which the heroine escapes the archaic castles that constrain female desire, here Radcliffe depicts the world before later heroines destroy it. The castle is fortified in an ironic strengthening of the patriarchal bonds through a trade of sisters that shows women to be paradoxically interchangeable yet necessary to exchange, forcing them into exogamous marriages that have a distinctly endogamous feel. The apparent strengthening of familial ties is precarious, threatened by the incestuous desires underlying the sibling bonds. Radcliffe heightens the representation of sibling relationships in *A Sicilian Romance*, intensifying the bond into an overtly sexual desire that develops and complicates her subversion of normative social restrictions, particularly those concerned with male control of female bodies and the sexual constraints imposed on women.

THE INTEGRATION OF BROTHER AND HERO: HOW THE SIBLING BECAME THE LOVER

In *A Sicilian Romance* the heroine's father is one of two chief villains and poses a threat to her freedom, chastity, choice and a danger to her sister, brother and mother. Of Radcliffe's deployment of violence and threats against the heroine, Durrant claims that 'to Mrs. Radcliffe, the world outside the family is utterly perverse in its villainy'.[52] Durrant's reading, which posits Radcliffe's adherence to a nuclear family structure, overlooks both the father's potentially incestuous longings for his beautiful daughter, Julia, and his imprisonment of her, which is intended to force her acquiescence to an undesired marriage. It similarly disregards the brother's more overt incestuous desires for his sister, the murderous stepmother and the father's imprisonment and attempted murder of his first wife. Family is rendered as at once the seat of threats against female sexuality (the father confines his daughter's unruly desires to her chamber) and the potential for its liberation (the brother frees his sister in defiance of the father's law), acting as a core of potential villainy, coercion and enslavement.

The plot of this novel differs substantially from that of Radcliffe's first novel; Miles describes it as demonstrating 'a developed form that feminist critics have come to call the "female Gothic", a narrative in which a daughter seeks for an absent mother'.[53] Julia resides with her sister, Emilia, and Madame de Menon, their governess and companion, in the Castle of Mazzini. Their mother, Louisa Bernini, is believed to have died after bearing the two daughters and a son, Ferdinand, to the father, Ferdinand, the Marquis of Mazzini. Subsequently the Marquis marries Maria de Vellorno, a devious step-mother whose adulterous affairs with younger men lead her to hate Julia's lover, Hippolitus de Vereza. I argue that Radcliffe's Gothic novels move from using the figures of the brother and the hero as their principal male characters to those of the hero and friend, beginning with *The Castles of Athlin and Dunbayne* and concluding with *The Italian*. This shift, demonstrating Radcliffe's conflation of the hero and brother, constitutes a profound challenge to constructions of law and desire. The transition of brother to lover is perhaps nowhere more important to examine than in *A Sicilian Romance*, the final Radcliffe novel in which the heroine has a brother.

The relationship between Ferdinand and his sisters is complicated by the fact that the two daughters have been raised in seclusion by Madame de Menon. They have not seen their brother for years and cannot identify him by sight. When, after the lengthy absence, the Marquis, his second wife and Ferdinand return to the Castle of Mazzini to refurbish it and host a series of parties there, confusion between the identity of Ferdinand and that of the novel's hero, Hippolitus, occurs: 'Julia pointed out to her sister, the graceful figure of a young man who followed the marchioness, and she expressed her wishes that he might be her brother.'[54] That Julia desires a handsome young man to be her brother – though this man is in fact Hippolitus – indicates an immediate blurring of the boundary between sibling and lover.[55] Already Julia conflates the instant erotic desire she experiences on seeing Hippolitus with her familial love for her brother: she believes that the physical attraction she feels for the stranger proves a pre-existing kinship. This explains her later disappointment and confusion when she discovers Hippolitus is not in fact her brother, or, indeed, a relative: 'the eager eyes of Julia sought in vain to discover her brother, of whose features she had no recollection in those of any of the persons then present. At length her father presented him, and she perceived with a sigh of regret, that he was not the youth she had observed from the window' (I, pp. 35–6). Julia's regret that the unknown man she desires is not her brother is explicit and locates her understanding of consanguineal kinship bonds as compatible with – perhaps even productive of – physical attraction. Julia's sense of the mutual nature of sibling love and attraction establishes from the narrative's outset that this unification of desires is a natural consequence of the brother–sister bond.

Julia's hope that her brother is the object of her attraction is united to her desire that Ferdinand will alleviate the control of her father and stepmother. Francisco Vaz da Silva discusses the role of the hero as saviour and supplanter of the father, describing 'the universal dragon-slayer theme in which "to kill the monster means to incorporate it into oneself, to take its place. The hero becomes the new monster, clothed in the skin of the old"'.[56] These folkloric allusions, which da Silva locates as the basis of Freud's Oedipus complex, explain the son's role as slaying the father and assuming his position as ruler of the kingdom and husband of the mother. I argue that when the traditional Oedipal theme is complicated by the father's incestuous pursuit of the daughter the son's sexual role emerges in relation to the sister, rather than to the mother. In either case, the defeat of the father results not in the liberation of the daughter but in the creation of a new monster in his place. The folkloric tradition of this pattern, in which the son usurps the father, is thus an important one to regard in light of Radcliffe's plot developments throughout her career. As Radcliffe rewrites the myth, the son does not slay and take over the father's role. The father is always killed by another person: an evil, jealous, passionate man or woman who, far from usurping the role of the father and taking over the kingdom, is killed or dies themselves. In this reworking of the myth, the brother does not inherit the throne of patriarchy but is conflated with the hero and becomes the ideal other half of the heroine. The distinction between brother and hero is erased just as the distinction between brother and sister is negated, paradoxically, through the incestuous union. As da Silva argues, 'the sexual drive minimizes ontological division after the model of mingling with one's own flesh and blood. And such mingling, of course, is what incest is about.'[57] This definition of incest suggests that the integration of the brother with the hero is a means for Radcliffe to allow her heroine a return to the pre-divided state, before marriage and before the incest taboo itself.

The brother, Ferdinand, and the lover, Hippolitus, love and interact with Julia in equal measure. Ferdinand demonstrates the shift from the previous figure of ideal mate to one who has clear sexual desires for his sisters (particularly Julia) that cause his conflation with the hero and thus his subsequent elimination from the texts in the role of the brother. Even before Ferdinand is confused by Julia with her eventual lover, he is the figure of a hero or saviour to both his sisters: 'The purposed visit of their brother, whom they had not seen for several years gave them great pleasure ... and [they] hoped to find in his company, a consolation for the uneasiness which the presence of the Marchioness would excite' (I, p. 32). A similar disordering of roles is engendered when Ferdinand replaces himself with Hippolitus: 'the confusion of Julia may be easily imagined, when Ferdinand, selecting a beautiful duet, desired Vereza would accompany his sister' (I, p. 50). Ferdinand replaces himself in his sister's arms with Hippolitus, who acts as Ferdinand's physical surrogate regarding Julia throughout the novel. When the Marquis discovers Julia and Hippolitus's love that will hinder his plan for her to marry the obsessive and wealthy Duke du Louvo, Hippolitus and Ferdinand decide to rescue her. Her brother says: '"I love you too well tamely to suffer you to be sacrificed to ambition, and to a passion still more hateful"' (I, pp. 140–1). Julia is distressed because, although she wishes to flee with Hippolitus, she is fearful of damaging her reputation. Ferdinand encourages her thus: '"Do not suffer the prejudices of education to render you miserable. Believe that choice which involves the happiness or misery of your whole life, ought to be decided only by yourself"' (I, p. 143). Ferdinand regards Julia as more capable than their father of making decisions regarding her future happiness.[58] He embodies the qualities of the ideal mate whose desire is to see the woman he loves happy and who wishes that she make her own decisions on solely those grounds. Much as with Osbert and Mary we can see here the potential in the sibling relationship for happiness.

After Julia agrees to elope with Hippolitus he says he may now call her 'my love' but it is interestingly Ferdinand who next uses this appellation when he and Hippolitus return to her room the night of the planned escape. '"Come, my love," said he, "the keys are ours, and we have not a moment to lose"' (I, p. 152). Ferdinand and Hippolitus have, like Laura and Julia and Alleyn and Osbert, become interchangeable at this point; the sister can safely marry the hero and thus the brother. However, the family offers no security here; rather it is precisely from family and home that Julia must flee.[59] Julia, 'almost fainting', gives her hand to both Hippolitus and Ferdinand, an indication that she sees them both as the hero. When the trio hear noises behind them, Julia 'hung upon Ferdinand' while Hippolitus 'vainly endeavoured to soothe her' (I, p. 154). Julia places herself physically in the hands of both men. It is soon hereafter that Hippolitus is wounded and disappears from the text while Ferdinand remains to assist and comfort Julia, completing the reversal of roles from Radcliffe's first novel, in which the brother is wounded and held hostage while the lover offers support to the heroine.

The scenes in which sexual desire and tension between Julia and Ferdinand are most clearly demonstrated are those in which Ferdinand makes repeated midnight visits to his sister's room in order to discover the origin of the mysterious noises therein. Radcliffe uses deliberately sexual pacing and language to underscore the incestuous desires between the protagonists. Importantly, these desires do not cause terror in the heroine; rather, Ferdinand's presence reassures Julia, who, with her sister Emilia, begs his assistance in their chamber.[60] Ferdinand feels an intense urge to comply, accounted for by his desire to resolve the mystery of the southern side of the castle: 'his imagination ... inspired him with an irresistible desire to penetrate the secrets of this desolate part of the fabrick. He very readily consented to watch with his sisters in Julia's apartment; but as his chamber was in a remote part of the castle, there would be some difficulty in passing unobserved to hers' (I, pp. 84–5). Ferdinand's urgency to 'penetrate' the secrets of his sisters' room is rooted in sexual desire and mirrored by his psychological need to ascertain the source of the unknown sounds. Miles describes the narrative style in instances such as these as creating 'tension between Radcliffe's surface narrative, which appears to go in a conservative direction, and her subtext, which moves in quite other ways, [and] is the source of Radcliffe's aesthetic dynamism'.[61] The dangers in passing to Julia's room unobserved highlight the necessity to hide the midnight visit from observation, hinting at its sexual nature. The description resembles that of a secret assignation more than a brother visiting innocently his sisters' chamber. Perry describes incest as 'the meaning of the gothic novel' that represents through its repeated depictions of 'a girl singled out, against her will, in her own domestic space, for the sexual attentions of a father, an uncle, or a brother' the dangers of male tyranny.[62] In these bedroom scenes, although Julia is in her own private domestic space and her brother's attentions are implicitly sexual in nature, she invites her brother into her room, an active participant in the incestuous desires. Rather than the brother being complicit with male tyranny through an undesired sexual pursuit, his position in the family is aligned with the sister's as equally fearful of paternal threats and power, thus necessitating the secrecy of his visits.

Alan Richardson claims that 'in eighteenth-century novels ... the incestuous love (actual and apparent) is inspired *before* the revelation of any kinship bond. The same holds true for the British gothics that feature incestuous couplings for their shock value and to further intensify an atmosphere of moral squalor.'[63] However, in this novel the question of whether incestuous love is inspired before or after the revelation of kinship is vexed. The siblings' reunion functions in some ways as a revelation of kinship bonds because, although Julia knows Ferdinand is her brother, they have been parted for so long that she no longer recognises him. That the incestuous desires are present before the sibling reunion and intensify thereafter serve the opposite function of Richardson's explanation of such desires inspired before kinship revelations. Ferdinand's desires and the encouragement they receive from Julia create an atmosphere of heightened arousal rather than one of shock or immorality; they add a pleasing tension to the narrative. As Julia waits for her brother she 'began to fear that Ferdinand had been discovered, when a knocking was heard at the door of the outer chamber. Her heart beat with apprehensions, which reason could not justify' (I, p. 85). Hearing nothing for several consecutive nights, Ferdinand grows frustrated with waiting; he wants to 'penetrate' the mystery in his sisters' room without further delay. He 'determined, if possible, to gain admittance to those recesses of the castle which had for so many years been hidden from human eye' (I, p. 86). While one result of this search 'gives us ... the "female Gothic", a narrative in which a daughter seeks for an absent mother' the more immediate and tangible effect is that of the sibling interaction.[64]

The description of the castle's passages is highly reminiscent of Ferdinand's sisters, hidden from the world for years and suddenly coming to life. Julia's sexual development that occurs in response to Ferdinand's and Hippolitus's arrival mirrors the castle's internal stirrings. The language here is explicit. The castle represents Julia's genitalia: a hidden, unseen area that is awakening and to which entry is sought by the brother. When penetration of the castle wall seems imminent, Ferdinand 'removed the tapestry, and behind it appeared, to his inexpressible satisfaction, a small door. With a hand trembling through eagerness, he undrew the bolts, and was rushing forward, when he perceived that a lock with-held his passage ... he was compelled to submit to disappointment at the very moment he congratulated himself on success, for he had with him no means of forcing the door' (I, pp. 88–9). Ferdinand cannot access the castle's secret areas because his father has the necessary keys; the Marquis bars entrance to the impenetrable castle recesses just as he bars entrance to Julia's body by Hippolitus, holding her chastity captive under lock and key.[65] But if Hippolitus is the hero, why is it Ferdinand who seeks entry? The brother, I argue, functions as the hero in his need to defeat the imprisoning paternal power to gain access to the unexplored areas of the castle and, metaphorically, his sister's sexuality. The conclusion to this usurpation of the heroic role by the brother is for Julia to marry Hippolitus, the non-blood-related brother-substitute and for Ferdinand to join the army. Ferdinand never finds a non-kin substitute for Julia as Osbert does for Mary and having used Hippolitus as his surrogate he is unable to regain Julia; consequently, he remains unmarried. In *A Sicilian Romance*, Radcliffe has moved from her first novel's plot towards the more patriarchal-order destructive/escapist plots of her later novels, in which the brother, in his new role as the hero, becomes part of the heroine's created world. This completely reimagined and female-constructed world is, however, difficult to understand without examining how Radcliffe leads us there via her first two novels through the use of transgressive and idealised incestuous desires.[66]

In Radcliffe's novels a conflation of the brother and the hero creates the somewhat uneasy sense that the ideal spouse with whom the heroine escapes the patriarchal castle is the sibling. The uneasiness derives, in part, from the way that incest is traditionally viewed in scholarship on the Gothic: as oppositional to Romantic portrayals of incest and as representative of the threats of male power. Richardson describes Romantic incest as fundamentally different from Gothic incest because it is portrayed 'not as a perversion or accidental inversion of the normal sibling relation, but as an extension and intensification of it'.[67] However, Ferdinand and Julia's relationship is natural and ideal, corresponding more closely to Richardson's description of Romantic, rather than Gothic, portrayals of incest. Scholarly arguments that place Romantic sibling desires and Gothic representations thereof at opposite ends of a spectrum are prevalent, yet incest in the Gothic is so varied that an overarching generic consolidation of its depiction becomes an impossible task. In tracing the evolutions in representations of brother–sister incestuous desires, the sibling bond emerges in Radcliffe's novels as an idealised, egalitarian bond that necessitates male and female cooperation to escape paternal power.

SIBLINGS AND LOVERS: DEFYING THE 'LAWS OF DELICACY'

Eleanor Sleath is one of the more obscure Gothic writers, her works being almost lost until Michael Sadleir, book collector and novelist, discovered a copy of Sleath's 1798 work *The Orphan of the Rhine* during the mid-1920s. Sadleir, who had been searching for the books listed in Jane Austen's *Northanger Abbey* (1817), proved the existence of the novel previously presumed a creation of Austen's imagination.[68] Some forty years later, Gothic scholar Devendra P. Varma, who acknowledged the difficulties in tracing the author definitively, located Mary Eleanor Sleath (born 1763) or her brother's wife, Eleanor Martin Sleath, both of Leire, as the most likely candidates for the text's authorship.[69] Yet in spite of the claims of romance novelist Carolyn Jewel to have 'rediscovered' Eleanor Sleath, factual material to support any one attribution remains to be found.[70] Although interest was kindled by the find of Sleath's novel in the 1920s, little criticism since has focused on Sleath's works in their own right. Instead, most focuses, misleadingly, either on *The Orphan of the Rhine*'s inclusion within Austen's *Northanger Abbey* list or on the novel's relationship to the works of Radcliffe.[71] When Sleath has been compared to Radcliffe it has been negatively; one contemporary reviewer, after describing Radcliffe's 'creative genius', writes 'if we have sinned in suffering ourselves to be seduced by the blandishments of elegant fiction, we endure a penance adequately severe in the review of such vapid and servile imitations as *The Orphan of the Rhine*'.[72] The language of seduction used in the review corresponds to the eighteenth-century view of women novelists as morally jeopardised and Gothic novels as particularly sexually dangerous, suggesting that Sleath is a temptress whose wares are so second rate that their consumption is a punishment.[73] In spite of such criticism, the novel deserves a place within the genealogy of the Gothic on its own merits: that is, as a novel of complex, layered incestuous relationships that are both unique in the reactions they cause in those surrounding the sibling pair and radical in their conclusion.

The Orphan of the Rhine tells the story of the beautiful Julie de Rubine, who, having been orphaned, is sent to live with her aunt, who attempts to force her into an undesired marriage. Julie marries the Marchese de Montferrat to escape the forced marriage and bears a son, Enrico, before the Marchese sends them away, telling her that their marriage was a sham and her infant is illegitimate. Four years later the Marchese gives Julie a baby girl to raise and moves them to the Castle of Elfinbach. Julie presumes the infant is the illegitimate offspring of the Marchese and his last known mistress, the Signora di Capigna. The four-year-old Enrico and infant Laurette are raised as siblings and although no information is ever given to the girl about her father, she knows the Marchese is responsible for her protection. The exact blood ties between the children are unknown to Julie, Enrico or Laurette, but Julie believes them to be half-brother and -sister. Enrico and Laurette know only that they have been raised together by Enrico's mother, who has cared for Laurette, since infancy, as a mother.

As we have seen, the Westermarck effect that posits children reared together will likely not be capable of sexual attraction towards each other – 'generally speaking there is a remarkable absence of erotic feelings between persons living very closely together from childhood' – indicates the development of any sexual attraction between Enrico and Laurette to be unlikely.[74] Westermarck's claim – 'their aversion to sexual relations with one another displays itself in custom and law as a prohibition of intercourse between near kin' – suggests that the natural aversion to sexual relations felt by those who live together from a young age has been absorbed into the collective cultural consciousness and is reproduced in the legal bans on incest.[75] The theory unites biological understandings of the incest taboo that argue the aversion is a natural repugnance to protect against inbreeding with a sociological position that focuses on co-rearing as creating aversion. It thus reveals how societies implicitly and explicitly acknowledge understandings of the taboo as both natural and socially constructed and enforced. Although he does not use the term, Westermarck identifies this implicit social ban on incest as 'custom'. It is an extension of what Foucault describes as a type of discipline within power relations that functions to prohibit a behaviour that threatens the dominant social ideology.[76] The legal ban is the explicit prohibition – or punishment, in Foucauldian terms – of such behaviour.[77] Foucault's models of power and their relation to incest have been examined by Vikki Bell, who points out that these models, particularly juridico-discursive power 'in the capacity to command and to receive obedience' and disciplinary powers 'that "imprison" the one who is being abused', inform feminist analyses of incest.[78] My interest in these analyses, Foucault's understanding of knowledge and power and Bell's account of their overlap, lies in how their intersections permeate representations of Gothic incest. That this is so reveals understandings of incest avoidance as having been historically located in both legal bans on the practice as well as prohibitions that are enforced by the dominant sexual and familial ideologies.[79] These cultural and legal prohibitions on incest are challenged in Gothic works such as Sleath's, as they are in Radcliffe's, and demonstrate a resistance to the dominant ideology of heteronormativity.

David Livingstone Smith, whose research concerns the biological roots of human nature, breaks Westermarck's claim into three distinct hypotheses, one of which corresponds closely to the situation of Enrico and Laurette: 'protracted childhood coresidence inhibits sexual desire and promotes sexual aversion'.[80] Smith uses Arthur P. Wolf's studies of Taiwanese *simpua* marriage (arranged marriages in which an infant girl is adopted by the family of the boy she is to marry and is raised with him by his parents) to conclude that 'these negative effects [infidelity, divorce and infertility caused by sexual aversion] only occur if the *simpua* bride is adopted before her third birthday, which led [Wolf] to believe that the first three years of life are a sensitive period for imprinting on siblings'.[81] Although Enrico is four when Laurette joins the family, Laurette herself is only an infant, making Sleath's treatment of Laurette as attracted equally and reciprocally to Enrico problematic in terms of the Westermarck effect. As the novel progresses Sleath shows the romantic love develop between Enrico and Laurette mutually, but, as is also the case in Eliza Parsons's *The Castle of Wolfenbach* (1793), the sexual attraction manifests after an absence occurs during which the female goes through puberty.[82] What is particularly interesting about the relationship between Laurette and Enrico (and Radcliffe's model of sibling incest) is how both Radcliffe and Sleath prefigure Westermarck's position that kin aversion manifests itself as custom and law and Foucault's description of power and discipline. Radcliffe, as we have seen, foreshadows such insights through the evolution of her brother figure into the hero; Sleath does so through her depiction of natural sibling desires that defy laws and customs. In their novels, sibling love and co-rearing does not create a natural aversion that is confirmed by the cultural and legal prohibitions; rather sibling love, erotic love and romantic love are mutually informing expressions of emotion that are not naturally exclusive. In this regard, Sleath's use of Enrico as brother and lover epitomises the model of sibling love as ideal romantic love that Radcliffe has set her readers up to expect, frequently framing the relationship between Enrico in Laurette in terms of legal language. The use of this language shows Sleath's treatment of incest and its legal prohibition, rather than stemming from a natural sexual aversion, as denouncing laws that arbitrarily limit human behaviour. Far from being a servile imitator of Radcliffe, Sleath, in her depictions of constraining laws, both works within Radcliffe's established pattern of heroines fighting against unfair legal systems regarding female inheritance and property and furthers the understanding of laws as unfairly limiting sexual desires.

In *The Orphan of the Rhine* the sexual desire between the siblings is established quickly and shown to be reciprocal. After Enrico returns from his first two years in the army he is described from Laurette's perspective as 'tall and finely proportioned; his eyes were full of fire, yet occasionally tender; and his countenance, which was frank, open, and manly, being animated with the most lively expression, betrayed every movement of his soul' (p. 123). Enrico describes Laurette, now fourteen, as having: 'just attained the age when the playful simplicity of childhood is exchanged for the more fascinating charms of the lovely girl ... [H]er features, which were soft, pensive, and interesting; and though not exactly answering to the description of a perfect beauty, possessed something beauty alone could not have bestowed' (p. 123). These descriptions are followed by Julie's – now known by her pseudonym, Madame Chamont – uneasy realisation that romantic emotions are developing between Enrico and Laurette:

> Madame Chamont was not insensible to these emotions, nor unsuspicious of the cause; she observed, with tender anxiety, the looks of her son when the subject of his departure was touched upon, and saw the colour fade from the cheek of Laurette as the necessity of it was mentioned, with evident concern. The suspicion that she was the daughter of the Marchese de Montferrat, and consequently nearly allied to Enrico, was a sufficient cause for distress; and as every circumstance she had collected seemed to confirm the justice of the supposition, the evidence, upon the whole, nearly amounted to conviction. (p. 125)

Madame Chamont is nearly certain that Laurette is the daughter of the Marchese and thus Enrico's half-sister, but her feelings of distress are couched in a fascinating use of legal terms. Sleath uses words such as 'suspicion', 'collected', 'confirm', 'justice', 'evidence' and 'conviction' to describe Madame Chamont's reaction to witnessing her son and Laurette falling in love. Madame Chamont's designation of what she believes is a half-brother/sister blood tie as 'nearly allied' is a pointed refusal to label the alliance incestuous.

That Madame Chamont characterises the relationship through legal language rather than in the terminology of morality or nature, coupled with her refusal to cast the siblings' bond as incestuous, indicates that her objections to it are based in its legal prohibition and, specifically, in the possibility of evidence being used to convict the lovers of a crime. If, as she suspects, Signora di Capigna and the Marchese are the parents of Laurette, making Enrico and Laurette half-siblings, her knowledge would render her a party to the incestuous relationship. Sleath's characters show a natural propensity towards incest that undercuts Westermarck's claims that aversion is caused by co-rearing. It presents sibling love as a normal development yet threatened by the law that is assumed to be a reproduction of the natural – or nurtured – aversion to incest. Sleath's siblings, raised in isolation beyond the implicit prohibition of incest that Westermarck calls 'custom', are similarly unaffected by the explicit 'law' of which their mother, familiar with social prohibitions on desire, is very aware.[83] Incestuous sibling desire adheres to the Radcliffean model of brother as hero and also depicts incest as the expected consequence of an upbringing outside of the prohibitive customs and laws of a society that uses these prohibitions to maintain its hegemony.

The legal focus on incest is sustained when Madame Chamont discovers that Signora di Capigna, the Marchese's mistress who she believes is Laurette's mother, never had a child. This pleases her, as she concludes:

> if Laurette was not the daughter of this unfortunate … it appeared highly probable that she was the orphan child of some deceased friend of the Marchese's, whom pity had induced him to patronize; and possibly, should time and reflection fix the attachment between her and Enrico upon a still firmer basis, no adverse circumstances might prevent their union. (p. 136)

Madame Chamont moves with ease from having believed for fourteen years that Enrico and Laurette are half-brother and -sister to being convinced that they are of no relation. Knowing the character of the Marchese, having once ascertained Signora di Capigna is not the mother of Laurette, surely the assumption would be that Laurette is the fruit of another illicit union of the Marchese's and thus still Enrico's half-sister. The possibility that the Marchese was induced by pity to patronise an orphan is an unlikely conclusion for the scorned mother of his neglected son to draw. However, not only does Madame Chamont not even touch upon the possibility that Laurette is the Marchese's daughter, but she also refers to the half-brother–sister tie as no more than an 'adverse circumstance' that might have prevented her children's union. Madame Chamont was, after all, so little bothered by the prospect of Enrico and Laurette forming a lasting attachment that she never even hinted to Enrico that he might be indulging in an incestuous love. She does not see incest as horrifying or repulsive, but rather as having the potential to be proved illegal. Once the possibility of proof of a blood tie through Signora di Capigna is removed, instead of desiring firm knowledge of Laurette's birth parents, she refuses to entertain any further possibilities of kinship that would place Laurette in the 'adverse' sister relationship and approves of their union. Incest is not so horrifying to Madame Chamont as the possibility of her children's love being thwarted, further evidence that her previous objections are based on legal rather than moral grounds. Madame Chamont merely requires proof that the evidence she had been aware of was false, any further proof is unnecessary; the letter of the law has been fulfilled. She is concerned with eluding potential punishment, not in adhering to implicit customs framed as morality dictated by the social structures.

As Enrico's feelings for Laurette develop he stresses the unfamiliar quality of other girls: 'whose manners contrasted with hers were coarse or unnatural; her superiority was too evident not to attract his admiration, and that admiration was of too exalted and refined a nature not to terminate in a softer passion' (p. 125). Laurette is the standard by which Enrico measures other women who fail to meet his expectations, in part, because of their 'unnatural' manners. While 'unnatural' may mean 'affected' it seems more likely that the unnatural quality Enrico attributes to other women is meant literally. Their manners seem such to him because they are different from Laurette's, which are the ones to which he has been accustomed his whole life. They are not familiar because they are not familial. This sense deepens when we consider manners as 'the morals, the general way of life'; Enrico's identification of the customs of others as unnatural constitutes a significant commentary on the morality, customs and habits of society in contrast to his attraction to Laurette, which is cast as a normal emotional development unaffected by the arbitrary customs of the wider society.[84] Sleath thus suggests that incestuous feelings are inherent. Positioning Laurette as the natural choice for Enrico, given her questionable and potentially illegitimate origins, further naturalises, or legitimates, both her origins and incestuous desires.

Laurette's feelings for Enrico are similarly bound up in the language of custom and law that at once distinguishes between the two restrictions on incestuous behaviour while blurring the boundaries between them. Sleath uses the term 'manners' to describe these customs or social norms and casts them as unnatural and so regulated that, in spite of being unenforced by legal punishment, they nonetheless become law. These social norms, or manners, are imposed to a greater extent on women, who must regulate not only incestuous behaviour, but also the very appearance of sexual desire of any kind: 'Laurette, whose feelings were not less awakened or acute, was condemned by the laws of delicacy, which are sometimes severe and arbitrary, to conceal them under an appearance of tranquility' (p. 127). Gayle Backus claims that 'with the nuclearization of the family, the incest taboo … came to depend on the contingent goodwill, integrity, value and self-discipline of individual fathers and brothers'.[85] Yet Sleath's depiction of Laurette's love constitutes a formulation of female incestuous desire of which understandings of incest as sought by the male omit the possibility. Although bound by social rules to hide her feelings, Laurette experiences the same intensity of desire as her brother. Sleath's designation of the customs that restrict Laurette's expression of natural feelings as 'severe and arbitrary' affirms that 'the laws of delicacy' are social standards that uphold norms of gender and sexuality through normative behaviour expectations until they are as constrictive as a punishable law. Foucault's understanding of observation as a discipline that enforces behaviour is relevant here, as is Judith Butler's discussion of gender as performance. Laurette is forced to perform appropriate feminine tranquility because custom forbids her expression of desire.[86] Laurette is 'condemned' or found guilty for her desires and her self-imposed punishment is silence. However, Laurette eventually transgresses these modes of discipline and punishment when she can avoid the social repercussions to which her desire exposes her.[87] Sleath departs from representations of female sexuality such as Beatrice de las Cisternas's masculine and unnatural passions in *The Monk*, depicting Laurette's desires as natural, though restricted by customs and laws that are indeed severe and arbitrary.

Enrico and Laurette's growing desires shed light on and complicate Westermarck's theories regarding non-blood kin and Greenberg's alternative studies of genetics and attraction. As Smith argues

> GSA both supports and detracts from the cogency of [Westermarck's hypothesis]. On the one hand, it demonstrates a clear relationship between early co-residence and incest avoidance. Reunited relatives do not have an opportunity to develop sexual aversions that would have protected them from incestuous passion. On the other hand, it suggests that inhibitions against incest must operate against an especially potent prior attraction: sexual feelings experienced by reunited relatives are often especially intense, suggesting that sexual aversions between co-reared non-kin and co-reared kin are not entirely comparable.[88]

Smith's account suggests Enrico and Laurette should not develop incestuous feelings because their early co-residence would cause sexual aversion but this is clearly not the case and GSA is somewhat at a loss to explain how Enrico and Laurette are capable of sexual attraction towards one another.[89] The eventual revelation of their lack of a blood tie may contain the answer. Greenberg argues that co-reared kin develop a strong sexual aversion to one another in response to a genetic predisposition towards a strong attraction, while co-reared non-kin do not have the same initial attraction and do not develop a corresponding and intense aversion. Thus, Enrico and Laurette, who do not share a genetic attraction, would not become averse to one another. Smith's 'shared mother hypothesis' seems relevant here. It bases its theory on incest avoidance between co-reared children on a slightly different footing; the mother figure with which a given child identifies becomes that child's mother and the child consequently responds to the mother figure's kin as equally his/her own relatives.[90] According to this model, Laurette would be averse to Enrico because she has always identified Madame Chamont as her mother and, consequently, Enrico as her sibling. Alternatively, however, the hypothesis that 'the lack of a single, consistent, unambiguously maternal figure might create a situation in which most of the adults ... are treated as potential kin' might suggest that even if Laurette did not identify Madame Chamont as her mother she would likely be sexually averse to Enrico based on her uncertainty of their kinship.[91] The potential for kinship would create sexual aversion towards any possible mates not clearly distinguished as non-kin. This aversion theory has ramifications for all Gothic novels in which a heroine's birth parents are unknown and for understanding her reactions towards the advances of older men. In terms of anthropological explanations of incest avoidance, Westermarck's hypothesis does not allow for the attraction between Laurette and Enrico, Smith's almost forbids it, but Greenberg's allows for the possibility.

Throughout the remainder of the novel, having made clear their mutual love, Enrico and Laurette identify themselves simultaneously as siblings and lovers. After finding Laurette, who is being sexually pursued by the Marchese at his estate, Enrico says: '"I resolved to hasten to the castle; by these means to soften, if I could not eradicate my grief, and to convince myself whether you, my Laurette – my more than sister, was in safety"' (p. 190). By having Enrico characterise Laurette as 'my more than sister', Sleath refuses to let the reader forget the original, and still potentially present, tie between the pair. Enrico views Laurette as his sister, but now something more as well. The sibling tie has not evaporated but has been enhanced by romantic love. This is akin to the definition of Romantic sibling incest discussed earlier. When Laurette expresses her concerns regarding Enrico's safety, 'the blush that suffused her cheeks, and the tremulous accent in which the words were delivered ... breathed more than sisterly affection' (p. 184). Far from being 'too safe a writer to truly explore issues of sexuality', Sleath forces a re-examination of the boundaries of sexuality and family.[92] Romantic love and sexual attraction are an intensification of, not a departure from, sibling love.

This is confirmed when Laurette asks Enrico why he gazes earnestly upon a portrait of the Madonna; his response is: '"because it resembles … my too charming sister; she whose image is ever present to my mind, and who is dearer to me than my existence"' (pp. 198–9). Enrico uses the term sister, rather than lover, to define his primary relationship with Laurette. Doing so in the context of viewing a painting of the Madonna compares Laurette to the virgin mother; a move that seemingly erases her sexuality yet simultaneously recalls *The Monk*, in which Ambrosio's sexual attraction to Rosario/Matilda is heightened by her resemblance to a painting of the Virgin Mary. Sleath unites increased sexual desire with intense emotional attachment and frames both by a context of forbidden or effaced sexuality that mirrors incestuous desire; sexuality is found in a traditionally taboo place.[93] After they have confirmed their mutual desire, Enrico asks Laurette in a letter: 'but why, Laurette, will you forget that I am your brother? Why would you deprive me of the sacred power of protecting you, the primary wish of my soul; of defending you from future injuries, or of redressing them if committed?' (p. 236). Enrico does not want Laurette to forget he is her brother, that his primary wish is to protect her even if this is equally his wish as her lover. He has, after all, been raised with her as his sister regardless of their actual blood tie; there will be no sudden realisation that they are not related for either Enrico or Laurette. The relationship between them does not require any such revelation because it was never an obstacle to them, either because they never believed themselves to be blood kin or because it was irrelevant to their feelings. For Enrico and Laurette, the terms 'brother' and 'sister' will be forever, inextricably, linked to that of 'lover'.

In seeming contrast to her ability to overlook brotherly bonds that have been in place since birth, Laurette assures the Marchese that she cannot disregard the idea of a paternal bond and love him romantically: '"I was taught from the earliest period of my existence, to consider you as my only surviving friend; and, when personally unknown to you, to honour and revere you as a parent; – forgive me when I say no other sentiment can be excited"' (p. 244). Smith's shared mother hypothesis, which states that 'the mother's behavioural markers of one's probable father and siblings activate different intensities of sexual aversion', functions here in relation to the parent.[94] Laurette is averse to a union with the Marchese due to Madame Chamont having raised her to view the Marchese in a paternal role. But Laurette's argument only further complicates her romantic love for Enrico, which easily overcomes the same boundaries she cites as prohibiting her from viewing the Marchese as more than family. It also recalls Manfred's attempt to claim incest as grounds for divorce in Walpole's *Otranto* in order to pursue an equally incestuous relationship with his contracted daughter-in-law – Laurette names the parental bond an insurmountable obstacle to a union with the Marchese so she can pursue her own desires for Enrico. Indeed, the only familial feeling the Marchese holds for Laurette is via his son, for whom he still maintains some semblance of fatherly feeling. This paternal feeling spares Enrico when the Marchese discovers him to be his rival for Laurette but also heightens his rage: 'had his rival been any other than his own son, he would probably have meditated some dreadful revenge; but the ties of blood … prevented him from exercising any actual cruelty, though it tended not to mitigate his resentment, but rather added warmth to the violence of his unrestrained passions' (p. 237). As discussed in Chapter 1, the paternal figure fears not only the removal of his object of sexual desire and opportunity to use the female as an object of exogamic exchange, but also the dissolution of his power via a younger generation's endogamic choices.[95]

Gillian Beer says of Sleath's work that 'the heroine's female condition of passivity, isolation, and privation is strongly identified with silence both within and without doors … In women's Gothic the woman author writes while the heroine is mute' in order to rebel against the muting of women.[96] Beer correctly locates the author as one who challenges the status of women and Sleath does so in part through Laurette, who, although not silent or passive, is 'condemned' to 'conceal' her feelings by the society she inhabits. This concealment allows for a position of absolute refusal of male propositions while maintaining desire for her sibling. Laurette refuses to consent to the Marchese's sexual desires and marriage proposals and overhears his murderous plans. She is subsequently imprisoned by the Marchese and, when Enrico finds her, he realises from viewing 'her thin emaciated form' (p. 287) that she has been starved to the point of near death.[97] Laurette's noncompliance with patriarchal demands of marriage for male sexual gratification and her very existence (as heiress to the fortunes the Marchese has illegally claimed and her discovery thereof) cause the near erasure of her body. Her ability to speak – to refuse, to bear witness against the Marchese – is a threat to the dominant paternal figure. The female body that voices resistance or defiance, particularly in favour of the brother, becomes the site of punishment by the patriarch who demands compliance to the heteronormative exogamic culture.

The complications of the novel's incestuous world culminate with Enrico inheriting the Marchese's fortune in a plot twist that reveals the marriage between the Marchese and Madame Chamont to be legitimate. But the hero's legitimacy has consequences: Enrico discovers Laurette is also legitimate and was orphaned when the Marchese killed her father to steal her inheritance; the money that Enrico inherits is rightfully Laurette's. Enrico conceals from Laurette the murder of her father by his and the novel ends with their wedding. Such a conclusion effectively negates the potential implications of Enrico's inheritance having rightfully belonged to Laurette and brings to the reader's attention the laws that govern female property; had Laurette been the recipient of the Marchese's wealth rather than Enrico he would still have gained control of the fortune with their marriage.

Sleath expresses through sibling kinship in *The Orphan of the Rhine* a defiance of unnatural social customs and laws, an organic development of romantic love stemming from sibling love and a reliance on individual choice in spouse selection. Westermarck's, Smith's and Greenberg's hypotheses on incest avoidance, genetic sexual attraction and shared mothering contribute to understandings of the complicated nature of kinship, siblings, attraction and aversion and the deployment of the incest taboo in Sleath's novel. Foucault's, Bell's and Butler's insights into the power relations underlying discipline and punishment and the performative quality of gender offer further important models through which to theorise incestuous behaviour in the text. Sleath's treatment of siblings blurs the lines between brother and lover, demonstrating that siblings and spouses are far from antithetical. This understanding of incestuous love as a heightened culmination of brother–sister affection that ends happily and prosperously locates Sleath as a radical writer of the Gothic who presents patriarchal control, the incest taboo and social dictates of female behaviour as at once severe and arbitrary.

THE ROMANTIC GOTHIC: NARCISSISM AND INCEST

Emily Brontë's *Wuthering Heights* is the fullest expression of the brother–sister incestuous bond, distinct from other Gothic novels in its representation of sibling desire as an apex of, paradoxically, equality and domination. The almost fifty-year gap between Brontë's text and the Gothic novels analysed in this chapter is bridged by the tradition of Romantic narcissistic incest that has been established in the interim.

Brontë's novel is best re-examined within the genealogy of brother–sister incest in the Gothic that is itself frequently read within the later context of the Romantic incest model. This repositioning places Brontë's novel as simultaneously aligned with the Gothic texts and the Romantic tradition preceding it, allowing discussion of the distinct paradigms of incest from which the novel borrows and departs.[98] If Westermarck's, Greenberg's and Smith's theories combine to help explain the formation of incestuous desires within Sleath's work, one need look no further than Greenberg to explain the magnetic attraction between Catherine and Heathcliff. While the concept of GSA as such was of course unknown to Brontë, the intensity of desires that manifest as recognition in her characters is a nineteenth-century representation of what was then understood as the *cri du sang*.[99] Catherine and Heathcliff's relationship, re-examined from this new vantage point, can be identified as a spectacular portrayal of sibling incest's power of attraction and the concurrent subsumption of individual identities within the network of kinship.

In spite of the importance of the incestuous desires between Catherine and Heathcliff to understanding *Wuthering Heights*, the classification of their relationship as incestuous, though part of critical discourse for some decades now, is variously assented to and resisted within the scholarly community.[100] Some scholars hesitate to include the possibility of incest as part of their focus. Marianne Thormählen writes that the element of incest 'would go some way towards accounting for the kinship one senses between them ... But if Catherine and Heathcliff are indeed related by blood, they will hardly know it themselves ... Consequently, talk of "incest" seems a little off-target.'[101] Yet if the potential for incest is overlooked, along with its contextualisation within the conventions of Gothic and Romantic sibling incest, analysis of the relationship veers off course. The argument that Catherine is an egomaniac who views Heathcliff as an extension of self speaks to the flaws in overlooking the incestuous nature of the Catherine–Heathcliff bond: 'nor does she [Catherine] feel erotically attracted to him [Heathcliff]; "one does not mate with one's self, with one's kind", as one critic has pointed out'.[102] Thormählen's point relies on denying the presence of incest in general and its function as an established convention of Gothic and Romantic texts.[103] Other scholars similarly dismiss the possibility of incest. In the words of William A. Madden, 'Mrs. Leavis revives the unprovable and, in my judgment, unnecessary assumption that Heathcliff is Mr. Earnshaw's illegitimate son.'[104] Characterising the incest potential as a theory 'unprovable' and 'unnecessary' reveals an anxiety regarding a consanguineal bond that would render Catherine and Heathcliff half-siblings. Scholarship that seeks to avoid the incestuous implications of the novel argues the existence of a blood relationship is not capable of being proved, echoing the legal language of evidence Sleath employs to challenge such requirements. The demand for proof and the assertion that its absence renders a consideration of incest irrelevant effaces incestuous and female desire from the body of the text in a reinforcement of the gender and sexual ideologies that Gothic representations of sibling incest seek to subvert.

The consequences of denying the incestuous element of Catherine and Heathcliff's relationship are a denial of their love and a reduction of it to a pathological egotism. When, for example, Thormählen states that 'I have avoided referring to the bond between Catherine and Heathcliff as "love" ... because the nature of their passions fits no description of the concepts known to me', she disregards the established conventions of Gothic and Romantic incest in which the representation of their love is, in part, grounded.[105] Without taking the possibility of blood kinship into account, the Catherine–Heathcliff bond is instead viewed as a function of egomania: 'Catherine's inability to recognise the reality, even existence, of human needs and wishes outside her own is itself a sign of mental disturbance, and her self-identification with Heathcliff is another ... Catherine and Heathcliff might be called schizoid.'[106] Identifying the Romantic, narcissistic sibling love/self-love convention at the heart of the Catherine–Heathcliff relationship is crucial to understanding the bond without classifying it as schizoid; one need look no further than to similar instances of incestuous sibling love in many Romantic texts.[107]

My discussion of Catherine and Heathcliff as siblings is not without precedent. William R. Goetz argues: 'the novel presents a narrow, conspicuously defined set of relationships that practically begs to be considered in light of the incest prohibition and rules of exogamy' and that 'even if we do not accept the speculative hypothesis that Heathcliff is ... a half-brother to Catherine, it is indisputable that Heathcliff's adoptive place in the family turns him into a brother of Catherine'.[108] Goetz's assertions highlight the multi-layered nature of the incestuous links between Catherine and Heathcliff, the fusion of ambiguous blood ties and their shared childhood. Alan Richardson points to Romantic literature's emphasis on sibling incest to argue that 'the strength of the sibling relationship is founded more on a shared childhood than on the blood tie'.[109] Even so, the possibility that Catherine and Heathcliff share both childhood experiences and a blood tie is strong. Recent scholarship that examines race and slavery in the novel illuminates the power dynamics of Catherine and Heathcliff's relationship; Maja-Lisa von Sneidern cites a wealth of textual and historical evidence to argue compellingly that Heathcliff, brought home from the port city of Liverpool that was home to thousands of black slaves, is of African descent and that his 'racial otherness cannot be a matter of dispute'.[110] Susan Meyer points out that locating Heathcliff's origins in 'England's largest slave-trading port' causes other characters to view him as a 'racial outsider' and that Mr Earnshaw gives Heathcliff the name of a son in an attempt to 'give him a more favourable social status'.[111] Such accounts locate Heathcliff as racial outsider yet, tantalizingly, they also do not preclude the existence of kinship, but suggest that Heathcliff's illegitimacy could originate with Mr Earnshaw and a mistress of African descent. Detaching Catherine and Heathcliff's relationship from its incestuous aspect based on the lack of proof of a blood tie thus becomes increasingly problematic from several perspectives. My designation of the bond as incestuous relies not only on the potential that Heathcliff is an illegitimate half-sibling, but also on the understandings of kinship that define as family those with whom one is co-reared and the presence of this convention in Romantic literature and draws on the intensity of the attraction as exemplifying the pull of blood experienced by reunited kin in current studies of GSA.[112]

Gail Finney's treatment of incest in the works of the German Romantics provides a useful definition of the narcissistic Romantic sibling love present between Catherine and Heathcliff: 'the myth of Narcissus ... reveals the underlying nature of the incestuous bond: erotic energy is transferred from the narcissistic individual to the object most like himself, his sibling'.[113] This reflective self-love is further magnified by Heathcliff's obscure origins and his status as Catherine's adopted brother. Heathcliff is at once a reflection of Catherine and her creation, her possible blood kin and her adopted brother. Any one of these facts makes a discussion of incest relevant to the text; all four render it essential. The model of Romantic narcissistic incest serves as the basis of John Allen Stevenson's argument that Brontë purposely crafts illegitimacy and mysterious origins for Heathcliff to necessitate the contemplation of Heathcliff as Mr Earnshaw's son, rendering him Catherine's half-brother and mirror-image lover.[114] Stevenson argues that Heathcliff is 'the forbidden outsider and the forbidden brother' who 'perform[s] a paradoxical double-role, both brother and other ... [that] demonstrates the dangers of both incest and excessive exogamy'.¹¹⁵ In contrast, I argue that the presence of Romantic narcissistic incest confirms Heathcliff's identification with Catherine and, moreover, his representation as other is produced through his degradation at the hands of Catherine's other brother, Hindley. In this context, Heathcliff's othering is a failed attempt by Hindley, who fears Heathcliff's potential to usurp both his position as older brother and his inheritance, to prevent the dispersal of wealth and property that could occur if Heathcliff is identified as an Earnshaw.

The othering of Heathcliff via Hindley (and to an extent through the servant, Nelly's, characterisation of him as alien and foreign) is temporarily successful as it propels Catherine into marrying Linton, the similar though non-related marriage choice that ends so disastrously. In an early analysis of the novel, Lord David Cecil argues that destructive marriages in *Wuthering Heights* occur from unlike marrying (Cathy to Linton and Heathcliff to Isabella); I extend this argument to contend that only like marrying like creates a non-destructive marriage.¹¹⁶ Indeed, every disastrous event that occurs in the novel does so because Catherine cannot marry Heathcliff – her kin – and instead chooses the unlike or non-kin. Heathcliff, the half-brother, the blank slate onto which she projects herself, is her true love – her soul – and her only real potential mate in the novel. Even critics who conclude Catherine is an egomaniac regard her and Linton as simply too different ever to be reconciled with each other. In contrast to Catherine and Linton, Stevenson argues that the bond between Catherine and Heathcliff

> has some of the practical effects of an actual wedding between them, effects that mirror the dangers of incest as Lévi-Strauss describes them. Their love for each other encloses them in Wuthering Heights, making it impossible for the Earnshaw household either to give or receive [women] … Her brother/lover has enclosed her heart, if not her body, in Wuthering Heights, and she finds herself unable to participate in that process of separation from the household of her parents and incorporation into the family of her husband that constitutes marital exchange.¹¹⁷

Stevenson asserts that Heathcliff's incestuous love for Catherine exemplifies the dangers of Lévi-Strauss's theory, acting as a 'paradoxical double crime in terms of conventional marriage customs, at once a hoarding and a theft', placing Catherine as the object of transfer. This is true of her relationship with Linton but not with Heathcliff.¹¹⁸ Her daughter and Hareton later repeat this endogamic move but again it is not shown as a danger. The 'hoarding and theft' Stevenson ascribes to Heathcliff are not actualised through marriage to Catherine – society as represented through the class spectrum of Nelly and Hindley has rendered that impossible. The question of likeness is framed by the eternal bond between Catherine and Heathcliff (regardless of its perception to others) that is presented as the most important of their lives. The social demands of parity in class and exogamy that forbid incest must be transcended for Catherine and Heathcliff to unite. Their likeness – be it born of projection, genetics or nature – draws them together and when thwarted leads to disaster; it is a similarity of self that is capable of realisation only in nature or the afterworld. Society and its prohibitions that forbid their love and demand Catherine's exchange must be left behind for the self to be reconciled to the self. Catherine cannot be with her brother/lover, herself, her soul, until the boundaries imposed by the incest taboo are disintegrated with death.

In Romantic and neo-Romantic literature, Finney states that 'narcissism in the guise of incest is a particularly effective expression of the individual's exclusion from society, since it adds the solitude of self-love to the guilt of a sexual taboo'.[119] Her reading of the twins Siegmund and Sieglinde in Wagner's *Die Walküre* (composed 1854) concludes that 'the attraction between the two intensifies rapidly. Its narcissistic overtones echo and re-echo. For what joins them is their common isolation, their shared suffering as members of a strange breed ... which all others shun.'[120] The attraction and shared isolation of the siblings locates the work as operating in the tradition of *Wuthering Heights*, which Finney describes as an example of 'the siblings-as-soulmates configuration', in which incest is 'committed in conscious defiance of the norms of the society that has excluded them' and designates Catherine and Heathcliff 'typically Romantic heroes, outsiders by virtue of their inherent social position or because of an exceptional sensibility which leads them to cast in doubt or completely reject their society's values'.[121] Catherine and Heathcliff's relationship is situated alongside Wagner's in terms of the protagonists' common status as outsiders and their incestuous love that transcends the values of the society that rejects them and the event of death itself. Catherine and Heathcliff's bond is unique, embodying neither solely the siblings-as-soulmates incestuous narcissism of Romanticism nor the isolated individual narcissistic incest of neo-Romantic works. Rather, Brontë's novel unites these incestuous conventions and exhibits a variation of the Gothic's egalitarian and idealised brother-as-hero paradigm that corresponds to the work's status as both a late Gothic and a late Romantic novel. Catherine and Heathcliff's love does not simply fit the incest as Romantic narcissism model, though it is aligned to what Finney describes as 'an irresistible, unconsciously generated passion, [where] the Romantic lover is defeated by his conscious rebellion against the society which has stigmatized him'.[122] Brontë's lovers, though self-obsessed and self-destructive, are very definitely lovers who define themselves through and by their love and identification with one another.

Catherine's cry of '"I am Heathcliff"' is the ultimate identification and integration of self with other that, even without the existence of a consanguineal bond, renders them kin through the declared melding of identity (p. 82). The affirmation of self and kinship through identification with the sibling that Catherine displays here is similar to that which Rooney observes in Sophocles' *Antigone* through Antigone's burial of Polyneices – an act that affirms her brother's existence and 'with this her own existence in that the brother and sister are conjoined, co-conjured, interdependent, similar but not identical beings'.[123] Although Goetz sees the marriages of Catherine to Edgar and Heathcliff to Isabella as fundamentally supporting the exogamic rules of marriage detailed by Lévi-Strauss, this overlooks the complex endogamic nature of the unions that Goetz points to as appearing in the repetition of characters' names. The surface appearance of exogamy is in actuality flawed and in danger of collapse: 'these doublings or overlappings of names … they insist upon that general threat of incest that overhangs society, the threat of a union between characters who are *too "alike"*'.[124] The repetition of names, as I have already argued, is common in Gothic novels and the subsequent creation of an ever-diminishing familial circle that is reborn in future, near-identical generations causes relationships to be endowed with incestuous undertones. Goetz's view of Catherine's marriage to Linton as 'the surmounting of the incest temptation and the willingness to leave the parental home and to become part of the system of exchange' is difficult to reconcile with her continued relationship with Heathcliff.[125] What is perceived as a willingness to leave the parental (or paternal) home is undercut by her desperate need to return to the wild nature of the heath. Rather than overcoming the incestuous temptation of Heathcliff, she joyfully welcomes him back upon his return, risking her marriage to resume a relationship with him.

Catherine's self-identification with Heathcliff situates them as kin who are positioned as equally outside the kinship circles of the Earnshaws, who refuse fully to incorporate Heathcliff, and the Lintons, to whom both Catherine and Heathcliff remain perpetual outsiders. It is their self-reflexive love that excludes them from subsumption into another family that causes all other relationships they undertake to fail, rather than the Freudian explanation that Catherine's unsuccessful marriage with Edgar is due to her inability to transition from childhood to adulthood and overcome the Oedipus complex.[126] Madden notes the outsider status of Catherine and Heathcliff and although he argues it motivates Catherine's 'attempt to re-enter society through marriage to Edgar' he recognises it as 'an attempt to evade the basic truth about herself, her being wedded to Heathcliff as a fellow outcast from that society … Heathcliff is inseparably connected in Catherine's mind with her beloved moors "out there" beyond society.'[127] Catherine's entrance into the exogamic system fails, not because she wants to return to Heathcliff as an aspect of her childhood, but because her attempt at exogamy in Heathcliff's absence is unable to lessen her incestuous love for him.

Indeed, Catherine never overcomes her love for Heathcliff; the narcissistic, outsider nature of their bond makes this impossible. To overcome Heathcliff would be to overcome herself. Her renunciation of Heathcliff is only ever a verbal one that when overheard by Heathcliff instigates his departure. Catherine never resists the love she claims would degrade her; Heathcliff simply leaves her behind to answer Linton's proposals. On his return their relationship is the same as ever, much to her husband's disapproval. In fact, Catherine sides with Heathcliff against Edgar during an argument between them, saying to her husband: '"if you have not the courage to attack him, make an apology, or allow yourself to be beaten. It will correct you of feigning more valour than you possess"' (p. 114). Catherine does not choose Edgar and exogamy over Heathcliff, evident in her defiant refusals to stop seeing Heathcliff. This is reinforced particularly in her death scene when she cries at the prospect of Heathcliff releasing her from his arms even though Edgar approaches: '"Oh, don't go, don't go. It is the last time! Edgar will not hurt us. Heathcliff, I shall die! I shall die!"' (p. 164). The notion of being without Heathcliff – who is as integral to her survival as herself – prompts a syntactic confusion over whether it is Heathcliff's proposed absence or an awareness of the severity of her illness that causes her to declare she will die. Heathcliff, of course, remains with her, stating: '"Hush, hush, Catherine! I'll stay. If he shot me so, I'd expire with a blessing on my lips"' (p. 164). Heathcliff and Catherine defy not only propriety (or custom) but threats of violence and death (or punishment) in order to remain in each other's arms.

Catherine and Heathcliff are duplicated in the younger generation by Catherine's daughter, Cathy Linton, and Hareton Earnshaw, the son of Catherine's brother Hindley. The novel's culmination in their eventual union, which is made possible only after obstacles identical to those faced by Catherine and Heathcliff are overcome, constricts the already endogamic circle created by their names and appearances. While Goetz claims that 'likeness in physical appearance … has been offset by a difference, or removal, in blood kinship' to explain their marriage, this union feels even more incestuous than that of the preceding generation.[128] Cathy's marriages to her cousin Linton and then to her cousin Hareton resume rather than amend her mother's story. Cathy makes the same misguided first marriage to a weak, blonde Linton (the result of blackmail and lies which call into question Catherine's motivations for marrying Edgar Linton given the other parallels between the marriages) and then makes the correct marital choice in the form of the dark, brooding, handsome, strong Hareton. If Cathy is happy in her second marriage it only reinforces the misery of the first one, to which Catherine's marriage to Edgar Linton is the mirror. To interpret their first-cousin blood tie as a weaker consanguineal bond than the adoptive brother–sister bond of Catherine and Heathcliff ignores the near-identical structure of Cathy and Hareton's existence, that of (after Edgar Linton's and Linton Heathcliff's deaths) two teenagers under the roof of an abusive father figure. Before their love develops Cathy and Hareton have become Catherine and Heathcliff, foster-siblings sharing the domestic space of a violent patriarch. But while Hindley stood in the way of a union between Heathcliff and Catherine by degrading Heathcliff and the existence of the Lintons provided an alternative marriage option, Brontë has removed any such threat to the happiness of this younger generation. Cathy and Hareton are more isolated from society than Catherine and Heathcliff were and are placed within a disruptive, fractured home environment even more conducive to and receptive of incestuous sexual union than that of their predecessors.

The unstable and isolated family that Brontë creates for Hareton and Cathy is in anthropological terms explicable as the consequence of incestuous desires; Brontë's reversal of what would become common knowledge in anthropology offers an alternative model of incestuous cause and effect. Malinowski states: 'the sexual impulse is in general a very upsetting and socially disruptive force … incompatible with any family relationship ... A society which allowed incest could not develop a stable family; it would therefore be deprived of the strongest foundations for kinship.'[129] Brontë's unstable family structure follows the incestuous desires of Catherine and Heathcliff and precedes the sexual impulse of Cathy and Hareton, in effect, becoming part of its cause. Brontë allows no exogamic possibility. Cathy and Hareton are the only option for each other, and in their relationship, rather than a weakening of kinship, the blood tie is strengthened and clarified. They look alike, they are unquestionably blood kin, they become foster-siblings and they will be married; the possible consanguineal ties that trouble Catherine and Heathcliff's relationship are here an absolute. It is within the fractured kinship circle of Wuthering Heights that Cathy and Hareton combine notions of family and desire, defining one another, eventually, as both kin and beloved.

Cathy creates Hareton in her image just as her mother did with the 'gypsy' Heathcliff, teaching him to read, write and behave properly. Although Hareton initially is kind to his cousin, her anger at her forced marriage to Linton and habitation at Wuthering Heights escalate tensions that damage their tentative friendship. When Cathy seeks Hareton's friendship again, apologising and flirting with him, she does so in a language that blends consanguineal kinship, ownership and desire: '"Come, you shall take notice of me, Hareton – you are my cousin and you shall own me"' (p. 313). Cathy is not an object of exchange, she is the agent of it, choosing to give herself to Hareton and take him in return. Hareton steadfastly ignores her until 'she stooped, and impressed on his cheek a gentle kiss' (p. 314). With the kiss Hareton and Cathy begin the transformation from kin and foster-siblings to lovers, the same transformation that Heathcliff and Catherine underwent. Scenes of Cathy teaching Hareton reading and pronunciation heighten the sense of a shared childhood, of siblings learning and developing together. It is not that 'the threat of incest ... loses the greater part of its force' but that the threat of incest is finally realised.[130] Endogamy is not threatened, it is actualised; the effect of their sexual impulses towards one another functions not to fragment a stable family structure, but rather, to allow its creation.

Wuthering Heights is the climax of sibling incest in the Gothic, in part, because of its Romantic influences. The self-reflexive sibling incest evidenced in the works of Romantic writers features in Brontë's treatment of Heathcliff and Catherine. Despite Heathcliff's seeming dominance over all the characters, he and Catherine are undeniable equals in their relationship because he has been created from Catherine's imposition of herself onto him. Their bond, however, is deeper than just this reflexive nature. Likely half-brother and -sister and certainly adoptive siblings, their shared experiences as social exiles, as the unwanted children of Wuthering Heights, heighten the incestuous and exclusive nature of the relationship. Brontë creates a community in which Catherine is propelled into an exogamic marriage as an object of exchange; the inevitable failure of the union and exchange engender the breakdown of the social world. For the attempted exchange, just like incestuous relationships, ends without any exchange at all: Brontë ensures this with the future generation, a mirror of Catherine and Heathcliff who unite the properties of Thrushcross Grange and Wuthering Heights and choose to live at the Grange. Rather than property being exchanged and expanded on, the social world becomes ever smaller. Cathy and Hareton embody the incestuous relationship Catherine and Heathcliff shared but failed to realise; they fulfil its promise by having no non-kin marital choices within their society or paternal agents to require Cathy's exchange outside the family.[131] Their status as orphans and shared isolation allow them to become their own agents and owners, capable of giving or keeping themselves as they wish. Brontë's treatment of incest is a revolutionary reimagining of the causation and consequences of familial sexual desires. Self-reflexive sibling love is shown as a lasting bond that transcends barriers of disparate class, birth, wealth and education in its egalitarian nature and creates a stable and complete family structure in counterpoint to what is approved of by society and state.

These depictions of incest challenge the established models of sibling love and trouble the traditional placement of Gothic texts as working in Lewis's paradigm. Radcliffe's paradigm of the brother/lover conflation establishes the brother as an equal and a friend, a beloved companion of the heroine, before integrating him with a physically and emotionally similar lover. The model established, brother as unified with lover, is shown as an almost unattainable goal in a society that forces exogamy and one that can only be realised once the integration of roles is completed. This formation of sibling incest is altered within *The Orphan of the Rhine*, where Sleath reworks Radcliffe's model by focusing more strictly on the unnatural taboos that society places on desire and behaviour to control and limit female action, allowing for a radical acceptance of the possibility for sibling incest with the brother himself.[132] In *Wuthering Heights* the Radcliffean model is complicated by Brontë's deployment of the conventions of Romantic sibling incest and the distortion of the hero-villain into the bad uncle before he is immortalised as the eternal brother-lover. Generations mirror previous generations in an incestuous cycle, but rather than this depiction ending on a note of degenerative failure, the endogamic union of Cathy and Hareton creates an egalitarian relationship that suggests wider social and political changes and, as Rooney claims, such brother–sister sympathy and love might serve as a revolutionary inspiration for such transformations.[133] Although there is seldom one clear, distinct message to be extracted from the varieties of and forms incestuous desire takes in the Gothic, there is an overwhelming insistence to re-evaluate the demands and laws of patriarchal society. The construction of rules and laws that enforce and govern behaviour is often shown as nothing more than a veneer of civilisation that keeps in check any desires – female or incestuous – that threaten its hegemony. In the representations of sibling incest, its potential for equality and its natural occurrence, the laws that society defines as natural are exposed as unnatural constructions that are enforced to maintain male control over female bodies and behaviour.

NOTES

1 Eleanor Sleath, *The Orphan of the Rhine* (London: The Folio Press, 1968), p. 184. Subsequent references will be given in the text.
2 See Lena Dominelli's 'Betrayal of trust: a feminist analysis of power relationships in incest abuse and its relevance for social work practice', *British Journal of Social Work*, 19:1 (1989), 291–308.
3 Ruth Perry, *Novel Relations: The Transformation of Kinship in English Literature and Culture 1748–1818* (Cambridge: Cambridge University Press, 2004), p. 377.
4 Caroline Rooney, *Decolonising Gender: Literature and a Poetics of the Real* (New York: Routledge, 2007). Rooney refers to this quality in terms of Lord Byron's incestuous relationship with his half-sister Augusta Leigh and Goethe's description of this relationship as 'poetical' (p. 29). Rooney argues the destruction of patriarchy is possible through the sibling bond, examining Sophocles' *Antigone*, in which the sister stands against the state for her dead brother, and points to Nelson Mandela's view of Antigone as symbolic of struggles against government (p. 19).
5 Leslie White, 'The definition and prohibition of incest', *American Anthropologist (NS)*, 50:3(1) (1948), 425. See also Claude Lévi-Strauss, *The Elementary Structures of Kinship* (London: Taylor & Francis, 1969), p. 25.

6 The paternal threat model of incest that is often applied to brothers in scholarship is also apparent in Kate Ferguson Ellis's examination of the threatening father figure and incest in *The Contested Castle: Gothic Novels and the Subversion of Domestic Ideology* (Urbana: University of Illinois Press, 1989) and in Margot Gayle Backus's *The Gothic Family Romance: Heterosexuality, Child Sacrifice, and the Anglo-Irish Colonial Order* (Durham, NC: Duke University Press, 1999).
7 Sarah Sheriffe, *Correlia, or The Mystic Tomb. A Romance*, 4 vols (London: The Minerva Press, 1802), I, pp. 196–7.
8 White, 420–5.
9 Alan Richardson, 'Rethinking Romantic incest: human universals, literary representations, and the biology of mind', *New Literary History*, 31:3 (2000), 553–72. See also Gail Finney, 'Self-reflexive siblings: incest as narcissism in Tieck, Wagner, and Thomas Mann', *German Quarterly*, 56:2 (1983), 243–56.
10 See David Haig, 'Asymmetric relations: internal conflicts and the horror of incest', *Evolution and Human Behaviour*, 20:2 (1999), 83–98; Justin H. Park, 'Is aversion to incest psychologically privileged? When sex and sociosexuality do not predict sexual willingness', *Personality and Individual Differences*, 45:7 (2008), 661–5; and David Livingstone Smith, 'Beyond Westermarck: can shared mothering or maternal phenotype matching account for incest avoidance?', *Evolutionary Psychology*, 5:1 (2007), 206.
11 Perry examines incest in the Gothic as an exaggerated trope common to sentimental novels and eighteenth-century literature more generally (*Novel Relations*, pp. 375–6).
12 Perry's comprehensive *Novel Relations* explores the appearance of the *cri du sang* throughout the eighteenth-century novel.
13 E. J. Clery, *The Rise of Supernatural Fiction* (Cambridge: Cambridge University Press, 1995), p. 120.
14 Examples of such siblings include Ambrosio and Antonia in Matthew Lewis's *The Monk* (1796), Isabella and Linton in Emily Brontë's *Wuthering Heights* (1847) and the brother and sister in Regina Maria Roche's *The Children of the Abbey* (1796).
15 See Maurice Greenberg and Roland Littlewood, 'Post-adoption incest and phenotypic matching: experience, personal meanings and biosocial implications', *British Journal of Medical Psychology*, 68:1 (1995), 29–44; and Roland Littlewood, *Pathologies of the West: An Anthropology of Mental Illness in Europe and America* (London: Continuum, 2002).
16 Tamas Bereczkei, Petra Gyuris and Glenn E Weisfeld, 'Sexual imprinting in human mate choice', *Proceedings of the Royal Society B: Biological Sciences*, 271 (2004), 1129.
17 Bereczkei, Gyuris and Weisfeld, 1129.

18 Maurice Greenberg's studies document family members who, after reunification with previously unknown kin, experience borderline obsessive attraction that often culminates in sexual affairs. See Greenberg, 'Post-adoption reunion: are we entering uncharted territory?', paper read at the Hilda Lewis Memorial Lecture given to the British Association for Adoption and Fostering (5 October 1993), 1–22. Paper available online at www.geneticsexualattraction.com/AAPostAdoptionReunion.pdf [accessed 21 May 2009].
19 'Forbidden love: pull of attraction felt between adoptees, biological family members', *CBC News*, 7 May 2009, www.cbc.ca/canada/story/2009/05/06/f-gsa.html [accessed 5 June 2009].
20 Alix Kirsta, 'Genetic sexual attraction', *Guardian*, 17 May 2003, www.guardian.co.uk/theguardian/2003/may/17/weekend7.weekend2 [accessed 16 November 2009].
21 Emily Brontë, *Wuthering Heights*, ed. Pauline Nestor (London: Penguin Classics, 1995), p. 82. Subsequent references will be given in the text.
22 White, 433.
23 Radcliffe's treatment of uncles is analysed in Chapter 3. Examples of Romantic narcissistic incest include Victor and Elizabeth in Mary Shelley's *Frankenstein* (1818) and Astarte and Manfred in Byron's *Manfred* (1817).
24 See Kate Ferguson Ellis, 'Can You Forgive Her? The Gothic Heroine and Her Critics', in David Punter (ed.), *Companion to the Gothic* (Oxford: Blackwell, 2000), pp. 257–67; Ellis, *The Contested Castle*; Ellen Moers, *Literary Women: The Great Writers* [1976] (Oxford: Oxford University Press, repr. 1985); Juliann Fleenor, *The Female Gothic* (Montreal: Eden Press, 1983); and Eve Kosofsky Sedgwick, *The Coherence of Gothic Conventions* (New York: Arno Press, 1980) for feminist treatments of the Gothic as written by women as a distinct Female Gothic genre that exposes the dangers of patriarchy.
25 Fred Botting and Dale Townshend (eds), *Gothic: Critical Concepts in Literary Cultural Studies* (London: Routledge, 2004), p. 56.
26 Ellis, 'Can You Forgive Her?', p. 257.
27 Richardson, 'Rethinking Romantic incest', 554. See also his article 'The dangers of sympathy: sibling incest in English Romantic poetry', *Studies in Literature 1500–1900*, 25:4 (1985), 737–54; and Eugene Stelzig, '"Though it were the deadliest sin to love as we have loved": the Romantic idealization of incest', *European Romantic Review*, 5:2 (1995), 234–9.
28 Scholars such as Clery in *The Rise of Supernatural Fiction* and Lauren Fitzgerald in 'Female Gothic and the Institutionalization of Gothic Studies', in Diana Wallace and Andrew Smith (eds), *The Female Gothic: New Directions* (Basingstoke: Palgrave Macmillan, 2009), pp. 13–25 work against the dominant scholarly positioning of Lewis and Radcliffe, arguing instead that Lewis reacted to a Radcliffean tradition.

29 For analyses of Radcliffe's work as a conservative response to Lewis's radical work see particularly Steven Blakemore, 'Matthew Lewis's black mass: sexual, religious inversion in *The Monk*', *Studies in the Novel*, 30:4 (1998), 528; and Vartan P. Messier, 'The conservative, the transgressive, and the reactionary: Ann Radcliffe's *The Italian* as a response to Matthew Lewis' *The Monk*', *Atenea*, 25:2 (2005), 39.

30 I do not intend to suggest Radcliffe did not respond to Lewis, rather, that analyzing incest in the genre without understanding Lewis as first responding to Radcliffe's oeuvre and tradition of sibling incest will produce a limited understanding of the incest thematic. For recent scholarship that offers important insights into Radcliffe's novel and its engagement with Lewis's work, see Jerrold E. Hogle's chapter 'Recovering the Walpolean Gothic: *The Italian: Or, the Confessional of the Black Penitents* (1796–1797)', in Dale Townshend and Angela Wright (eds), *Ann Radcliffe, Romanticism and the Gothic* (Cambridge: Cambridge University Press, 2014), pp. 151–67.

31 E. A. Baker, 'Introduction', Matthew Gregory Lewis, *The Monk*, ed. Tom Crawford [1907] (New York: Dover, repr. 2003), pp. iii–xii. Subsequent references will be given in the text. Baker's description of Radcliffe 'soothing' the reader's alarm before it 'exceeds the point of pleasant excitation' portrays Radcliffe as inhibiting the fulfilment of orgasmic terror.

32 Terror in the Gothic is produced after a finely drawn atmospheric scene evokes fear, while horror is evoked through depictions of graphic violence or gore. Clery points to this divide in *The Rise of Supernatural Fiction* (p. 110), as does Robert Miles in *Ann Radcliffe: The Great Enchantress* (Manchester: Manchester University Press, 1995), p. 44.

33 Baker, p. viii.

34 Clery, p. 110.

35 Fitzgerald, p. 13.

36 Moers, p. 137.

37 Radcliffe's inclusion of material from Horace Walpole's *The Mysterious Mother* (1768) as epigraphs in *The Romance of the Forest* (1791) and *The Italian* is consistent with an evaluation of her oeuvre as consciously subversive. The reproduction of Walpole's 'disgusting' tale discounts public opinion (read: social control) and attaches the spectre of horrifying maternal incest to Radcliffe's own – according to critical accounts – comparably cautious representations of incest, asserting the counter-hegemonic nature of her work. See Ellen Malenas Ledoux's forthcoming book *Fantastic Forms of Change: Mass Persuasion and Policy in Gothic Writing, 1764–1834*, which examines Radcliffe's use of Walpole's works in her epigraphs.

38 Claudia L. Johnson, *Equivocal Beings: Politics, Gender, and Sentimentality in the 1790s* (Chicago: University of Chicago Press, 1995), pp. 127–8.

39 Johnson, p. 76.

40 Michael Gamer, *Romanticism and the Gothic: Genre, Reception, and Canon Formation* (Cambridge: Cambridge University Press, 2000), p. 69. Gamer argues that 'few writers … have responded so directly to periodical criticism. Each successive work saw previous "errors" corrected', viewing these corrections as negotiations that enabled Radcliffe to continue publishing. Gamer's analysis helps to understand why Radcliffe's earlier works are overlooked: her first novels are frequently read as conventional and inexperienced compared to the progressive modifications of her later works to reflect criticism.

41 Miles in *The Great Enchantress* and Hoeveler in *Gothic Feminism* note that siblings appear in Radcliffe's first two works but are not present in the later novels.

42 Ann Radcliffe, *The Castles of Athlin and Dunbayne: A Highland Story* (London: T. Hookham, 1789), p. 41. Subsequent references will be given in the text.

43 Antonia in Lewis's *The Monk*, Adeline in Radcliffe's *The Romance of the Forest*, Julia in Radcliffe's *A Sicilian Romance*, Ellena in Radcliffe's *The Italian* and Laurette in Sleath's *The Orphan of the Rhine* are among the many heroines subjected to a masculine gaze that turns sexually aggressive.

44 Hoeveler discusses the wounded hero in *Gothic Feminism* as have George E. Haggerty in *Queer Gothic* (Urbana: University of Illinois Press, 2006) and 'Psychodrama: hypertheatricality and sexual excess on the Gothic stage', *Theatre Research International*, 28:1 (2003), 20–33 and Miles in *The Great Enchantress*.

45 Radcliffe works against the representation of male social elevation as impossible in eighteenth-century novels such as Samuel Richardson's 1740 *Pamela, or Virtue Rewarded* (Oxford: Oxford University Press, 2008). In Richardson's novel Mr B says 'a Man ennobles the Woman he takes, be she *who* she will; and adopts her into his own Rank, be it *what* it will: But a Woman, tho' ever so nobly born, debases herself by a mean Marriage, and descends from her Rank, to his she stoops to' (p. 422). The subtext is that a woman debases herself through a union predicated on her sexual desire while the male's role as the head of the patriarchal family permits both his sexual desires and the elevation of the low-born woman he desires. Radcliffe's presentation of Mary as mentally elevating Osbert to her brother's rank challenges the rejection of female desire and ability to ennoble the male's social status.

46 See David Durrant, 'Ann Radcliffe and the conservative Gothic', *Studies in English Literature, 1500–1900*, 22:3 (1982), 520–8.

47 While Osbert's jealousy never causes him to harm his sister, in Radcliffe's subsequent works such passions incite the incestuous and/or prideful crimes of the father and then uncle figures.

48 Durrant, 520.

49 The pastoral, Edenic upbringing to which Durrant claims Radcliffe forces her heroines to return is also undermined by the neglected adolescence in *A Sicilian Romance*, the abandonment and near coercion into becoming a nun in *The Romance of the Forest* and the orphaned existence of Ellena in *The Italian*.
50 Miles, p. 74.
51 The baroness's criticism of this system reinforces reading Radcliffe as equally condemnatory of the limitations of the legal institutions to protect female interests, a criticism that will find full expression in *The Mysteries of Udolpho* (1794).
52 Durrant, 525-6.
53 Miles, p. 90.
54 Ann Radcliffe, *A Sicilian Romance*, 2 vols (London: T. Hookham and Carpenter, 1790), I, p. 34. Subsequent references will be given in the text.
55 See Ruth Perry, 'De-familiarizing the Family; or, Writing Family History from Literary Sources', in Marshall Brown (ed.), *Eighteenth-Century Literary History: An MLQ Reader* (Durham, NC: Duke University Press, 1999), pp. 159-72. Perry, in an analogous reading, refers to the sibling desire in Aphra Behn's *The Dumb Virgin; or, The Force of Imagination* (1688) as a 'confusion of family feeling and erotic love' (p. 163). Perry argues, however, that the sisters in Behn's work can mistake another man for their brother because 'so weak is the voice of blood' ('De-familiarizing the Family', p. 163). In contrast, I argue that Julia mistakes Hippolitus for her brother because of her desire to discover that the attraction is inspired by consanguineal kinship.
56 Francisco Vaz da Silva, 'Folklore into theory: Freud and Lévi-Strauss on incest and marriage', *Journal of Folklore Research*, 44:1 (2007), 3.
57 Da Silva, 5.
58 The role that the language of individual choice and rights plays in the context of incestuous relationships in the Gothic is examined in Chapter 4.
59 Durrant, 523.
60 The assertion that the brother/father/uncle threatens the heroine in the Gothic is here undermined by the sister's entreaty of the brother to come to her; her desire creates the situation meant to represent male threats (see Perry, *Novel Relations*, p. 389).
61 Miles, p. 176.
62 Perry, *Novel Relations*, pp. 388-90.
63 Richardson, 'Rethinking Romantic incest', 554. Richardson usefully summarises the Westermarck effect, arguing that 'British Romantic writers did come up with a model for representing sibling incest with remarkable parallels to Westermarck's hypothesis ... [I]t is in the unique and specific character of Romantic-era culture and discourse that an interpretation of the literary Westermarck effect must be sought' (563).

64 Miles, p. 90.
65 The father's control of his daughter's sexuality extends here to control of his son's sexuality. The brother is as incapable as his sister of defying patriarchal control at this point, which renders the siblings equally oppressed by and desirous of escaping paternal authority.
66 The incest is transgressive in that it ultimately allows penetration through the locked areas of the castle (metaphorically, Julia's genitalia) and is idealised in its portrayal of oppressed siblings working together to escape the confines of the paternal castle.
67 Richardson, 'Rethinking Romantic incest', 555. Richardson argues that Romantic portrayals of incest are unique in their paradoxical and ambivalent presentations of the bond as at once ideal yet capable of being viewed as unnatural (569).
68 Peter Otto, 'The Sadleir-Black collection', *Gothic Fiction*, www.adam-matthew-publications.co.uk/digital_guides/gothic_fiction/Introduction1.aspx [accessed 20 November 2009].
69 Devendra P. Varma, 'Introduction', Sleath, *The Orphan of the Rhine*, p. viii.
70 Carolyn Jewel intended to deliver a paper, 'Eleanor Sleath: a writer rediscovered', at the March 2008 Popular Culture Association Annual Conference; however, notes on the conference show that she was unable to attend, http://teachmetonight.blogspot.com/2008_03_01_archive.html [accessed 20 January 2010]. Jewel states she 'discovered what no one else knew; that Eleanor Sleath was a wealthy widow who married the Reverend John Dudley under rather scandalous circumstances' in an interview with Megan Frampton, 'Friday with Carolyn Jewel!', *Risky Regencies: The Original, Riskiest, and Forever the Friskiest Regency Romance Blog*, 13 February2009), http://riskyregencies.blogspot.com/2009/02/friday-with-carolyn-jewel.html [accessed 20 January 2010]. However, I am unable to find any material to support these claims and Jewel offers no sources.
71 Many of the references to *The Orphan of the Rhine* appear in catalogues of *Northanger Abbey*'s Gothic list or in discussions of Austen's and/or her heroine, Catherine's, reading habits. See, for example, L. Erickson's 'The economy of novel reading: Jane Austen and the circulating library', *Studies in English Literature, 1500–1900*, 30:4 (1990), 573.
72 Review of Eleanor Sleath, *The Orphan of the Rhine* (1798), *The Critical Review, or, The Annals of Literature*, 27 (1799), 356.
73 Varma, p. ix. The religious language of the review offers implicit support of Varma's argument that Sleath, unlike Radcliffe, was likely Catholic.
74 Edward Westermarck, *The History of Human Marriage* (London: Macmillan and Co., 1903), p. 80.
75 Westermarck, p. 80.

76 Michel Foucault, *Discipline and Punish: The Birth of the Prison*, trans. A. M. Sheridan-Smith (London: Penguin, 1979), pp. 136–9.
77 Michel Foucault, *The History of Sexuality Volume I: An Introduction*, trans. R. Hurley [1979] (Harmondsworth: Penguin, repr. 1981), pp. 83–9. Foucault describes the juridico-discursive model of power as a ruler or head of state's ability to create laws and punish those who disobey them that he argues has 'gradually been penetrated by quite new mechanisms of power that are probably irreducible to the representation of the law' (p. 89).
78 Vikki Bell, *Interrogating Incest: Feminism, Foucault and the Law* (London: Routledge, 1993), pp. 60–3.
79 Foucault refers to this enforcement in *Power/Knowledge: Selected Interviews and Other Writings 1972–1977*, ed. Colin Gordon, trans. Colin Gordon *et al.* (Brighton: Harvester Press, 1980), stating that 'we are forced to produce the truth of power that our society demands ... in order to function' (p. 93).
80 Smith, 203.
81 Smith, 205.
82 Parsons's novel (explored in the following chapter) depicts an aggressive uncle whose sexual desires for his niece begin after she develops physically during his absence.
83 Perry uses a similar situation in Eliza Haywood's *The Force of Nature; or, The Lucky Disappointment* (1724) to argue that Haywood's siblings who are raised together (though ignorant of their kinship) 'can hardly be said to illustrate the voice of blood, since they grew up together and their love developed from deep and familiar knowledge of one another rather than from mysterious, unseen forces'. She concludes, contrary to my reading of Enrico and Laurette, that the '*cri du sang* motif, central to [the] plot without ever providing definitive proof of the instantaneous power of kinship, come so close to the traditional use of the topos that their subversive differences almost seem like denials of its force' (Perry, 'De-familiarizing the Family', p. 163).
84 The definition of 'manner' as 'a custom, a habit' and of 'manners' as 'the morals, the general way of life' is found in John Ash, *The New and Complete Dictionary of the English Language*, 2 vols (London: Edward and Charles Dilly and R. Baldwin, 1775), I.
85 Backus, p. 43.
86 See Foucault's treatment of the panopticon in *Discipline and Punish* (p. 200) and his argument that disciplinary power necessitates surveillance to create 'comparative measures that have the "norm" as their reference' (p. 193); see also Judith Butler, *Gender Trouble: Feminism and the Subversion of Identity* (London: Routledge, 1990), pp. 175–86, particularly her argument that 'gender is also a norm that can never be fully internalized; "the internal" is a surface signification, and gender norms are finally phantasmatic, impossible to embody' (p. 179).

87 In *Discipline and Punish* Foucault describes self-regulation as the effect of observation: 'he who is subjected to a field of visibility and who knows it assumes responsibility for the constraints of power' (p. 202). Bell uses Foucault's understanding of this type of disciplinary power to argue that 'if power is exercised and not possessed, contingent rather than static, feminist opposition to the various operations of power may expect to find more gaps and weaknesses in power's operations' (p. 41). Laurette demonstrates what Bell theorises – an ability to find the gap in the power operations through the eventual expression of her incestuous love for her brother.
88 Smith, 206.
89 See Greenberg, 'Post-Adoption Reunion'.
90 Smith, 208.
91 Smith, 209.
92 Beth Kilkenny, 'Representation of the repressed: women and the feminine in Eleanor Sleath's *The Orphan of the Rhine* and *The Nocturnal Minstrel*', *The Corvey Project at Sheffield Hallam University*, http://extra.shu.ac.uk/corvey/corinne/1%20Sleath/Sleath%20critical%20essay.htm [accessed 8 July 2009].
93 *The Monk* often locates sexual desire in a forbidden context of religious vows, imagery and setting; Sleath combines religious imagery and a familial context that, unlike Lewis's novel, de-emphasises the taboo nature of the sexual desire.
94 Smith, 210.
95 This is similar to da Silva's discussion of the dragon-slayer myth, the themes of which are identifiable in Radcliffe's use of the incestuous siblings to defeat the father in *A Sicilian Romance*.
96 Gillian Beer, '"Our unnatural no-voice": the heroic epistle, Pope, and women's Gothic', *Yearbook of English Studies*, 12 (1982), 151.
97 Her imprisonment and starvation are noticeably similar to that of Louisa Bernini in *A Sicilian Romance*.
98 This tradition is examined in Richardson's 'The dangers of sympathy', 737–54.
99 Perry, 'De-familiarizing the Family', p. 161. Perry describes eighteenth-century French comedy and tragicomedy novels in which 'a sudden and instinctive sympathy between strangers that signaled consanguinity – enabled family members ... to recognize one another in time to avert, betrayal, incest, and murder' (p. 161). She argues that in French dramas characters sometimes 'confuse the force of blood with romantic love and mistake the magnetism of kinship for erotic attraction to someone who is really a sibling' and that this literary convention reappears in English fiction in the latter half of the eighteenth century as a 'plot in which biology asserts itself as intuition' (p. 161).
100 For an early treatment of the incest potential see Eric Solomon, 'The incest theme in *Wuthering Heights*', *Nineteenth-Century Fiction*, 14:1 (1959), 80–3.

101 Marianne Thormählen, 'The lunatic and the devil's disciple: the "lovers" in *Wuthering Heights*', *Review of English Studies*, 48:190 (1997), 185.
102 Thormählen, 186.
103 Wade Thompson, 'Infanticide and sadism in *Wuthering Heights*', *PMLA*, 78:1 (1963), 69–74.
104 William A. Madden, '*Wuthering Heights*: the binding of passion', *Nineteenth-Century Fiction*, 27:2 (1972), 132.
105 Thormählen, 196–7.
106 Thormählen, 190.
107 Samuel Taylor Coleridge's *Osorio* (1797) and Ludwig Tieck's *Der blonde Eckbert* (1797) include examples of Romantic sibling incest.
108 William R. Goetz, 'Genealogy and incest in *Wuthering Heights*', *Studies in the Novel*, 14:4 (1982), 360, 363.
109 Richardson, 'The dangers of sympathy', 740.
110 Maja-Lisa von Sneidern, '*Wuthering Heights* and the Liverpool slave trade', *ELH*, 62:1 (1995), 174. Von Sneidern argues that 'the Catherine/Heathcliff dyad is peculiar in its passion and commitment' (177), asserting this is due to the master/slave nature of their bond. Consequently, the pleasures 'of a conventional marriage pale when confronted with the addictive pleasure of absolute possession free of restraint and control of "human" passions' (178). Von Sneidern also points out the similarities between Heathcliff and Hareton, noting that 'although Hareton is Hindley's by blood, we are inclined to think of him as Heathcliff's "immaculate" creation, embodying his masculinity and vigor – traits systematically denied a racial hybrid, but afforded the racial other and racial ancestor' (187). She notes that a 'disquieting element that stubbornly persists at the ending of the novel is imagery of bondage, chillingly domesticated and civilized' (187).
111 Susan Meyer, *Imperialism at Home: Race and Victorian Women's Fiction* (Ithaca, NY and London: Cornell University Press, 1996), pp. 98–9.
112 Catherine and Heathcliff fall into both the category of co-reared kin as they share a childhood and that of reunited kin as they are past the age of reverse sexual imprinting, generally agreed to be before the ages of three to eight, when they begin their co-residence. See Smith, 203; Joseph Shepher, *Incest: A Biosocial View* (New York: Academic Press, 1983); and Chuang Ying-Chang and Arthur P. Wolf, 'Marriage in Taiwan, 1881–1905: an example of regional diversity', *Journal of Asian Studies*, 54:3 (1995), 781–96 for discussions of the critical period of reverse sexual imprinting.
113 Finney, 243.
114 John Allen Stevenson, '"Heathcliff is me!": *Wuthering Heights* and the question of likeness', *Nineteenth-Century Literature*, 43:1 (1988), 62.
115 Stevenson, 73–5.

116 Lord David Cecil, *Early Victorian Novelists* (London: Constable, 1934), pp. 152–67.
117 Stevenson, 77.
118 Stevenson, 78.
119 Finney, 245.
120 Finney, 248.
121 Finney, 248.
122 Finney, 253.
123 Rooney, p. 21. Rooney's argument is situated in the context of Judith Butler's work *Antigone's Claim: Kinship Between Life and Death* (New York: Columbia University Press, 2000), in which, Rooney argues, Butler is concerned with giving 'the rhetorical speech act precedence over an action that would otherwise precede it so that the speech act appears to be the originating phenomenon. This is a matter of attempting to defend the logo-centric theory of performativity, together with the theory of gender as performativity, from the ways in which Antigone might occasion a call for the rethinking of such theories' (Rooney, p. 21).
124 Goetz, 365.
125 Goetz, 367.
126 Goetz, 368.
127 Madden, 149.
128 Goetz, 369.
129 Bronislaw Malinowski, 'Culture' in Charles G. Seligman (ed.), *Encyclopedia of the Social Sciences*, 15 vols (New York: Macmillan: 1930), IV, p. 630.
130 Goetz, 369.
131 Cathy's marriages to her cousins as endogamic exchanges are examined in Chapter 4.
132 Smith, Wolf, Shepher and Westermarck believe that co-residence is detrimental to incestuous sexual attraction; Littlewood in *Pathologies of the West* argues for the inverse: that it is a lack of co-residence that allows for incestuous desire in the many incest cases that he and Greenberg interviewed that involved 'first-degree relatives who are unfamiliar with each other [and] later have sexual access to each other', noting that such situations 'were a common theme of nineteenth-century Romantic literature' (pp. 136–7).
133 Rooney, pp. 19–26.

3
Uncles and nieces: thefts, violence and sexual threats

'My uncle's behaviour was to me unaccountable, he was for ever seeking opportunities to caress me.'

Eliza Parsons, *The Castle of Wolfenbach* (1793)[1]

The relationships between heroines and their uncles in the Gothic novel are ones in which sexual threats are underpinned by financial entanglements and legal issues, often to a greater extent than is the case with other familial relationships. Representations of family, finance, property, law and ownership are examined frequently by scholars of the Gothic, but within the context of uncle–niece relationships that are complicated by incestuous desires these ideas are embedded in sexual language and meaning.[2] Incestuous relationships between uncles and nieces abound in Gothic fiction; in fact, even in novels where the primary incestuous focus is on a different consanguineal bond, there is often still an uncle in the background, his presence being part of the plot construction that drives persecution and usurpation. Susan Staves refers to the laws regarding married women's property in the long eighteenth century as a patriarchal code 'that justified the dominance and privilege of men by deference to their superior abilities to create good order in families and their duty to provide and support for subordinated women and children in their families.'[3] In the Gothic this code is revealed as inadequate through its manipulation and enforcement by the figure of the uncle and becomes entangled with the representations of incestuous desires and violence that are equally justified and supported by the familial and social structures that grant male control of female bodies and property. Eugenia C. DeLamotte argues that 'the mysterious crime at the heart of most Gothic plots is a transgression of legal barriers as well as, in many cases, a transgression of the stronger barriers of taboo – incest, the murder of a brother, patricide'.[4] Within the realm of uncle–niece relationships these transgressions are combined with representations of property, genealogies and ideologies of gender and sexuality. Through an exploration of these thematics and the manner in which incestuous desires and threats become difficult, if not impossible, to extricate from their presence, a new paradigm of incest as both mutually enforcing and threatening to the patriarchal power structure and hegemony emerges.

Maggie Kilgour says of Walpole's *The Castle of Otranto* (1764) that the conclusion is 'a tidy way of suddenly resolving, in a highly oedipal text, the potential conflict between past and present, or guilt about the representation of the overthrow of a tyrannical father, by showing the father to have been a usurper all along'.[5] If this is true of Walpole's work, then later Gothic novels take up this Oedipal drive in a different way, exposing the figure of the uncle as usurper of both the rightful father and the niece. Although many scholarly accounts claim that one of the hallmarks of the Female Gothic is a tendency to show the father as tyrannical, employing the paternal figure as one who persecutes the heroine to impress upon readers the dangers of patriarchy, more commonly it is the uncle who is the usurper: the tyrannical figure who threatens the lineage, fortune, property and namesake of the heroine.[6] Because of the scholarly trend to view the father as representative of patriarchal dangers there is a corresponding tendency to overlook the figure of the uncle, who, in fact more frequently than the father, represents a physical, sexual and financial threat to the heroine. While the conflict between past and present in these novels is still very much a part of the plot, the resolution reveals, not a Walpolean false lineage from a servant who murdered the master, but a brother who murdered a brother and often the sister-in-law as well. The danger is not positioned outside the family line, but within it, not from the serving class but a member of the aristocracy who threatens the women of his own bloodline. Here it is not the heroine who transgress the incest taboo, often viewed as fundamental in maintaining the kinship system of exchange that reinforces the patriarchal power structure, but the uncle.[7] In order to understand how the uncle is capable of violating the tenets of the incest taboo that uphold his power while remaining a figure representative of the dangers of the dominant male hegemony and its corresponding ideologies, it is essential to look at the contexts in which the uncle violates the taboo.[8]

In the previous two chapters I have examined novels in which the incestuous desires between fathers and daughters and brothers and sisters are central; but even in texts that focus on these configurations there are still uncles looming within the storylines. Ann Radcliffe's *The Castles of Athlin and Dunbayne* (1789) and *The Romance of the Forest* (1791) feature uncles who either threaten incestuous desires or are murderous, imprisoning heroines and usurping their property. In Emily Brontë's *Wuthering Heights* (1847) Heathcliff plays a dual role, shifting from the brother/lover into the threatening uncle with ease, propelled towards kidnapping, imprisonment and the theft of property from his niece. Angela Wright has recently pointed out that feminist critics have begun to focus increasingly upon the relationship between the law – particularly property law – and the Gothic.[9] The centrality of law is often related in these Gothic novels to the figure of the uncle, the most common predatory or persecutory male figure who appears consistently and often initially makes himself felt as a desirous or lustful force towards the heroine before being revealed as blood kin. Often entrenched in murderous, incestuous plots driven by lust for the heroine, her mother or the familial titles and property belonging to an older brother, the uncle is a shadowy figure within the Gothic that seems representative of the genre itself. An assemblage of motives, desires and drives, a compilation of good and bad, condemned and saved, hideous and handsome, the uncle often acts as the Gothic text: joining together the old and new, the figure of the uncle represents and acts out seemingly oppositional roles. These contrasting positions have often caused scholars to treat the Gothic genre as having a limited ability to be radical or transgressive. As Kilgour points out, the Gothic novel seems to 'denounce precisely the transgressive qualities with which it was associated', dividing scholars on the question of whether the genre is conservative or radical.[10] Part of what appear to be inconsistencies in the form are mirrored in the figure of the uncle, himself representative of both the older, aristocratic order and the destruction of it. Resembling the genre itself, the uncle adheres to and abuses the dominant cultural structures to usurp powers traditionally denied to his position.[11]

The incestuous desires of the uncle towards his niece are bound up with generations of thefts of property and person. The heroine, frequently herself a physical reflection of her mother, acts as a younger generation onto which the uncle can project his sexual longings, usually thwarted previously by the marriage of her mother to his older brother.[12] With the niece another opportunity is born to rewrite his own history, to use the property, title and wealth stolen from her father to attempt to force a union with the heroine. Sexual desires are consistently tied together with murderous desires, thefts of property and/or title and legal manoeuvrings. Law or legal language is often a recourse to which the uncle retreats, backing himself up with legal documents (real or forged) and legal standpoints (valid or not) in order to try to force his claims on the heroine's body or property.[13] Binding incestuous desires together with persecutory intentions does seem a way of, as Kilgour puts it, 'cloaking familiar images of domesticity in gothic forms' in order to enable 'us to see that the home *is* a prison, in which the helpless female is at the mercy of ominous patriarchal authorities'.[14]

The combination of incest and law serves also to highlight the vulnerability of the heroine in the face of unwanted sexual desires complicated by questions of legality and the inalienable right of the heroine to make decisions regarding her body. By uniting the persecution of the heroine's body with concepts of liberty and law, Gothic writers mobilise the female body to enter the typically masculine arena of political rhetoric. Kilgour points to the association of the Gothic with British freedom from tyrannical laws as capable of being used both to demonise and idealise the past.[15] This notion is examined by Diana Wallace in her analysis of Gothic and legal institutions that traces this association to Margaret Cavendish's 1662 'Female Orations'.[16] Wallace, while focusing on 'the haunting idea' as Gothic and legal metaphor, makes important connections between legal institutions and the Female Gothic fixation on loss of female identity and property through the institutions of marriage and inheritance. I argue that because of their frequent positioning as the younger brother, Gothic uncles often inhabit a similar position to the heroines in terms of inheritance and identity, being unable to lay legal claim to familial property or title.[17]

Eighteenth-century legal scholar Sir William Blackstone famously described the English constitution and legal system as an inheritance: 'an old Gothic castle, erected in the days of chivalry, but fitted up for a modern inhabitant'.[18] Wolfram Schmidgen discusses Blackstone's metaphor of law and the Gothic castle as an allusion that 'ties together the themes of property, common law, and the English constitution in a single image'.[19] This notion of inherited rights is important in relation to the figures of uncles and nieces, who are both portrayed as being denied their inheritances of property, title or rights. In contrast to the heroines, the uncles use violence and force to usurp the inheritances denied them and the positions of power and wealth held by their older brothers, displacing them as the bastions of patriarchy. Along with positions of patriarchal power, estates and titles that uncles usurp through their violent crimes, they inherit generations of female bodies from their brothers. In one sense, the figure of the uncle allows a reaffirmation of individual freedom over social contract or law before revealing the ultimate futility of a reaffirmation that results in a mere displacement of power rather than an abolition of its structures. As such, the uncle's compromised place within patriarchy makes him a useful figure to writers of the Gothic as he becomes reflective of the form and underscores the Gothic's location at the centre of radical discourse.

Representations of incest place desires, bodies and sexuality within the context of debates on freedom, choice and the ethics of tyrannical laws. In order more clearly to understand how writers of the Gothic used the figure of the uncle to represent a variety of legal and domestic dangers, it is necessary to examine a diverse selection of Gothic novels. *The Castle of Wolfenbach* by Eliza Parsons precedes the more celebrated works of Ann Radcliffe as well as the scores of Gothic novels written in the latter's style. It is therefore a useful text to look at both in terms of possible influences on Radcliffe's works but also as a novel that, in spite of being relegated to a mere footnote in discussions of Jane Austen's *Northanger Abbey* (1817) list of Gothic novels, is one that deserves recognition for raising questions of ownership, independence and the origins of desire. Radcliffe's two most famous novels, *The Mysteries of Udolpho* (1794) and *The Italian* (1797), are essential works to examine in a chapter considering uncle–niece incest and questions of property as both texts explore these topics in divergent ways. In *Udolpho* Radcliffe uses the figure of an uncle by marriage to depict the implications of property transfer upon marriage and the system of inheritance. While avoiding explicit incestuous situations, she positions the heroine as an object of both persecution and exchange by her uncle, who uses other male figures as proxy sexual threats to force compliance. In *The Italian* Radcliffe explicitly unites incestuous sexual desire and murderous desire, deploying the uncle as a figure conflicted over whether to rape or kill his niece, whom he has already left without property or title. When the common threads of legality and sexuality that are apparent within these different Gothic narratives by women are unpicked a pattern emerges that links the figure of the uncle with sexual, incestuous threats, creating a subversive commentary on tyrannical persecution, oppression and the hypocrisy of 'natural' law.[20]

NATURALLY ARISING DESIRES: RAISING THE NIECE TO BECOME THE WIFE

The heroine of Parsons's *Wolfenbach* is Matilda Weimar, a young woman raised by her uncle, Mr Weimar, in a remote location in Austria. Matilda holds little affection for her uncle and guardian in spite of his extreme fondness towards her. Although Weimar takes a minimal interest in Matilda while she is young, once she goes through puberty and turns fifteen he grows intensely attracted to her. After Matilda overhears a conversation between Weimar and a servant that implies he plans to rape her she flees to Germany, seeking refuge at the Castle of Wolfenbach, where she meets the Countess Wolfenbach and with her help escapes to Paris to the Countess's sister and brother-in-law (the Marquis and Marchioness de Melfort). When Matilda next sees Weimar he tells her she is not his blood kin but is rather an unknown orphan he raised and fell in love with and proposes marriage. Matilda refuses, running away first to England and then to a convent in France before being abducted by Weimar and taken onto a ship. Overtaken by Turkish pirates, Weimar stabs Matilda and reveals the truth of her origins: she is his niece, the daughter of his older brother whom he killed for the inheritance. He switched Matilda as an infant with her wet nurse's dead daughter, taking her to Austria where he subsequently raised her as his niece. Matilda finds her mother and a joyful reunion with her and her love interest, the Count de Bouville, ensues.

Parsons's novel unites themes of inheritance, incestuous desires, threats of rape and female imprisonment with thefts of female-held property and the usurpation of the patriarchal position by the younger brother. Parsons embeds the thefts, usurpation and crimes in a heavily coded language of Gothic incestuous desires. The uncle, in stealing from the older brother, takes not just his property but his daughter, laying claim to Matilda's body as his own. Weimar's shifting desires towards Matilda show that his position as her father has culminated in the ultimate betrayal of power but also that such abuses of power and incestuous desires are the natural result of the available familial, legal and marital models. The abuses that occur are exacerbated in a perpetuation of thefts, crimes and incestuous violence against women that reveal the threat of what Gothic scholar Ruth Bienstock Anolik refers to as the possession of women in marriage.[21] Weimar's incestuous threats and thefts of property are bound together, underscoring the function of the female body as a commodity to be exchanged between a patriarch and a non-kin male. That his desires and usurpations negate the necessity for this exchange locates the paradox at the heart of what Foucault refers to as the deployment of alliance and the deployment of sexuality.[22] Parsons's novel demonstrates that incestuous desires and threats are the inevitable and unavoidable products of the power relations created by the customs and laws intended to prohibit incest in order to shore up eighteenth-century ideologies of kinship and sexuality.[23]

It is apparent from the development of the plot that the novel follows an ostensibly recognisable Gothic arc, complete with persecutions, revelations and reunions. What is intriguing about the novel's depictions of incest is not only the way various characters react to Weimar's incestuous desires but also the way the desires develop and how Parsons links incestuous urges with questions of ownership, birth and property. This unification necessitates an examination of usurpation, violence and sexuality that is pointed towards by Kilgour in her reading of Radcliffe's *Udolpho*, in which she states: 'below the surface narrative lurks a story of usurpation. What is unusual, too, is that the suggested dispossession and perhaps murder is of a female by a male. Is this a subversive myth of the usurpation of female property and power by a patriarchal order?'[24] The question applies to all Gothic novels in which a heroine is deprived of inheritance and freedom by a male villain. When the male villain is also a family member who tries to force incestuous relations onto the younger female relative, the myth becomes not one of mere property usurpation but of sexual domination and physical violence. This type of dispossession and attempted murder of females is quite common in Gothic representations of uncles and nieces. Rather than understanding this frequent (though widely varying) plot line as a subversive myth, it is a sophisticated blending of traditionally masculine powers – sexual, financial and legal – that are manifested in the form of the uncle and wielded over the niece to expose the threats implicit in the dominant ideology.[25] The niece's position is one of legal (and at times physical) powerlessness rather than of moral or emotional helplessness; her persecution and usurpation by the uncle is one that is accommodated – and, in a sense, demanded – by the laws of society that are frequently articulated in the Gothic in the very terms of desire and incest: as naturally occurring or unnaturally imposed.[26]

Uncle Weimar's incestuous longings for Matilda begin, not when she is a young child in his care, but after she is a teenager and (perhaps more interestingly from an anthropological viewpoint) after he has returned from an absence of nine months.[27] Although as a child Matilda felt 'a repugnance to return his caresses', when she is fifteen he leaves for France and for the first time she feels affection for him: 'nothing could exceed the tenderness of his behaviour at parting, and for the first time in my life I was affected; I returned his embraces and shed some tears' (pp. 10–11). He returns after writing to her constantly; and although Matilda 'was overjoyed to see him … the pleasure I felt and expressed fell very short of the rapture and transport with which he embraced and praised me; he dwelt on the improvement in my person with such delight, that I felt confused and uneasy; the attention which used to give me pleasure was now painful, and I repulsed his caresses involuntarily' (p. 11). When explaining to the Countess Wolfenbach why she fled from her uncle Matilda focuses on the attention Weimar lavished on her and his expectations of her responses to him that were disappointed by her hesitant or confused reactions. Weimar's sexual attraction for Matilda, though perhaps beginning earlier, is clearly pinpointed by Matilda as being inspired by the improvement in her person that has occurred during his absence.[28] Scholars often see incest in the Gothic as allied to that deployed by the Romantic writers, as a trope that 'suggests an abnormal and extreme desire (a violation of natural familial ties) that is antithetical to and subversive of social requirements'.[29] However, rather than being shown as 'unnatural' incest is often portrayed instead as a natural desire, as a 'more than' familial love; rather than a violation of familial love it is an extension of it.[30] The result of this representation is frequently a subversion of the legal as well as the social requirements regarding sexuality, exchanges of women and exogamous marriages. Parsons's Matilda is positioned in relation to her uncle's sexual persecution that is tied to his legal and financial control over her. Although she is able to escape the authority he has over her that facilitates his incestuous desires, they are presented as the natural consequence of his control over her body and property.

Weimar's fixation on Matilda is revealed as sexual in nature, not only by his dwelling on her appearance and the rapture with which he greets her, but also by the books he has brought back with him. Weimar has made purchases on his trip away that Matilda views as akin to pornography, from which she instinctively recoils. The incident is, as far as I know, unique in early Gothic fiction. An uncle shows his young niece lewd images that distress her:

> [H]e had brought me a present of some books and drawings, both of which he knew would be acceptable to me ... the latter were very beautiful, but the attitudes and want of decent drapery confused and hurt me, for although I had never received any particular lessons on delicacy or modesty, yet there is that innate virtuous principle within us, that shrinks involuntarily from any thing tending to violate that sense of decency we are all, I believe, born with; I therefore could not examine them with the accuracy I wished, much less praise them, as I saw he expected. (p. 12)

Weimar expects (or desires) Matilda to respond to the drawings with praise; whether he intends her to be aroused by them is arguable, but what is clear is that the sexual advances and desires here are linked to inappropriate images the uncle shows the niece.[31] Her inability to view them with anything but distress is testimony to her innate virtue, a modesty that makes her shrink from the images and her uncle; she identifies the incident as unsettling although she cannot fully articulate why.[32] It is also an act typical of male abusers, who take advantage of their power. In her article addressing abuses of power Lena Dominelli describes the overall denial that meets claims of the family structure promoting abuse: 'the public has generally resisted the feminist message that incest is widespread in our society and that it arises from the social legitimation of unequal power relations within the family'.[33] This abuse of power is frequently cited in scholarly examinations of the Gothic to equate incest in the genre with representations of male abuse. In spite of its overapplication to all forms of incestuous relationships in the Gothic, the relevance of this paradigm to the incestuous advances of uncles that stem, in part, from the unequal distribution of power in the family structure is readily apparent. The feminist claim that father–daughter sexual abuse 'is a characteristic of a patriarchal society' explains how the social structure perpetuates abuses against women within the context of family.[34]

The application of this sociological understanding of incest to the representations in the Gothic, though limiting in certain configurations that defy its construction as an abuse on the part of the paternal figure, is highly relevant in examinations of the uncle. The nature of incestuous sexual abuses as a violation of the taboo that is essential to the maintenance of the power structure that allows such abuses is a paradox relevant here. The uncle's disruption of the power structure that seemingly reinforces his position of authority while concurrently jeopardising it through the violation of the taboo is further complicated through his simultaneous transgression of the structure of primogeniture and inheritance that does not occur with father–daughter violations. The uncle disregards a taboo that endangers his usurped power in order to strengthen his individual authority over the niece as well as his usurped position in the patriarchy. The incestuous threats serve as more than literalisations of paternal power, inscribing the uncle's abuses within a network of usurpations that repeatedly represent the female body as the site of these transgressive thefts. His paternal role is appropriated, as are all positions of power over female bodies and finance; the incestuous desires arise naturally in an unnaturally constructed configuration of family, economics, sexuality, power and discipline. All control is a false usurpation: the uncle demonstrates the implicit falsity of all hegemonic ideologies.

Seventeenth-century English theologian and clergyman Jeremy Taylor's understanding of incestuous unions is taken up by scholar Ellen Pollak in her comprehensive analysis of incestuous representations in English literature to discuss the transgressive nature of the uncle–niece relationship.[35] Pollak examines Taylor's argument (whose views influenced many later debates on marriage and kinship law) that only marriages between parents and children/children-in-law were against the prime laws of nature and that although unions between siblings were incestuous and illegal, they did not constitute a violation of the natural law. Neither were marriages between uncles and nieces a violation of the natural law as they did not overturn 'the proper order of familial authority' as the unnatural union of parent and child would.[36] Pollak's treatment of Taylor is intriguing because it illuminates both the widening gaps between divine law and natural law and how civil law was affected by these shifts. These ideas are further taken up by T. G. A. Nelson, who argues that Taylor's perspective reveals the contradiction between (in relation, specifically, to brother–sister unions) the natural propensity towards incest as checked by laws that have become so ingrained within us that they are now natural: 'such marriages have been outlawed, to the extent that the law against them has become a kind of secondary law of nature'.[37] Foucault refers to the paradox that Nelson examines as a system of knowledge produced through the ongoing reproduction of power, stating that 'we are forced to produce the truth of power that our society demands, of which it has a need in order to function'.[38] That systems of law and inheritance are designated in the Gothic as natural and unnatural in their reproduction is critical to examining how they are presented as lending themselves to abuses of power manifested as incestuous desires and threats, becoming a site of resistance to such reproductions without depicting the desires as inherently unnatural. More important for a discussion of Weimar and Matilda is the possibility that Weimar's position as uncle is not the relationship that would cause his marriage to his niece to be perceived as unnatural, but his usurped position as her familial head. Taylor's views indicate that seventeenth- and eighteenth-century society would object to the disruption of familial authority resulting from Weimar's marriage to Matilda as his ward rather than to the idea of a natural law being violated by his marriage to her as his niece.[39] Weimar's role as Matilda's guardian and the familial patriarch puts him in a position of authority that, in conjunction with the usurpations of these roles, reinforces the depiction of incestuous desires occurring naturally within the unnatural structures of family and society.[40]

Matilda's account of her uncle's behaviour to the Countess of Wolfenbach continues with further examples of his excessive praise and touching:

> From this time my uncle's behaviour was to me unaccountable, he was for ever seeking opportunities to caress me, his language was expressive of the utmost fondness, he praised my person in such glowing colours as sometimes filled me with confusion. In short, madam, not to tire you, within three months after his return I began to be extremely uneasy at freedoms I scare knew how to repulse. (p. 12)

Matilda's confusion at her uncle's advances is caused by her inability fully to comprehend the sexual nature of his caresses and compliments and how to stop him.[41] She knows she does not like his behaviour but does not quite know why or what to do about it. This changes abruptly when Matilda overhears a servant counsel her uncle to tell her they are unrelated and do to her what he likes. The conversation convinces Matilda that whether or not Weimar is her uncle, he poses a clear threat to her person (her physical form, her virginity, her chastity) and she flees his estate. Matilda's flight and subsequent adventures underscore the tensions within scholarship's understanding of the Female Gothic as paradoxically conservative and radical in its destruction of the patriarchal past and its reconfiguration as a reformed ideal. Kilgour describes the Gothic as at once dismembering the present and re-membering the past into something pure and idealistic, stating that: 'the gothic is better at dismemberment than re-memberment, at parody than the construction of an alternative'.[42] Kilgour's argument and Kate Ferguson Ellis's analysis of the Gothic heroine's attempt to destabilise and then reform the nuclear family exemplify scholarly divergences on the function of the Gothic as a space in which writers articulated subversive views on patriarchy and family.[43]

These divergent understandings of the Gothic's ability to reform (or re-member) the past into a new bourgeois family structure emphasise the difficulties scholarship has encountered in determining what the heroine achieves at the end of the Gothic novel. Does she re-member the dismembered and idealised past into a reformed family structure – and fail in doing so effectively, as Kilgour suggests – or does the Gothic fail as subversive if the heroine's aim in destabilising patriarchy is only to reform it, as Ellis's argument suggests? Matilda is a heroine who does neither. She does not fail in re-membering the past because she never attempts to do so; rather, she dis-members her present and creates a new family structure with an equal partner. That Matilda does not destabilise the family structure to reform it is a consequence of its extant weaknesses. The presence of undesired incestuous advances demonstrates that the available family structure permits unequal power relationships and is thus fundamentally compromised, necessitating the heroine's escape from its archaic structure. Rather than reform it, she must leave it behind forever. Matilda's escape from her uncle's home propels her forward into an even more violent family structure, that of the Countess Wolfenbach's home – her prison – in which she has been kept by a jealous and murderous husband for almost two decades and from which Matilda also escapes. The patriarchal underpinnings of the family and society are exposed as inherently unstable as they permit the legal imprisonment of women by their male family members and perpetuate a system of chronic injustice.

Matilda's perception of incest is intriguingly ambiguous. When she reflects on her loyal servant Albert, implicitly comparing him to her uncle, she views him as superior to the depraved Weimar: 'how much superior are their sentiments to those of better understanding and cultivated talents, when their minds are depraved by the indulgence of irregular passions!' (p. 23). Albert, although devoid of cultivated talents, has not been corrupted by the indulgence of irregular passions as Weimar has.[44] But it cannot be incest that Matilda calls an irregular passion, because at this point she is no longer certain of Weimar's having a consanguineal tie to her and so her description of his passions as irregular applies rather to their exploitative nature and the force he planned to use on her.[45] In a contrasting perception of their connection, Matilda says to her uncle: 'heaven can witness for me how grateful I was for your kindness, until my delicacy was alarmed by freedoms I thought improper from our near connexion' (p. 61). Here, Matilda implies that it is the blood relationship that makes the freedoms alarming rather than the freedoms themselves that disturb her, contradicting her earlier assertion that Weimar's actions disturbed her innate sense of delicacy and modesty. It is an interesting turn of phrase when examined in conjunction with other Gothic heroines, such as Radcliffe's Ellena or Sleath's Laurette, who are represented more frequently as uncomfortable with caresses or freedoms taken by those outside of the family, by men who are not kin, and who consequently view proof of blood as a green light for caresses that would be otherwise inappropriate.[46] Matilda's honesty (like Laurette's) is, however, in this instance questionable given the context of her statement: she is refusing an offer of marriage from the man she believed her whole life to be her uncle after he has announced he is not blood kin and is thus capable of marrying her legally.

Weimar relies on the notion of obligation to persuade Matilda to marry him as a repayment for his financial investment in her upbringing. Matilda says to her uncle on his offer of marriage that she feels unable to refuse him if he is not her uncle because of this debt, but that she will never love him:

> The conversation I overheard is ever present to my mind, and could I forget that, then my reverence for my uncle would return, and I should shudder at the idea of a nearer connexion. When I think of it, and indeed, Sir, I have endeavoured to think of it, an unaccountable repugnance makes the idea horrible to me; yet after all, if you persist in wishing me to become your wife, I do not think myself at liberty absolutely to refuse, but I tell you candidly, I never can love you; that though I will obey you and do my duty, I know I shall be miserable, and in that persuasion surely 'tis impossible I can make you happy. (pp. 67–8)

Matilda's first reason for resisting the marriage is not her memories of Weimar raising her as a niece but her knowledge of his plan to force himself on her. She phrases it so that her refusal is couched in terms of her inability to forget that conversation, which, even if forgotten, would then cause her to view him again as her uncle, making the idea of marrying him horrible. She constructs a logical paradox that makes it impossible for her to marry him based on the tautology of his position as a potential rapist or as blood kin. Nonetheless, she undercuts the refusal this construct allows her by admitting that if he persists in his proposals she will marry him because she feels she owes him.[47] The obligation Matilda feels to her uncle is viewed primarily as a financial one, which is reinforced by Charlotte De Melfort's attempt to eliminate the debt on financial terms. Charlotte, acting as Matilda's protector, intervenes as a buyer in the market of female bodies and undermines Weimar's male privilege of purchasing and ownership. Trying essentially to buy Matilda from Weimar, Charlotte says she will give him the money for the expense he incurred in raising her to have adoptive claim to her (p. 102). It is made clear that Weimar's right to Matilda, once he has asserted that she is not his blood kin, is based on monetary obligation and that he will use this perceived debt to attempt to force Matilda into marriage.

Charlotte deploys Weimar's argument of financial obligation against him, freeing Matilda from a marriage repulsive to her by purchasing Matilda from her uncle in an act of exchange that reverses the traditional commerce in female bodies.[48] Her intervention reveals that it is in fact these exchanges and the ownership of women by family that reduces their bodies to currency, entailing incestuous and endogamous desires.[49] She further tries to use money to liberate Matilda in England, offering her '£400/year [to] make her independent – under no obligation to any young man' (p. 97) to free her from any obligations to Count de Bouville, Weimar or any other man. Matilda too finds the idea of obligation unsettling, preferring to belong to only herself rather than have potential debts used to force her compliance.[50] When Weimar tells Matilda her illegitimacy makes it unlikely that she will find any man other than himself willing to marry her, she says: 'I never will owe the obligation to any man, nor have the chance of being upbraided, that I belong to nobody' (p. 68). Matilda uses Weimar's assertion of her illegitimacy as an undesirable trait to renege on her verbal agreement to marry him by claiming that she will not let her obscurity (both her potential illegitimacy and her lack of fortune) degrade any potential husband. Matilda claims that rather than cause any such degradation she will become a lay-sister, a suggestion that indicates she will submit to celibacy rather than be an unequal partner in a marriage. When Weimar agrees to let Matilda stay with the De Melforts for a year, so long as she forms no attachment to any other man and writes to him, the same scenario of proposed marriage and refusal is repeated with Matilda's lover, Count de Bouville. Matilda declines to marry and disgrace him because of her obscure origins, preferring instead to go to a convent. She rejects being a party to any relationship that places her under an obligation, financial or as an object of pity or disdain due to her illegitimate birth, leaving behind both Bouville and her uncle.

Matilda's resistance to the institution of marriage as offered by her uncle is presented as a natural disinclination predicated on both a distrust and dislike of Weimar coupled with her inability to view him as non-related given her upbringing. Her reluctance is strengthened by having met and fallen in love with the handsome and wealthy Bouville; her desire for Bouville jeopardises her uncle's continued control over her body. Robert Miles argues that Gothic representations of the institutionalisation of marriage in the eighteenth century are tied to threats against inheritance via desire: 'the plot of the Gothic romance is a threat to primogeniture, the arranged marriage gone wrong through the advent of a desire that proves literally unruly'.[51] Miles argues that unnatural sexuality characterised anything that resisted the institutionalised discourses of marriage and procreation in the eighteenth century. In Parsons's novel the sexuality that withstands marriage is Matilda's; her natural desires for Bouville oppose a marriage that embodies the heteronormative ideologies of power and violence. Weimar's desires, although developing naturally in the context of his power over his niece's body, become unnatural as they endanger female liberty, desire and property ownership. Male sexuality formulated within the available power networks, particularly in relation to an already existing control over a female, engenders female resistance to marriage. Sexuality cannot develop into anything other than a threat within the confines of the existing ideologies and their reification in the family structure of Weimar and Matilda. Although all desires arise naturally, that they do so from within the uncle–niece configuration as Parsons delineates it – fraught with prior usurpations of property, name and body – brings about their manifestation of heteronormative structures that renders them unnatural threats to female desire, property and body.

Miles calls Parsons's novel a core Female Gothic narrative 'where the daughter leaves, or is abducted from, the castle of a Baron intent on making his daughter marry dynastically'.[52] Yet in Parsons's novel Matilda does not leave because her father wants her to marry dynastically, she flees because her uncle threatens rape and proposes marriage.

As Weimar explains his attraction its development corresponds to Matilda's maturation and initially resists the tradition of institutionalised marriage: 'as Matilda grew up, I became passionately fond of her; my love increased with her years, and I determined to possess her ... I did not first intend marrying; I had an aversion to that tie' (p. 150). However, he would have succumbed to the institution of marriage had Matilda accepted him if that was the only way to indulge his sexual desire for her: 'it was my intention to have married you, unless you rejected me – in that case you must take the consequence' (p. 151). Weimar's desire works against Miles's assertions regarding unnatural sexuality resisting marriage and Parsons's novel as a narrative of flight from a dynastic marriage as it is traditionally understood. Rather, unnatural sexuality (Weimar's desires) eventually subscribes to the cultural convention of marriage as it is within this institution that such urges are indulged under the sanction of the heteronormative society whose laws and customs corroborate male desires. The marriage Weimar proposes is literally dynastic – within the same family line – however, it is not the father who attempts to enforce this incestuous marriage but the uncle, whose prior usurpation locates the proposed dynastic marriage as a further consequence of the unnaturally constructed intersections of desire, marriage and sexuality.

A discussion of rights and laws demonstrates the incestuous desires of the uncle to be a crossover between the control over women afforded to non-kin and kindred men – an unfairly weighty blend of authority over female sexuality, property and exchange in marriage. The convent in France to which Matilda retires offers her no protection from Weimar; although her uncle 'could not oblige her to marry him' (p. 100) nor prevent her entry to the religious house he can remove her from it by an order of the King. When the convent surrenders Matilda to Weimar she says to him: 'how you mean to dispose of me, or by what right you assume yourself master of my destiny, I know not; but of this you may be assured, no force shall prevail upon me to act contrary to my own inclinations and judgment; and since I am not your niece, you have no legal authority over me' (p. 142). Matilda believes that Weimar is not a consanguineal relative and therefore has no legal claim to or authority over her. Were Weimar Matilda's blood uncle her virginity would be safe (Matilda's understanding of kinship and sexual desire as incompatible has been enforced by Weimar's false assertions that he only loves her because she is not his kin), but the lack of a blood tie jeopardises her chastity just as its presence puts at risk her whole body and future because it would grant Weimar control of those. Kinship and law are tied together paradoxically, as the presence of kinship grants male relatives legal control over female bodies and property while prohibiting (theoretically) sexual acts and marriage between kin, while the absence of blood ties renders the female unprotected and at the sexual mercy of all non-kin.[53] The relationship between kinship and the law in the eighteenth century forces women to be the objects of exchange – financial property – or the objects of desire – sexual property. Uncle–niece incest merges these forms of female commodification to locate the niece as an object of both sexual and financial value, who, in the uncle's ideal market, circulates within the confines of the castle. Matilda's refusal to submit to Weimar's false authority establishes her own inclinations and judgement as the superior power: she defies the subordinate positions afforded her through both consanguineal and non-consanguineal ties.

Matilda's belief that she is unrelated to Weimar is short-lived as he declares himself yet again to be kin, saying: 'well ungrateful runaway, you are once more in the custody of your true and natural protector' (p. 142). The use of the terms 'true' and 'natural' implies that the protection Charlotte provided Matilda was unnatural and false due to her status as a non-kin female. When Weimar tells Matilda that she must once more be his 'niece' to preserve her character, she replies: 'do you think I will give a sanction to your falsehoods, and permit myself to be made a slave of?' (p. 143). Matilda equates the blood bond to the bondage of slavery. Weimar's claim of kinship is – she believes – not only false but also a means of maintaining her reputation that she rejects, risking her public character rather than be repositioned as kin and slave. Weimar kidnaps Matilda, forcing her onto a ship, and when after two days at sea there is gunfire Weimar tells Matilda she has been their ruin, promptly stabbing them both (p. 144). The uncle who has tried to coerce and force his niece into a sexual relationship instead plunges a knife into her, figuratively raping her. Neither is wounded fatally (Matilda covers her breast, receiving a wounded arm) and while recovering Weimar tells Matilda that he would rather she die than marry another, admitting that he is her uncle. Weimar further confesses to the murder of his elder brother, switching Matilda at birth and subsequent removal to Austria, where he raised and fell in love with her. He regrets the murder, not the incest, telling his niece: 'yet even at this moment I adore Matilda' (p. 151). He never views the incestuous desires, which developed alongside Matilda and intensified after the nine-month absence that allowed him to re-form her into a sexually mature and accessible woman, as criminal or unnatural.

Weimar's confessions restore kinship status and legal claims to name and property to his niece. He states: 'I acknowledge Matilda to be the only child and heiress to the Late Count Berniti's estates, which I have unjustly withheld' (p. 147). The blood tie is a legal one that gives her the ability to marry the man of her choice; blood – or genealogy – grants freedom of choice once it no longer entails being under Weimar's authority. Weimar believes 'the restitution of her estates would sufficiently prove his penitence for the intended wrong done to her' (p. 159), though it is unclear what Weimar is referring to as 'the wrong' – his initial intended rape, his general incestuous designs on her, his attempts to force her to marry him under false pretences or his final plot to keep her imprisoned as his sex slave if she refused to marry him. When her uncle recuperates and establishes himself as a monk, Matilda reads a letter from him describing his state of repentance: 'this letter affected Matilda greatly; she remembered the care he had taken of her youth, though she shuddered when she considered him as the murderer of her father' (p. 175). It is her uncle's crime of fratricide, the murder of her unknown father, that makes her shudder rather than the incest Weimar desired (and threatened) to commit with her.

The figure of Weimar in many ways foreshadows the figure of Radcliffe's Schedoni, another uncle who does not know whether he should rape or kill his niece. But it is not only Radcliffe who takes cues from Parsons's plot and character. Austen, another author who focused on money, property and family, had at least heard of Parsons's novel, as is proved by her inclusion of it in her *Northanger Abbey* list; that she perhaps also used it as inspiration for parts of her plots is supported by my earlier comparisons of *Wolfenbach* with *Mansfield Park* (1814). Other points of similarity to Austen's fiction include Matilda's false belief that her lover, Count de Bouville, is already married to another woman, one undeserving of his worth, Mrs Courtney. Matilda cannot bear to inquire about the two for fear of hearing about their marriage (p. 165), much as Elinor fears Edward is married to another scheming woman, Lucy Steele, in *Sense and Sensibility* (1811) only to be proved wrong. Moreover, the revelation of Bouville's continued single state as revealed by the Marchioness (p. 168) is highly reminiscent of the revelation of Edward's continued bachelorhood in Austen's novel. Another strong similarity to *Sense and Sensibility* occurs when the Countess asks Matilda if she loves Bouville, to which Matilda replies: 'If, madam ... to prefer him to any other man I ever saw; if to confess that I think him deserving of the highest esteem from every one he honours with his acquaintance; if this is to be called love, I must answer in the affirmative' (p. 171). This evokes Elinor's near confession to Marianne about Edward: '"I do not attempt to deny," said she, "that I think very highly of him – that I greatly esteem, that I like him."'[54] Both heroines struggle with questions of money, emotions and the marital statuses of their lovers. That Parsons's work influenced that of other writers who focused at length on the ties of kinship and property reveals that the Gothic, while so frequently thought of as a genre obsessed with constantly recycled conventions, possesses a much broader range of concerns reflected in their reimagining in later non-Gothic novels. Not only do Gothic novels demonstrate their thematic range from the diversity of texts they influence, but they are also themselves engaged with the broader concerns of the various genres of fiction that precede and follow them.[55]

RAPE BY PROXY: WITHDRAWING PROTECTION TO FORCE SUBMISSION

The wealth of criticism that focuses on representations of property in Radcliffe's novels, according to certain lines of scholarship, recapitulates the Gothic narratives of female victimhood and resistance. Lauren Fitzgerald, for example, writes that Ellen Moers's examination of property in *The Mysteries of Udolpho* demonstrates the ways feminist critics 'often reproduce the plots and characters of their object of study' by casting writers like Radcliffe in the role of the heroine beleaguered by male critic villains.[56] Such criticism is not unjust; much scholarship has been devoted to repositioning Radcliffe in light of Matthew Lewis and her male critics such as Sir Walter Scott, while even more has focused on ownership, inheritance and property in her novels.[57] Fitzgerald ultimately links feminist criticism's fixation on property to a desire to reclaim the textual property of women writers and ownership over a literary tradition.[58] It is, indeed, impossible to overlook so central a focus of Radcliffe's texts, particularly when the themes of property are intriguingly united with threats of incestuous sexual violence, which we have already seen in play in Parsons's work. E. J. Clery states that Radcliffe, 'by regularly endowing her female characters with inherited fortunes, foregrounds the ideological inconsistencies of the property laws relating to women of her time'.[59] Clery's well-made claim focuses on the flaws of the legal system and its failure to protect female control and ownership of property and wealth.[60] Recent critical work by Radcliffe scholars such as Miles hints at a link between the threats of sexual violence and property thefts: 'the true risks posed by Radcliffe's plots are not the rapes threatened with a surprising frequency in such a proper writer, but the alienation of property and place'.[61] This conclusion tends to minimise the threat of rapes and their prevalence, yet the imbrication of body and property is central to the texts. Radcliffe's novels consistently navigate the legal complexities of female inheritance and its usurpation by male relatives – specifically the uncle – and risks of sexual violence, presenting incestuous threats as inextricable from property theft by relatives. Because threats to female-owned property become united with dangers to the female body – which is valuable to men through its potential for exchange – male usurpations of female inheritances become themselves an incestuous violation.

In *The Mysteries of Udolpho* Radcliffe addresses property, inheritance and incestuous violence when Montoni threatens the heroine, Emily St Aubert, with rape by proxy through a withdrawal of his protection if she fails transfer her property to him. Emily is raised in the domestic tranquility of the family home La Vallée and falls in love with the Chevalier Valancourt while travelling with her father before she is orphaned by his death. Madame Cheron, Emily's paternal aunt and guardian after her parents' deaths, objects to the Chevalier as unworthy of Emily. Forced to leave France with her aunt, who has married the aristocratic Italian, Montoni, Emily becomes little more than a piece of property Montoni attempts to marry off to the highest bidder in exchange for money to pay off his numerous debts. At Montoni's remote and ancestral Castle Udolpho, Emily's aunt dies and Montoni continually pressures Emily to sign over her properties (and those left to her by her aunt) to him. Montoni threatens to withdraw his protection of her, leaving her vulnerable to rape before Emily escapes, takes possession of her properties and marries Valancourt. The aspects of the story most relevant to an analysis of uncles, nieces, incest and property are those that take place at Castle Udolpho and it is on those that I will most closely focus.

In her examination of father–daughter incest, Angie Ash states that 'explicit violence may not always be necessary to force a daughter's submission: rather, the threat of its uses, or the coercive nature of the father's behaviour in the family, may be sufficient to ensure the victim's cooperation'.[62] Radcliffe's novel represents a distortion of Ash's description that locates threats of violence as ensuring sexual submission. It is not that physical violence forces sexual acquiescence, but that threats of sexual violence are designed to extort submission to financial desires. Montoni's withdrawal of his protection underscores the sexual violence Emily will experience if she does not submit to his will – to his desire for her property. Montoni will use rape by proxy to secure his acquisition of female property that he feels is unjustly withheld from him. Radcliffe reveals that female inheritance threatens male control of women (and their bodies) and is potentially disruptive of the patriarchal structure that is re-established through the uncle's threats against the niece's female body. This body, itself a commodity or property within the existing structures of family, law and sexuality, becomes a contested site of ownership.

From early in the novel Radcliffe depicts Emily as forced into relative dependency on the will and authority of others, a position to which she consistently refuses to acquiesce. Montoni, her aunt, her maternal uncles, even the kindly Count de Villefort, all attempt to dictate her actions and/or control her property. At the point she decides to encourage their marriage, Madame Cheron says of Emily to Valancourt: '"Well, I will take upon me to answer for her. But at the same time, sir, give me leave to observe to you, that I am her guardian, and that I expect, in every instance, that my will is hers."'[63] This ownership of Emily's will by Madame Cheron is extended to Montoni when Madame Cheron tells Emily that '"From this hour you must consider the Signor Montoni as your uncle – we were married this morning"' (p. 141). In a rather Gothic twist on the transfer of a woman's property to her husband upon marriage, Emily is shown as the commodity in this transfer. When her aunt controls Emily, it is by legal guardianship due to her age; as Emily points out to Valancourt: 'in little more than a year, she should be her own mistress, as far as related to her aunt, from whose guardianship her age would then release her' (p. 147). Montoni, taking over as head of the family from Madame Cheron upon their marriage, becomes Emily's familial head and assumes control over her based on this power. Ash writes: 'power in the family lies with the patriarchal head, the father. That power is literal and symbolic. Literally, it denotes, for example, economic power and physical power.'[64] Montoni is quick to take advantage of this role via his attempts to sell and steal from Emily. He is not, however, alone in this assumption of power based on familial hierarchy; Monsieur Quesnel, Emily's maternal uncle, takes control of her land, seemingly in her interest, by renting out her paternal estate, La Vallée: 'that Mons. Quesnel should let it, without even consulting her on the measure, both surprised and shocked her, particularly as it proved the absolute authority he thought himself entitled to exercise in her affairs' (pp. 194–5). Emily repeatedly rejects the attempts made to control her and force her submission to the assumed authority of those surrounding her, identifying their actions as indicative of unlimited power unjustly wielded.

Even when threatened with a permanent break from Valancourt, Emily has no desire to flee to her uncle, Quesnel, as she is certain 'in flying to him she would only obtain an exchange of oppressors' nor does she assent to the clandestine marriage proposed by Valancourt, although this would 'give her a lawful and generous protector' (p. 203). Emily will not marry until she has no need for a protector; this is almost always the case in the Gothic, in spite of critical trends to see Gothic heroines as in perpetual need of or search for a protector.[65] When Emily questions Quesnel regarding La Vallée she describes him as 'conscious of possessing absolute power' (p. 213). Like Montoni, Quesnel believes his authority is unconditional. His arrogance proves that power distribution on arbitrary lines of gender and class creates petty tyrants. Quesnel also presses Emily to marry against her will, siding with Montoni in trying to coerce her into marrying the wealthy Morano. He is furious with her refusal to do so; Emily describes the 'cruelly exerted authority of M. Quesnel and Montoni' (p. 215). Montoni's financial ruin makes him more desperate and brutal than Quesnel, who exerts authority merely as a matter of right rather than to benefit himself directly. Emily's guardianship rests more firmly in Montoni's control via his wife, which gives him undue influence over Emily that he exerts to the full extent. Indeed, Montoni is so furious with her continued refusal to marry Morano and so sure of the breadth of his authority that he informs her that: 'he would no longer be trifled with, and that, since her marriage with the Count would be so highly advantageous to her … it should be celebrated without further delay, and, if that was necessary, without her consent' (p. 216).

In Montoni's mind, his niece has no right to refuse a financially advantageous marriage; her will is moot, his power total. When Emily questions what right he has to exert such authority over her, Montoni replies: '"by the right of my will; if you can elude that, I will not enquire by what right you do so"' (pp. 216–17). Emily is only reassured by the thought that the marriage could not be valid if she refused to repeat the ceremony before the priest: 'she trembled, more than ever, at the power of Montoni, which seemed unlimited as his will, for she saw, that he would not scruple to transgress any law' (p. 219). In fact, Montoni need not transgress many laws to accomplish his goals; as Lee Holcombe writes, the family is 'a microcosm of the larger society, authoritarian in nature and carefully constructed as to hierarchies and duties ... As such it had been buttressed by the provisions of the law.'[66] That Montoni's will and authority are unjust is clear, but the legal implications of this become irrelevant when his control extends to Emily's body once she is removed to Castle Udolpho and is physically at his mercy. Claudia Johnson refers to 'the brutal silencing of female protest compelled by Montoni's authority' that 'erase[s] female subjectivity'.[67] In Venice, before the removal to Udolpho, Emily had some hopes of legal recourse but once cut off from any pretence of society or lawfulness, Montoni's authority becomes absolute and Emily's refusal to capitulate becomes an act of defiance and bravery.

The removal to the castle and Emily's escape from the marriage to Morano are due, in part, to Montoni learning that Morano has lost his fortune and is penniless. Morano arrives at Udolpho and sneaks into Emily's room at night to attempt to liberate her from the castle and Montoni, begging Emily to leave with him, telling her that Montoni is '"a villain who would have sold you to my love ... Can I love you, and abandon you to his power?"' (p. 262). Morano confirms what Emily had suspected: that Montoni did attempt to sell her to the Count, a clear exchange of his niece's body and chastity for direct financial gain. Emily realises this and consequently concludes that Montoni must have another, wealthier, purchaser in mind for her: 'that Montoni had formerly sold her to Morano was very probable ... [A] scheme of stronger interest only could have induced the selfish Montoni to forego a plan, which he had hitherto so strenuously pursued' (pp. 262–3). Montoni then enters the room and says to Morano: '"was it that you might repay my hospitality with the treachery of a fiend, and rob me of my niece?"' (p. 266). The language repeated throughout this scene is that of economics – buying, selling, robbing, repayment – all locating Emily as a commodity, valuable for its youth, beauty and chastity. It is interesting to note that Radcliffe's heroines never marry exceptionally wealthy older men; Radcliffe never allows her heroines even the appearance of selling themselves.

One of the ideas that is consistently reiterated throughout the novel is that male demands for female acceptance of and submission to their unlimited control over their bodies and fortunes produce incestuous sexual violence; that the social structures that require obedience from women create a power relationship in which female compliance to all male desires is expected. Montoni suggests Emily set up her own attempted abduction and tells her she should '"learn and practice the virtues, which are indispensable to a woman – sincerity, uniformity of conduct and obedience"' (p. 270). Kilgour says of Montoni that 'his main vice is not lust but avarice' and 'his vision of female maturity is that of total acquiescence to male authority; in his terms, self-control means complete abdication of female control and will to male sublime power'.[68] Montoni's repeated attempts to trap Emily linguistically into admitting her properties are his or that she is somehow out of control, wilful and bad for attempting to keep them for herself always terminate in his outrage at her defiance of his will. Montoni embodies the patriarchal familial head representative of a society that typically punishes women for being assertive, and Emily's avowals of her status as rightful owner of the estates provoke a backlash that culminates in sexual intimidation as punishment and threat.[69] Montoni is not ostensibly driven by sexual lust – although he takes advantage of it in others, exploiting his employees' desires for Emily to set them against each other and threatening to unleash them on Emily to force her acquiescence. However, his lust for her property and use of sexual threats demonstrate that his desires are as equally grounded in an exploitation of the female body as the incestuous threats of uncles like Weimar.

Radcliffe highlights the lack of kinship between Montoni and Emily to accentuate the impropriety of their living arrangements if her aunt is deceased, merging ideas of improper relations with a description of Montoni's will (or desire). After Emily believes Montoni has murdered her aunt she asks him to let her return to France. He refuses absolutely. Emily says: '"I can no longer remain here with propriety [...] and I may be allowed to ask, by what right you detain me." "It is my will that you remain here," said Montoni ... Emily, considering that she had no appeal from this will, forbore to dispute his right' (p. 361). Montoni tells her that her aunt is still alive and allows Emily to see her. Montoni's previous threat to his wife that she would 'understand the danger of offending a man, who has an unlimited power over you' (p. 305) has been realised; Madame Montoni is near death, imprisoned in the east turret. After she dies Montoni demands the properties in France that she would not sign over to him from Emily, who has inherited them, and she realises that he will not give up his authority over her.

> [S]he then feared Montoni was about to employ some stratagem for obtaining [the estates], and that he would detain her his prisoner, till he succeeded. This

thought, instead of overcoming her with despondency, roused all the latent powers of her fortitude into action ... For Valancourt's sake also she determined to preserve these estates, since they would afford that competency, by which she hoped to secure the comfort of their future lives. (p. 379)

Although it is not clear how Madame Montoni's estates pass to Emily, escaping Montoni's control, Holcombe describes the establishment of married women's separate property as partially concerned with parents who wanted to ensure 'that if there were no children of a marriage the property would not pass to their daughters' husbands but would return to their own families'.[70] It seems likely that since Montoni hounded his wife for these properties that she was 'allowed to dispose during her lifetime of real property settled upon her' and was further permitted to dispose of this separate property by will.[71]

Along with the possession of the estates Emily also inherits Montoni's avarice and schemes and cruelty; but what Radcliffe evokes in her heroine is not fear but fortitude. Willing to give up the estates to secure her aunt's health or safety, she is now able to undergo extraordinary suffering and imprisonment to preserve them. Although DeLamotte refers to the repeated imprisonment of Emily as a 'portrayal of the heroine's activity [that] centres on a portrayal of her feminine passivity', it is more that her forced passivity portrays the imposition of culturally enforced male control over female bodies.[72] Emily wants the estates because through them she can provide for Valancourt and herself; this is an uncommon example of a Gothic heroine calmly resolving to undergo imprisonment and torment to maintain financial independence. April London refers to this kind of 'individualist ethic' as one that resists familial demands in favour of personal integrity as a recurrent feature in eighteenth-century novels.[73] Emily's fortitude is reinforced by what she knows to be Montoni's unjust abuse of misplaced power over not only herself but also over her aunt before her. Montoni's anger and abuse, part of her inheritance, impress upon the reader the repetition of paternal authority and constraints throughout generations of family until the cycle is broken and the inadequacy of even the most liberal laws regarding women and property to protect women from their husbands and 'protectors'. When it is later revealed that Castle Udolpho is not justly Montoni's, but the property of Signora Laurentini, a female relative whom he attempted to court and marry for both love and money, an even more distinct pattern of usurpation that ties property to body emerges. Signora Laurentini, long missing, also dared to resist Montoni's advances and though Emily eventually discovers she is still alive, Montoni has simply taken over her castle as his own in her absence.

Just as Montoni attempts to usurp ownership of the estates, so too does he unjustly usurp control of Emily's body, another piece of valuable property. Miles argues that Emily's status 'is that of property, either to be bartered away – as Montoni attempts to do – or discarded, put out of sight, once her entitlements have fallen within the net of male acquisitiveness'.[74] When Montoni is unable to complete the transaction of Emily's sale to Morano, he attempts to coerce her out of her inheritances. He tries to trick Emily into signing papers but she refuses to sign anything she has not read. Montoni tells her that ' "I, as the husband of the late Signora Montoni … am the heir of all she possessed; the estates, therefore, which she refused to me in her life-time, can no longer be with-held … and I think you have more sense, than to provoke my resentment by advancing an unjust claim" ' (p. 380). Emily replies, ' "I am not so ignorant, Signor, of the laws on this subject, as to be misled by the assertion of any person. The law, in the present instance, gives me the estates in question, and my own hand shall never betray my right" ' (pp. 380–1). Emily affirms her knowledge of her legal rights while defying Montoni's threats against her person – the dual promise of freedom or risk of continued imprisonment at the castle. Montoni also, interestingly, uses the language of 'just' and 'unjust' to assert his claims on Emily's land in an inverted representation of the morality of the situation. While attempting to use incorrect legal information to fool Emily he clarifies that if she does not abide by his will he will exert his own over her body. This threat is made more potent when Emily realises the real power Montoni has over her is not his ability to keep her captive at the castle but that he can expose her to the desires of his group of bandits.

It is this vulnerability to rape if she does not comply with Montoni's will rather than the possibility of imprisonment that weakens Emily's resolve to retain the properties. Montoni follows through with his threat: Emily is accosted by one of Montoni's officers but breaks free and locks herself in her room, reflecting:

> It appeared to her, that Montoni had already commenced his scheme of vengeance, by withdrawing from her his protection … To retain the estates seemed to be now utterly impossible, and to preserve her life, perhaps her honour, she resolved, if she should escape the horrors of this night, to give up

all claims to the estates, on the morrow, provided Montoni would suffer her to depart from Udolpho. (p. 385)

However, Emily's decision to relinquish the estates is dismissed when she hears a song from her region of France being sung beneath her window; the possibility that the anonymous singer is Valancourt reinforces her determination. Montoni sends for her, saying: '"I ... give you another opportunity of retracting your late mistaken assertions concerning the Languedoc estates ... Dare my resentment no further, but sign the papers"' (p. 393). Emily replies: '"If I have no right to these estates, sir ... of what service can it be to you, that I should sign any papers, concerning them? If the lands are yours by law, you certainly may possess them, without my interference, or my consent"' (p. 393). What appears to be a rather cavalier attitude from Emily is a thinly veiled assertion that she is certainly aware of her legal rights and is choosing to engage in verbal sparring with Montoni over her inheritance. She proves herself more than a match for him. The usurpation of women's property rights by men is, as demonstrated, an essential focus of the Gothic and is noted by Kilgour, who argues: 'from Walpole Radcliffe inherits a concern with inheritance itself, and the question of the rightful ownership of property'.[75] Indeed, the omnipresence of disputes over 'rightful ownership' and their unification with the bad uncle figure in Radcliffe's works is overwhelming.

Montoni's violence and designs towards Emily cause her to reflect: 'if he did not intend to destroy her, with a view of immediately seizing her estates, he meant to reserve her ... for some more terrible design ... remembering Signor Brochio and his behaviour in the corridor, a few preceding nights, the latter supposition, horrible as it was, strengthened in her belief' (p. 407). Emily now fears that Montoni is going to give her to the men to punish her for refusing to sign the papers. Sexual threats are wielded for financial defiance with the additional benefit of gratifying his vengeance. The commodification of the female body as an object of male exchange makes it impossible for the male subjects in such exchanges to allow the possibility of a commodity owning property – physical property such as the estates or control over their own bodies.[76] What Miles calls the bartering away of Emily in marriage is also implicitly a threat that she will be bartered away for sex.[77] Marriage, no longer a viable prospect given the remote location of Udolpho, has given way to the possibility of enforced prostitution, a likelihood alluded to through

Montoni's treatment of Emily and the arrival of prostitutes at the castle for the bandits' pleasure. Emily overhears Signors Bertolini and Verezzi discussing her: 'each seeming to claim some former promise of Montoni' (pp. 430–1). These men pursue Emily through the castle's dark passages in an iconic Gothic flight that concludes with her making it safely to her room with the help of her servant Annette. When Emily tells Montoni of the attempted attack and begs for his protection, he replies: '"you know the terms of my protection … if you really value this, you will secure it"' (p. 436). His assertion 'shewed Emily the necessity of an immediate compliance with his terms; but she first demanded, whether he would permit her immediately to depart, if she gave up her claim to the contested estates' (p. 436). Demanding female submission to male control through threats of rape is a situation Kathleen Barry defines as sexual slavery: 'regardless of how they [women] got into those conditions they cannot get out: and where they are subject to sexual violence and exploitation' and is characteristic of Emily's position.[78]

Emily attempts to buy her freedom and safety from rape through the forfeiture of her estates to Montoni, effectively purchasing herself.[79] Afterwards, Emily 'endeavoured to believe, that Montoni did really intend to permit her return to France as soon as he had secured her property, and that he would, in the mean time, protect her from insult' (p. 437). Of course, by 'insult' she really means rape and molestation.[80] Unfortunately, Emily's belief in her safety is shaken by Montoni's dishonesty and her continued imprisonment and she fears that he has taken her payment for her freedom without ever intending to grant it: 'She not only doubted, whether Montoni ever meant to release her, but greatly feared, that he had designs, concerning her, … Montoni had lost large sums to Verezzi, so that there was a dreadful possibility of his designing her to be a substitute for the debt' (p. 445). Montoni asserts absolute power over Emily, regardless of his lack of legal claim to her estates or person, to acquire money through the sale of her body or the acquisition of her property. DeLamotte points out that: 'the real tyranny at issue in Gothic romance had not been superseded; it still existed in the patriarchal family of the eighteenth century, in which fathers could legally, if they wished, be virtual tyrants'.[81] The element of sexual threat by proxy charges this tyrannical situation with an incestuous current magnified by the familial structure that fosters this atmosphere of oppressor/oppressed.[82] It is likewise exacerbated by what Johnson describes as Emily's 'fearful attraction to the very qualities that make Montoni so forthrightly misogynist'.[83]

Montoni places himself as Emily's paternal protector only to threaten the removal of his protection in order to force her submission of property, ultimately revealing the notion of paternal protection as oxymoronic in the extreme.

To Emily, property and money offer an escape from oppression that allows freedom of choice; it enables female independence from familial and male rule. Emily wants her estates 'for Valancourt' while ruminating that they could 'contribute little to the happiness of a life, in which Valancourt had no longer an interest' (p. 560).[84] The use of 'interest' ironically combines both emotional and financial connotations; Radcliffe implies Emily is a proper female who does not show excessive interest in money beyond what it can provide for her family, while at the same time undercutting this conservative attitude with Emily's persistence in securing her estates. On the surface her desire seems conventional enough – to establish financial security for her family – but in addition to gaining her inheritance and estates she achieves freedom from any male: protector, pursuer, family or benefactor. After Emily escapes from Udolpho, Montoni is killed and the mystery surrounding the castle and its inhabitants clarified. As Kilgour puts it: 'Udolpho now passes to the impoverished Mme Bonnac so that it is restored to a female line, now a non-aristocratic one' and the same happens to the estates of Madame Cheron and St Aubert, which pass to Emily.[85] Still separated from Valancourt, Emily sells her aunt's chateau at Toulouse to purchase her father's childhood home from her uncle Monsieur Quesnel, to whom St Aubert had been forced by financial necessity to sell it some time ago. Emily considers her financial security as the cause of her freedom and independence, if not happiness: 'and now, when she had escaped from so many dangers, was become independent of the will of those, who had oppressed her, and found herself mistress of a large fortune, now, when she might reasonably have expected happiness, she perceived that she was as distant from it as ever' (p. 619).

Like many Gothic heroines, Emily must navigate the terrors of the patriarchal structure before securing her hero and home. Radcliffe's novels are not bildungsromans in which the heroine develops: the heroine remains constant; it is the unjust world in which women are subject to incestuous threats and thefts that must be and is changed. Valancourt's return and explanations restore him to Emily and after their marriage they reside in La Vallée, 'the retreat of goodness, wisdom, and domestic blessedness!' (p. 672). Kilgour says that Radcliffe's 'heroine's circular journey is a transformative one, in which the end both recovers and revises the beginning' and if Emily's return to La Vallée with Valancourt is read as revising the initial scenes of her childhood, Kilgour's reading seems accurate.[86] La Vallée, however, is not so much a revised ancient estate but a more modern version altogether; additionally, Emily is the only Radcliffe heroine who had a particularly happy childhood home and the sole Radcliffe heroine without a murdered parent. Emily can return to La Vallée without it being a restoration of conservative values because it represents a family structure removed from the cycle of violence, imprisonment and male ownership. Like La Vallée, Udolpho reverts to female ownership after Montoni is killed and, indeed, all of Montoni's properties are eventually revealed as rightfully belonging to women; his (mis)use of their structures reconfigured after his death. His sexual threats against Emily are an echo of his undesired sexual advances to Signora Laurentini, as are his usurpations of rightfully female spaces. Emily's ability to withstand Montoni's threats through her legal knowledge, strong sense of justice, ability to endure imprisonment and suffering and awareness of her rights epitomise the Gothic heroine; a woman who overcomes patriarchal threats against property and body to establish her own familial structure.

TO RAPE OR TO MURDER? LUST AND VIOLENCE IN *THE ITALIAN*

Radcliffe's *The Italian*, her most critically praised work over time, hinges upon the multi-layered relationship between Schedoni and Ellena di Rosalba that positions the heroine alternately as Schedoni's intended victim, daughter and niece. While the layering of roles is not unique in the Gothic, what distinguishes this deployment of the convention is that Ellena occupies these positions concurrently with her recasting as the object of his lust and murderous designs and as the daughter of his previous rape victim. Such a reconfiguration casts Ellena as the embodiment of his past crimes; Schedoni's attempt at their reinscription upon her echoes his previous usurpations of the female body and purse in a violent incestuous cycle. Ellena's future is imperilled as a direct result of both Schedoni's prior incestuous crimes – the marriage into which he forced his widowed sister-in-law and his subsequent legally sanctioned rapes of her – and his present ones.

The novel follows Ellena and her lover Vivaldi as they flee from the machinations of Vivaldi's mother, the Marchesa di Vivaldi, and her confessor Father Schedoni, whom she enlists to abduct and murder Ellena. Throughout, Ellena encounters previously unknown members of her family: a sympathetic nun, Olivia, is revealed as her mother and Schedoni, while attempting to murder and/or rape Ellena, confesses his belief that he is her father. Ellena is in fact Schedoni's niece, the daughter of his older brother di Bruno and his wife. Schedoni's position as the younger brother in the family structure is the impetus behind the murder of his older brother and usurpation of di Bruno's title and property, wife and family. He steals from his older brother his wealth and his female family members, the usurpations from the outset combining thefts of money and bodies. When Schedoni squandered his patrimony granted via the laws of primogeniture, his brother could no longer afford to support him; this and Schedoni's envy of di Bruno's unencumbered estate and beautiful wife prompted Schedoni to have his brother killed.[87] Schedoni displaces his brother as the patriarchal head, literally taking over his place in the family, marrying his sister-in-law and assuming control of the estates. The usurpation of what the laws governing inheritance denied is the younger brother's way of contravening the system. Kilgour argues that the law 'ensures unbroken succession and so maintains the continuity of tradition'.[88] In light of this understanding of the law, the figure of the usurping uncle paradoxically represents the destruction of tradition and the epitome of patriarchy's constraints of women. Schedoni's incestuous designs on his niece are complicated by his murderous impulses that are interlinked as the symptoms and requirements of his desire for power. The figure of the uncle becomes incapable of separating acts of theft, violence and incest, displacing the heroine's father through an act of rebellion that condemns the legal system that created him just as it positions him as its new enforcer.

The meetings between Ellena and Schedoni evoke alternately a sense of safety or possible rescue with her fears and his murderous lust. In Ellena's first confrontation with Schedoni outside the house where she is held hostage she views Schedoni as a figure of potential protection. This idea is dispelled when she catches a glimpse of his eyes and face: 'his air and countenance were equally repulsive … [Ellena] shrunk as from an enemy' (p. 263). Her instinct to trust him is replaced with dread at his features – Ellena fails to identify him as kin or as a protector. When Schedoni reveals he is acting in collusion with the Marchesa and Ellena faints, his initial hatred and desire to kill her are lessened as he gazes upon her unconscious form and is touched by feelings of pity and compassion, although he still plots to have her killed.[89] When the assassin Spalatro refuses to do so, Schedoni reluctantly takes up the knife, questioning why he did not kill her earlier and must steel himself for the task: 'the wine, with which Schedoni also had found it necessary to strengthen his own resolution, did not secure him from severe emotion, when he found himself again near Ellena' (p. 276). This hesitation manifests before Schedoni has any reason to believe Ellena is related to him – she is nothing more than a stranger who stands in the way of his advancement within the church.

That Schedoni feels reluctance to harm her hints at a feeling of familiarity or kinship strengthened by the image of her innocence, youth and beauty. Whether it is a sense of kinship, the stirrings of lust or both, Schedoni's reluctance to kill Ellena is palpable. He enters her chamber to find her sleeping and as he watches, she smiles. Schedoni shudders to see her smile in her murderer's face, her innocence affecting him. At this moment his murderous intent becomes loaded with sexual undercurrents. The following passage, often quoted in analyses of the novel, bears repeating due to the unification of sexual and physical threats by a family member:

> He searched for the dagger, and it was some time before his trembling hand could disengage it from the folds of his garment; but, having done so, he again drew near, and prepared to strike. Her dress perplexed him; it would interrupt the blow, and he stooped to examine whether he could turn her robe aside, without waking her … His agitation and repugnance to strike encreased with every moment of delay, and, as often as he prepared to plunge the poniard into her bosom, a shuddering horror restrained him. (p. 279)

Of this passage, Clery writes: 'finally Schedoni lifts the dagger (in a gesture which carries resonances of sexual assault), but is halted by the sight of a miniature of himself hanging round her neck, which reveals him to be her father'.[90] I would put it even more strongly: Radcliffe uses Schedoni's dagger as a metaphorical penis, turning his attempted murder into contemplated rape.[91] The action becomes less physical assault with sexual resonances than voyeuristic sexual assault with murderous resonances. Even the 'shuddering horror' which restrains him from plunging the poniard into Ellena's bosom carries orgasmic implications.

Ellena's lack of experience with a father figure or protector causes her to require proof of kinship before submitting to the caresses and control that Schedoni immediately assumes as his paternal right.[92] After

Schedoni pulls aside Ellena's dress (in preparation to stab her) and sees the miniature around her neck he demands to know who the portrait represents. Ellena tells him it is her father and says: '"I never knew a father's care, nor till lately did I perceive the want of it. – But now – … if you are not as a father to me – to whom can I look for protection?"' (p. 279). Schedoni paces, weeps, sighs and confesses to Ellena that he is her father, although he is labouring under a misapprehension: he is in fact her uncle. As Perry puts it, it is: 'a scene in which murder with incestuous overtones is averted at the last possible minute by recognition of a blood tie'.[93] Ellena believes Schedoni and calls him 'father', although it is unclear whether she is using his religious title or acknowledging his status as her kinsman, as moments later she realises: 'whatever might be the proofs, that had convinced Schedoni of the relationship between them, he had not explained these to her … it was not sufficient to justify an entire confidence in the assertion he had made, or to allow her to permit his caresses without trembling' (p. 281). Ellena is not well-enough convinced of her paternity for her to allow Schedoni's touch without fear; she questions the proofs of a blood tie that would allow his caresses to be appropriate. The immediate recognition of kinship is lacking and so: 'she shrunk, and endeavoured to disengage herself; when, immediately understanding her, he said, "Can you doubt the cause of these emotions? These signs of paternal affection?"' (p. 281). Ellena's reply – '"Have I not reason to doubt … since I never witnessed them before?"' – underscores her fears of Schedoni's caresses being sexual in nature (which they very well may be) and her inability to differentiate between sexual and paternal caresses and emotions as she has never experienced either (p. 281). Ellena has lacked paternal protection, affection and, as Schedoni points out, tenderness. However, these are also familial trappings she has never missed until her abduction and attempted assassination.

Ellena points out her inexperience with paternal signs of affection in order to distance Schedoni until she can evaluate the evidence that has convinced him. The proofs that have satisfied Schedoni are yet unknown to her and therefore his caresses are sexually threatening.[94] Evidence, not assurance, is required in lieu of an instantaneous familial recognition, such as the one she felt for her mother.[95] While imprisoned at the convent Ellena is drawn to Olivia: 'the regard of this nun was not only delightful, but seemed necessary to her heart' (p. 115), a feeling that is later justified by the discovery that Olivia is her mother.[96] Kinship is evidenced by an instant fixation or attraction and subsequent feelings of mutual sympathy and understanding. Schedoni's belief that Ellena is his daughter is rendered questionable given her initial, terrified, emotional response to him. Later, this sense is reiterated when Ellena thinks: 'there were moments when she shrunk from the relationship of Schedoni with unconquerable fright. The first emotions his appearance had excited were so opposite those of filial tenderness, that she perceived it was now nearly impossible to love and revere him as her father' (p. 353). Ellena attempts to ascertain kinship by examining the miniature and comparing it to Schedoni: 'Ellena did trace a resemblance in the bold outline of the features, but not sufficient to convince her, without farther evidence, that each belonged to the same person' (p. 282). Schedoni subsequently provides details that persuade her of their blood tie, promising that she will 'be restored to her home' (p. 283). That Ellena is never able to overcome her initial fear and instinctual dislike of Schedoni contextualises her emotional response as a sort of ancestral memory of his acts of violence against her parents.

Ellena's conflicted perception of the attempted attack at least partly influences her ambivalent acceptance of Schedoni as family. After his revelation of kinship Schedoni leaves Ellena alone; she sees the dagger he dropped and considers the possibility that he was going to kill her, although she quickly disregards that thought, preferring to view him as the hero who foiled Spalatro's plan. Schedoni, on the other hand, manages to move from feelings of guilt and horror at the murder/rape he nearly committed to chastising himself for the crime because a marriage between his daughter and Vivaldi would elevate him even higher than he could have imagined. A conversation filled with layers of meaning regarding the dagger occurs between Ellena and Schedoni when she offers it to him as an object of gratitude for his saving her from an assassin: '"last night while I slept upon this mattress, unsuspicious of what was designed against me, an assassin entered the chamber with that instrument in his hand"' (p. 293). Radcliffe draws attention to the dagger (weapon and metaphorical penis), the attack (a veiled attempted rape and attempted murder), Ellena's misconceptions (that the attacker was someone other than her father/uncle, that the attack was only murderous in intent, that Schedoni saved her from another man), conspicuously highlighting Ellena's continued ignorance regarding Schedoni. The reader knows she is wrong about his character, so is it possible she is also wrong about his identity? Her attempt to return the dagger to him, given its metaphorical status, is fraught with sexual and sacrificial implications. Ellena struggles to reconcile the dark and alarming presence of Schedoni with a father figure; indeed, 'Ellena, whenever her eyes glanced upon him, suffered a solemnity of fear that rose almost to terror' (p. 299). These feelings of fear and terror, however naturally occurring to her, do not preclude Ellena from putting her life in danger to preserve Schedoni when threatened by Spalatro.

The scene combines references to Schedoni's 'rescue' of Ellena with sexual imagery, causing the interaction to be loaded with incestuous meaning. When Schedoni asks Ellena where his would-be assassin has gone, Ellena perceives his intent to kill their attacker and hesitates to answer because she fears for both his safety and the life of the wounded man. She instead begs him to leave: '"Do not, by remaining here, leave me a possibility of grieving for you. What anguish it would occasion you, to see me bleed; judge, then, what must be mine, if you are wounded by the dagger of an assassin!" Schedoni stifled the groan which swelled from his heart, and abruptly turned away' (p. 315). The language Ellena uses to describe a physical attack is sexually evocative, carrying with it allusions of lost virginity through the references to her bleeding and the mention of the dagger. Ellena reminds her father/uncle of what she believes was his protection of her the night before while he remembers drawing aside her dress in anticipation of using his dagger, frantic to disengage it from the folds of his robe. The scene is effective not only because the reader is aware that Schedoni remembers, not saving Ellena, but almost killing her, but also because of the charged sexual atmosphere of the attempted murder and Ellena's continued ignorance thereof. Schedoni's groan that 'swells' further strengthens a reading of his thinking back with mingled lust, horror and regret on the sexual nature of his assault. Perry argues that the near attack on Ellena by Schedoni 'suggests rape rather than murder'[97] but it is the very conflation of the two acts that makes the scene so terrifying and layered in meanings. The unification of near murder and near rape demonstrates that the uncle's desire for increased wealth and power is a lust that he will attempt to act out by commodifying, sexualising and victimising the female body.

It is essential to understand Schedoni's incestuous lust as not only sexually and physically threatening but as equally concerned with the usurpations that are embedded in these violations against generations of female bodies. Some scholars resist identifying sexual violation in the uncle's actions: Miles, for example, suggests of Schedoni that 'incestuous rape is not actually meditated' but springs to the reader's mind because of similar scenes in *The Monk* and *The Castle of Otranto*.[98] Certainly it does, but these are also scenes and texts with which Radcliffe was familiar and aware of evoking. Writing at the peak of Gothic popularity and the swirl of controversy surrounding *The Monk*, Radcliffe would have been keenly attuned to the effect her reworking of these scenes creates. While in *The Monk* the act of incestuous rape ends with the murder of the heroine, Radcliffe does not permit rape or murder to be committed; both acts are interrupted by a revelation of familial ties that in Lewis's novel comes post-rape. Ellena's blood tie to Schedoni saves her from sexual violence and murder while at the same time places her in the control of male hands that seek to barter her off for their benefit.[99] As Kilgour argues: 'in retelling his [Lewis's] story in *The Italian*, she [Radcliffe] reasserts narrative law and order, restoring the correct version he has corrupted, and re-establishes her authority, insisting on both the duty and the power of the author to control the plot she originated'.[100] Radcliffe also exposes Lewis's rape of Antonia by her half-brother as sensationalist scene-writing hinging on the age-old convention of men blaming women for tempting them into the act. Radcliffe's avoided incestuous rape/murder scene locates such threats as symptoms of a social structure that disempowers younger brothers and women in a perpetuation of unbalanced power and wealth.[101] Schedoni's rape of his brother's wife establishes that he is able to commit sexual violence and tie together murder (of brother), rape (of sister-in-law) and usurpation (of title and estates).[102] Incest functions very differently here from its deployment in configurations that focus on its potential for creating ideal relationships or social structures.[103] By positioning uncle–niece incest alongside murder, thefts and usurpations, such thefts and violence are portrayed as unnatural yet endorsed and normalised by the inherently aberrant structure of familial power in the existing patriarchal order.

The link between representations of violence and incest in the Gothic is noted by Wright, who argues that the 'genre's treatment of violence, murder and incest is linked symbiotically to issues of sexuality and gender within the fiction'.[104] These concerns are further united with theft, inheritance and the law as well. In the uncle–niece configuration the act or desire of incest is not cast as unnatural or deviant but, when represented as violent or forceful, the actions of ownership, theft and usurpation that it underpins are so presented. Incestuous desires and sexual threats are bound up with the desire to own female bodies and possessions, of which rape and sex become another form of theft and control.

Incest is not unnatural; however, the forcing of it – the unlawful seizure of property and the unlawful seizure of sexuality – is inherently unjust and sanctioned by a social structure governed by the laws that prohibit female inheritance and ownership of property and body. Emily's attempt to purchase herself from Montoni and his men and Charlotte's purchase of Matilda from Weimar emphasise this issue of incest as a form of male ownership of female bodies. As women cannot own themselves (their bodies as property) before marriage, after marriage the ability to gain female self-control and ownership becomes even more improbable.[105]

Undesired incest functions to denaturalise the male usurpation of female bodies and properties. Incest's unification of sex and family mirrors, in a distorted fashion, the concept of inheritance – itself a combination of wealth and family. Much as inheritances seized wrongfully are presented as unjust usurpations, forced or threatening incest is likewise grounded in the language of unnatural desires. Intertwining familial theft with familial rape, the Gothic presents the complex relationship between patriarchal structures of inheritance, family and sexuality and demonstrates how such structures allow men to use sex as a weapon against women, particularly those who defy the structures by ownership of property or wealth.[106] When women assert their natural claims of ownership of themselves and their property, they are raped, imprisoned and murdered. The men who commit these acts of theft and violence are the younger brothers who did not inherit either title or fortune and have thus been impeded in their quests for female companionship in favour of their older, titled, landed brothers. The younger brothers reconstitute themselves as dominant by murdering the sibling they feel has displaced them through the privilege of birth and strip the women who have inherited when they could not, taking by force and sexual aggression what they were unable to inherit.

The usurpation of what was denied by inheritance laws allows the younger brother to break the legal system of succession and tradition. Schmidgen argues regarding Blackstone's metaphor of the Gothic castle that it 'can be completely intertwined with the common law. That complexity is only increased by Blackstone's allusion to the popular notion of English constitutional rights as an inheritance.'[107] If English constitutional rights are an inheritance they are inherited by primogeniture, for it is clear that women were no more liable to receive justice under the law than to receive property when they had a male sibling. Primogeniture, which is responsible for Schedoni's being entitled only to a small allowance as a younger brother, explains, in part, his actions. But in spite of his own rebellion against the system of property inheritance and continuity, Schedoni positions himself as patriarchal head of first Olivia and then Ellena. Once Schedoni has declared himself Ellena's father, Ellena finds herself under paternal protection that is depicted as worthless. Schedoni refuses to listen to Ellena regarding her safety, future and desires, discounting her concerns regarding Spalatro, refusing to answer her questions about Vivaldi's whereabouts and ultimately lying to her. He informs Ellena that she will be placed in a convent instead of returning to her home as he promised and when she suggests her preferred convent he does not respond. Whatever protection Schedoni's paternal status lends to Ellena is negated by the control he assumes over her life.

Schedoni's paternal authority echoes the maternal ownership the abbess and the Marchesa attempted to wield over Ellena by stripping her of a voice in her future choices after her abduction and imprisonment, exemplified by the abbess's command that Ellena: '"must determine either to accept the veil, or the person whom the Marchesa di Vivaldi had, of her great goodness, selected for her husband"' (p. 109). Ellena's indignation at what she privately calls the tyrannical injustice of this proposal is evidenced through rebellion as she states: '"I am prepared to meet whatever suffering you shall inflict upon me; but be assured, that my own voice never shall sanction the evils to which I may be subjected, and that the immortal love of justice, which fills all my heart, will sustain my courage no less powerfully than the sense of what is due to my own character"' (p. 110). Like Emily, Ellena is defiant; she has a strong sense of entitlement based on her inner worth of character. Scholarship is divided on the question of Ellena's defiance or passivity; Johnson suggests that despite her refusal to relinquish Vivaldi, 'Ellena is the most classically feminine of Radcliffe's heroines, a model of passive fortitude enduring the action of others upon her rather than initiating her own.'[108] In contrast, Miles finds that Ellena's unwillingness to surrender her lover is unconventionally defiant, arguing that she 'shows herself a true Gothic heroine in subordinating her desires to those of dynastically-minded parents ... she also proves an atypical one, when, under the threat of having to abandon Vivaldi, she admits and refuses to relinquish her desire, and this, as much as dignity, is shown to be "due to her own character".'[109] Ellena's resistance is typical of most Gothic heroines who claim to abide by the dynastic requirements of the older generation while inwardly resolving to do the opposite. Kilgour notes the rebellious nature of this defiance, arguing that: 'the lovers themselves are revolutionary figures in their resistance to these false systems which unnaturally impede the fulfilment of their individual desires'.[110] Ellena (and Vivaldi) challenge the ancient and archaic systems that preceded them and revise the system – and its unnatural repression of desire – into a model that allows for individual choice and desires.[111]

This new structure is presented at the novel's end when individual desires are finally realised and the cycle of incestuous thefts has ended. When Vivaldi asks Olivia for Ellena's hand in marriage she consents if his father does and, having ascertained that Ellena is not Schedoni's daughter but that of the respectable Count di Bruno, he accedes to the union. As Kilgour describes it, the novel enables a reconciliation 'achieved by the removal of false figures of authority, and the gradual emergence of good models already present in the system. Schedoni turns out to be a false father, so that Ellena is not contaminated by her origins ... the text trots out the familiar themes of fraternal rivalry, jealousy, fratricide, and a usurpation of both property and wife'.[112] The couple marries and a fete is held at one of Vivaldi's estates that they choose as their main residence: a 'scene of fairy-land' (p. 473) that stands on the entrance of a valley to the bay, with pleasure gardens and shores sloping to the water. There are groves of magnolia, ash and palms, elegant halls and views; from the estate one can see 'beyond the rich foliage the seas and shores of Naples, from the west; and to the east, views of the valley of the domain, withdrawing among winding hills wooded to their summits' (p. 473). This idyllic retreat is less a gradual emergence of a model already present in the text but appears as the Garden of Eden, a new world that has sprung whole out of nothing. While Ellis describes the Female Gothic as a narrative in which 'the heroine exposes the villain's usurpation and thus reclaims an enclosed space that should have been a refuge from evil but has become the very opposite – a prison' – this only partially describes the narratives which more generally involve the heroine leaving the prison behind rather than reclaiming it.[113] Gothic heroines find new refuges, new structures in which to create an idealised egalitarian sphere. The domestic world Vivaldi and Ellena choose is untouched by the presence of the past and is radical in its democratic nature. The servant Paulo declares that they are in a paradise they had to travel through purgatory to reach, reiterating that they are in an Eden wherein all ranks of people are welcome and received as the couple shares their abundance and joy.[114] The archaic constraints and structures of a social system that denies love based on genealogies and perpetuates thefts of female bodies and property by male family members are nowhere present in Ellena and Vivaldi's egalitarian society.

When examining the role of the uncle and his actions towards his brother, sister-in-law and niece, a layered critique of the dominant social structuring of family and the participants within it coalesces. By killing his brother and taking his wife, the uncle displaces the patriarch to establish himself as familial head.[115] The uncle thus fulfils a conventional role: the abuse victim turned abuser, becoming complicit with the system having claimed a position of power within it.[116] Such an understanding makes reading the Gothic as a conservative textual form impossible: the uncles are not too rebellious, but rather not rebellious enough. The familial structure that places the uncle as the protector post-displacement of the elder brother lends itself to the usurpations, incestuous desires and abuses even when the uncle inherits this role without committing murder.[117] The uncle then threatens the lineage, namesake and inheritance of the heroine, who, as a female free of a father to control her property and body, represents a dangerous threat to the hegemonic order.[118] While the uncle and niece often experience uncomfortably close roles, existing in the margins of the society that denies them access to power, the Gothic uncle ultimately joins the system. One of the reasons the Gothic's radical ideas are so contested is because of how the transgressions within the genre are simultaneously celebrated and punished.[119] The complex and paradoxical figure of the uncle subscribes to the usurpations and violations of the female body that render his incestuous acts a mode of upholding the dominant hegemony's ideologies of sexuality and laws.[120] Kilgour's explanation of Gothic incest as abnormal and subversive of social requirements, reconfigured in light of incest's frequent portrayal as normal and natural in the genre, can be used to understand how incest is depicted as natural and normal while subverting social requirements and unnatural while maintaining them.[121] Incest in the Gothic is thus naturalised due to its location as abnormal and transgressive by the laws of a heteronormative society.

When women are denied their inheritance – of rights or of estates – it is because neither the constitutional freedoms nor legal protection of property apply to them. The uncle is representative of the patriarchal order: a thief who has stolen property, title, wealth and freedom. Uniting these thefts with sexual threats reiterates the way the structure of inheritance and law steals rights and wealth through a denial predicated on gender. Just as primogeniture grants wealth and title to one brother but not to the other, society grants all its protection and benefits to only one gender. The uncle's incestuous desires, whether (like Weimar's) developing naturally to be exploited later, arising solely from the desire to force compliance (as Montoni's) or inextricably linked to past crimes and present ones (as Schedoni's are), are all unified with thefts of property and physical violence, illuminating the cyclical nature of injustice and abuse within a contained system and reiterating the necessity of the heroine's escape from and destruction of it in order to be free from the genealogy of usurpations. The incestuous violence underscores the family structure that inherently promotes such abuses, itself a microcosm of the larger social structure.[122] Incestuous threats, rape and violence are impossible to disentangle from their use as weapons to enforce the ownership and control of female bodies and properties and as productions of the uneven power distribution affected by a patriarchal culture that demands such controls. The uncle seems to represent, more than any other male family figure in the Gothic, the threat of patriarchy in general terms, shadowy, lurking men who are intent on a combination of thefts from women – of their bodies through kidnap and rape, of their property through usurpation of property and title, of their lives through murder. There is almost always an element of incestuous sexual abuse tied to thefts of property, a highlighting of the ties between body and purse, female genitalia and property seizure. Authors of the Gothic were perfectly aware of the way the female body figured into the exchange of money and property necessary to preserve patriarchy and through the figure of the uncle are able to literalise how dangerous the traditional structuring of family is to female liberty and desires.

NOTES

1 Eliza Parsons, *The Castle of Wolfenbach* (London: The Folio Press, 1968), p. 12. Subsequent references will be given in the text.
2 In addition to Sue Chaplin's important studies of the Gothic and law, recently, chapters in Diana Wallace and Andrew Smith (eds), *The Female Gothic: New Directions* (Basingstoke: Palgrave Macmillan, 2009) by Diana Wallace, Marie Mulvey-Roberts and Lauren Fitzgerald have focused on the intricacies of Gothic heroines, estates, and legal rights within marriage, applying William

Blackstone's 1765 legal text and its Gothic themes to representations of ownership of property, knowledge and women in the genre.

3 Susan Staves, *Married Women's Separate Property in England, 1660–1833* (Cambridge, MA: Harvard University Press, 1990), pp. 25–6.

4 Eugenia C. DeLamotte, *Perils of the Night: A Feminist Study of Nineteenth-Century Gothic* (Oxford: Oxford University Press, 1990), pp. 21–2. DeLamotte then focuses on the 'deep structures' of women's psychological experiences relating to and in the Gothic genre, whereas my focus is on the legal, social and anthropological overlappings of transgression and what this nexus means for traditional scholarly treatments of incest within the Female Gothic.

5 Maggie Kilgour, *The Rise of the Gothic Novel* (London: Routledge, 1995), p. 20.

6 See Diane Long Hoeveler's *Gothic Feminism: The Professionalization of Gender from Charlotte Smith to the Brontës* (Liverpool: Liverpool University Press, 1998), in which she describes Gothic heroines as imagining their fathers are trying to rape or kill them (p. 57). A scholarly tradition that views the father as persecutor or the heroine as imagining this to be true when this is often not supported by closer textual analyses has been imposed on Gothic novels; this is particularly true of the novels by Radcliffe examined in this chapter.

7 Juliet Mitchell believes patriarchal structures enforce the incest taboo to maintain control of the exchange of women, an exchange jeopardised by incestuous relations that would unbalance the power of the father (or father figure) in *Psychoanalysis and Feminism: Freud, Reich, Laing and Women* [1974] (repr. as *Psychoanalysis and Feminism: A Radical Reassessment of Freudian Psychoanalysis*, New York: Basic Books, 2000).

8 The appearance of law and property as a thematic alongside uncle–niece incest necessitates an examination of exchange. The threats and violence against female bodies aligned with property seizure reifies the concept of female exchanges between men.

9 Angela Wright, *Gothic Fiction: A Reader's Guide to Essential Criticism* (Basingstoke: Palgrave Macmillan, 2007), p. 135.

10 Kilgour, p. 8. Kilgour further identifies the wealth of criticism that argues that 'whatever radical and subversive implications the gothic might have are radically limited by its own inconsistencies' (p. 9).

11 As the uncle adheres to the available structures of law and power to usurp and grasp at the powers denied to him as the younger brother, so too does the Gothic adhere to a generic structure. The Gothic deploys the sexualities perceived by society as aberrant that are inherent in the genre to undermine gender and sexual ideologies, ultimately showing the futility of using/abusing forms grounded in such uneven distributions of power as capable of only further entrenching one in the existing power relation, advocating instead the position taken by the heroine – to abandon the extant forms.

12 This is the case in Parsons's *Wolfenbach*, Radcliffe's *The Castles of Athlin and Dunbayne*, *The Romance of the Forest* (1791) and *The Italian* (1797) and Eleanor Sleath's *The Orphan of the Rhine* (1798), in which fratricide and sister-in-law rape are part of the plot.

13 One of the most important examinations of the Gothic and law is Sue Chaplin's *The Gothic and the Rule of Law, 1764–1820* (Basingstoke and London: Palgrave Macmillan, 2007), in which she argues that 'Radcliffe's cryptic, Gothic, *maternal* spaces are subversively implicated in the law's economy of familiarization, remembrance and retribution' (p. 96) and that 'Radcliffe's female Gothic interrogates more deeply than [Sophia] Lee's possibilities and problematics of feminine inheritance within a legal temporality that is radically "out of joint"' (p. 96).

14 Kilgour, p. 9.

15 Kilgour, p. 14.

16 Diana Wallace, '"The Haunting Idea": Female Gothic Metaphors and Feminist Theory', in Wallace and Smith, *The Female Gothic: New Directions*, pp. 27–31.

17 In Parsons's *Wolfenbach*, Radcliffe's *The Castles of Athlin and Dunbayne*, *The Romance of the Forest* and *The Italian* and Sleath's *The Orphan of the Rhine*, younger brothers are bypassed by familial riches and usurp their older brothers' wealth, titles, wives and daughters.

18 Sir William Blackstone, *Commentaries on the laws of England. Book the second. By William Blackstone, Esq. vinerian professor of law, and solicitor general to her majesty*, 4 vols (Oxford: Clarendon Press, 1768), II, p. 268.

19 Wolfram Schmidgen, *Eighteenth-Century Fiction and the Law of Property* (Cambridge: Cambridge University Press, 2002), p. 166.

20 A more detailed analysis of eighteenth-century understandings of natural law and their application to Gothic representations of obligation, incest and individual rights can be found in the following chapter.

21 Ruth Bienstock Anolik, 'The missing mother: the meanings of maternal absence in the Gothic mode', *Modern Language Studies*, 33:1/2 (2003), 27.

22 Michel Foucault in *The History of Sexuality Volume I: An Introduction*, trans. R. Hurley [1979] (Harmondsworth: Penguin, repr. 1981), argues that: 'the deployment of alliance has as one of its chief objectives to reproduce the interplay of relation and maintain the law that governs them; the deployment of sexuality, on the other hand, engenders a continual extension of areas and forms of control' and that since the eighteenth century the deployment of alliance has been displaced by the deployment of sexuality (p. 106).

23 Sociologist Vikki Bell suggests that Foucault's argument places incest 'at the crossroads between the two sex deployments … because whereas the deployment of alliance forbids incest, the deployment of sexuality actually incites it' in *Interrogating Incest: Feminism, Foucault and the Law* (London: Routledge,

1993), p. 95. Foucault's chronology of the deployments of alliance and sexuality positions my examinations of representations of incest and its prohibition in eighteenth-century Gothic novels as written in the context of the deployment of alliance. I use Bell's point to argue that Gothic representations of incest prior to this deployment locate tensions between the prohibition of incest and incestuous desires as incited through the unequal power relations necessary to maintain the deployment of alliance.

24 Kilgour, p. 121.

25 What Foucault refers to as laws designed to reproduce the system of alliance (p. 106) are represented in the Gothic as the unnatural control of women, the exchange of women and laws surrounding female inheritance and property that incite incestuous threats. Such structures of law served to maintain male control over female bodies in order to exchange them and reproduce kinship circles while locating power within the hands of male kin. That the female body becomes a commodity under male control necessitates its sexualisation and thus its location as a potential site of incestuous desires and threats.

26 See Ellen Pollak's *Incest and the English Novel, 1684–1814* (Baltimore: Johns Hopkins University Press, 2003). Pollak argues that during the long eighteenth century legal impediments to marriage were being questioned and 'incest was increasingly being naturalized within emergent theories of natural law' (p. 19).

27 Although anthropological theories on sexual aversion would point towards Weimar being disinclined to commit incest with his niece, his separation from her occurs at a critical moment in physical development – the change between pre- and post-pubescence.

28 See Judith Lewis Herman with Lisa Hirschman, *Father–Daughter Incest* (Cambridge, MA: Harvard University Press, 1981), in which they argue that the common reaction of fathers to their daughters' reaching adolescence is often an attempt to establish total control over their emerging sexuality (p. 117). In Jane Austen's *Mansfield Park* (1814), the portrayal of Sir Thomas Bertram 'noticing' his grown-up niece, Fanny Price, bears similarities to Parsons's scene.

29 Kilgour, p. 12.

30 This notion, analysed in greater detail in the preceding chapters, bears brief repetition to demonstrate how differently incest functions within the uncle–niece relationships than in those previously explored.

31 Instances of older male relatives showing pornography to their younger female relatives occur frequently in case studies on present-day incest abuse such as those detailed in Jean Renvoize's *Incest: A Family Pattern* (London: Routledge & Kegan Paul Ltd, 1982).

32 See Jennie Batchelor's analysis of Sarah Scott's *Millenium Hall* (1762), in which she argues that the gifts offered to a young ward by her older male guardian

and her reciprocal 'gift' of gratitude constitute an 'obligation he forces upon Louisa [that] will lead only to her destruction'. Jennie Batchelor, *Women's Work: Labour, Gender, Authorship, 1750-1830* (Manchester: Manchester University Press, 2010), p. 47. That Matilda resists the obligation of gratitude intended by the gift giving that Batchelor notes eighteenth-century readers 'perceive[... as an inevitable prelude to seduction' (p. 47) positions her as withstanding the sexual advances of her uncle that would have been anticipated by the novel's readers.

33 Lena Dominelli, 'Betrayal of trust: a feminist analysis of power relationships in incest abuse and its relevance for social work practice', *British Journal of Social Work*, 19:1 (1989), 291-308.

34 Angie Ash, *Father-Daughter Sexual Abuse: The Abuse of Paternal Authority* (Bangor: University College of North Wales, 1984), p. 9.

35 Pollak, pp. 36-8.

36 Pollak, p. 37.

37 T. G. A. Nelson, 'Representations of Incest in Dryden and his English Contemporaries', in Elizabeth Barnes (ed.), *Incest and the Literary Imagination* (Gainesville, FL: University of Florida Press, 2002), p. 122; see also pp. 117-37.

38 Michel Foucault, *Power/Knowledge: Selected Interviews and Other Writings 1972-1977*, ed. Colin Gordon, trans. Colin Gordon *et al.* (Brighton: Harvester Press, 1980), p. 93.

39 Pollak, p. 38.

40 Herman and Hirschman define incestuous behaviour as any sexually motivated act that violates a relationship between a child and adult in a position of familial power, regardless of blood kinship (p. 27). I widen this definition to include adults, so that incest is any sexual behaviour (implicit or explicit) between people in a familial relationship regardless of consanguineal ties as well as between blood kin unaware of the bond or between blood kin who are aware of it but were not raised in a familial relationship.

41 Austen echoes this with Edmund Bertram's comments regarding Sir Thomas's admiration of Fanny that distress her in *Mansfield Park*, ed. Margaret Drabble (New York: Signet, 1996), p. 181.

42 Kilgour, p. 31.

43 Kate Ferguson Ellis, 'Can You Forgive Her? The Gothic Heroine and Her Critics', in David Punter (ed.), *Companion to the Gothic* (Oxford: Blackwell, 2000), pp. 264-5.

44 With this manoeuvre Parsons effectively disintegrates the class boundaries between servant and master, elevating Albert above Matilda's uncle via his virtue and lack of depraved/incestuous desires.

45 This lends weight to Herman's definition of incest as based more on an abuse of power than a transgression between blood kin. Matilda's distress responds

to her uncle's plan to force her, an easy task given his position of authority, not to the possibility of his kinship (which is at this point unclear to her).

46 The different ways heroines regard family or non-family members who caress them is analysed further in Chapter 4 in an examination of the presence or potential presence of a blood tie as alternately permitting or prohibiting physical and emotional closeness not allowed to a non-consanguineal relation.

47 See Cynthia Klekar and Linda Zionkowski (eds), *The Culture of the Gift in Eighteenth-Century England* (Basingstoke: Palgrave Macmillan, 2009) for an excellent treatment of gift exchange and theories of obligation in eighteenth-century England. Parsons invokes the language of obligation and liberty in a way that depicts the eighteenth-century understandings (evidenced in works such as Jean-Jacques Rousseau's *The Social Contract, or Principles of Political Right* (1762) and *Emile, or On Education* (1762)) of women as obliged to perform duties for family (and thus society) without the freedoms or liberty awarded to men as an unfair demand productive of female misery and enslavement.

48 See Luce Irigaray, *This Sex Which is Not One* [1977], trans. Catherine Porter and Carolyn Burke (Ithaca, NY: Cornell University Press, 1985), in which Irigaray argues against the traditional anthropological understanding of the exchange of women as essential to culture: 'the exchanges upon which patriarchal societies are based take place exclusively among men. Women, signs, commodities, currency all pass from one man to another; if it were otherwise, we are told, the social order would fall back upon incestuous and exclusively endogamous ties that would paralyze all commerce' (p. 192).

49 This furthers my reading of Foucault's deployment of alliance as not exclusive of the deployment of sexuality. What Foucault discusses as 'the link between partners and the definite statutes' (p. 106) – the laws governing alliance and exchange – are themselves structures of power pertinent to the deployment of alliance. Such structures of dominance and submission are inherently sources of pleasure that, as representations of incest in the Gothic make clear, charge the laws and statutes governing kinship with a sexual element made explicit in the male control of female bodies within the family. For an excellent treatment of Foucault's denial of eroticism inherent in power structures, see Leo Bersani, 'Foucault, Freud, Fantasy, and power', *GLQ: A Journal of Lesbian and Gay Studies* 2 (1995), 17–19.

50 Charlotte's attempts to free Matilda from male control provide a clear link to the sentimental novel, which often criticised women's dependence on men – writers such as Charlotte Smith, Sarah Scott and Frances Burney used the form of the sentimental novel to depict a female protagonist's struggles and highlight the dangers of female dependency on male authority figures, often family members.

51 Robert Miles, *Gothic Writing, 1750–1820: A Genealogy* (London: Routledge, 1993), p. 25.
52 Miles, *Gothic Writing*, p. 98.
53 We will see later how in Radcliffe's *The Italian* the sudden appearance of a blood tie grants a total stranger authority over the previously (relatively) autonomous Ellena.
54 Jane Austen, *Sense and Sensibility*, ed. Claudia L. Johnson (New York: W. W. Norton, 2002), p. 18.
55 We can see this in many examples, such as in how *Wolfenbach* influences not only *Sense and Sensibility* but is itself influenced by Sarah Scott's earlier *The History of Cornelia* (1750) and *Millenium Hall* (1762) regarding notions of unfair female obligation, relentless pursuits by men and criticisms of female dependence.
56 Lauren Fitzgerald, 'Female Gothic and the Institutionalization of Gothic Studies', in Wallace and Smith, *The Female Gothic: New Directions*, p. 15.
57 See Jerrold E. Hogle's recent chapter 'Recovering the Walpolean Gothic: *The Italian: Or, the Confessional of the Black Penitents* (1796–1797)', in Dale Townshend and Angela Wright (eds), *Ann Radcliffe, Romanticism and the Gothic* (Cambridge: Cambridge University Press, 2014), pp. 151–67, in which he re-examines *The Italian* as both a response to Lewis's *The Monk* and, importantly, as an attempt to achieve the blending of new and old forms of romance that Walpole outlines as his goal in *Otranto*.
58 Fitzgerald, pp. 12–16.
59 E. J. Clery, *The Rise of Supernatural Fiction, 1762–1800* (Cambridge: Cambridge University Press, 1995), pp. 126–7.
60 Fitzgerald, pp. 17–20.
61 Robert Miles, '"Mother Radcliffe": Ann Radcliffe and the Female Gothic', in Wallace and Smith, *The Female Gothic: New Directions*, p. 51.
62 Ash, p. 39. Ash's discussion is in the context of the father's violent threats to enforce the daughter's sexual submission, but its applicability to the uncle–niece binary is apparent.
63 Ann Radcliffe, *The Mysteries of Udolpho*, ed. Bonamy Dobrée (Oxford: Oxford University Press, 1998), p. 138. Subsequent references will be given in the text.
64 Ash explores how this power subordinates women economically, politically and legally, fastening them into institutions that ensure their continued subordination.
65 For example, Hoeveler writes in *Gothic Feminism* that heroines seek the most malleable and feminised male protector they can to manipulate him (pp. 36–50).
66 Lee Holcombe, *Wives and Property: Reform of the Married Women's Property Law in Nineteenth-Century England* (Toronto: University of Toronto Press, 1983), p. 6.

67 Claudia L. Johnson, *Equivocal Beings: Politics, Gender, and Sentimentality in the 1790s* (Chicago: University of Chicago Press, 1995), p. 99.
68 Kilgour, p. 120. Emily, interestingly, the female, English version of Rousseau's eponymous Emile, refuses to submit to the vision of female compliance to male authority that Montoni desires and that reflects Rousseau's attitudes towards female education and placement in society detailed in *Emile*, particularly in Book V.
69 For further contextualisation of how sexual threats are linked to women's fears of other types of assaults, see Kenneth F. Ferraro, 'Women's fear of victimization: shadow of sexual assault', *Social Forces*, 75:2 (1996), 667–90.
70 Holcombe, pp. 38–9. Holcombe describes the ability of married women to retain separate property in several ways via the Court of Chancery, which allowed this to be done in equity, and generally accepted any trust created for a married woman.
71 Holcombe, p. 43. Because Madame Montoni refused to sign documents that would give Montoni possession of her states and left hidden papers for Emily that appear to give her possession of the estates (or reinforce Emily's right to the estates if they were already assigned to return to the family), one can assume she had 'unrestricted rights over her separate property' (Holcombe, p. 43), which, as Radcliffe shows, did not protect wives from a husband's avarice.
72 DeLamotte, p. 181. This description is followed by an analysis of the constraints Gothic heroines face in having to maintain female decorum while preserving themselves. DeLamotte concludes that Gothic heroines escape via mental transcendence in contemplation of the sublime, yet Gothic heroines also manage physical escapes.
73 April London, *Women and Property in the Eighteenth-Century Novel* (Cambridge: Cambridge University Press, 1999), p. 25. London argues that the inevitable conclusion to the individualist ethic is either to establish the hero as landed gentry and cause the heroine's end via figurative death in marriage, or, failing this, a literal death. While this dichotomy tends to overlook other outcomes (such as endings where the heroine is established as the partner with property or novels where the hero's status as landed gentry was never questioned), the idea of the individualist ethic is essential to understanding Gothic heroines and their integrity.
74 Robert Miles, *Ann Radcliffe: The Great Enchantress* (Manchester: Manchester University Press, 1995), p. 137.
75 Kilgour, p. 120.
76 See Irigaray, p. 84; pp. 171–89.
77 See further discussion of this in Miles's *Ann Radcliffe*, p. 64.
78 Kathleen Barry, *Female Sexual Slavery* (New York: New York University Press, 1978), p. 163.

79 Emily's 'purchase' of herself is akin to that of Charlotte's purchase of Matilda from her uncle in *Wolfenbach* and contributes to the destruction of the system of exchange that Irigaray describes as denying the woman as object/commodity such self-possession: 'how can such objects of use and transaction claim the right to speak and to participate in exchange in general? Commodities, as we all know, do not take themselves to market on their own' (p. 84).

80 Johnson argues, by contrast, that Emily and her aunt 'possess more in the way of manly spirit than men do in the novel. Any emancipatory import this chiasmus might support, however, collapses; a woman's heroism stops with her body. She cedes her property as soon as Montoni threatens her with gang rape', pp. 108–9.

81 DeLamotte, p. 156.

82 DeLamotte discusses Emily's self-defence and conscious worth in contrast to Samuel Richardson's *Clarissa* (1747–48), noting the ambiguity of Gothic writers in showing that consciousness of virtue is not enough to save the heroine; escape or salvation must remove them from the threat in another way as well (pp. 32–5). This inability of consciousness of worth to protect the Gothic heroine draws attention to the necessity of the law or society to offer protection that mere chastity and innocence will not.

83 Johnson, p. 104.

84 Johnson describes Emily as 'framing her resistance to Montoni in Wollstonecraftian terms of rights' and notes her 'suffering to keep her property for Valancourt' while he is gambling in Paris (p. 108).

85 Kilgour, p. 138.

86 Kilgour, p. 161.

87 Ann Radcliffe, *The Italian*, ed. Deborah Rogers (New York: Penguin, 1995), p. 417. Subsequent references will be given in the text.

88 Kilgour, p. 25.

89 The compassion Schedoni feels reflects DeLamotte's understanding of the Gothic heroine's ability to evoke pity in the villain as ambiguous and inadequate compared to Richardsonian heroines. Her argument applies here as Ellena's ability to inspire Schedoni with pity and hesitancy to murder her is ultimately inadequate; it is rather the chance of familial recognition that spares her.

90 E. J. Clery, *Women's Gothic: From Clara Reeve to Mary Shelley* (Tavistock: Northcote House, 2000), p. 82.

91 Johnson likewise notes the sexual violence of the scene, describing Schedoni as attempting to 'penetrate/murder the sleeping girl' p. 127.

92 Schedoni's understanding of a 'father' gives him the right at once to touch and command his presumed daughter.

93 Ruth Perry, *Novel Relations: The Transformation of Kinship in English Literature and Culture 1748–1818* (Cambridge: Cambridge University Press, 2004), p. 102.
94 See Chapter 4 for further analyses of proofs of kinship as allowing caresses or behaviour that would otherwise be considered inappropriate.
95 See Chapter 2 for an examination of the proofs and evidence necessary to establishing kinship or denying the possibility of a consanguineal bond.
96 Johnson argues that the intensity of the attraction between Ellena and Olivia 'momentarily threatens to overturn the heterosexual plot altogether by privileging erotic sisterhood' but that this potential is 'finally reabsorbed into the heterosexual economy: once Olivia is identified as Ellena's long-lost mother, her importance subsides' (p. 135).
97 Perry, p. 395.
98 Miles, *Gothic Writing*, p. 171.
99 Ironically, although Schedoni wants to exchange Ellena for increased status via a marriage to Vivaldi – a marriage she also desires – he cannot. He compromised his ability to promote this marriage by having agreed with the Marchesa that Ellena is a scheming girl prior to his discovery that she is his kin.
100 Kilgour, p. 169.
101 Perry states 'the effect of these legal innovations in marriage settlements of the late seventeenth century was to diminish the proportion of a family's resources that went to female offspring and younger sons' (p. 213).
102 Olivia, Ellena's mother and Schedoni's sister-in-law, is not explicitly described as being raped by Schedoni, but as her marriage to him was forced, it follows that the sex was non-consensual.
103 See particularly Chapter 2 for analyses of the Gothic's representations of brother-sister incestuous relationships as ideal and egalitarian in nature.
104 Wright, p. 147.
105 Though this generalises the laws that moved female-held property to husbands and excludes exceptions (such as entailments or primogeniture instances where property remained in the family when a female was the sole remaining family member) that have been discussed in the section on Radcliffe's *Udolpho*, it reflects how these laws are represented in the Gothic. For a further examination of the restraints imposed by women's commodification see Irigaray, p. 84.
106 Examples of this include the repercussions suffered by Madame Cheron for attempting to keep her own property in *Udolpho*, Olivia for resisting her brother-in-law in *The Italian* and Matilda for refusing her uncle in *Wolfenbach*.
107 Schmidgen, p. 166.
108 Johnson, p. 134.

109 Miles, *Gothic Writing*, p. 171.
110 Kilgour, p. 177.
111 I argue this in contrast to readings of Radcliffe's conclusions by scholars such as David Durrant in 'Ann Radcliffe and the conservative Gothic', *Studies in English Literature, 1500–1900*, 22:3 (1982), 519–31, who believes that the endings symbolise a return to a safe bourgeois familial structure headed by a genial patriarch.
112 Kilgour, p. 179.
113 Kate Ferguson Ellis, *The Contested Castle: Gothic Novels and the Subversion of Domestic Ideology* (Urbana: University of Illinois Press, 1989), p. xii. Just as Ellena leaves her prisons, so too does Emily leave Castle Udolpho, Julia flees the patriarchal castle in *A Sicilian Romance* and Laurette abandons an ancestral home turned prison in *The Orphan of the Rhine*.
114 In contrast, Johnson argues that the 'purely imaginary landscape of fairyland' and Paolo's 'effusive absurdity' at the novel's conclusion indicate the extent to which Radcliffe must go to reconcile the 'plethora of last-minute adjustments too strained to stand up to scrutiny' and 'establish an epithalamium' (p. 136).
115 This blurring of roles between father and uncle is most pronounced in the confusion over Schedoni's status as father or uncle to Ellena, a position that is unclear due to both his belief he is her father based on her miniature and his having married and fathered a child with Ellena's mother.
116 See Bersani, who argues that 'the oppressed, having freed themselves from their oppressors, hasten to imitate them' (22).
117 Montoni, like Heathcliff in Emily Brontë's *Wuthering Heights* (1847), inherits a position of power over his niece by marriage.
118 The uncle's assumption of the paternal role is an attempt to reinscribe control over the relatively free body of the heroine that, in its assumption, highlights the sexual and incestuous nature of such a position of power.
119 See Fred Botting, *Gothic: The New Critical Idiom* (London: Routledge, 1996), pp. 4–11.
120 An ongoing topic of scholarly debate on the Gothic is whether the genre represents (overall) a radical commentary with pro-revolution themes or a conservative, bourgeois understanding of family and society.
121 See the Introduction and Chapter 5 for a more detailed examination of how male incestuous desires, while prohibited, are often normalised in incest discourse while female incestuous desires are prohibited and considered deviant and unnatural.
122 Ash describes the behaviour of family members as reflective of broader social relations and power structures, and that the historic view of 'women and children as property of their male protectors … has supported the use of male aggression to maintain dominance' (pp. 4–5).

4
More than just kissing: cousins and the changing status of family

> 'My Welch cousin is the very thing for a tête à tête.'
> Charlotte Smith, *Emmeline* (1788)[1]

Amongst the many tangled familial relationships in the Gothic that are fraught with incestuous desires and passions, cousin relationships occupy a curious space in which the incestuous nature of the bond is at once diminished and heightened by its relative acceptance by both English society and the law. Cousin marriages may be more permissible than other relationships between blood kin because the consanguineal tie, in terms of shared genetic material, is weaker than those between the more taboo incestuous relationships, such as mother–son, father–daughter or brother–sister. The difficulty in coming to a clear consensus regarding the incestuous nature of cousin marriage is demonstrated by the irreconcilable differences between leading scientists and anthropologists on cousin incest. Sociobiologist Joseph Shepher argues that 'most cultural forms of mating', including preferential cousin marriages, 'represent cultural regulations aimed at *optimum* inbreeding'.[2] Shepher defines incest as 'mating between relatives, called inbreeding' and that 'as a technical term, *inbreeding* is reserved for cases in which discernible traces can be followed back to common ancestors within two to three generations'.[3] Certainly cousins count in this regard, their shared relations being grandparents. But not everyone agrees with this definition of incest. Biologist William Shields contends that while extreme inbreeding is 'associated with incest', incest is defined only as 'parent-offspring or full sibling matings'.[4] However, while children generally lose sexual interest in the siblings with whom they are raised, geneticist Patrick Bateson argues that people also tend 'to choose partners who are a bit different, but not too different', making the case that cousins fulfil this urge to mate with the similar.[5] So similar, in fact, that Shepher demonstrates that while paternal uncertainty means that all cousin marriages are not genetically equal, nonetheless, 'to marry your mother's brother's daughter is to marry the closest kin of your generation who is not from your own clan'.[6] First cousins share 12.5 per cent of their genetic material, compared to the 50 per cent shared with full siblings and parents, or the 25 per cent shared with grandparents; one is as genetically similar to one's first cousin as to a great-grandparent and half as related as to a half-sibling.[7]

Genetic and anthropological reasons for and against cousin couplings may seem to be coming from irreconcilably different schools of thought, but they both examine the seemingly contradictory nature of cousin marriage or mating. Genetically, such relationships can either benefit or harm a group depending on the presence of detrimental recessive alleles, making it a gamble, health-wise.[8] In anthropological terms, cousin marriage can result in either endogamy or exogamy, depending on the descent pattern of the social group and the type (cross or parallel) of cousin marriage.[9] While Claude Lévi-Strauss's view is that cross-cousin marriage is exogamous and parallel-cousin marriage is endogamous, other anthropologists, such as Martin Ottenheimer, challenge this assertion: 'close kin marriage does not necessarily result in social or genetic isolation. Marriages within a group may lessen the number of affinal connections between that group and others, but there are many other ways for alliances between groups to be established: trade, agreements, treaties, adoptions and the like.'[10] It seems, inevitably, that a consensus on either the genetic or anthropological consequences of cousin marriage is impossible to achieve. What becomes clear is that relationships between cousins are capable of benefiting or harming a family group in terms both physical and social.

The social aspects of cousin marriage that anthropologists have observed are equally scrutinised by historians and scholars who examine family and marriage in eighteenth-century British society. Ruth Perry analyses the change in kinship structures throughout the eighteenth century as emphasising conjugal ties over consanguineal, stating that 'the overdetermined emphasis on conjugality in English culture and the shedding of wider kin ties grew out of another economic imperative related to, but distinct from, issues of lineal inheritance or romantic love'.[11] Perry argues that the need for increased personal wealth in the changing economic structure contributed to making cousin marriage desirable, particularly among the members of the upper classes.[12] Cousin marriage became a viable option to allow the transfer of property from one paternal family to another while at the same time allowing the bulk of an estate or title to remain within the wider family line. In these instances cousin marriage is viewed, not with the horror of incestuous couplings that would destroy a patriarchal structure of exchange, but as a union that ought to be encouraged. Alternatively, it is just as possible for certain cousin marriages to do the opposite: to create an endogamic family that allows for title or wealth to remain in the family but does not allow for property or fortune to increase, or for the cousin to inhabit a position either outside of or socially inferior to the family. In these cases cousin marriage would ultimately damage the patriarchal structure that demands the exchange of women and would thus require a prohibition.[13] The changing structures that allowed the cousin to, in certain circumstances, become a desirable marriage choice positions this family role as alternately kin or non-kin, one that is capable of a flexibility that renders it particularly profitable to politically conservative and radical writers of the Gothic.

One of the difficulties faced in attempting to trace representations of cousin incest in Gothic novels is not a lack of representations but an overabundance. The variety of cousin relationships has led me to include a greater number of texts here than in the previous chapters, in order more fruitfully to tease out the social, legal and anthropological implications of their representation. The Gothic novels included do not focus solely on first-cousin marriage or relationships, but rather on a sampling representative of the range of cousin relationships, including first cousins, half-cousins, cousins by marriage, double cousins (the offspring of two sets of siblings) and cousins by adoption. Each of these different relationships is deployed in the novels to which they belong to emphasise a unique concern regarding questions of kinship and through a detailed analysis of the nature of the relationship, the relevance of the blood tie becomes clear. How cousins are viewed within the novels, as family members or as non-kin, is one of the ways we can understand whether the author is privileging the conjugal or the consanguineal bond. Some of the cousins examined equate their familial bond to that of siblings, placing their love on an even more consanguineal and egalitarian footing with parallels to the positioning of the brother-as-lover, while for others the cousin bond is utterly insignificant to their romantic love.[14] Interestingly, Perry reads the legality of cousin marriage in the eighteenth century as implicit compensation for the loss of brother–sister kinship: to allow cousin marriage 'is to assume that there is no sibling unity that transcends generations and that the sibling tie is dissolved by adulthood and marriage ... Marriage between the children of siblings also strengthens consanguineal ties, cementing the connections among members of natal families of origin in the next generation.'[15] Perry's point reinforces the idea that conjugal ties were increasingly more important than consanguineal ties and establishes the desire to link related families through marriage as based on economic necessity as well as a sense of familial obligation. The characters in the Gothic are driven to participate in cousin marriage from a variety of different motivations (duty and honour, threats, romantic love, sexual desire, financial need). Such a range of motivations and responses to cousin marriage establishes the complicated nexus the cousin as kin and/or spouse position inhabits, being at once legal and questionable, pressed for by family members and alternately repulsed by them.

It is essential to keep in mind when analysing kinship systems and marriage that people readily manipulate their kinship bonds to attain the most desirable result.[16] The very history of cousin marriage in England shows this to be the case. Henry VIII, for example, to pursue his own matrimonial desires, instituted legislature that allowed first-cousin marriages when previously such marriages had been illegal.[17] Cousin marriage remained an issue of debate throughout the seventeenth and eighteenth centuries in spite of Henry VIII having persuaded the church to accept it. Ellen Pollak points towards Samuel Taylor's *Marriages of Cousin Germans* (1673) and later works such as John Fry's *The Case of Marriages between Near Kindred* (1756) as evidence of the ongoing controversy.[18] Pollak states, referring to the various changes in statutes following the 1503 papal bull that allowed Henry to marry Catherine: 'Henry's determination to make the rules bend to dynastic and personal interests made them seem arbitrary.'[19] This ongoing confusion over the (il)legitimacy of cousin marriage continued for centuries, beyond even Chief Justice Vaughn's 1669 declaration of the legality of cousin marriage, and especially between secular and spiritual courts because the declaration 'challenged canon law'.[20] The challenge, however, did little to jeopardise the ecclesiastical courts' control over marriages between persons within the prohibited degrees for some centuries to come. As Polly Morris observes, 'In eighteenth- and nineteenth-century England ... canon law treated incest as an aspect of the church's regulation of marriage and dealt with it in the ecclesiastical courts.'[21]

The question of whether eighteenth-century literary representations of cousin marriage offer a suggestion of impropriety or immorality is contested by scholars in the field. Perry suggests such unions are presented as culturally accepted, stating that 'eighteenth-century fiction corroborates the cultural standing of these legal regulations. There is not the slightest indication of the least impropriety in first-cousin marriage in eighteenth-century novels.'[22] Pollak, however, argues in relation to Jane Austen's *Mansfield Park* (1814) character Sir Thomas Bertram that 'his scruples also pertain to the moral character of close kindred marriages. Although its respectability was much debated, cousin marriage in and of itself was not illegal.'[23] Such disagreements speak to the contested nature of the marriages that, while not illegal, occupied an uneasy place between acceptable and unacceptable unions between kin and continue to cause scholarly divide on their deployment in the literature of the time. Pollack's examination of the writings of Bishop Simon Patrick (1626–1707) underscores the extent to which law and religious and social values coalesce in late seventeenth/early eighteenth-century discourse on matrimony between family members. 'Commenting on Leviticus, Patrick acknowledges that moral determinations concerning the legitimacy of close kindred marriages are not solely matters of conscience but are also intimately tied to the vagaries of inheritance and property, as well as to prevailing definitions of honor – or, as it was sometimes also termed, honesty.'[24] Concerns over conjugal legitimacy may account for the low occurrence of such marriages: 'it was uncommon in practice in aristocratic circles in the eighteenth century, when only one percent of aristocrats married their first cousins'.[25] These moral and legal concerns regarding cousin marriage and incest eventually gave way to questions of a political and philosophical nature.

Pollak notes this shift, arguing that in respect of the earlier debates on cousin marriages that tended to locate the point of argument in 'the discourse of Reformation anticlericalism and seventeenth-century natural law, eighteenth-century writing about incest eventually reconstitutes its subject as part of a discourse of natural liberty'.[26] Pollak's understanding of this emergent discourse – which privileged the nature of the human subject over the institutions of law – exemplifies the philosophical changes leading up to the French Revolution. These eighteenth-century philosophical discussions of natural liberty and rights, such as those of Jean-Jacques Rousseau, used notions of contract theory and obligation to the state to argue that women's duties within the state should be to raise good citizens through their status in the family.[27] Such political and philosophical positioning of women as fundamental participants in the formation of good citizens cast their role in the language of both state and familial obligation. Eighteenth-century feminist thinkers such as Mary Wollstonecraft worried that the notions of contract theory and obligation to the state were manipulated unfairly by men in order to uphold familial models that denied women the right to exist as citizens and the freedom of choice, forcing them instead to exist as dependants within the familial structure.[28] Wollstonecraft intervened in Rousseau's debate, arguing that women must be citizens in order to fulfil this role and asserted the necessity of female citizenship and rights.[29] The social and familial demands on women without benefit of liberty and rights were thus repositioned as an unfair burden: an obligation without the corresponding gift of freedom or choice. Perry picks up on this in her analysis of how eighteenth-century spousal selection took on a new weight when tied up in these notions of individual rights.[30] Representations of cousin marriage, which so often depict the competing demands of family and individual desire, are thus equally grounded in the discourse of republicanism, natural rights and obligation inherent within these debates and become endowed with political significance in their appearance in the Gothic – a genre preoccupied with subversion and rebellion. Gothic writers used the genre's convention of incest and the contemporary discourse of natural liberty to charge representations of cousin marriage with an endogamous and disruptive potential that questions notions of female obligation to families (read: states) that would deny them the gift of individual rights and choice.[31]

Cousin relationships in the Gothic frequently subvert the importance placed on blood ties and compliance with familial marital demands and negotiate a focus on individual desires and choice. These themes develop and manifest in the different varieties of the Gothic I examine: the Radcliffean Gothic, the anti-Gothic and the sentimental Gothic. By locating the cousin as either kin, non-kin or a combination thereof, in order to trouble contemporary understandings of family and outsider, the figure of the cousin becomes the most readily manipulated figure through which writers could locate anxieties over the changing status of family and marriage. Cousin marriage is a versatile union in which incest is legal while still capable of being opposed on moral, familial, financial and emotional grounds. As such, the role of the cousin is of particular interest to writers of the Gothic, who can use it to represent an aristocratic, patriarchally sanctioned incest, a threatening familial force, an ideal spouse reflective of self or a sibling-like friend incapable of being viewed sexually. Through these different representations of the cousin as fluctuating between inside and outside the natal family, Gothic writers reveal their moderate, conservative or radical views regarding the struggles between the individual and the family.

Beginning with Charlotte Smith's *Emmeline* (1788), which blends the genre of the sentimental eighteenth-century novel with the Gothic, the cousin is ultimately rejected as a spousal choice in favour of non-kin. Smith's constant repositioning of Emmeline as kin and non-kin shows such classifications to be based on economic and social structures similar to the structure of the patriarchal family and render them irrelevant to the heroine, who privileges individual choice. It is an important place to start examining the figure of the cousin because it is the novel that most clearly demonstrates the struggle of the individual against a larger and more powerful institution – in this case, the heroine's family – in a radical rejection of kinship ties with parallels to the French Revolution. As such it stands at the beginning, chronologically, thematically and contextually, of the debates on kinship and conjugality that are played out via the role of the cousin that develop in the subsequent Gothic novels. In *Clermont* (1798) by Regina Maria Roche, the mysterious familial ties surrounding the heroine and her lover (her almost double cousin) emphasise instant familial attraction and female choice in spousal selection. Roche complicates an endogamic union sought by kin that creates a static family unit by making the marriage a love match based on the heroine's instant attraction to a penniless suitor. The novel is unusual in having the male love interest discovered to be the destitute son of an illegitimate younger brother; he is kin, but is compromised by his father's illegitimacy and his own lack of fortune.

Anna Maria Bennett's *Ellen, Countess of Castle Howel* (1794) is a sentimental novel with Gothic elements that positions the cousin as sibling-lover and highlights the tensions between economic familial duty and individual choice, establishing the egalitarian consanguinity of the cousin/sibling as synonymous with romantic love. Cousin marriage is represented as a mature and sensible choice in Elizabeth Thomas's 1816

Purity of Heart, or, The Ancient Costume, which identifies kin as ultimately safe in comparison to the unknown non-kin. The author makes clear in her preface that the novel is written to ridicule Lady Caroline Lamb's Gothic novel *Glenarvon* (1816). As such, the novel is a sort of anti-Gothic, an interesting piece of the incestuous milieu, literary and public, surrounding the Gothic novel and its writers and readers. *The Sons of the Viscount and the Daughters of the Earl: a Novel; Depicting Recent Scenes in Fashionable Life* (1813) by Selina Davenport, while not strictly a Gothic novel, revolves around a castle, an abandoned abbey, a feud and a family secret. These highly Gothic themes and settings surround the multiple sets of cousins who are married and/or pressured to marry each other and present the role of cousin as one capable of fulfilling a variety of positions (sibling, spouse, protector, friend, beau) at once. The cousin becomes a safe option for the heroine to treat as a suitor without endangering her reputation; with him she can explore emotional and physical desires rendered socially acceptable by their kinship tie. Finally, *Jane Eyre* (1847), Charlotte Brontë's Gothic novel, and Emily Brontë's *Wuthering Heights* (1847) use intriguingly contradictory portrayals of cousin love and hate to disrupt notions of female respectability, familial obligation, individual choice and social requirements, revealing as erroneous the understanding of the cousin as safe. Jane Eyre's reiteration of the marriage service that describes husband and wife becoming one flesh dismisses the notion that consanguinity creates family as it confirms her husband as her true kin, the final privileging of the conjugal bond. This variety of Gothic and Gothic-themed texts shows how the role of cousin was understood, portrayed and manipulated to privilege either conjugal or consanguineal bonds, emphasising the contemporary ideological uncertainties of cousin marriage and the cousin as kin. It is as a consequence of its uncertain status, as inside or outside of the family, that the cousin becomes the most versatile figure through which Gothic writers of conservative or radical political persuasions can engage with questions of inheritance, family, conjugality, individual choice, sexual desires and duty, often revealing their political orientation in the process.

EMMELINE AND *CLERMONT*: FAMILIAL OBLIGATIONS AND INDIVIDUAL CHOICE

Charlotte Smith's *Emmeline* deploys the insatiable desire of a male relative to trouble sentimental notions of the family as a safe haven. The novel negotiates the value of kinship and portrays a shifting definition of family through the depiction of cousin desires that are prohibited by family on the grounds of money and pride. Perry locates in the novel the 'conflict between romantic love and filial obligation … [M]orally impeccable heroines always cast their lot with the consanguineal rather than the nuptial principle – proving their moral worth by siding with families against upstart lovers.'[32] Smith's novel initially designates its eponymous heroine as the illegitimate daughter of Mr Mowbray, an elder son who died while Emmeline was in her infancy. Emmeline is raised in the family seat by the indulgence of her uncle, Mr Mowbray's brother, Lord Montreville. His son, Lord Delamere, meets and instantly desires his indigent cousin, much to Lord Montreville's displeasure. The novel follows Delamere's parentally forbidden pursuit of Emmeline, her refusals and eventual acceptance of his proposals when his father reluctantly relents. Emmeline uncovers her birthright and fortune, is freed of her engagement with her cousin and marries the man of her choice, Godolphin. Emmeline's exogamic marriage displaces her uncle's ill-gained fortune out of his family and her cousin's death represents the end of the Mowbray and Montreville family lines. Endogamy is revealed to be a potentially resuscitative force for the family that Emmeline ignores, leaving the family to die out instead.

Emmeline's conflict, regarded as she is by her uncle and his wife as less than kin, is made easier; she can be both the morally impeccable heroine and choose the non-kin lover, in spite of a promise to marry her cousin, because she has been relieved of filial obligation. The disruption of Emmeline's sense of familial obligation reveals traditional understandings of family as flawed and calls into question the motivations behind her aunt's and uncle's actions. Smith's deliberate repositioning of Emmeline as kin and non-kin throughout the novel illuminates the changing importance of consanguineal family, only ultimately to place her within a new family, one she has discovered and chosen for herself. Not only does the novel's chronology place it ahead of the texts to come, but its treatment of cousin incest as being alternately dangerous and desired, inhabiting a first forbidden and then permissive place, also foregrounds the representations that follow and their attempts to negotiate the demands of kin and non-kin. Emmeline's fluctuating status as family, mirroring the contemporary view of the cousin, renders the demands of consanguineous relations inferior to individual choice.

Emmeline's supposed illegitimacy leaves her potentially vulnerable to the sexual designs of her cousin, Frederic Delamere, as she would not be were she legitimate kin, and makes her a non-viable marriage option. Rehearsing a conventional sentimental literary trope, Delamere falls for Emmeline instantly: he 'fix[es] his eyes on her face ... examining the beauties of that lovely and interesting countenance which had so immediately dazzled and surprised him' (I, p. 42). Although struck by Emmeline's beauty, Delamere has no interest in marrying her; his desire is initially only sexual: '"I like her so well that I think it's a little unlucky I did not come alone. My Welch cousin is the very thing for a tête à tête"' (I, p. 45). Lord Montreville perceives the danger and determines to stop the situation lest 'his son should form an attachment prejudicial to his ambitious views' (I, p. 48). This seems a perfect literary example of Adam Kuper's point that 'the formal rules [of cousin marriage] do not determine how the game is played. People act selfishly on the whole, but they can usually find some socially acceptable justification for their actions ... the genealogies offering different options, kinship terms themselves open to manipulation.'[33] Lord Montreville manipulates Emmeline's kinship status to suit his inclination, claiming her as his niece when demanding her obedience and casting her off as illegitimate when his son expresses an interest in her.

The ambitions that Montreville has for Delamere complicate his more general sense of Mowbray family pride. When the castle steward tells Lord Montreville that he would like to marry Emmeline, 'family pride made a faint struggle in his Lordship's breast on behalf of his deserted ward. He felt some pain in determining, that a creature boasting a portion of the Mowbray blood, should sink into the wife of a man of such inferior birth' (I, p. 50). But family pride in relation to Emmeline is not enough when pitted against ambitions for his son and so he agrees to the marriage. When Emmeline refuses the proposed union she is sent away with a small yearly stipend contingent on staying away from her cousin. Montreville clarifies that, '"to Mr. Delamere, my son, the heir to a title and estate which makes him a desirable match for the daughters of the first houses in the kingdom, you can have no pretensions"' (I, pp. 61–2). Regardless of their kinship, Emmeline's fortuneless state and questionable birth render her unmarriageable. Perry states that Montreville, 'opposes the marriage between Emmeline and his son, Delamere, not because they are first cousins – which appears to be irrelevant – but because she has no fortune'.[34] Montreville's determination to sacrifice Emmeline, despite her 'portion of the Mowbray blood' to the greater ambitions he has for his son show the soluble nature of kinship and the disposability of women. The natal family and legitimate kin are given higher preference than lineal kin such as Emmeline. Smith shows definitions of family and blood are fluid, susceptible to change for material benefits. Although Montreville overlooks the blood tie between himself and Emmeline, Delamere uses it as a partial justification for his desires. When Emmeline's friend Mrs Stafford will not counsel Emmeline to elope with a man whose family would not own her, Delamere asks '"And who, Madam, has said that I dare not own her? Does not the same blood run in our veins?"' (I, pp. 126–7). Delamere points to their relationship as cousins as being grounds for their union to be accepted; he sees their kinship as proof she is not beneath him.

These multiple ways of viewing the cousin bond are reiterated when Mrs Stafford says to Montreville (thinking he is foolish for prohibiting the marriage), '"Miss Mowbray will reflect as much credit as she can borrow, on any family to which she may be allied"' (I, p. 153). The irony is apparent: Emmeline is already allied, consanguineously, to Montreville's family; the affinal connection he so strenuously opposes has nothing to do with her character and everything to do with her lack of fortune. Viewing Emmeline as an outsider, as non-kin, is dangerous for her uncle and his wife because they give her no incentive to deny Delamere's proposals. When Delamere presses his suit for a secret marriage, Emmeline 'feared her resolution would give way … [S]uch unabated love […] was seducing; and the advantages of being his wife, instead of continuing in the precarious situation she was now in, would have determined a mind more attentive to pecuniary or selfish motives' (I, pp. 238–9). Emmeline weighs the considerations of her obligations to Montreville and her loyalty and friendship with Augusta (Delamere's sister) over the pecuniary advantages of a secret marriage, but it is her friendship with Augusta and a general disinclination to unite herself to Delamere that make her unwilling to upset her family, not a sense of obligation to her uncle. Emmeline discusses Augusta's family members as if they are exclusive of her own, rather than her kin too. Her aunt also accuses Emmeline of non-kinship, telling her: '"you would like to hide your own obscurity in the brilliant pedigree of one of the first families in Europe. But know, presumptuous girl, that the whole house shall perish e're it shall thus be contaminated"' (II, p. 37–8). Lady Montreville views Emmeline as conniving and artful, a dangerous outsider attempting to trick her way into a 'pedigree', posing a threat to both the family's ambitions for Delamere and its very bloodline.

Although Emmeline has everything to gain from an alliance with Delamere she cannot consider him as non-kin: 'and had rather the friendship of a sister for him than any wish to be his wife' (I, p. 179). Describing Delamere, Diane Long Hoeveler writes that 'the dominant and threateningly odious suitor has about him an incestuous air of familiarity'.[35] Delamere, though hardly odious, certainly occupies a more incestuous role than cousin. He and Emmeline are put into a sibling context by both her resemblance to his sister – 'there was in figure and voice a very striking similitude between her and Emmeline' (II, p. 173) – and by Emmeline's attachment to him, which is 'the affection of a sister' (II, p. 172). This is similar to how the cousins in *Mansfield Park* relate to one another for a large part of the novel. In her analysis of Austen's treatment of the cousin union Eileen Cleere writes: '[Fanny's] move from cousin to sister to wife in relation to Edmund has generated a large body of criticism about sibling incest.'[36] But while Fanny loves Edmund as a brother and a lover, Emmeline is unable to make this shift.[37] When Montreville and his wife eventually concede to the marriage, Emmeline's promise to marry Delamere is reluctantly given; she claims she can only love him as a sibling. The affinity of values and social situation that make cousin marriage desirable do not here apply.[38]

Emmeline is released from her promise to marry Delamere and falls in love with Captain William Godolphin. Her origins are proved to be legitimate when she finds her parents' marriage certificate and her father's will, which 'confirmed every claim which they both gave Emmeline to her name and fortune' (IV, p. 21), a fortune previously claimed by Montreville. When Delamere proposes again Emmeline refuses him but her birthright and claim to Castle Mowbray is now (ironically) an impediment to a union with Godolphin:

> [S]he reflected on the character of Delamere, and remembered that his father would now claim an authority to control her actions – that one would think himself at liberty to call any man to an account who addressed her, and the other to refuse his consent to any other marriage than that which would now be so advantageous to the family – she saw only inquietude to herself and hazard to the life so dear to her, should she suffer the passion of Godolphin openly to be avowed. (IV, p. 152)

The restoration of her name and fortune positions her as legitimate kin with wealth – a viable option for Delamere now that her uncle desires their marriage to regain the lost estate and money. Emmeline's reflection demonstrates what Hoeveler describes as the 'sense of powerlessness experienced by a woman in the grip of two generations of patriarchal power'.[39] The status of niece is paradoxical. As Cleere writes, she is 'simultaneously inside and outside of the family', capable of being exchanged in either direction.[40] Like Fanny in *Mansfield Park*, Emmeline is 'the compromise between exogamy and incest, the sexual commodity that can be either exchanged outside the family, or "made the most of" within the family'.[41] Smith's and Austen's heroines are family and not quite family, a moveable good through which 'endogamy itself becomes an economic strategy'.[42] Emmeline is aware this strategy motivates her uncle's acquiescence to Delamere's wish to marry her; she says, '"the authority of my uncle … 'till I am of age, will probably neither restore my fortune nor consent to my carrying it out of his family"' (IV, p. 175). This recirculation of property and kin within the structure of the family is noted by A. H. Bittles, who argues that it allows 'the maintenance of family structure and property; and the strengthening of family ties'.[43] Strengthening the family structure through cousin marriage would, however, benefit the Montrevilles while placing Emmeline even more under familial power and she rejects this authority, resolving instead to wait out the familial demands.

Emmeline declines the endogamous exchange that would further entrench her in the structure that allows Montreville's assumption of paternal authority and demands for her obligation. Scholars such as Cynthia Klekar point to Emmeline's awareness of Montreville's generosity, which leaves her obligated to his paternal authority; Klekar argues that Emmeline is unable to 'escape the asymmetrical cycle of exchange that subjects her to competing forms of male control'.[44] Klekar suggests that Emmeline's 'promises to Montreville and Delamere cast the heroine's reliance on patriarchal authority in the language of the gift and obligation, depicting these relations as ostensibly based on filial affection'.[45] Yet Emmeline's earlier acquiescence to Montreville's demands that she not marry Delamere let her fulfil her own wish to refuse him. Emmeline's engagement with the language of paternal obligation allowed her to appear compliant with her uncle's request; however, her seeming participation with the patriarchal ideology was not grounded in filial affection or obligation but because it corresponded with her desires. Smith reveals the falsity underlying notions of paternal gifts and corresponding female obligation. Klekar asserts that in Smith's work: 'women can manoeuvre within but never escape from the sense of obligation to a patriarchal ideology'.[46] However, it is not Emmeline's sense of obligation that Smith cultivates when she describes Emmeline's 'indebtedness' to her uncle for 'suffering' her to live in the castle, or her 'sacrifice' in continuing to refuse Delamere's proposals. Smith ironically points to Montreville's greed and foolish insensibility to both Emmeline's legitimacy and rights to the castle and demonstrates that Emmeline uses her uncle's demands for her obligation to his will to assert her own.

Klekar suggests that Emmeline lacks self-assertion and individual rights; that Emmeline is only freed of Delamere when he dies; and that Smith is 'unable to imagine a narrative conclusion in which self-assertion, a claim to individual rights, or reason can release the heroine from her obligations'.[47] But, in fact, Emmeline is freed before Delamere dies in a duel, when Montreville returns her signed promise to marry his son. Emmeline's refusal to become engaged again to Delamere, in spite of his pleas, those of his sister and the acquiescence of Montreville, is a strong expression of self-assertion given her fears regarding Delamere's and Montreville's power over her. To deny Emmeline's self-assertion is to diminish her bravery and defiance of her cousin's will and her uncle's desires to see the fortunes united. Emmeline's individual rights are self-asserted and hard won. To ignore them, and Smith's ironic undermining of the idea of obligation, is to misunderstand Smith's beliefs regarding individual rights.[48] The novel is a radical rejection of notions of female economic value, familial dependence and obligation to kinship bonds. Rather than being obligated to the familial structure, Smith shows Emmeline's roles as cousin and niece as ones that require no sense of obligation because these roles are in permanent flux depending on the caprices of her relatives.[49] Her status as kin is alternately claimed or denied, and this constant repositioning causes notions of kinship obligation to become moot, leaving her free to escape familial bonds and marry the non-kin man of her choice.

Roche's *Clermont*, in seeming opposition to *Emmeline*, concludes with a close kinship marriage highly sought by the cousins' fathers. But the endogamic union that seems to privilege consanguineal bonds also, as seen in uncle–niece relationships, exposes the dangers of patrilineal descent systems that bestow wealth upon the elder son. The novel's heroine, Madeline Clermont, uncovers family secrets, falls in love, is abducted, nearly raped and murdered and is eventually repositioned as a wealthy heiress who marries her (almost double) cousin. Madeline's father, Clermont, is a man without a history, living a simple life below the status to which his educated background seemingly entitles him. The novel is discussed in scholarship almost exclusively in terms of Austen's

Northanger Abbey (1817) list.[50] However, *Clermont* is worthy of much closer analysis as it subverts its location of kin as a family-approved marriage choice. Roche manufactures this subversion by initially depicting the protagonists' mutual desire as an instant attraction that occurs prior to the revelation of kinship and is disapproved of by the heroine's father. Allowing for a close kin marriage that is based on love rather than the blood tie or familial urgings privileges choice while incidentally accommodating the family's wishes. The complex genealogies that are unravelled throughout the novel eventually lead to recognition and familial acceptance for Madeline and her father, and the very complexity of the bonds of kinship makes Roche's work fascinating. Family is represented at once as friend and foe, the seat of companionship and cheerful domesticity and equally capable of inspiring jealousy and murder. Relationships interweave and overlap; sets of siblings marry sets of half-siblings and legitimacy and inset narratives are interwoven in such layers that it is only through careful analysis that the true bonds of kinship can be understood. Roche's representations of family show individual romantic choice located within seemingly inescapable consanguineal bonds, allowing self-assertion while exposing the dangers of kinship.

Kuper analyses the preference of the bourgeoisie for 'marriages within the kinship network' and points to Goethe's characters in *The Man of Fifty* (1829) who are 'cousins ... expected to marry each other in order to preserve their patrimony'.[51] He argues that sets of elite and upper-class families in the eighteenth century 'coalesced into clans that persisted for several generations' to protect their fortunes, particularly in volatile times.[52] This seems an appropriate place to start an analysis of Roche's novel in which an upper-class family is presented in light of the marriage choices of its members. Roche depicts individuals marrying outside of their kinship circle with people unapproved of by their families with disastrous consequences and this mistake, made by the older generation, is righted in the next. But the marriage of Madeline and Henri de Sevignie is not motivated by a desire to appease familial demands or to correct previous mistakes; rather it represents an individual choice made by both the cousins before their familial bond is revealed. Their fathers' desire to see Henri and Madeline wed to protect the patrimony and unite family fortune with family name reveals that the older generation is continually misguided despite their children's correct ability to assert personal choice that happens to coincide with their family's desires. The cousins' mutual attraction and love cause them to risk parental disapproval to be together before the plot revelations render this unnecessary. But rather than being the happy coincidence Perry deems revelations of this sort to be in eighteenth-century novels, here the disclosure is cast in a darker endogamic light that hints at the danger of such close family ties.[53]

Madeline and de Sevignie share an instant attraction portrayed as a 'magic spell' that renders Madeline incapable of movement, suggesting that she is pulled into a stasis by her cousin and the bonds of kinship he represents: 'as if riveted to the spot by a magic spell, she stood immoveable' while the stranger 'wildly, yet delightedly, gazed on her'.[54] Although a stranger, de Sevignie is accepted into the family fold until Clermont sees his love for Madeline and, concerned by his inability to locate himself within a family and provide a personal history, orders him to leave them. De Sevignie's lack of history and kinship network is perceived as ominous. But Madeline's other suitor, D'Alembert (her second cousin, Clermont's cousin), has too much history, is too connected with her family's past, making him an even greater danger (he wants to kill his wife to marry Madeline, who is, unbeknownst to her, heiress to a fortune). Eventually we learn that de Sevignie is Madeline's cousin; in fact, they are almost double cousins as his mother and Madeline's mother were sisters and his father is Clermont's half-brother. De Sevignie is ignorant of this as he was raised in obscurity in an effort to conceal his true origins.

The plot, uncovered via memories and inset stories, requires some summary. Clermont was the son of Count Montmorenci and his first wife. The count, knowing his father would disinherit him if he discovered his marriage to his penniless wife, denies the union. Clermont's mother leaves him to be raised by friends (the De Valdores), eventually dying in a nearby convent. Clermont's father, meanwhile, commits bigamy by marrying a rich heiress with whom he has a son, Philippe – the recognised heir. Clermont discovers his true origins and meets and befriends his younger half-brother, Philippe. The two travel, meeting sisters, and Clermont marries one, Geraldine, not knowing his half-brother has secretly married the other, Eleanora. Philippe and Clermont's uncle by marriage, D'Alembert, is heir to his brother-in-law Montmorenci's estate if Clermont and Philippe are dead or disinherited, and, in a further criss-crossing of familial and affinal ties, is father-in-law to Viola De Valdore – the daughter of Clermont's adoptive sister. Due to D'Alembert's conspiring, Clermont wrongly believes Philippe guilty of an affair with Geraldine and stabs his half-brother. Clermont has since lived in obscurity, believing his brother dead, but after Madeline meets her grandfather,

Montmorenci, as she flees from young D'Alembert (Clermont's cousin/ Viola De Valdore's husband), Clermont is re-established as his father's heir. The senior D'Alembert threatens to reveal Clermont's crime and forces Madeline to promise she will marry his son in exchange for his silence (Viola, reported dead, is in fact imprisoned so the young D'Alembert can marry Madeline). Eventually the truth is revealed: Philippe survived the wound and was kept imprisoned by D'Alembert. De Sevignie (who is nearly identical to his father, Philippe) was raised by D'Alembert's colluding servants.[55] After learning this, de Sevignie rescues Madeline and Clermont from their imprisonment by the D'Alemberts. Clermont is restored as the heir of the Montmorenci estates, Philippe forgives him and Madeline and de Sevignie marry.

These relationships are excessively incestuous even for the family-centred plots of Gothic novels, creating a series of affinal and consanguineal ties that repeatedly cross. Marriages unite families – the De Valdores and the D'Alemberts, the Montmorenci half-brothers with the sisters Geraldine and Eleanora, and proposed marriages would unite Madeline with the D'Alemberts and de Sevignie with the D'Alemberts – though both Madeline and de Sevignie are, in the end, shown to be Montmorencis. In fact, throughout the novel, the number of people originally thought to be unrelated diminishes until virtually all the characters are proved to be related to one another through blood or marriage. In this way, Roche effectively dissolves differences between affinal and consanguineal kin. When D'Alembert proposes to Clermont that his son and Madeline should marry she refuses, but her grandfather favours the union because 'he highly approved of the projected alliance: he wishes to have the fortunes of the family united' (IV, p. 41). A marriage between his granddaughter and nephew would unite the family fortunes through an affinal connection to a blood connection, reinforcing the kinship tie with a legal one. But Madeline replies: ' "The fortunes of the family! ... and are such the considerations that sway the great world? Ah! no wonder, if the union of fortunes, not of hearts, is alone considered, that misery, vice, and dissipations from such connections should ensue" ' (IV, pp. 41–2). Her position is clear: to marry to unite family fortunes is essentially sinful; it is the heart that should be consulted. Madeline asserts her right to individual choice (similarly to Emmeline), but, ironically (and unlike Smith's heroine), she unknowingly falls in love with, other than her father, her closest living kin. Scholars are divided on the cultural and legal implications of first-cousin unions; Pollak's examination of the influence of property and inheritance laws on the status of cousin marriage demonstrates the desirability of these unions, just as Cleere points out their economically frugal nature. Madeline faces familial pressure to marry D'Alembert because of the desire, exacerbated by the lack of a direct male heir, to consolidate wealth in the family.

Madeline's uncle, Philippe, views her as a potential gift to his son via marriage that would reimburse him for his suffering.[56] Philippe tells Clermont, '"by giving your daughter to my son, you can make me amends for all my sorrows"' (IV, p. 322). Clermont readily consents:

> '[I]n seeing the precious offspring of Elenora and Geraldine united, the most ardent wishes of my heart will be accomplished: in giving her to de Sevignie, I give her to a man, in whose favour I felt a predilection from the first moment I beheld him – a predilection, excited not only by his manner, but his strong resemblance to you. Take her' (he continued, presenting her hand to de Sevignie), 'take her with the fond blessing of her father.' (IV, pp. 322–3)

Clermont's words are powerfully loaded with the language of exchange and ownership coupled with that of kinship recognition. If ever there were an eighteenth-century case of genetic attraction, it is clearly articulated here.[57] Clermont and his brother see Madeline as a peace offering, a gift from Clermont to Philippe's son that will compensate Philippe for years of misery. In an exchange reminiscent of the incestuous uncles examined earlier, the younger brother demands the daughter of the elder.[58] The overlapping familial bonds cast Madeline and de Sevignie's proposed marriage as incestuous; as one-and-a-half first cousins, they share three out of four grandparents – all but their paternal grandmother. Even half-siblings share only two out of four grandparents. Yet their bond does not give Clermont or Philippe pause; indeed, it strengthens their desire for the union. Perry's belief that 'marriage in some sense neutralizes siblinghood so that sibling incest taboos are not transmitted to the next generation'[59] underscores the extent to which Clermont and his brother's siblinghood and that of their sibling wives must be neutralised to promote the union between their children. However, far from offsetting the tie of siblinghood, Clermont and Philippe reconfirm it.[60] Clermont points to Geraldine and Eleanora's sisterhood as the reason he wants their children united and declares de Sevignie's resemblance to his brother caused an instant predilection for his nephew.[61] Endogamy is achieved through the union of Madeline and de Sevignie and the family has closed itself off from outsiders, inhabiting a closed-circuit environment.

In spite of this endogamic ending, Roche achieves a curious balance between conjugal and consanguineal ties, privileging choice but causing it to exist within the blood tie. For whenever it appears she is granting blood ties primacy we are quickly reminded that the most egregious crimes of the novel (murder, attempted murder, attempted rape, kidnapping, imprisonment) are perpetrated by family against family. In allowing Clermont to 'give' Madeline to her cousin – who is as related to her as a half-sibling, or, as closely related as Clermont is to Philippe – Roche allows her heiress heroine to marry the penniless son of the illegitimate Philippe. (Montmorenci's bigamous second marriage renders Philippe illegitimate, although this plot consequence is never mentioned.) This overlooked outcome of Montmorenci's bigamous marriage is that the lover is both kin and an outsider, like Emmeline's status before she discovers her legitimacy, except that for de Sevignie's father there is no legitimacy to find. Madeline's choice is de Sevignie before she knows he is kin, before their union is sought by their parents; Roche allows individual liberty but undercuts it by making kinship selection seem inevitable. In so doing, the dangers implicit in the exogamic exchange of women so necessary to patriarchy (there are virtually no examples of happy marriages in the novel) and the threats of being pressured into a kinship marriage to maintain family fortunes are underscored and given equal weight. Roche hints that only marriage to kin for love can manage to escape either of these traps of women as exchange, but the language of Clermont that offers Madeline as a gift renders this option a highly uneasy compromise.[62] Such an ending, subversive in its exposure of dangerous consanguineal demands, threatens to destabilise the radicalism of its own endogamy did it not ultimately privilege Madeline's desire for her cousin.

INSTRUCTION OR DESTRUCTION:
THE DANGERS OF NON-KIN UNIONS

In *Ellen, Countess of Castle Howel* Anna Maria Bennett couples the sentimental and the Gothic in a plot line that focuses on Ellen Meredith, her husband – who also serves as a father figure – and her cousin by adoption and second husband, Percival Evelyn. The incestuous implications of Ellen's marriage to her first husband, Lord Howel, are explicit: he sees her as an engaging child he wishes to educate and help raise properly, but also loves and marries her. Ellen, although she grows to love her much older husband, is always in love with her cousin by adoption. Percival is only able to marry his beautiful and wealthy cousin after finding his true name and genealogy. Bennett's novel is distinctive in its handling of the reformation of its chief villain, Lord Claverton, who turns out to be Percival's father. The incestuous bond between Percival and Ellen, unsubstantiated by blood, is nonetheless depicted as a relationship between kin through their sibling-like bond formed in early childhood.[63] Their constant attachment to one another and eventual union demonstrate the interchangeability of familial and sexual emotions, the ease with which non-kin becomes kin through a shared childhood and the need to balance individual liberty with familial duty.[64] Bennett portrays desires and romantic relationships as inherently incestuous but reveals the egalitarian cousin-sibling incestuous bond as most closely aligned with the brother-as-lover.

Bennett distinguishes Percival as Ellen's true choice by positioning them as equals. In a socially accepted model of the sibling–lover relationships analysed previously, the cousin can fulfil the role of the sibling in a legal marriage, being an equal other half and viable marriage option. In opposition to the sibling-like bond she shares with Percival, Ellen is viewed as a child by the other men cast in the role of lover (and lover-villain), a beautiful girl whose innocence and unformed mind (and body) is appealing. Lord Howel, 'undertook himself to begin the formation of a mind so open and naturally ductile'[65] before 'his heart claimed a different interest in' the 'beautiful and amiable child' (I, p. 176). Lord Howel's love for Ellen is, like Ellen's love for Percival, an example of familial or near-familial love evolving into or existing alongside romantic love, though it positions him as the father/instructor. Lord Claverton, a friend of Ellen's uncle, also views her as a child and his sexual desires are focused on this quality, explicitly centred on entrapping and ruining Ellen: ''Tis true, beautiful as Ellen was, it was the beauty of a tall child; but neither did *that matter*, it was a fault every day would mend' (I, p. 34). He reflects upon seeing her: 'Heavens! What an object for attention – for admiration – for ruin!' (I, p. 42). These very different types of men (Lord Howel is kind, intelligent and generous while Lord Claverton is dissipated and calculating) expose the pervasiveness of masculine desires centring on a younger girl they can either educate or ruin. Male passions are revealed as incestuous when shown to focus on the malleable, childish and immature qualities of their objects of desire. Percival, however, both kin and contemporary, sees Ellen as an equal companion instead of an object for instruction or destruction and, as such, proves himself her true partner. By creating this companionate, sibling-like bond with the adopted cousin, Bennett's heroine marries the forbidden brother without having completely to deconstruct the family structure to allow it, as Brontë does in *Wuthering Heights* or Eleanor Sleath does in *The Orphan of the Rhine* (1798). The cousin is here a viable alternative to the brother-as-lover so often presented as the ideal relationship in the Gothic.

Ellen's uncle Edmund Meredith is so attentive to his ward, Percival, that many believe Percival is Edmund's illegitimate child: 'Mr. Meredith's attention to his morals and learning was incessant, and as he grew up the affection of a father, was blended with the instruction of a tutor, in so much that many people gave him the credit of being one' (III, pp. 70–1). Percival views Edmund as his adopted father and he is treated as kin by the Meredith family. Before the truth of Percival's birth is revealed (he is the legitimate son of Lord Claverton and his deceased wife, daughter of the conniving neighbour who nearly cheats the Merediths out of their family seat, Code Gwyn) Ellen believes Percival is not only her adopted cousin, but also her cousin by blood:

> Ellen's infant years had passed in the exchange of kindnesses with Evelyn, without thinking of enquiring about his parents; as love began to usurp his sway in her young heart, Evelyn's *self* still more engrossed her, but ... since she had by accident heard the report of the country, her own observation on her uncle's extreme fondness, and Evelyn's implicit duty, had partially confirmed these reports. (IV, p. 190)

Part of what has caused Ellen to believe that Percival is her blood cousin is the 'implicit duty' that Percival shows her uncle. Similar to Smith's use of irony to undermine notions of familial obligation, Bennett's unification of family ties with notions of duty and obligation creates an association that renders family burdensome.[66] Likewise, the passage depicts these infant years together as inspiring the cousins' mutual love. Relevant here is Kuper's claim that the casual nature of cousin relationships facilitated romantic love: 'cousins grew up in friendly intimacy ... free to mix unchaperoned, cousins readily fell in love'.[67]

Percival and Ellen's shared childhood and mutual love corroborates Kuper's findings, rather than those of statistical geneticist Steven Buyske and anthropologist Alex Walter. Buyske and Walter argue that 'early childhood cosocialization makes a male over 3000 times more likely to be rejected as a marriage partner later in life ... daily social contact in the first seven years ubiquitously disqualifies individuals as marriage candidates for female participants'.[68] Ellen and Percival's childhood does not disqualify Percival as a marriage candidate; rather, it cements his place in Ellen's heart. Their relationship develops similarly to the sibling bond Enrico and Laurette share in Sleath's novel; Percival and Ellen's unchaperoned childhood allows for the strong development of emotional attachment that moves seamlessly into romantic love. The connection is a familial tie supplemented with passion; 'a stronger attachment than that which grew up between Evelyn and our heroine, could not perhaps be' (III, p. 169),[69] and 'as Percival was three years older than Ellen, he led in all their infant sports, and became her habitual protector' (III, p. 72). Their childhood bond develops and Ellen is described as: 'the companion, who from his infant state, became a part of his vital existence' (III, p. 74). While initially positioned as a protective figure who leads Ellen, Percival's location as leader is destabilised through Ellen's maturation. Ellen becomes integral to Percival's existence because of how they are raised together; this is intriguing because it seems to repudiate traditional anthropological views on how kin is rendered unattractive.[70]

Bennett shows the cyclical and confining nature of kinship obligations through Ellen's first marriage. Code Gwyn, the family seat, is threatened by a neighbour who has put the Meredith family deeply into his debt, in large part because they are generous landowners.[71] In order to keep the ancient castle in the Meredith family Ellen's relatives persuade her to marry Lord Castle Howel, the paternal figure who undertook her education.[72] The marriage required by the bonds of familial duty preserves the Gothic relic that represents 'imperfect laws'.[73] After Ellen's marriage to Lord Howel and the birth of their child, she still harbours romantic feelings for Percival: 'Ellen could not help remembering, the companion of her youth; she could not help feeling how superior he tower'd, both in person and understanding, above any young man she knew; but he was not her husband, the tender kind husband' (III, p. 170). She is torn between her conjugal tie to Lord Howel and the sexually attractive Percival. Klekar's analysis of obligation to family is relevant here; Ellen is obligated to her family because they raised her after she was orphaned and to her husband whose wealth has saved her family home. After Lord Howel's death and the restoration of Percival's birthright, any barrier to a union with Ellen is removed. As Smith's Emmeline disrupts the tradition of familial duty and obligation that plagued female marital choices by casting off family, Ellen also avoids the snare of consanguineal pressures in her second marriage choice by marrying her childhood love.

Bennett strikes a complicated balance between the demands of consanguineal, conjugal and affinal ties and personal desires, showing her heroine burdened with familial obligations that negate her ability to assert individual choice, yet fulfilling her obligations before choosing a second spouse. By making this spouse Percival Evelyn, Bennett creates an alliance that escapes the exchange of women (in this marriage, only Ellen and Percival benefit and Ellen's widow status means no father figure controls her exchange) and eludes the common societal reasons for allowing cousin marriage: to preserve a familial estate or fortune. As non-kin, Percival is excluded from the patriarchal reason for permitting cousin marriage and their union falls outside the traditionally proscribed option of either exogamous or endogamous to fulfil both positions. As such, this marriage between cousins/non-cousins represents a negotiation between familial duties and individual choice that concludes by privileging the ties of romantic love grounded in equality and individual choice and the security of near family.

Elizabeth Thomas's novel *Purity of Heart, or The Ancient Costume* is written in an anti-Gothic mode and demonstrates that the fulfilment of duty rather than individual desire or choice is essential to happiness. The heroine, Camilla, avoids making her own spousal selection when she marries her parentally endorsed cousin in a relationship close to Bennett's depiction of Ellen's marriage to Lord Howel. Camilla's marriage, based on filial duty, proves her to be the 'morally impeccable heroine' Perry describes by siding with the 'consanguineal rather than the nuptial principle'.[74] An attack on Lamb's *Glenarvon*, *Purity of Heart* has a preface in which Thomas describes how her motivations for writing the novel stemmed from the dangerous and profane impressions left on her by Lamb's novel:

> The novel of Glenarvon ... and its horrible tendency, its dangerous and perverting sophistry; its abominable indecency and profaneness, struck her with such force, that she could not resist the wish which started into her mind, of ridiculing it. The speeches of Lady Calantha Limb, are many of them copied from Glenarvon; and the greater part of them may be fairly inferred from the incidents and conduct of the Hero, and the Heroine of that work ... if the world has indeed saddled the production of Glenarvon on the right owner, she hopes and believes it is one solitary incident of depravity which cannot be paralleled.[75]

I include much of Thomas's preface because the language used to describe Lamb's novel is important in establishing the milieu surrounding not only Thomas's own work, but also that of *Glenarvon* and the incestuous Byron-Lamb-Leigh scandal, which is itself reminiscent of a Gothic text. In attempting to ridicule the excesses of the Gothic, Thomas reveals her understanding of the form to be one that grants individual choice and desires precedence over the demands of family and duty. Thomas's text and commentary are highly illuminating in their positioning as a literary antidote to the subversive radicalism of Gothic sentiments. The novel, in its declared intention of ridiculing Lamb's work for its profaneness and depravity, offers the antithesis of Lamb's Lady Calantha in the heroine, Camilla.

In *Glenarvon* Lady Calantha (meant to represent Lady Caroline) is intended to marry her cousin William to preserve the family estate and title – the marriage does not take place and is rendered undesirable by its economic motivation and the murderous machinations of William's mother, Calantha's aunt. Lamb presents cousin marriage as a contract entered into under familial pressures and doomed to failure, yet presents an equally dire portrait of the relationship between Calantha and Glenarvon (the character representing Byron), based on sexual desire and attraction. Thomas's novel replaces the heroine with Lady Camilla, but keeps Lady Calantha as her antithesis. The portrayal of cousin marriage, devoid of love in Lamb's novel, becomes the type of marriage that Camilla chooses and fights to preserve. Disappointed in love with her first fiancé, Camilla obeys her parents' advice to marry, selecting a cousin of whom her mother approves. Camilla's cousin/husband proves unfaithful and after her first lover returns to England Camilla battles rumours and the threat of divorce to win back her husband. Thomas's novel and her declared intention in writing it place consanguineal and conjugal duties as compatible in moral characters and expose their conflict with dangerous individual desires. Incest is depicted as a horrifying taboo via Calantha's characterisation, while cousin marriage is portrayed as a responsible choice for virtuous women. Camilla's and Calantha's representations imply that sexual desire is incompatible with virtue in women and that such rampant desires inevitably lead to horrific incestuous couplings and unstable, unfeminine behaviour. But if Thomas's aim is to condemn female sexual desire by uniting it with the incestuous and unfeminine and to sanctify female obligation and duty to family and husband, her lacklustre portrayal of the latter compromises her purpose.

The marriage of Camilla and Sir Lusignan is described in loveless terms: 'Camilla had ... in compliance with the wishes of her parents, selected ... her present husband; who was the only surviving son of the elder brother of her mother; and who was in the possession of a very large fortune ... together with a baronetcy, which gave him the title of Sir Lusignan Dellbury' (pp. 33–4). Thomas establishes Sir Lusignan's pedigree as kin, wealthy, titled and one of many candidates for Camilla. Camilla evinces no preference for him but accepts him to comply with her parents and because his character and military achievements have fixed his position in the public world:[76]

> The many amiable qualities of Sir Lusignan, the pleasure which her mother seemed to take in his society, the high character he bore in the world, and the splendour which military achievements had thrown around him, all contributed to fix the choice of our heroine; and her parents in giving her to their nephew, felt certain that they had secured her happiness. (p. 34)

Sir Lusignan, a member of her family, is unlikely to cause any disruptions as Camilla's first lover, the erratic Lord Ellesmere, did. Ellesmere, non-kin, is dangerously emotional, violent in his passions and temper and jeopardises Camilla's position in society before she breaks their engagement due to his demanding nature.[77] Camilla's cousin is far from demanding. At first he plays the doting lover, but once they are married, Sir Lusignan 'slighted and forsook her' (p. 35). His inattention contrasts the obsessive love Ellesmere displays for her and, intriguingly, Thomas suggests this inattention is superior to being an object of sexual desire; better to be forsaken for mistresses than be treated as one.[78]

Camilla's overinflated sense of familial duty and wifely obligation engender a childlike dependency on her husband that robs her of what Perry points to as the more radical implications of a consanguineal relationship that 'advantages women with respect to gender politics and sexual power'.[79] Camilla puts herself into the parent/child binary from which Ellen must escape in order to find happiness in Bennett's novel, saying to her cousin/husband, '"in my dependence upon you, Dellbury, I wish always to be a child"' (p. 37). The role of the wife is made equivalent to that of the child by virtue of its dependency. Her obedience to her husband is reiterated when her father tries to persuade her to divorce her husband; while she pleads the marital tie over the consanguineal, she remains dutiful to family as her conjugal bond is also a blood one. The only instance in which Camilla defies parental authority is to abide by the higher authority of her cousin/husband. Camilla states '"from the moment I gave myself to Sir Lusignan, I lost my individuality ... I can think only as the wife of Sir Lusignan; to make him happy, to dwell in his house, to nourish his children, to pray for his reformation, and to wait ... for his return; this, this is my duty"' (pp. 140–1).[80] Camilla views herself, her possessions and her children as the property of Sir Lusignan.[81] Her complicity in the patriarchy's placement of children and possessions under the husband's domain and adherence to conjugal and consanguineal ties is shown as Camilla's duty as a virtuous woman, regardless of how it renders her powerless and inactive.[82] Her refusal to divorce Sir Lusignan fulfils Camilla's duty to him as both husband and family, privileging the marriage and blood bond in a subordination of her individual rights and liberties to consanguineal and conjugal duties.[83] Camilla ignores his affairs, remains faithful and, when he departs with his current lover, tracks him to the continent and takes a residence near him. Presented throughout as almost saintly in her behaviour, Camilla is more the angel of the house of Victorian fiction than a Gothic heroine.

Part of what distinguishes *Purity of Heart* as a conservative text is the way it sets itself up as a foil to Lamb's novel; designed to react against a radical Gothic work it becomes anti-Gothic. In spite of Thomas stating that *Glenarvon* is a work of dangerous depravity, her representation of Calantha at times glamorises her. Calantha is so unfettered by social restrictions that this portrayal comes across as less a condemnation than a comparison of two women fighting to save their relationships. That Calantha does so through an act of trasvestitism troubles Camilla as it empowers Calantha. While Camilla waits to hear from her husband, Calantha joins a Prussian corps and dresses as an officer to fight in the Algerines: '"De Lyra ... was taken prisoner by the barbarians, and I am going ... to save my love. O how exquisite will be my delight in fighting against these renegades, in rescuing him"' (p. 191). Calantha explains if the fight fails, she will take off the uniform, charm the enemy captain and then stab him. Camilla's response, '"you are beyond nature horrible"' (p. 193) demonstrates the unnatural way she sees Calantha. It is unnatural for women to act, to fight, to prefer their lover to their husbands and to declare it to the world: it is unnatural for a woman to speak of 'stabbing' a man when tradition specifies that act as the special prerogative of men.[84] Calantha bends gender ideologies in, not only her actions, but also her costume. This is an important point; the novel concludes in Sir Lusignan's words: '"Virtue, Camilla, is the ancient costume of Britain; let us not cast it aside for foreign frippery and tinsel"' (p. 273). To Sir Lusignan and the system for which he and Camilla stand, virtue is a British quality and Calantha has compromised her nationality as well as her gender in casting it aside and donning the Prussian uniform in favour of freedom and choice. In Thomas's novel, foreign costumes (or customs) are highly dangerous to British values of virtue and female nature.[85]

Calantha's character is that of a transgressor. Unlike Camilla, Calantha cannot be swayed by family pressure; she has no sense of obligation to conform to social mores or gender and sexual ideologies. She says to Camilla: '"I love to step over every bound, to run to every verge, to post myself on every promontory. I love to scale fences, break walls, throw aside props, and walk alone; I love to run fearlessly forward, in spite of the maxims of the world; to do that which no one has ventured to do"' (p. 181). Camilla, in response to this speech, says, '"the woman who moves out of that beaten path, which custom has prescribed for her footing, will generally make some false steps"' (p. 182). Camilla is content only to follow in the beaten path prescribed for women; Calantha's desires move her beyond attempts to control her. Thomas attempts to privilege Camilla's sense of duty, obligation and custom and to cast Calantha as a dangerous and unnatural madwoman. Calantha cites incest as an example of how much allure the taboo holds, '"As if love is not twenty times more attractive, when it is forbidden, and sinful ... it would have tempted me to fall in love with my great grandfather, if I had had the awful prohibition always before me"' (pp. 175–6). Thomas's deployment of cross-generational incest, the type of incest considered the most distasteful,[86] demonstrates the unnatural and horrific nature of Calantha's desires in contrast to cousin incest, which is represented as having little to do with desires. Camilla and Sir Lusignan are restored to one another after she nurses him through a fever and he forgoes his adulterous ways to enjoy domesticity with his wife.[87] Camilla, however, never views him with the desire and liberty of choice that make the cousin the flexible kin/non-kin role inhabiting both familial and sexual roles that it is in the Gothic. Thomas's depiction of the cousin as entrenched in the kinship bond despite being a marriage choice unintentionally reinforces Gothic novels (and specifically *Glenarvon*) that identify a strict fulfilment of duty as incompatible with individual choice.[88]

What becomes of Calantha and her lover is never related and so the reader is left with two contrasting images: the angelic Camilla who patiently waited for her adulterous husband and the transgendered

Calantha, described by Camilla as having a 'masculine daring in her air and manner, which terrified and alarmed ... so totally dissimilar from all other women' (pp. 67–8). The two women embody binary representations of incest: Camilla's first-cousin marriage is desired by her parents as a safe matrimonial option that keeps her childlike and submissive to her husband's will, while Calantha claims she so loves the forbidden that she would desire her great-grandfather. The representations of incest and gender intended to make Calantha ridiculous may succeed in places, but Thomas's ridiculing of *Glenarvon* also effectively resuscitates Lamb's Calantha from a watery grave and turns her into a sword-wielding soldier on the brink of rescuing her imprisoned lover. In the end, Thomas seems incapable of escaping from this highly Gothic plot line; in spite of the attempt to position Camilla and Sir Lusignan as the domestic ideal, it is Calantha with her transgressive desires who lives to fight, avoids Camilla's beaten path and continues to 'run fearlessly forward, in spite of the maxims of the world'.

THE BURDEN AND BENEFIT OF KINSHIP: THE MANY ROLES OF THE COUSIN

The Sons of the Viscount and the Daughters of the Earl by Selina Davenport is a sentimental Gothic novel with similarities to *Emmeline*. But while Emmeline's cousin defies paternal orders to abandon her, the protagonists of Davenport's novel struggle to obey parental commands. Angeline and Elvira De Courci are orphaned sisters raised in their ancestral castle by an aunt and under their uncle's care. Lord Fortescue, owner of the nearby Fortescue Abbey, has forbidden his sons, Henry and Sidney, any contact with the De Courcis. In spite of the prohibition, Sidney meets and falls in love with Elvira. In the following London season Elvira marries another man in a fit of pique at Sidney. Meanwhile, though Henry and Angeline are attracted to each other, Henry is obliged to marry his cousin. Eventually Henry's wife dies in childbirth, Sidney marries his sister's friend and Elvira dies. The secret that caused the Fortescue–De Courci enmity is revealed (Lord Fortescue's sister was engaged to Elvira and Angeline's father, who had sex with her before the wedding, causing her to be 'ruined' and die) and Henry and Angeline overcome the paternal ban on their union. Incestuous marriages between cousins are portrayed as highly sought by the older generation: Henry's father promotes his marriage to his cousin; Lord De Courci tries to persuade his son Lord

Reginald to propose to his cousin Elvira; and Angeline's cousin Desmond is advanced as a potential suitor. But just as the older generation advocates these unions, they are undesired by the cousins themselves. The younger generation is more outward-looking, moving beyond the realm of kinship to find spouses from other, forbidden families. The role of the cousin is multifaceted, portraying the subordination of individual desire to family duty and honour while ultimately rewarding choices that defy paternal expectations. The cousin's position as alternately kin or non-kin incorporates the respectability of family protection with the potential for romantic attachment, reflecting the ease with which the familial bond can coexist with sexual desire and granting cousin relationships a flexibility and liberality denied in other male–female courtships.

Lord Fortescue phrases his ban on involvement with the De Courcis in the language of blood, telling his sons '"never to let the pure and noble blood of the Fortescues be contaminated by mixing with that of the detested Earl's"'.[89] Much as Emmeline's blood is described as a contaminant to the Montreville line, Lord Fortescue believes pure bloodlines can be sullied by mixing with impure ones.[90] Henry's marriage to his first cousin, the daughter of Lord Fortescue's brother, has been arranged for some time. Perry refers to the preference of the aristocracy for first-cousin marriage, explaining that:

> [T]he marriage-of-incorporation did not pose the same kind of threat to the consanguineal family as the marriage-as-alliance because by extending and adding to the natal family it shored up the principle of consanguinity. The marriage-as-alliance on the other hand expressly put the interest of the new unit above the interests of either of the spouses' natal families.[91]

Marriage-as-alliance, already attempted by the Fortescue family, ended with the corruption and death of Lord Fortescue's sister and the dissolution of Lord Fortescue's engagement with Lady Desmond, Lord De Courci's sister. Now Lord Fortescue looks to his own family for his son's spouse in a relationship that Perry would describe as a marriage-of-incorporation, which will 'shore up the principle of consanguinity' that is so important for Lord Fortescue to maintain.[92] Incest, in this case, is sanctioned and promoted by the older generation, which has the interest of the natal family at heart.

Familial resemblances – physical traits and personalities – are represented as a method of making compatible pairings. Lord De Courci promotes cousin marriages in his family, requesting his son, Lord Reginald, to marry his niece, Elvira. He says: '"Reginald will not make a bad beau for Elvira; and should the young Lord Desmond resemble his mother … he will be an excellent companion for my little Angeline"' (I, p. 149). Lord De Courci, knowing his sister's qualities, decides that if his nephew resembles her he will be a good spouse to Angeline. But when Lord De Courci tells Reginald he wants him to marry Elvira, his son replies: '"My heart will never feel any other affection for Elvira but that of a relation"' (I, p. 188). Reginald's statement, juxtaposed with his feelings for Angeline, demonstrates the cousin bond as one in which kinship affection and romantic affection can become interchangeable. While Reginald says he will only ever see Elvira as a relation, he views Angeline as a potential mate: his 'heart immediately acknowledged a preference, which increased as he became more intimately acquainted with [Angeline's] virtues' (I, p. 157). The instant attraction he feels for Angeline is grounded in the language of siblings: 'Lord Reginald took her hand, and with the affection of a brother carried it to his lips. "With such a companion as you, my dear cousin, the country would be a paradise at any season of the year"' (I, p. 161). Davenport uses the word 'brother' to desexualise the attraction Reginald feels for Angeline. But Reginald explains to his new wife Mary Evelyn: '"had my heart been free from the magic of thy charms, my Mary, it would certainly have been devotedly attached to my cousin Angeline"' (I, p. 208). The language of fraternal affection is at once belied by Reginald's description of his bond with Angeline as one in which kinship is not incompatible with desire.[93]

Davenport suggests that endogamy is the inevitable consequence of familial pride as, in order to keep valuable women within the family and to marry a spouse at the same level of birth and blood, kin must marry kin. Elvira's beauty makes her a possession that her uncle is eager to maintain. Lord De Courci says to her, '"I wish to secure you, my beloved niece, in my own family. When you are presented, some happy man may run away with my charming Elvira; and I shall lose all the pleasure I have promised myself from her society"' (I, p. 190). Lord De Courci promotes cousin marriage to keep a prized beauty in the consanguineal family (he is, like Sir Thomas, being economical), believing that her perfect form and face make her highly valued. De Courci is already titled, landed and wealthy, so the need for exchange is lessened. Elvira's beauty and the pleasure her uncle takes in her company make retaining her more advantageous than an exchange and De Courci is eager to 'secure' her in his own natal family, where he will have continued access to her society.[94] Lord De Courci is furious with his son's lack of familial duty in refusing to propose to Elvira, not merely because Reginald defies his parental command, but also because he will lose his niece to an outsider (again, the uncle tries to control access to the niece's body either himself or by proxy).[95]

That cousins are perceived as safe companions in terms of sexual reputation is an idea Davenport portrays particularly through the relationship between Angeline and her cousin Desmond. When the cousins meet they are instantly attracted to each other; Desmond thinks Angeline's amiable nature renders her 'an object to inspire the tenderest affection, the most lasting friendship; and he regarded her in the light of a beloved sister' (I, p. 191). Angeline is equally fond of Desmond, and their family and friends desire their marriage as their status as cousins makes the potential union an appropriate option. As Leonore Davidoff and Catherine Hall point out, 'cousins were favoured as close friends ... The fact that cousins could marry, however, could make the relationship of male–female cousins problematic ... Male cousins could be called upon to perform general masculine functions of advice and protection, if not support.'[96] Lord Desmond feels that Angeline is like a sister and they also look alike; they 'would have passed for brother and sister' (I, p. 163). While the older generation hopes that they will marry, the cousins view their bond as a sibling one, though their relationship is charged with sexual undertones. When Desmond discovers Angeline crying, 'accustomed to look upon him as a brother she threw her white arms around his neck, and wept unrestrained, while his lordship, pressing her still closer to his bosom, wiped away her tears' (II, p. 160). Desmond is described as a brother rather than a cousin, but there are still frissons of sexuality in the interaction. The label of brother does not preclude desire, as seen in Sleath's depiction of the siblings Laurette and Enrico, but it is here shown as a safe way of exploring desires.[97] Desmond is positioned as an almost-suitor, a companion who offers the safety of kinship with the power of attraction.

The cousin is a person with whom the heroine can indulge sexual desires, constant attention and familial affection without the censure of society. No other role allows for an unmarried woman to hold constant discourse with a man in such a way without being married or engaged to him. The cousin's status as kin makes him a safe person with whom the heroine can dance, flirt, appear in public, be alone and have as a constant escort and companion without a loss of reputation. He can be relied on for the kind of physical comfort (such as hugs and 'brotherly' kisses) that would be proscribed with a non-relative and the heroine can use his presence to discourage unwanted suitors. When Desmond faints, Angeline 'pressed her lips to his cold damp face – her tears, her sobs, alone possessed the power to reanimate him. He groaned as he again felt the pressure of her lips to his' (IV, p. 6). Henry, in love with Angeline, views this interaction as enviable but they are actions that Angeline can commit without risk of her reputation specifically because it is her cousin, a relation, who receives her kisses.

Henry's marriage to his cousin Lucinda is similar to Perry's description of Edmund and Fanny's marriage in *Mansfield Park* as one that will 'strengthen consanguineal bonds and consolidate family feeling'.[98] While Lucinda loves Henry as a husband, he describes his attachment to her as solely familial and their marriage as a duty he was obligated to fulfil.[99] Henry says '"my uncle's partiality made him desirous that the happiness of his child should be committed to my care. My dear father's heart was also fixed upon the match"' (I, p. 128). As Lucinda's cousin, Henry is a safe option for her father to fix upon; he knows that Henry will provide protection and constancy to his daughter because he knows that his character and understanding of familial obligation will render him a good husband. Thomas's *Purity of Heart* also attempts to show the cousin as a safe option encouraged by the family; though she endangers this positioning of kin as safe with Sir Lusignan's repeated infidelity, he is eventually redeemed through Camilla's goodness (as Lucinda is not), which rewards filial and conjugal duty and obligation. On Henry and Lucinda's wedding day, Lord Fortescue says to Lucinda: '"would that your father was here, my dear child, to witness this happy event, to behold the long desired wish of his heart gratified!"' (I, p. 184). His phrasing is akin to that in Roche's *Clermont* regarding the parents' desires to see Madeline and De Sevignie married; but in Roche's novel, the cousins both wish for the union. This is not the case in Davenport's text, where the cousin marriage is destined to fail.

The parental generation that so earnestly desires Henry and Lucinda's union is blinded to the cousins' incompatibility. Henry says, '"I love Lucinda with brotherly affection [...] but the differences in our tastes, in our inclinations, are so striking ... I foresee we shall lead a life but little consonant to my taste or wishes"' (I, p. 178). Henry knows the marriage will be unhappy as he and his cousin have little in common and his affection for her is fraternal. His father does not realise this until after the marriage, 'convinced, when too late, that his niece was not the woman calculated to make happy such a heart and mind as his beloved Henry's'

(II, p. 63). Davenport complicates the meaning of 'brotherly' when even after Henry impregnates Lucinda he continues to describe his feelings for her as brotherly. After Lucinda dies in childbirth, Henry reflects again on Angeline, whom he continues to love despite his father's ban on the De Courci family. Henry describes to Angeline his marriage to Lucinda as follows:

> 'The engagement ... was made by my father and uncle ... Duty and honour overcame, for a time, the secret prepossession of my heart, but even these were insufficient to wholly banish the angel form of her who alone had taught me the sweet feelings of a lover. Attached from childhood as a brother to my cousin ... I mourn her loss as a beloved sister.' (IV, pp. 174–5)

Even the duty and honour that Henry feels for the Fortescue family are insufficient to let him forget Angeline, his forbidden love of choice. Once Lord Fortescue releases the ban on Fortescue–De Courci marriages, Henry weds Angeline without defying the paternal prohibition.

Davenport's novel is rife with endogamous marriages and near marriages and more are implied than are supported by consanguineal ties. Lady Desmond describes the childhood relationships between herself, her brother and the Fortescue siblings by saying, '"From infancy ... we seemed to be but one family, and as we grew up to years of maturity our affection increased"' (II, p. 149). The original inhabitants of the abbey and the castle grew as one family, intimacy developing alongside familial love. Those previously engaged couples, as sets of siblings, would have made Elvira, Sidney, Desmond, Angeline, Reginald, Cecil and Henry all double cousins. The families, structured as separate and forbidden, are only so divided because of the ban that severed what had promised to be one large family united through marriages and sibling ties. In a statement that equates love to an inheritance, Cecil says to her father of her feelings for Desmond, '"But is it to be wondered, that his child's heart should not prove insensible to the merits of the son of his once adored Emma?"' (III, p. 191). Indeed, the children of the De Courci and Fortescue families seem destined to fall in love with each other.

The paradoxical representations of cousin relationships show them to be analogous to a sibling bond but also sexualised. Just as the De Courci and Fortescue families are delineated as kin who love and sexually desire one another, the cousin tie allows for the coexistence of familial and erotic love. The role of the cousin, shown through the relationships of Desmond, Reginald and Angeline, offers practice in relating to the opposite sex, protection from undesired suitors, shared mutual sensibilities and desires and opportunities to display affection in ways forbidden to non-kin. The relationships between cousins are rife with opportunities to explore emotions and physicality in a socially acceptable way, protected from disgrace by the consanguineal bond that allows sexual attraction within the safety of a familial relationship. In Davenport's text cousins can be family or lovers, but they must make this decision for themselves without the interference of an older generation who, blinded by family pride and honour, attempt to wrest individual rights from their children in favour of tightening consanguineal bonds.[100] A careful balance between family duty and individual desire is essential for happiness.

REJECTING THE COUSIN AS FAMILIAL OBLIGATION OR DUTY

A later debate in the Gothic is interesting because in the more than thirty years between Davenport's novel and those of the Brontë sisters, while political reforms occurred, the essential position of women as lacking citizenship remained unchanged. Historian Constance Rover points to the Reform Act of 1832 as one that, while enfranchising male persons, provided an explicit statutory bar to women's voting.[101] The ongoing exclusion of women from the political and public arena in spite of the newly afforded rights granted to men makes these later representations of cousin marriage in the Gothic and their privileging of female rights over familial obligations demonstrably relevant to an analysis of the Gothic's subversive and politicised use of such unions. In Emily Brontë's *Wuthering Heights* (1847) two disparate cousin marriages underscore the extremes of dangerous consanguinity and patrimonies and the rejection of exogamy in favour of familial anarchy. The first union, between Cathy Linton and Linton Heathcliff, represents the violent power and destructive nature of paternal authority wielded by Heathcliff as a perverse inheritance from Mr Earnshaw and his son, Hindley. The second marriage, between Cathy and her cousin Hareton Earnshaw, allows an endogamic union that stems from an overabundance of overlapping family ties yet is utterly devoid of familial interference. Charlotte Brontë's *Jane Eyre* (1847) also features a heroine with two very different male cousins; and though only one of them proposes, she rejects the offer in favour of a marriage of questionable respectability. In *Wuthering Heights* the consequences of patriarchy are apparent in Heathcliff's schemes for his son's marriage to Cathy while these consequences are absent in the ensuing union of Cathy and Hareton. Both heroines marry husbands who are masculine, dark and powerful; in Emily Brontë's novel the sexualised hero is the cousin and in Charlotte Brontë's he is non-kin, but both novels reflect a rejection of the duties that coincide with family in favour of individual rights and desires.

Pauline Nestor, in her introduction to *Wuthering Heights*, argues against the conclusion of scholars such as David Cecil who suggest that the union of Cathy and Hareton brings a restoration of order to the novel. Instead, she focuses on the 'ever-present potential for reversion' in the novel: 'we cannot assume that the change in Hareton is any more secure'.[102] Nestor's point about the 'precarious nature' of conversion is convincing, as is her scepticism regarding the novel's ending as representing a restoration of order. Heathcliff's determination to destroy the Earnshaw and Linton familial lines has been partially realised; certainly, there are no Lintons left as Cathy Linton has become a Heathcliff and is on the verge of becoming an Earnshaw. Neither, however, is there any real order; the two large estates are managed by two young people, but primarily by the old housekeeper, Nelly. Wuthering Heights is on the verge of being left to the servants when the young couple moves to the Grange and it is hard to imagine Hareton playing convincingly the role of landed gentry, no matter how well his cousin has taught him to read. But what the ending means, and how Brontë structured the familial ties in order to arrive there, ought to contribute to the way the novel's conclusion should be read.

Nestor writes that 'the transgressive power of the novel is further evident in its flirtation with the fundamental taboos', of which incest resonates in the 'intermarriages of the second generation, in which Catherine marries her two cousins in succession, virtually without ever meeting an eligible male outside her family'.[103] The novel's incestuous insinuations are apparent from the outset and Catherine's marriages, made without any extra-familial courtship, heighten the claustrophobic sense of endogamy and confusion over character roles and relations. The narrator, Lockwood, not knowing the genealogies of his landlord, incorrectly guesses first that Catherine is Heathcliff's wife, then Hareton's: '"The clown at my elbow … may be her husband. Heathcliff, junior, of course. Here is the consequence of being buried alive: she has thrown herself away upon that boor, from sheer ignorance that better individuals existed!"'[104] Lockwood, the unreliable narrator, manages to get everything wrong and right at once. Catherine is not Heathcliff's wife (though he wanted her mother to be), she is not Hareton's (though she becomes his wife) and Hareton is not

Heathcliff's son (though he resembles him more than he does his father Hindley). But his incorrect/almost correct assumptions reflect the distorted genealogies and incestuous endogamy of the household he has stumbled upon. Wuthering Heights is established as a location filled with overlapping and confusing relationships of kinship and marriage, where almost all the characters are related to each other via both blood and marriage.[105] They also all resemble each other in different ways; Nestor discusses the confusion of names and resemblances, writing that 'lineage seems unclear … Cathy's nephew Hareton resembles her more closely than her daughter Cathy, while Hareton seems the truer son of Heathcliff than his biological offspring Linton'.[106] In this exceptionally small family group, lines of blood and resemblance intersect. Both the family and their crossing ties of consanguineal and affinal connections allow Heathcliff to achieve his goal of securing Linton's estate and fortune for his own.

Catherine's first encounters with her cousins are far from the instant attraction/recognition-filled meetings common in the Gothic. She meets Hareton when she is thirteen and he is 'a great, strong lad of eighteen' (p. 193). She initially thinks his father is the owner of Wuthering Heights and is upset to find out that this is not the case, mistaking him for a servant.[107] Another servant corrects Cathy, telling her, '"Though Mr Hareton, there, be not the master's son, he's your cousin"' (p. 195). Cathy is appalled: '"my cousin is a gentleman's son – That my –" she stopped, and wept outright; upset at the bare notion of a relationship with such a clown' (p. 196). Cathy is aggrieved to discover she is kin to a servant; when she hears her father will be bringing home her cousin Linton she is overjoyed: she 'indulged the most sanguine anticipations … of her "real" cousin' (p. 199) who will be the 'gentleman's son' Cathy believes her cousin should be. Cathy's meeting with Linton, however, also fails to meet her expectations. The 'pale, delicate, effeminate boy' with a 'sickly peevishness' (p. 200) does little more than sob and complain before Heathcliff sends for him to live at Wuthering Heights.

In spite of Linton's initial poor impressions Cathy desires to renew their acquaintance and her father, because of the kinship tie, eventually acquiesces. Both Heathcliff and Linton seek a union between the cousins, though for opposing reasons. Heathcliff confides his plan to Nelly:

'My design is as honest as possible … That the two cousins may fall in love, and get married. I'm acting generously to your master; his young chit has no expectations, and should she second my wishes, she'll be provided for, at once, as joint successor with Linton.' 'If Linton died ... Catherine would be the heir.' 'No, she would not ... there is no clause in the will to secure it so; his property would go to me; but, to prevent disputes, I desire their union, and am resolved to bring it about.' (p. 215)

When Linton is irritable and sickly Cathy placates him, stroking his hair and saying ' "Pretty Linton! I wish you were my brother"' (p. 238); an interesting shift in roles from a cousin with whom she has just been exchanging love letters. As in Davenport's and Bennett's novels and *Emmeline* and *Jane Eyre*, the cousin bond is again manipulated into one of siblinghood, regardless of romantic desires.[108] Edgar hopes that the cousins may form an attachment and wed primarily because Linton, his male next of kin, will inherit his property and he wants Cathy to be able to stay in Thrushcross Grange after his death. Nelly states that Linton 'had a natural desire that she might retain, or, at least, return, in a short time, to the house of her ancestors; and he considered her only prospect of doing that was by a union with his heir' (p. 259). Linton's desire for this seems woefully naïve; he is aware of Heathcliff's ability to manipulate and the power he has over his son but he still hopes that the cousins could have a happy marriage. Brontë emphasises not only the injustice of patrimony, but also Linton's childlike trust in the system of inheritance and kinship, a trust that is proved to be ill-founded. Heathcliff desires the marriage as a legal means to solidify his grasp on the Grange when Linton dies and, as Cathy's money would become her cousin's once married, to claim the fortune as well as the estate.

When Heathcliff tricks Catherine into accompanying her cousin into Wuthering Heights, locking her and Nelly in, Linton explains, ' "Papa wants us to be married ... he's afraid of my dying, if we wait; so we are to be married in the morning"' (p. 272). Nelly is outraged beyond Cathy, saying her charge would never marry such a weakling. The comparison to her other infant charge, Hareton, is clear; Hareton and Cathy are strong and alike and Linton is a weak 'changeling' unfit to marry Cathy. After Cathy is forced into the cousin marriage, Linton tells Nelly that his uncle Edgar is dying:

'I'm glad, for I shall be master of the Grange after him – and Catherine always spoke of it as her house. It isn't hers! It's mine – papa says everything she has is mine. All her nice books are mine – she offered to give me them, and her pretty bird, and her pony Minny, if I would get the key of our room, and let her out: but I told her she had nothing to give, they were all, all mine.' (p. 280)

Linton, vicious, weak and petty, delights in the benefits granted to him by his sex.[109] He is infuriated by the notion that Catherine should claim as 'hers' anything that is 'his' based on either the patrimony or their marriage that rendered her personal possessions also 'his'. Part of Perry's argument concerning cousin marriage in Austen revolves around an uneasiness occasioned by the motivation of wealth accumulation; she writes 'the possible paternal first-cousin matches … are tainted by social ambition and the venal desire for accumulation of wealth … because of the concentration of wealth and title in the male line. Maternal first-cousin marriage did not profit from this fact of inheritance.'[110] Linton exemplifies cousin marriage for wealth accumulation; manipulated into the match by his father, he delights in the rewards he reaps from the marriage.

Because Edgar Linton realises on his deathbed Heathcliff's goal of gaining Cathy's personal property as well as the Grange, 'he felt his will had better be altered – instead of leaving Catherine's fortune at her own disposal, he determined to put it in the hands of trustees … By that means, it could not fall to Mr Heathcliff should Linton die' (p. 282). The lawyer, however, is under Heathcliff's command and the will remains unaltered. Cousin marriage is exposed as a sham sought to gain control of property and fortune and marriage in general is presented as fraught with the danger of being under the command of tyrants who gain control of female property and fortune. Linton dies within a month of his marriage to Cathy, though it is too late for her to retain any of her personal possessions. Heathcliff is now owner of everything relating to the Grange and Cathy; as described by Nelly, Linton: 'bequeathed the whole of his, and what had been her moveable property to his father … The lands, being a minor, he could not meddle with. However, Mr Heathcliff has claimed, and kept them in his wife's right, and his also … Catherine, destitute of cash and friends, cannot disturb his possession' (p. 294). Cathy is far from reconciled to this appropriation; when Heathcliff upbraids her for daring to disturb bushes in the garden she says, ' "you shouldn't grudge a few yards of earth, for me to ornament, when you have taken all my land! … and my money … and Hareton's land, and his money" ' (pp. 319–20).

Instead of the landed aristocracy desiring this union between cousins to maintain familial wealth and title, it is sought by two servants; one because she raised and loves them both, one because she wants to see Cathy lowered.[111] After Linton's death Hareton makes overtures of friendliness to Cathy; he is attracted to his cousin as a 'child to a candle' (p. 296) but after she unleashes her temper on him – emphasising his ignorance – he will have nothing to do with her. This does not long continue. Cathy, trapped indoors or within the boundaries of the garden on Heathcliff's orders, is bored beyond measure. Echoing Lockwood's earlier remarks regarding 'the consequence of being buried alive' (p. 13), Cathy looks to Hareton for companionship. Zillah, the housekeeper, wants to see Cathy's pride lowered, saying to Nelly: '"you happen to think your young lady too fine for Mr Hareton … but, I own, I should love well to bring her pride a peg lower"' (p. 295). A potential union between the two is shown as degrading to Cathy, who nonetheless persists in seeking a relationship with her cousin. Apologising for her previous bad behaviour – '"I should like you to be my cousin"' (p. 312) – she uses their kinship as a basis for a friendship that would be impossible without it, given his position as a destitute, uneducated servant.[112] Cathy says, '"Come, you shall take notice of me, Hareton – you are my cousin, and you shall own me"' (p. 313). They fall in love and Nelly says to Lockwood that '"the crown of all my wishes will be the union of those two"' (p. 316). The lowering that Zillah refers to is akin to the degradation Catherine feared through a union with Heathcliff, her inferior in social class, though it was her union with her social equal, Linton, that was so unhappy.[113] Brontë represents surface and social differences – such as Hareton and Heathcliff's darker complexions and lack of status – as minor impediments while underscoring consanguineal likeness as crucial to conjugal happiness.

With no families to whom Catherine owes obligation and duty and no paternal figures against whom to fight, the estates have evolved into a state of near anarchy, with the housekeeper in charge and the heiress marrying the former stable boy. When Lockwood returns he asks Nelly for the master in order to pay the rent and Nelly tells him, '"it is with Mrs Heathcliff you must settle … or rather with me. She has not learnt to manage her affairs yet, and I act for her; there's nobody else"' (p. 309). Now engaged to her cousin Hareton, Cathy is prepared to return to the Grange as mistress. Although it is not explicitly stated, it seems Wuthering Heights is now Hareton's property in the absence of a will, given his family's ancestral ownership of the estate. Nelly's words '"there's nobody else"' are the stark truth: Cathy is alone in the world; all the Earnshaws, Lintons and Heathcliffs, with the exceptions of Hareton and her, are dead. This reiterates Lockwood's words regarding Cathy and Hareton – is she only marrying him because there is no one else? Brontë takes care to show the evolution of their relationship and

Hareton's manners, but she is equally careful to position an unreliable narrator and Zillah to trouble our conception of their potential happiness. Regardless, what is explicit is the absence of family besides the cousins; there can be no consanguineal obligation or duty that presses them to wed. Cathy and Hareton are free to assert their individual rights, but by the time this is true, they have already been raised in the highly incestuous environment of Thrushcross Grange and Wuthering Heights. If Cathy has seen only three eligible males in her life, Hareton has seen only her. Heathcliff uses consanguineous marriage to achieve the exact opposite of the traditional reasons permitting it – maintaining estates, wealth and lineage – in a distortion undertaken to disperse and destroy these symbols of the Linton and Earnshaw families. The ending may be many things, but Nestor is right, a return to order it is not. Brontë's final cousin marriage is agreed upon for none of the traditional reasons therefore and is achieved in the absence of any familial interference in the cousins' spousal selection.

The novel that perhaps most clearly embodies the shift from the privileging of consanguineal obligations to the increasing importance given to individual choice is Charlotte Brontë's *Jane Eyre*. While her sister's novel shows an eventual removal of family members until there is no one left but the cousins-in-love, Charlotte Brontë's novel places her heroine within a family but without familial ties. Jane Eyre is raised in her uncle's home but the Reed family is unkind to the niece/cousin they treat as inferior and Jane discovers sympathetic family only later in the three Rivers cousins. Jane rejects her cousin St John Rivers's marriage proposal and its basis in his desire for respectability, instead marrying Rochester in a celebration of mutual love. Critics such as Eugenia C. DeLamotte point to the novel as having a 'domestic' ending with a sexually tamed husband.[114] I argue in contrast that the novel's conclusion emphasises the role of the sexual desires between Jane and Rochester in creating a kinship bond between the two. The importance of sexuality to the novel is pointed out by John Maynard, who refers to the 'process of emotional and sexual maturation' that Jane undergoes before returning to and marrying Rochester.[115] *Jane Eyre* is a strong assertion of female rights and desires, presenting a radical realignment of what constitutes consanguineal and conjugal bonds. Showing the sacrament of marriage that unites husband and wife in a bond of kinship as essential to Jane's understanding of her relationship with Rochester, Brontë equates the conjugal tie to the consanguineal in a love-based egalitarian union.

In her Rivers cousins Jane finds perfect sympathy with her female kin, but none with her male kin. Jane compares St John Rivers to a statue with a 'high forehead, colourless as ivory'[116] and understands that 'he might well be a little shocked at the irregularity of my lineaments, his own being so harmonious' (p. 396). Jane and St John do not resemble each other; she is unattractive to him and he seems like a marble sculpture to her. Ambitious and unhappy in his profession as a minister, Brontë portrays St John as the icy antithesis to Jane's fiery temperament. DeLamotte writes: 'The ice-cold St John ... offers religious ecstasy, enlightenment, release. But in the imagery associated with their relationship Jane suffers torture, darkness, and imprisonment instead.'[117] In contrast, in her female cousins, Jane discovers a pleasure 'arising from the perfect congeniality of tastes, sentiments, and principles' (p. 402). Jane divides her inheritance of £20,000 between herself and her Rivers cousins, splitting the wealth four ways to give each cousin freedom; in dismantling the inheritance Jane does away with the system of keeping wealth intact through the generations by dispersing it amongst the kin laterally.[118] Dispersal of wealth weakens the total power of a family but increases the individual power of its members, a revolutionary idea that St John hesitates to agree to. When he suggests that she could marry well with the fortune intact, Jane says (perhaps unconsciously describing St John and then Rochester): '"I do not want a stranger – unsympathising, alien, different from me; I want my kindred: those with whom I have full fellow-feeling"' (p. 447). They agree to view each other as siblings; St John says '"I feel I can easily and naturally make room in my heart for you, as my third and youngest sister"' (p. 447), while Jane thinks: 'it seemed I had found a brother: one I could be proud of – one I could love' (p. 444).

In Brontë's novel opposites destroy each other; like must be allied with like in marriage but such a bond is not found with kin.[119] St John's relationship with Jane develops but she finds he gains a control over her through a withholding of emotion she finds unbearable. The cousins may think they share a sibling-like bond but in his treatment of Jane, St John comes closer to Lord Howel's education of Ellen; he appears as a father figure rather than a brother. St John proposes that Jane marry him and accompany him to India, enumerating the qualities that make her a good missionary's wife. Jane contemplates the loveless marriage they would have and decides 'as his sister, I might accompany him – not as his wife' (p. 467). St John recoils at this idea but Jane knows that their natures are incompatible: 'I daily wished more to please him; but to do so ...

I must disown half my nature' (p. 460). St John uses respectability as a reason to press for the marriage, saying ' "How can I, a man not yet thirty, take out with me to India a girl of nineteen, unless she be married to me?" ' (p. 470). When Jane declares she will go only as his assistant he is icily enraged; her willingness to go with him without benefit of marriage makes him view her as sexually accessible. In a complete dissolution of the notion of the cousin as safe, St John reveals the bond as providing no protection for the reputation. Jane, however, does not regard preserving her reputation as incentive to marry without desire, offering him only her companionship. St John uses the language of heavenly duty and respectability rather than that of familial obligation and duty to persuade her to marry him but his rhetoric leaves her unconvinced.[120] Maynard refers to the choice between Rochester and St John as one between the 'two versions of the sexual openness and sexual suppressions that are built generally into the structure of the book'.[121]

After she rejects her sexless, icy cousin it is to Rochester and his fiery nature that Jane runs and she is rewarded for her rejection of endogamic celibacy with a virile and masculine lover. DeLamotte argues that 'the ideology of Gothic romance idealises female passivity and dependence. At the crucial moment Gothic heroines are rescued, almost always by a man',[122] stating that Rochester's cry for help is Jane's salvation from St John's marriage proposal. But this seems an odd kind of rescue, for Jane has already refused St John when she mentally hears Rochester's cry and goes to save him. Jane finds him missing an eye and a hand, nearly blind from the injuries sustained in the fire, though he looks remarkably unchanged. Jane reflects, looking at him, 'not in one year's space, by any sorrow, could his athletic strength be quelled or his vigorous prime blighted' (pp. 497–8). He is hardly the wounded hero rendered feminine, as scholars have frequently cast him.[123] DeLamotte, for example, perceives Rochester as somehow neutered, pronouncing him 'a husband whose sexual energies have been distinctly tamed'.[124] But this does not correspond to Jane's description of Rochester as strong and vigorous; the wound sustained damaged his vision rather than his genitals. While the wounding may have had a levelling effect on their relationship, it is premature to conclude his sexual energy has diminished.[125] In fact, Rochester's injuries have only made him more attractive to Jane: ' "it is a pity to see … the scar of fire on your forehead: and the worst of it is, one is in danger of loving you too well for all this" ' (p. 503). The mark of fire on his forehead, much like that of thunder on Satan in *Paradise Lost*, pulls Jane to him;[126] she is drawn to the darkness and signs of sin that brand him. St John's purity and punctilious duty to God were never the enticement that Rochester's fierce strength and desires are. Rochester describes St John as Apollo and himself as a Vulcan. The reference to Vulcan, the Roman god of destructive fire, emphasises his heightened sexuality and contrasts it to St John's marble sexlessness. It relates not only to Rochester's physical appearance – dark and powerfully built – but the mythical being is also associated with male fertility.[127] Jane's stated 'danger' in loving Rochester 'too well' after seeing the mark of fire alludes to a heightened sexual relationship, not a 'tamed' one. She is at liberty with him: 'there was no harassing restraint, no repressing of glee and vivacity with him; for with him I was at perfect ease, because I knew I suited him' (p. 504). Rather than having to repress half her nature as she did with her cousin, Jane finds in Rochester complete freedom of self-expression and sexuality that proves him to be truly kindred.

The kinship bond between them is reinforced with the imagery associated with their union, a melding of flesh and bodies both sexual and spiritual. After their marriage Jane reinforces their unification by saying 'no woman was ever nearer to her mate than I am: ever more absolutely bone of his bone and flesh of his flesh' (p. 519). When before their first failed marriage attempt Rochester employed 'the rhetoric of romantic love' Maynard suggests that 'the metaphors of his loving her as his flesh could emerge as emotionally real threats of incest'.[128] Now Jane joyfully embraces this rhetoric and its incestuous kinship implications. Stevie Davies notes that 'the Book of Common Prayer incorporates this kinship into the sacrament of the marriage service'.[129] Brontë affirms that Rochester is absolutely Jane's family through Jane's reiteration of the sacrament; that true kinship is of the soul. DeLamotte argues that Brontë sees domesticity as blissful only with 'the self-knowledge and mutual knowledge the male–female relationship at its centre is capable of accommodating … [A] vision of such radical equality of communication at the centre of a marriage was not common.'[130] However, this radical equality of communication is common in the Gothic. The main attraction between Gothic heroines and heroes is that they are perfectly sympathetic to each other, sharing the same tastes in music, art and literature and having the same views on philosophy and religion. Often from the same family, or from closely connected families, they frequently come from an equal footing of birth, education, age and sentiment; these similarities are all almost always present in the marriages that take place between the Gothic protagonists. This is partially what makes even non-incestuous relationships feel incestuous. Brontë's vision is radical, but for Gothic writers, it is far from uncommon. What makes Jane and Rochester distinct is Brontë's articulation of their non-consanguineal union as kinship through their nuptial vows and mutual love; their freedom with each other creates a consanguineous conjugal family.

Brontë causes the role of the cousin to shift from one of implicit safety and respectability to one of potential danger, even from such a highly respectable and sexless man as St John. In this shift Brontë draws attention to the erosion of familial bonds and the perception of safety therein, revealing kin-based male–female relationships as no longer socially privileged or even respectable. At a time in England when cousin marriage, increasingly acceptable and popular, was nearing an all-time high,[131] the role of the cousin became that of a potential mate rather than merely that of kin, and thus the respectability afforded by the consanguineal bond diminished. Jane tries to re-endow the cousin with respectability by offering to accompany him on his missions without benefit of marriage but succeeds only in making him question her morality. Brontë troubles the idea of consanguineal ties as equivalent to family, showing Rochester turn from lover to husband to family in a way Jane's blood kin never could. Hoeveler suggests that we see the 'incestuous suitor' rejected again in *Jane Eyre* and *Wuthering Heights* in the characters of St John Rivers and Heathcliff and that 'moving out of the family kinship clan and into an exogamous alliance, based on the property of one's own body rather than one's blood, proved to be an enormously anxious and ambivalent activity for middle-class women and writers'.[132] But as Perry has clearly demonstrated, the anxiety felt is at least partially due to a privileging of conjugal over consanguineal ties, not the notion of one's body as property; hardly a new idea for women who, be it based on blood or body, were quite accustomed to being the object of exchange. Jane's rejection of St John is a choice for life, vigour and virility that demonstrates the failure of St John's attempt to establish a new ideology in favour of cousin marriage based on female reputation and Christian duty. Brontë's depiction of these substitutes as inadequate establishes her text as truly radical in its privileging of individual choice and female sexual desires over respectability, familial obligation and heavenly duty.

The contested role of the cousin as legitimate marriage choice or not, kin or non-kin, lover or sibling, respectable or potentially dangerous, reflects the flexible nature of the cousin's role and the relative ease with which definitions of family could change.¹³³ The complexity of the cousin's situation allows for writers of the Gothic, so invested in subversions of patriarchal structures, readily to manipulate the bond in order to privilege individual rights and desires over duty and obligation. The Gothic, indebted to the philosophical and political discourses of the eighteenth century, took up the language of individual rights and social and familial obligation in its representations of cousin marriage. Participating in the prevailing discourses allowed writers to trouble the notion of female obligation to a patriarchal structure – such as the state or the family – that denied women individual rights. Representations of cousin marriage as an unfair familial demand and female obligation necessary to maintain ancestral estates and wealth demonstrate the hypocrisy of demanding obligation to a family structure that afforded women no rights within it and express anxieties regarding the underlying causes of this incestuous configuration's social acceptability. The grounds on which cousin marriage was permitted were thus exposed as perpetuating the family structure at the expense of women's rights, access to property and potential citizenship within the family and the state.¹³⁴ Yet, rather than these grounds designating cousin marriage solely as a conservative option, such unions occupy a versatile position in the Gothic. The flexible nature of the kinship bond, its frequent depiction as akin to an egalitarian sibling bond, the influence of familial pressure and the desires of the cousins render such marriages capable of fulfilling an obligation to the family or rejecting entrapment within the family structure.¹³⁵ How different Gothic novelists locate the figure of the cousin as kin or non-kin reveals radical, conservative or moderate views of the struggle between familial obligations and individual rights reinforced by the particular genre of Gothic (Radcliffean Gothic, anti-Gothic, sentimental Gothic). Entrenched within the kinship changes of eighteenth-century society regarding the importance of consanguineal, affinal and conjugal ties, locating the cousin in or removing him from the patriarchal structure reveals him as alternately rejected or desired by the heroine who refuses to participate in the dominant ideology of patrilineal inheritance, exchanges of women and demands of female obligation and duty.

NOTES

1 Charlotte Smith, *Emmeline, The Orphan of the Castle*, 4 vols (London: T. Cadell, 1788), I, p. 45. Subsequent references will be given in the text.

2 Joseph Shepher, *Incest: A Biosocial View* (New York: Academic Press, 1983), p. 98. Shepher uses Pierre L. van den Berghe's *Human Family Systems: An Evolutionary View* (1979) as a basis for his examination of cousins, inbreeding and incest.
3 Shepher, p. 85; p. 88.
4 William Shields, *Philopatry, Inbreeding and the Evolution of Sex* (Albany, NY: State University of New York Press, 1982), p. 34.
5 Patrick Bateson and Peter Gluckman, *Plasticity, Robustness, Development and Evolution* (Cambridge: Cambridge University Press, 2011), p. 65. See Chapter 2 for a summary of Maurice Greenberg's theories of genetic sexual attraction and Edward Westermarck's hypothesis of reverse sexual imprinting that suggest individuals are attracted to kin with whom they are not raised. Bateson and Gluckman argue that cousin unions of the third or fourth degree provide the 'optimal degree of relatedness' (p. 65).
6 Shepher, pp. 98–104.
7 Steven Pinker, 'Strangled by roots: the genealogy craze in America', *New Republic*, 237:3 (2007), 32–5.
8 Bateson and Gluckman, pp. 66–70.
9 Claude Lévi-Strauss, *The Elementary Structures of Kinship* (London: Taylor & Francis, 1969), p. 14; pp. 47–8.
10 Martin Ottenheimer, *Forbidden Relatives: The American Myth of Cousin Marriage* (Urbana: University of Illinois Press, 1996), p. 145.
11 Ruth Perry, *Novel Relations: The Transformation of Kinship in English Literature and Culture 1748–1818* (Cambridge: Cambridge University Press, 2004), p. 222.
12 Perry, pp. 230–1.
13 Examples include Emmeline in Charlotte Smith's eponymous novel, Hareton in Emily Brontë's *Wuthering Heights* (1847) and St John in Charlotte Brontë's *Jane Eyre* (1847).
14 For example, Henry Fortescue in *The Sons of the Viscount and the Daughters of the Earl* (1813) refers to his affection for his cousin as akin to his affection for his sister, while in *Clermont* (1798) Madeline and de Sevignie never discuss their kinship status.
15 Perry, p. 121.
16 Napoleon Chagnon, 'Male Yanamamo Manipulation of Kinship Classification of Female Kin for Reproductive Advantage', in Laura Betzig *et al.* (eds), *Human Reproductive Behaviour* (Cambridge: Cambridge University Press, 1988), pp. 41–4.
17 Randolph Trumbach, *The Rise of the Egalitarian Family: Aristocratic Kinship and Domestic Relations in Eighteenth-Century England* (New York: Academic Press, 1978), pp. 18–19.
18 Ellen Pollak, *Incest and the English Novel, 1684–1814* (Baltimore: Johns Hopkins University Press, 2003), p. 38.

19 Pollak, p. 30.
20 Pollak, p. 38.
21 Polly Morris, 'Incest or survival strategy? Plebian marriage within the prohibited degrees in Somerset, 1730–1835', *Journal of the History of Sexuality*, 2:2 (1991), 235.
22 Perry, p. 122.
23 Pollak, p. 165.
24 Pollak, p. 164.
25 Adam Kuper, *Incest and Influence* (Cambridge, MA: Harvard University Press, 2009), p. 23. Kuper notes that this rate increases sharply over the next century, peaking in the 1870s, when nearly 5 per cent of aristocratic marriages were between cousins, before dropping off dramatically in the following years (p. 23). See also Kuper's 'Incest, cousin marriage, and the origin of the human sciences in nineteenth-century England', *Past and Present*, 174:1 (2002), 158–83, in which he writes, 'in the nineteenth century, cousin marriage became more acceptable among the gentry and middle classes' (166), citing Nancy Fix Anderson, 'Cousin marriage in Victorian England', *Journal of Family History*, 11 (1986), 291 and Leonore Davidoff and Catherine Hall, *Family Fortunes: Men and Women of the English Middle Class, 1780–1850* [1987] (London: Routledge, repr. 2002).
26 Pollak, p. 44.
27 Jean-Jacques Rousseau, *The Social Contract*, trans. G. D. H. Cole (New York: Cosimo, 2008), p. 15; p. 77; and *Emile, or On Education*, trans. Allan Bloom (New York: Basic Books, 1979), pp. 362–77.
28 The historian Linda Colley notes this in *Britons: Forging the Nation 1707–1837* (New Haven, CT: Yale University Press, 2009), writing that 'stripped by marriage of a separate identity and autonomous property, a woman could not by definition be a citizen and could never look to possess political rights' (p. 243).
29 Colley, pp. 279–81.
30 Perry points to the political and economic changes of the day that emphasised individualism and individual rights but that for women 'did not expand the sphere of their social or political power' while often pitting their individual desires against 'the interests of the family' (p. 221).
31 For examinations of the role of gift exchange in eighteenth-century literature see Cynthia Klekar and Linda Zionkowski (eds), *The Culture of the Gift in Eighteenth-Century England* (Basingstoke: Palgrave Macmillan, 2009); and Jennie Batchelor's excellent synthesis of feminist theories on gift economy and their application to literary scholarship on eighteenth-century texts in *Women's Work: Labour, Gender, Authorship, 1750–1830* (Manchester: Manchester University Press, 2010), pp. 44–58.
32 Perry, p. 234.

33 Adam Kuper, 'Changing the subject – about cousin marriage, among other things', *Journal of the Royal Anthropological Institute (NS)*, 14:4 (2008), 727.
34 Perry, p. 122.
35 Diane Long Hoeveler, *Gothic Feminism: The Professionalization of Gender from Charlotte Smith to the Brontës* (Liverpool: Liverpool University Press, 1998), p. 38.
36 Eileen Cleere, 'Reinvesting nieces: *Mansfield Park* and the economics of endogamy', *NOVEL: A Forum on Fiction*, 28:2 (1995), 113–30.
37 Emmeline's love for Delamere is presented by Smith as a sibling-like love, but given Emmeline's upbringing – separate from Delamere – and that he has never behaved as a brother or cousin but only as a suitor, it seems unlikely that Emmeline finds Delamere an unacceptable choice because of the kinship bond, but rather because she simply is not in love with him.
38 Kuper, 'Changing the subject', 732.
39 Hoeveler, p. 45.
40 Cleere, 122.
41 Cleere, 129.
42 Cleere, 115.
43 A. H. Bittles, 'A background summary of consanguineous marriage' (unpublished manuscript, Centre for Human Genetics, Edith Cowan University, Perth, 2001), p. 5.
44 Cynthia Klekar, 'The obligations of form: social practice in Charlotte Smith's *Emmeline*', *Philological Quarterly*, 86:3 (2007), 271.
45 Klekar, 269–70.
46 Klekar, 277.
47 Klekar, 285.
48 Smith's views seem aligned with Wollstonecraft's *A Vindication of the Rights of Woman* (1792) and its rejection of Rousseau's demands for female participation in a state (here: family) that would grant women no rights. Smith, like Wollstonecraft, asserts women must have the same individual rights as men and shows Emmeline reject the structure of family and its concomitant demands for her obligation and denial of her rights.
49 Hoeveler points to this disruption in familial definitions, arguing that Smith presents the patriarchy as comprising 'a corrupt aristocracy and the old, kin-based order it implies and second the rising bourgeoisie characterized by its commitment to exogamous marriage' (p. 47).
50 Tenille Nowak, 'Regina Maria Roche's "horrid" novel: echoes of *Clermont* in Jane Austen's *Northanger Abbey*', *Persuasions*, 29 (2007), 184–93. Nowak's fascinating article offers a point-by-point comparison with Austen's novel to demonstrate Austen's inversions of Roche's plot and characters.
51 Kuper, *Incest and Influence*, p. 244.
52 Kuper, *Incest and Influence*, p. 247.

53 Perry, p. 369.
54 Regina Maria Roche, *Clermont*, 4 vols (London: The Minerva Press, 1798), I, pp. 30–1. Subsequent references will be given in the text.
55 A further cousin marriage is anticipated in a proposed union between de Sevignie and D'Alembert's daughter as a bribe to assure the silence of the servants who raised de Sevignie; a marriage between their foster-son and a member of the aristocracy would enrich and ennoble them. D'Alembert's daughter is de Sevignie's second cousin (his father's first cousin).
56 Philippe, similar to Weimar in Eliza Parsons's *The Castle of Wolfenbach* (1793), sees his niece's marriage as a method of repayment. Although Philippe envisions Madeline's union to his son as reimbursement for a debt of sorrow, while Weimar desires his niece marry him as a repayment for the money he spent raising her, both see the exchanges of their nieces' bodies through marriage as transactions that will settle debts. See Chapter 3 for a further analysis of obligation, debt and exchange in uncle–niece relationships.
57 See Tamaz Bereczkei, Petra Gyuris and Glenn E Weisfeld, 'Sexual imprinting in human mate choice', *Proceedings of the Royal Society B: Biological Sciences*, 271 (2004), 1129–34 for an account of human recognition of 'gene-related "strangers"' (1129).
58 That Madeline is intended as a gift for Philippe's son and not for Philippe (particularly given his status as her uncle – almost always a role fraught with incestuous desires for the niece) is an inversion of what Anne K. Mellor describes as 'the perverse desire of the older generation to usurp the sexual rights of the younger generation' underlying the Male Gothic's deployment of father–daughter rape in her work; *Mary Shelley: Her Life, Her Fiction, Her Monsters* (London: Routledge, 1989), p. 197.
59 Perry, p. 121.
60 This type of cousin marriage – parallel cousins – is slightly less common than cross-cousin marriages. John Maynard Smith points to the prohibition of parallel cousin unions as a leftover from primitive societies in *The Evolution of Sex* (Cambridge: Cambridge University Press, 1978), p. 144. Lévi-Strauss describes women as being received (as wife) or given (as sister or daughter), arguing that parallel cousin marriages are less common as 'parallel cousins come from families in the same formal position, which is a position of static equilibrium' (Lévi-Strauss, p. 138).
61 As Philippe and Clermont are half-siblings who married full siblings, the parallel cousin bond is doubled and, with it, the risk of two brothers sharing one sister. Richard D. Alexander points to this as a paternal uncertainty factor that renders parallel cousin marriage less than desirable in certain societies such as polygynous ones, where parallel cousins may also be half-siblings. See Alexander, *Darwinism and Human Affairs* (Seattle: University of Washington Press, 1979), pp. 177–88. The potential

then, is for Madeline and de Sevignie to be more than half, though less than full, siblings, a potential compounded by the charge of adultery levelled against Philippe.

62 Marcel Mauss in *The Gift: The Form and Reason for Exchange in Archaic Societies* [1925] trans. W. D. Halls (London: Routledge, 1990) examines the contractual nature of gift exchange (p. 4), while Luce Irigaray in *This Sex Which is Not One* [1977], trans. Catherine Porter and Carolyn Burke (Ithaca, NY: Cornell University Press, 1985) describes how our social structure makes women '"products" used and exchanged by men. Their status is that of merchandise, "commodities"' (p. 84). Madeline is positioned by her uncle and father as a commodity Clermont is obliged to offer his nephew, while she subverts this through her initiative as the pursuer in her interactions with de Sevignie.

63 See David Livingstone Smith, 'Beyond Westermarck: can shared mothering or maternal phenotype matching account for incest avoidance?', *Evolutionary Psychology*, 5:1 (2007), 202–22 for an analysis of childhood co-rearing causing sibling-like bonds between non-kin (203). See also Chapter 2's exploration of sibling incest, particularly in Eleanor Sleath's *The Orphan of the Rhine* (1798), in which the sibling bond and mutual love between the non-related Enrico and Laurette bears a marked resemblance to that of Percival and Ellen.

64 Perry's exploration of the demands of family obligation and individual desires as increasingly difficult to negotiate in eighteenth-century literature (p. 221) is relevant here; she identifies a nostalgia for stronger consanguineal bonds in many texts of the period (p. 373). In an inversion of this, Ellen's subsumption of her desires in fulfilment of family duty reveals the claustrophobic, unreasonable demands of kin.

65 Anna Maria Bennett, *Ellen, Countess of Castle Howel*, 4 vols (London: The Minerva Press, 1794), I, p. 122. Subsequent references will be given in the text.

66 This sense of a familial burden is supported by Ellen's marriage to Lord Castle Howel to preserve her family's home following family pressure, the representations of the Meredith children living at Code Gwyn who contribute little to its maintenance and Lord Howel's burdensome sister and aunts who demand his financial support and duty.

67 Kuper, *Incest and Influence*, p. 17. Kuper focuses particularly on upper-middle-class families in nineteenth-century England to argue that the casual and unchaperoned environments in which cousins associated facilitated the development of romantic attachments, a point that applies equally to the environment in which Ellen and Percival are raised.

68 Steven Buyske and Alex Walter, 'The Westermarck effect and early childhood co-socialization: sex differences in inbreeding-avoidance', *British Journal of Developmental Psychology*, 21:3 (2003), 362–3.

69 The representation of the mutual and natural development of Ellen and Percival's love echoes Alethea Brereton Lewis's *The Nuns of the Desert: or, The Woodland Witches*, 2 vols (London: The Minerva Press, 1805), which describes the love between two sets of half-cousins as follows: 'Formed by Nature to constitute each other's felicity … By pursuing their own wishes, each party gratified those of the other; so exactly consonant were their principles, their sentiments, and their dispositions. Nor was the union between Sophia Selwyn and Ferdinand less perfect' (II, p. 122).

70 The Westermarck effect, which posits that children raised together (whether blood kin or not) tend to become non-viable mates as they view each other as kin, typically when they share parental figures and are brought up in the same household, is bypassed here and often is with cousins who do not share parental figures and/or households. See Edward Westermarck, *The History of Human Marriage* (London: Macmillan and Co., 1903), pp. 320–30.

71 The Merediths' carelessness in undercharging their tenants and Lord Howel's inattention regarding the money he gives his sister are represented as acts of dangerous generosity. Inverting the typical Gothic trope of generosity being indicative of a moral and responsible character, in Bennett's novel it has potentially devastating consequences.

72 Ellen is coerced into being a gift for Lord Howel; her liberty of individual choice is denied in favour of fulfilling obligation to the family. That she is forced into this position due, in large part, to her family's overinflated sense of obligation to their tenants, reinforces the sense that traditional economies of gifts, exchanges, obligation and ownership have become onerous and incapable of proper management.

73 Code Gwyn is described as 'a large gothic mansion, built at a time, when imperfect laws and civil discord obliged the chiefs of the country to consult safety, more than pleasure and convenience, in the construction and situation of their houses' (I, p. 2).

74 Perry, p. 234.

75 Elizabeth Thomas, *Purity of Heart, or The Ancient Costume, A Tale, In One Volume, Addressed to the Author of Glenarvon* (London: W. Simplin and R. Marshall, 1816), pp. v–vii. Subsequent references will be given in the text.

76 Thomas here creates Sir Lusignan in a model recognisable as Rousseau's male citizen, whose role in the public world is contrasted to that of women in the private sphere. Sir Lusignan's public life is appropriately grounded in patriotic military achievements. See Rousseau, *The Social Contract*, pp. 36–9.

77 Ellesmere shares many qualities with *Emmeline*'s Delamere in this regard.

78 Perry argues that the kinship changes throughout the long eighteenth century positioned women 'as the sexual property of their husbands rather than as partners and co-owners of the marital household' as part of their increasing commodification (p. 251) and that 'if women were to stay put as the

sexual property of one man and one man only, they had to be trained to feel repugnance for physical relations with anyone else. The emphasis of woman's sexual allegiance to a mate, rather than her obedience to a father, also signaled the realignment of kinship along a conjugal rather than consanguineal axis' (p. 254). Camilla's representation negotiates sexual repugnance towards Ellesmere with sexual fidelity to her cousin/husband, blending fidelity and duty to both models of sexual allegiance and repugnance and obedience to family.

79 Perry, p. 124.
80 Camilla's role within Sir Lusignan's house is akin to that advocated for wives by Rousseau in *Emile*: 'the obedience and the fidelity she owes to her husband and the tenderness and the care she owes to her children are consequences of her position so natural and easily sensed that she cannot without bad faith refuse her consent to the inner sentiment that guides her, nor fail to recognize her duty if her inclinations are still uncorrupted' (p. 382).
81 This is quite different from Linton's speech over Cathy's possessions in *Wuthering Heights*, where the husband's ownership of wifely possessions is shown to be a cruel tyranny.
82 The negotiation between parental authority and individual choice or affinal ties is a common one in the eighteenth-century novel, particularly the Gothic. In Lewis's *Nuns of the Desert* the villain, Mr Selwyn, says to his daughters: '"you are already acquainted with your lot in future life; it being the result of both the wisdom and affection of those who have, as they ought to have, unlimited power over your destiny"' (I, p. 120). The girls defy their father's desire for them to become nuns, fleeing from the convent and renouncing his authority in favour of their own destinies (one sister marries her half-cousin, the other announces she will remain single) and the rebellion ends with both sisters happy.
83 Camilla exemplifies Rousseau's understanding of the ideal wife: she remains entrenched in the private sphere and in marrying her cousin she submits to both conjugal and familial obligations. Rousseau asserts that 'to please men, to be useful to them, to make herself loved and honored by them, to raise them when young, to care for them when grown, to counsel them, to console them, to make their lives agreeable and sweet – these are the duties of women at all times' (*Emile*, p. 365).
84 See Chapter 3 for an examination of the phallic knife wielded against women in the Gothic, particularly in scenes depicting uncles with incestuous desires for their nieces.
85 The dangers of foreign influence on British women is a convention of much literature written during and following the 1790s; Linda Colley examines the impact of the execution of Marie-Antoinette on British anxiety over the treatment of women during the French Revolution as it became clear that

domesticity was no longer safe for wives and mothers in France, arguing that 'in Great Britain, woman was subordinate and confined. But at least she was also safe. The twin themes of the peculiar safety of British women and of their danger from the French were played on assiduously by loyalist propaganda during the wars' (p. 262).

86 In *Pathologies of the West: An Anthropology of Mental Illness in Europe and America* (London: Continuum, 2002), Roland Littlewood examines the higher social stigma against cross-generational incest due to the sexualisation of power and the erosion of care-giving involved in such relationships (p. 145).

87 The illness may be what robs Sir Lusignan of his desire for extramarital affairs; Thomas draws on the Gothic tradition of wounded heroes but implies a lessening of sexual power not alluded to in earlier Gothic texts.

88 In a likely unintended consequence, Thomas acknowledges that notions of female obligation and duty will not result in liberation as Camilla never becomes a 'citizen' – she exists only as a dependant in Sir Lusignan's home; Calantha, conversely, becomes liberated from the confines of gender ideologies through her unruly and socially unacceptable desire that defies the demands of duty and obligation.

89 Selina Davenport, *The Sons of the Viscount and the Daughters of the Earl*, 4 vols (London: Henry Colburn, 1813), I, p. 42. Subsequent references will be given in the text.

90 In *Incest and Influence* Kuper argues that the 1858 Bemiss report that claimed both close kin unions and miscegenation caused birth defects due to bad blood was the impetus behind laws that banned biracial and cousin marriages in America (p. 249); Davenport's language reveals such ideas regarding contaminated blood were part of earlier understandings of family bloodlines. That Davenport locates the sullied blood within non-kin who are like kin displays an ambiguity similar to the Bemiss report's assertions regarding the danger of unions either too similar or too different.

91 Perry, pp. 230–1.

92 Perry, p. 230.

93 The cousin bond here demonstrates its flexibility, allowing cousins to relate to and identify one another as siblings and simultaneously feel attraction and desire for each other.

94 Irigaray's point about the commodification of women within the structure of exchange is relevant here, as Davenport's description of beauty demonstrates Elvira's true value is as an object; Davenport similarly plays with the Gothic convention of incestuous uncles, underscoring the dangers of endogamic desires and the paternal power that seeks to confine Elvira within the familial structure.

95 Like Philippe, Lord De Courci wants to control the daughter of his older brother; both here and in Roche's novel the uncle selects the beautiful niece for his son's wife. In the novels examined in Chapter 3 the younger brothers who threatened their nieces with rape, violence and theft had no sons to use as sexual substitutes.
96 Davidoff and Hall, *Family Fortunes*, pp. 353–4.
97 The sibling-like quality of their relationship that causes them to be compatible echoes the idealisation of such brother–sister relationships as that of Ferdinand and Julia in Ann Radcliffe's *A Sicilian Romance* (1790).
98 Perry, p. 123.
99 Like Bennett's Ellen, Henry is obligated to undergo a first marriage due to familial pressures before the fortuitous death of the spouse enables the marriage based on individual choice.
100 Davenport's depiction of familial obligation as largely incompatible with individual rights and choices is another example of a novel that struggles to conform to the overarching narrative of nostalgia for kinship identified in eighteenth-century literature as sentimentalising 'the consanguineal basis for obligation' (Perry, p. 8).
101 Constance Rover, *Women's Suffrage and Party Politics in Britain, 1866–1914* (London: Routledge & Kegan Paul, 1967), p. 3.
102 Pauline Nestor, 'Introduction', Emily Brontë, *Wuthering Heights* (London: Penguin, 2003), p. xxxi.
103 Nestor, p. xxix.
104 Emily Brontë, *Wuthering Heights*, ed. Pauline Nestor (London: Penguin, 2003), p. 13. Subsequent references will be given in the text.
105 Similarities to the overlapping, intergenerational kinship ties in *Clermont* are apparent.
106 Nestor, p. xxvi.
107 This is analogous to the analysis in Chapter 2 of Radcliffe's *A Sicilian Romance*, in which Julia hopes the handsome young Hippolitus is her brother.
108 Cathy's desire to identify Linton as a sibling is not concurrent with romantic feelings in spite of the love letters, as Brontë represents the epistolary exchange as resulting from Cathy's immaturity and frustration at being prohibited from visiting her cousin rather than a true desire or passion for Linton.
109 Cathy's attempt to buy her freedom from her cousin/husband is futile as he already owns her possessions. Brontë provides a parallel to the contemporary laws that denied citizenship without property ownership and shows the impossibility of female participation in the state. Colley's point bears repeating: 'stripped by marriage of a separate identity and autonomous property, a woman could not by definition be a citizen and could never look to possess

political rights' (p. 254). Cathy cannot buy her freedom from her husband and women could not buy the individual rights guaranteed by citizenship as both family and state repress female rights through the law.
110 Perry, p. 123.
111 Heathcliff echoes Zillah's sentiment that a union between Hareton and Cathy will end badly: '"if I see him listen to you, I'll send him seeking his bread where he can get it! Your love will make him an outcast, and a beggar"' (p. 321). Heathcliff means Hareton will be a beggar because he will cast him out with nothing, but also alludes to Catherine's love that sent him from Wuthering Heights to return, too late, as a permanent outsider.
112 This is parallel to the relationship Cathy's mother had with Heathcliff and is like that between Roche's Madeline and de Sevignie.
113 Brontë, like Davenport, displays an understanding (and rejection of) the beliefs underlying the later American bans against cousin and interracial marriage that Kuper describes as grounded in the idea that 'in the one case the "blood" was too similar, in the other too alien' in *Incest and Influence*, p. 249.
114 Eugenia C. DeLamotte, *Perils of the Night: A Feminist Study of Nineteenth-Century Gothic* (Oxford: Oxford University Press, 1990), p. 224.
115 John Maynard, *Charlotte Brontë and Sexuality* (Cambridge: Cambridge University Press, 1984), p. 137.
116 Charlotte Brontë, *Jane Eyre*, ed. Stevie Davies (London: Penguin Classics, 2006), p. 396. Subsequent references will be given in the text.
117 DeLamotte, p. 217.
118 DeLamotte, pp. 224–5.
119 As in *Wuthering Heights* and the sibling relationships examined in Chapter 2, like and like are ideally united in marriage to create sympathetic and egalitarian unions.
120 As in Cathy's voiced desire to have Linton as a brother, here the claims for a sibling bond are expressed rather than experienced. The desire for the bond is present, but the bond itself is not.
121 Maynard, p. 133.
122 DeLamotte, p. 222.
123 Hoeveler, pp. 221–2.
124 DeLamotte, p. 224.
125 Maynard argues regarding the maiming that: 'Rochester has received a blow but is anything but sexually impotent when Jane sees him' (p. 138).
126 Stevie Davies, 'Notes', Brontë, *Jane Eyre*, p. 577.
127 Eli Edward Burriss, 'The use and worship of fire among the Romans', *Classical Weekly*, 24:6 (1930), 45.
128 Maynard, p. 119.
129 Davies, p. 578.

130 DeLamotte, p. 226.
131 Kuper 'Incest, cousin marriage', 166–7.
132 Hoeveler, p. 38.
133 Kuper, 'Changing the subject', 727
134 The institution of family thus comes to represent other forms of arbitrary power systems, such as the legal and political institutions.
135 Pinker describes marriages between cousins as unions that 'enmesh them in a network of triangular relationships' (34).

5
Queer mothers:
female sexual agency and male victims

> [O]n genetic grounds, mother–son incest should be the rarest, brother–sister more common, and father–daughter the most common.
> Joseph Shepher, *Incest: A Biosocial View* (1983)[1]

In examining the occurrence of mother–son incest what is striking is just how infrequent examples of mothers and sons engaged in sexual relationships are, in both literature and life. And yet, as Karen Sanchez-Eppler states, 'If father–daughter incest has been found to be most prevalent in practice, erotic relations between mothers and sons have long dominated the symbolic discourse of incest.'[2] Her point is an important one that I believe illuminates a disjunction between the prevalence of scholarship featuring *Oedipus Rex* and Freud in discussions of incest and the actual limited occurrence of mother–son incest, particularly compared to father–daughter incest.[3] The disparity between the statistics on mother–son incest compared to those on other incestuous relationships is accounted for in biological terms by the genetic disadvantages of mother–son inbreeding.[4] Shepher's attempt to account for the rarity of mother–son incest through its corresponding low genetic gains moves from the biological to the social. Shepher argues that the incest inhibition proscribed by the maternal act of nurturance does not exist in mothers such as 'queens who did not have time for such everyday activities, upper middle-class mothers who were too busy with shopping and philanthropic activities, and prostitutes who had to supply their clients'.[5]

The shift from emphasising the incest taboo as biologically rooted to using a sociopolitical lexicon attempts to explain the conditions that lead to incest as both culturally created and unnatural. Mother–son incest is described here as a failure of women to act according to their biological nature as a consequence of social conditions that enable (or force) them unnaturally to work or otherwise abdicate their maternal obligations. Locating the socially proscribed gender ideologies that render mother–son incest unlikely as being biologically grounded or natural exposes the same understandings of mother–son incest that have underpinned both literary representations of and scholarly discourse on the topic. That research across a range of fields suggests there are links between positions of power, non-maternal instincts and dangerous sexual promiscuity illuminates the sociopolitical investment in maintaining the myth of biologically determined gender ideologies. These ideologies, enforced by the mother's position as nurturer or deviant, are equally informed by the sexual politics of power and desire as described by scholars such as George E. Haggerty in *Queer Gothic* (2006), Luce Irigaray in *This Sex Which is Not One* (1977) and Michel Foucault in *The History of Sexuality* (1976). Examining the intersections of sexuality and power within the representations of mother–son incest in the Gothic reveals the complexities of the radical destabilisations of gender and heteronormativity occurring therein.[6]

Leo Bersani argues that attempts to subvert heteronormativity through sadomasochism fail because the nature of s/m is a reproduction of the power dynamics that it seeks to subvert.[7] Bersani uses the presence of sadomasochism within gay sexual culture to demonstrate that the power dynamics of this type of sexual encounter are connected to the overall ideology of power relationships in society. In troubling the idea of sadomasochism as a challenge to authority, Bersani exposes the inadequacies of mere rearticulations truly to subvert ideologies.[8] I believe Bersani's argument can be applied to literary portrayals of rearticulated ideologies to reveal the paradoxical nature of these depictions as challenges to heteronormativity. In this respect Bersani's argument is particularly profitable in terms of incest representations that present sadomasochist structures as inherent in these relationships and in representations that reimagine similar incestuous configurations devoid of these elements.[9] Bersani states: 'S/M profoundly – and in spite of itself – argues for the continuity between political structures of oppression and the body's erotic economy.'[10] This understanding reveals that the models of sexuality and power available in the Gothic allow writers not merely to rearticulate, but also to literalise the political structures of oppression through incest. Such literalisations subvert the structure of male power and dominance by revealing its dangers to the male and female bodies that do not conform to heteronormative ideologies of power and desire. The Gothic, in novels by writers such as Ann Radcliffe and Eliza Parsons, challenges the notion of chaste maternity by revealing the mother as sexually desirable and aligning her rediscovery with her daughter's sexual awakening.[11] Gothic texts by writers such as Matthew Lewis, William Beckford, Eugenia de Acton and Charlotte Dacre rearticulate this subversion through a queering of desires that creates male victims of maternal desires or agency and disrupts cultural requirements of male dominance. Though these modes of the Gothic respond to the figure of the mother differently, both position her as aligned with sexuality and disruptive to heteronormativity's restrictive models of sexuality.

Heteronormative fears of maternal sexuality are exacerbated by the idea that mothers could use sexual agency, in a socially disruptive way, to seduce, force or coerce their sons into a sexual relationship. As Susan McKinnon puts it: 'Where sexual intercourse is thought to involve the "naturally" assertive, even aggressive, agency of men and the equally "naturally" passive acquiescence ... of women, it follows that paternal incest would be viewed in terms that stress its relative "normalcy" at the same time that maternal incest would be viewed in pathological terms.'[12] In re-examining accounts that claim father–daughter incest is engendered by the mother/wife's neglect of the family (for example, in seeking work outside the home, or if the husband is 'relegated' to positions such as child-minder or housekeeper) McKinnon reveals that such understandings view incest as 'caused' by the father/husband's relocation into a traditionally female function in the house. The horror 'with which women contemplate its [incest's] possibility, is due to the "naturally" nurturant role of women as mothers' – a role that men are presumed ill-equipped to fulfil. When fathers are forced into functions incompatible with their masculine, non-nurturing 'nature' that fails to contemplate incest with horror, male-perpetrated incest follows.'[13] Why then is it so monstrous for women to commit incest when it is represented as a natural consequence of their traditional position when this role is taken on by the husband? As McKinnon points out so succinctly, mothers are assumed incapable of assaulting their sons because 'they lack the sexual equipment necessary for direct sexual agency or assault. Without a penis women are assumed to be the acquiescent objects, not the active agents, of sexual acts.'[14] The idea of women as actively assaulting men sexually is such a troubling idea to normative definitions of female agency that the existence of such acts is often dismissed.[15] Though McKinnon refers to the way modern Americans view the role of the mother, its applicability to the British eighteenth- and nineteenth-century Gothic is aptly demonstrated in her assertion that: 'the only way to account for the contravention of the "natural" is by conjuring the "unnatural" – a woman whose intellectual deficiency or psychological pathology completely undermines her maternal nature'.[16]

This 'unnatural' mother, one capable of aggressive sexuality or sexual agency, is a figure often represented in the Gothic as a stepmother or similar relation. In this genre populated with incestuous relationships, mothers who are involved in sexual liaisons with their sons or daughters are hard to find.[17] Haggerty points to the erotic mothers of Radcliffe's novels, but he identifies an 'erotics of loss' rather than a physically or emotionally sexual relationship (though this does not preclude the possibility of a sexual element).[18] The heroine's birth mother is more often a victim of the patriarchy than a sexual aggressor.[19] Ruth Bienstock Anolik describes this latter type of mother as a figure in constant peril: 'the typical Gothic mother is absent: dead, imprisoned, or somehow abjected … Those Gothic mothers who are not actually dead are effaced by their husbands or other representations of the patriarchy in some way.'[20] This analysis of the mother is particularly relevant to scholarly discourse positioning the Female Gothic in opposition to the Male Gothic as in the latter the mother is often rearticulated into the most 'unnatural' mother of all: the incestuous mother capable of aggressive sexual agency or the power to refuse sexual access to the female body. An overrepresentation of mother–son incest in the Gothic written by men – predominantly homosexual men – and frequently absent mothers in the Radcliffean Gothic is apparent. Scholars such as Toni Bowers, Felicity A. Nussbaum and Ruth Perry have theorised that from the mid-eighteenth century onwards motherhood is characterised by the removal of the sexual from the maternal.[21] The Radcliffean Gothic reworks this tradition by removing the maternal from the narrative until the heroine can reclaim her mother as she simultaneously locates her own sexuality. The Gothic as written by authors such as Beckford, Lewis and Horace Walpole responds to the mother by relocating her as the sexual centre of the text as victim or perpetrator, making the chaste maternal monstrous through mother–son incest. Representing mothers as capable of sexual aggression and holding positions of power, male bodies are revealed as vulnerable to aggression and capable of submission. This use of the sexually aggressive incestuous mother radically destabilises the tradition of heteronormativity and conventional power dynamics that demand and naturalise male dominance and female submission. The Gothic, whether reclaiming the mother or demonstrating her sexual agency, exposes heteronormative society as at once creating and rejecting queer sexualities.

Part of the title of E. J. Clery's essay on Walpole, 'the impossibility of female desire', summarises the extent to which female desire is viewed as unimaginable and as such already queer, already placed outside the heteronormative realm, and thus transgressive.[22] Ruth Perry points out that 'gothic fiction ... was written in the closing decades of the eighteenth century by women and homosexual men'.[23] Because of what we know of the authors' sexual orientation and the genre's fixation on transgressive sexuality, the application of queer theory to Gothic texts has been widely made use of by scholars such as Max Fincher and Haggerty.[24] It seems particularly appropriate to apply this methodology to the instances of mother–son incest that combine the queerness of female desire with the queerness of male passivity and the queerness of incest. Bersani uses Foucauldian ways of thinking about pleasure to argue that the intolerance of homosexuality reveals: 'a more profound anxiety about a threat to the way people are expected to relate to one another, which is not too different from saying the way power is positioned and exercised in our society'.[25] If we replace the intolerance of queerness with the intolerance of incest, another type of sexuality that falls outside of the normative constructs, we can see how Bersani's point about anxieties regarding power relationships applies here. The incest that is the least heteronormative of all, I would argue, is mother–son incest, because of the reasons for its rarity advanced by sociologists, anthropologists and geneticists. Mothers using sexual agency to coerce their sons thoroughly disrupts traditional understandings of passive women and aggressive men and the maintenance of power implicit in these constructions. This type of incest, like homosexuality in Bersani's terms, reveals through its social production of intolerance similarly profound anxieties about power and social relations. What appeals to me the most about Bersani's use of Foucault to shape an understanding of the social intolerance of homosexuality and my desire to apply it to incest intolerance (read: social revulsion) – particularly incest of the mother–son variety – is that it speaks to my overall argument regarding power relations in the Gothic. For if, as Bersani states, there are connections between 'the way we take our pleasure and the way we exercise power' then there must certainly be something seriously destabilising to traditional power relationships – sexual and political – in the mere idea of mother–son sex.[26]

In order to explore the implications of the representations of mother–son incest I will analyse Walpole's *The Mysterious Mother* (1768), a Gothic play involving mother–son incest in which the mother seduces her son on the night of her husband's funeral. The text unites a condemnation of the Catholic church with anxieties over inheritance and female sexual agency. Walpole's play is unique not only in the clear description of sexual intercourse between mother and son, but also in its convoluted publication history and contemporaneous condemnation. Though Walpole's work is a play, the representation of incest functions much like that of mother–son incest in the Gothic novels I analyse due, in part, to its treatment as tragic and its presentation of aggressive female agency. In Beckford's novel *Vathek* (1786), Vathek's mother Carathis is the epitome of maternal evil. Obsessed with the dark arts and, though celibate, overly focused on her son's sexual encounters, she is fixated on being admitted to hell with a near-sexual desire. Her ability to manipulate Vathek into evil-doings to promote their descent to the Halls of Eblis, where the forbidden can be known, is, in itself, an incestuous structure that highlights the dangers of mothers educating sons and positions female power as masculinising. In Lewis's *The Monk* (1796) the titular character murders his mother in a sexually motivated act that Radcliffe would later rework in another violent and incestuous scene. I also briefly discuss *Ernestus Berchtold; or, The Modern Oedipus: A Tale* (1819) by John Polidori, a novel in which Polidori, perhaps most famous for *The Vampyre* (1819) and his role as Lord Byron's personal physician, depicts twin siblings haunted by their mother. Polidori's novel represents the mother as an erotic and ghostly figure, physically effaced while remaining maternal and seductive. In analysing these texts and their accompanying criticism it becomes clear that the figure of the mother tends to be characterised in one of two ways: either as overly maternal or non-maternal. Both of these characterisations, in their incestuous incarnations, reflect an extension and conflation of the two functions already present for mothers in the Gothic: that of the nurturing good mother or the sexual bad mother. In combining and exaggerating these roles, Gothic writers trouble the either/or dichotomy of good or bad, virgin or whore, absent or present mother that tends to dominate examinations of the maternal. Focusing on these Gothic texts that range from implied, explicit and violent depictions of mother–son incest, the absent or hyper-present mother is revealed as a figure impossible to ignore and highly disruptive to traditional models of female sexuality and desire.

THE MYSTERIOUSNESS OF MOTHERS HAVING DESIRES

Walpole's *The Mysterious Mother* is described by David Punter and Glennis Byron as a: 'tragic contemplation of human desire and suffering ... a darker, more serious and more psychologically complex vision of what Edmund ... calls "this theatre of monstrous guilt"'.[27] The play depicts the Countess of Narbonne's incestuous relationship with her son Edmund and his subsequent incestuous relationship with his daughter/sister, Adeliza. On the night of her husband's funeral the Countess discovers her son has a rendezvous planned with a servant. She disguises herself as the maid, intending to chastise Edmund, but is instead overcome with desire based on Edmund's physical similarities to his father and has sex with him. Edmund is sent away to war and his mother has their child, Adeliza, who is raised in the nearby convent as the Countess's ward. The Countess maintains possession of the castle and property while Edmund fights in wars for the next sixteen years, returning home to fall in love with Adeliza and marry her. This prompts the Countess finally to reveal all and go mad. She stabs herself, after which Edmund rushes to die in battle and Adeliza is sent (again) to a convent. The play has attracted much critical attention in part because of the agency of the mother in the incest scene, causing disagreement between scholars such as Robert Miles and Clery regarding the play's subversiveness or adherence to social and political institutions.[28] Regardless of the play's intention to uphold or ridicule the legitimacy of government and religious institutions, the figure of the mother, in her sexual agency, reveals anxieties about the female body as capable of having aggressive designs on unsuspecting (or passive) male bodies. The inversion of male/female gender ideologies and their respective sexual positions as aggressor or passive receiver is realised through the mother's desires and deviousness. Walpole queers the 'unnatural mother' of Gothic fiction into ultimately wielding the phallic sword on her own body in a final act of sexual aggression and suicide.

Contemporary criticism of the play is wide and varied; Haggerty points particularly to Coleridge's take on it: 'no one with a true spark of manliness, of which Horace Walpole had none, could have written it.'[29] Haggerty's reading places the 'unmanning' of Edmund as lying with the father–daughter incest aspect of the plot: 'Just as Edmund, the play's hero, is unmanned by the news that his bride is in fact his daughter, Walpole's interest in this incest plot unmans him because it places him in lurid relation to the erotics of family life.'[30] The 'unmanning' is a consequence of Edmund's ignorance regarding the incest; he is 'unmanned' or 'feminised' by his ignorant and passive position. Haggerty believes that Walpole's presentation of incest as a spectacle reveals his sexuality as it positions Walpole 'outside the normativity that he would attack'.[31] Coleridge's criticism of Walpole and scholarly understanding of the play's status as a challenge to normativity speak to the queerness of the play's subject matter: incestuous relationships the male hero enters into unknowingly and thus against his will. This 'disgusting' subject matter – men capable of victimisation at the hands of active female agents – was alluded to by Walpole himself.[32] In a preface to the 1781 edition of the play Walpole writes that the author: 'is sensible that the subject is disgusting … All the favour the Author solicits or expects, is, to be believed how unwillingly he has submitted to its appearance.'[33] Walpole's protests at letting the material out into the world unwillingly are substantiated by his hesitation to have it performed and perhaps also influenced by the play's reception, as by the time he wrote the preface the play had been circulating for over a decade.

Jeffrey N. Cox questions Walpole's hesitation to have the play performed as follows: 'the assumption has always been, from Walpole forward, that the play was unstageable because it presented mother-son incest'.[34] Cox believes that the play indicates that regardless of the presence of religion, unrestrained sexuality will not be contained. In the play's postscript Walpole's own discussion of (ir)rationality and sexual urges suggests an ironic treatment of conventional sexuality, claiming that 'in order to make use of a canvas so shocking, it was necessary as much as possible to palliate the crime, and raise the character of the criminal' (p. 253). To achieve this, Walpole links desire, reason and grief: 'To attain the former end, I imagined the moment in which she has lost a beloved husband, when grief, disappointment, and a conflict of passions might be supposed to have thrown her reason off its guard' (p. 253). Walpole attempts to justify the Countess's act of sexual agency by emphasising her grief, highlighting a lack of reason that 'might be' behind the incestuous encounter. But Walpole's intentions regarding the Countess's actions can perhaps be understood by his postscript: 'I have placed my fable at the dawn of the reformation; consequently the strength of mind in the Countess may be supposed to have borrowed aid from other sources, besides those she found in her own understanding' (p. 253). Walpole explains that the Countess's reason is beyond that found in typical weak (female) understanding and fixes on the historical context of the Reformation and its surrounding emphasis on free will. The explanation – which combines references to the Countess's strength of mind while describing her as irrational from grief – is curiously ambivalent. Nowhere in the play does Walpole expose the strong-minded mother as influenced by anything other than rational thought or desires. His explanation of her as deranged by grief thus becomes specious at best; a palliation designed to appease rather than be believed.

Such half-hearted explanations are hardly unique to Walpole's postscript; John Polidori makes a similar assertion in his novel *Ernestus Berchtold*. Written decades after Walpole's play it too features themes of mother–son and brother–sister incest. Polidori claims in his introduction:

> A tale that rests upon improbabilities, must generally disgust a rational mind; I am therefore afraid that, though I have thrown the superior agency into the back ground as much as was in my power, still, that many readers will think that the same moral, and the same colouring, might have been given to characters acting under the ordinary agencies of life; I believe it, but I had agreed to write a supernatural tale, and that does not allow of a completely every-day narrative.[35]

Both authors distance themselves from the 'disgusting' nature of their works, emphasising the impact of either grief or supernatural agency on their characters and their actions. The distinction frequently made between the explained supernatural and supernatural Gothic tales seems less important than the use authors made of these different elements to effect (or to claim to effect) the same end: abdicating responsibility for what readers would see as the disgusting subject matter of mother–son desires. The rejection of rational thinking is in fact Walpole's deliberate manipulation of rational and irrational elements in order to justify before disrupting the generic conventions of female agency and rationality.

The play's combination of tragedy, tale, satire and comedy resembles the generic mixture in *The Castle of Otranto* (1764).[36] In his postscript Walpole wrote: 'The subject is so horrid that I thought it would shock, rather than give satisfaction' and that 'the subject is more truly horrid than even that of Oedipus' (p. 251). Clery describes Walpole's delayed revelation of incest in the play as essential to its tragic effect which enabled incest to be depicted without offending audiences: 'incest as it appears within this literary schema was by no means shocking to polite theatre goers of the eighteenth century'.[37] But the Reverend William Mason, a contemporary of Walpole's who read his manuscript, found the agency of the mother objectionable: 'In Mason's view the Countess sacrifices all claims to pity by her active sexuality, her voluntary commission of incest'.[38] Rejecting the Countess's agency shows the desire to privilege tragedy as the appropriate mode in which to portray incest. Clery suggests that 'the reconstruction of the tale as a tragedy was an acknowledgement that in an age of sensibility, stories of female sexuality could only end in disaster' – Walpole's blending of forms reveals society's conception of female sexual agency as disastrous.[39] This adherence to viewing incest as tragic is described by Frank as a critical failure: 'Considering that high tragedy has been the privileged mode in Freud's centring of sexuality in the family through incest and its prohibitions, it is not altogether surprising that psychoanalytic accounts have failed to appreciate Walpole's parodic family romances'.[40] Incest itself is not repugnant as a theme but the structural changes Walpole uses to depict it are because they destabilise the traditional messages conveyed in incest tales or tragedies.[41]

Rather than read the revelation of incest as delayed, I argue that Walpole establishes secrecy and sexual transgression on the Countess's part from the beginning of the play, self-consciously offering the reader (or viewer) the idea of incest early on. A conversation between monks regarding the Countess establishes their belief that a sexual transgression underlies her self-imposed constant prayer and atonement without confession. Benedict says of the Countess's penance for this secret sin: ' "this woman was not cast in human mould" ' (p. 182). The monk unwittingly voices the church's perception of the incest that prompts her devotion as monstrously unnatural. Edmund says of his mother: ' "she herself was woman then; a sensual woman. Nor satiety, sickness and age, and virtue's frowardness, had so obliterated pleasure's relish – she might have pardoned what she felt so well" ' (p. 192). He believes that his mother, a 'real' woman with sexual desires, would have forgiven his sexual transgression with the maid. Edmund compares his active male sexuality to that of his mother and describes her change after his night with Beatrice: ' "her heart, never too partial to me, grew estrang'd. Estrang'd! – aversion in its fellest mood scowl'd from her eye, and drove me from her sight. She call'd me impious, named my honest lewdness, a profanation of my father's ashes"' (p. 193). The anger Edmund feels from the Countess follows a lifetime of maternal indifference and neglect.[42] Edmund thinks the sexual intercourse he engaged in was '"honest lewdness"' and does not understand that his mother's reaction is caused by her guilt, though it is clear to the reader that something serious is at play here. Edmund has fought in wars and is weary of his mother's banishment: '"to stain my sword with random blood"' (p. 194) no longer pleases him; he wants to return home. Walpole uses the Gothic metaphor of sword for penis in a typically bloody image, uniting it to incest via Edmund's desire no longer to stain his sword with foreign blood but to return it to his native soil, into the sheath, as it were, of family.

The argument that the revelation of incest is a shock at the play's ending becomes strained under the repetition of sexual allusions united to images of the mother, father and home; the reader expects some sort of incestuous reveal. Cox points to the Countess's passion for her husband 'that hurled her into the arms of her son'.[43] While Cox's language marginalises the mother's agency in the sexual act, implying she was mindlessly propelled by passion rather than cunningly disguising herself to deceive her son into sex, the play suggests this incestuous agency from the very start. Peter, the porter of the castle, says of the Countess regarding her deceased husband: '"I marvel not my lady cherishes his remembrance, for he was comely to sight, wond'rous and goodly built. They say, his son, Count Edmund's mainly like him"' (p. 179). The porter's description counters a tendency to overlook the Countess's action; comparisons between the physical appearances of (particularly cross-generation) family members often cause sexual desires. For the Countess, such desires are inspired by Edmund's 'wond'rous' physical similarities to his father.[44] The Countess calls herself a monster who has committed sins 'unheard of' and 'horrors', asking of Edmund: '"has not a mother's hand afflicted him enough?"' (p. 209). It is apparent her deeds are taboo transgressions rather than typical sins and she acknowledges her own agency by her reference to her hands as the cause of Edmund's miseries. When the Countess asks Adeliza if she loves her suitor (unaware it is Edmund) she replies '"yes, with such love as that I feel for thee. His virtues I revere: his earnest words sound like the precepts of a tender parent: and, next to thee, methinks I could obey him"' (p. 212). Adeliza's comparison of her love for Edmund to that for her mother indicates that her passionate love is based partly in unconscious familial recognition. By loading their speeches with the language commonly preceding familial or incestuous revelations, Walpole provides the play's readers and viewers with a context with which they would have been familiar.

A challenge to patriarchal power comes, as it often does, in the form of inheritance disruption. Clery finds in the Countess 'hints that female desire … might be impervious to the social desiderata of sexual reproduction and the patriarchal family, that it might even be at war with them'.[45] The disruption that female desire presents to the patriarchal family is manifested in the disordering of patrilineal inheritance caused by the Count's love for his wife. This excessive love, resulting perhaps from the Countess's noted strong sexual desire for her husband, puts her in the unusual position of power in her role as mother and wife.[46] Anolik writes: 'Gothic representations of marriage as dangerous and confining to the wife, and of motherhood as resulting in the disappearance of the mother, work to literalise and thereby reveal the horror implicit in two legal principles that governed the lives of women in England through the middle of the nineteenth century: *coverture* and primogeniture.'[47] Because the Countess defies this disappearance through the inheritance disruption, she becomes a highly dangerous figure: her rearticulation of the power structure has successfully destroyed the tradition of primogeniture.[48] Frank ties the inheritance of property to the inheritance of transgressive desires that she describes as perversions: 'the very means by which Edmund seeks to secure his patrimony invalidate it; his desire to marry Adeliza, his own daughter, reveals that in place of his father's estate, he has inherited his mother's perversion'.[49] The description of incest as an inherited trait bears resemblance to the generations of incest in other Gothic novels such as Regina Maria Roche's *Clermont* (1798) and Selina Davenport's *The Sons of the Viscount and the Daughters of the Earl* (1813), but Frank sees it as a perversion rather than an inversion that disrupts inheritance structures. Edmund's naïve hope that a marriage to Adeliza might reconcile his mother with him gestures ironically towards this genealogy of past and future incestuous acts: a multi-generational destruction caused by uncontrollable desires.

The consequences of the Countess's sexuality and sexual agency, which have already proved inimical to patrilineal inheritance, continue to derange social structures. Clery writes: 'the incest which is a consequence of female desire must blow the family apart'.[50] The Countess, who believes Edmund is dead, faints upon seeing him alive. Edmund says: ' "stand off, and let me clasp her in my arms! The flame of filial fondness shall revive the lamp of life, repay the breath she gave, and waken all the mother in her soul"' (p. 216). Of course, Edmund's 'filial flame' is the precise 'fondness' that has led to his banishment and the loss of his mother. On reviving, the Countess repeatedly asks if Edmund is Narbonne, a confusion of husband and son that confirms the idea that this conflation has happened before. Clery's point about Walpole's blending of the two types of incest narratives is evident here; Walpole implies a confusion or mistake between Edmund and his father (as occurs in incest tragedy), but it is by design (as in the incest tales) that the Countess has slept with her son.[51] The Countess asks Edmund: '"art thou my husband wing'd from other orbs to taunt my soul? What is this dubious form, impress'd with ev'ry feature I adore, and every lineament I dread to look on! Art thou my dead or living son?"' (p. 217). The confusion underscores the physical likeness and desirability of both father and son. When the Countess pulls away in horror from Edmund he says: '"to thy eyes I seem'd my father – at least for that resemblance-sake embrace me"', to which his mother replies: '"horror on horror!"' (pp. 217–18). It becomes clear that this confusion between father and son brings back the memory, now horrifying, of the Countess's sexual transgression. Walpole plays with the possibility of observing the tragic form, but it is already here implied that this text's seeming adherence to the accidental nature of incest in tragedy has been undermined by the Countess's agency and desires.

The Countess further troubles convention in her use of the knife/metaphoric penis of Gothic fiction. When she reveals her daughter is the child of sin she says: '"pity would bid me stab thee"' (p. 229). She is tempted to wield the phallic knife usually found in the hands of violent male aggressors against her daughter, but does not. Rather than simply invert the paradigm of male aggression and violence, Walpole implicitly acknowledges the limits of such inversions. Instead, Walpole mirrors the incest act by having the Countess take the sword from Edmund and stab herself with it. When the Countess explains her actions to her son she says she was in a state of grief and disappointed desire for her dead husband: '"my fancy saw thee thy father's image ... while thy arms twin'd, to thy thinking, round another's waist, hear, hell, and tremble! – thou didst clasp thy mother!"' (p. 246). Edmund's reply reveals his impotency to act against his mother: '"my dagger must repay a tale like this! Blood so distemper'd – no – I must not strike – I dare not punish what you dar'd commit"' (pp. 246–7). The Countess orders him: '"Give me the steel – my arm will not recoil!"' (p. 247). As she stabs herself with Edmund's sword, the Countess takes agency, again, away from her son in a final act of suicidal, metaphorical rape. The play concludes with Edmund rushing off to war as he commands the clergy to take Adeliza to become a nun.[52] He says: '"to th' embattl'd foe I will present this hated form – and welcome be the sabre that leaves no atom of it undefac'd"' (p. 248). He commits his 'hated' and fetishised body – hated for its submission to his mother's sexual agency and for its likeness to his father that made him the victim of maternal desires – to death by sabre. It is no coincidence that Edmund's attempt at suicide is a final act of submission to the sword of an other – this time, a male. His inability to perform the act himself is concretised in these lines as is the mysterious, disastrous, gender-neutralising results of female sexual agency that disempower the male at the hands of the mother. Beckford takes up these notions of male disempowerment caused by an active mother in *Vathek*, wherein transgressions of gender ideologies pervert the natural development of masculinity and femininity.

THE EVILS OF MATERNAL INFLUENCE

William Beckford, an Englishman notorious in his own time for his love affairs with adolescent males and his immense fortune, wrote the Oriental Gothic novel *Vathek*, which frequently has been analysed in relation to Beckford's sexuality and his relationship with his mother.[53] Though scholars such as Roger Lonsdale have questioned the designation of the novel as Oriental, Donna Landry argues that for Beckford, 'an Orientalised eroticisation of everyday life offered a licence for transgression, and a means of protesting against English society by pursuing queerness in various forms'.[54] It is this 'Orientalised eroticisation' that forms the basis of *Vathek*, a work preoccupied with transgression and queerness. Landry's analysis of *Vathek* points to Beckford's 'attraction to things that are horrifying ... and the illicit pleasure associated with that attraction' and underscores the extent to which the novel is discussed in light of its author's sexuality and personal life.[55] The novel follows the journey of the Caliph Vathek, who is a 'most curious' man 'much addicted to women' with 'indulgencies unrestrained',[56] on his descent into hell. *Vathek* fluctuates between focusing on the Caliph's desires for adolescents and his use as the tool of his manipulative and evil mother, Carathis.[57] Carathis, while given influence and importance in the narrative, is presented as evil, immoral and wicked in her desires. Incapable of maternal feelings, Carathis has incestuous desires towards Vathek that become apparent in her intrusions into his sexual relationships and her control over him. Fincher points to Carathis's 'implied incestuous desire for her son' as being located in her hatred of his lover, but I argue it is grounded in her position of gender-ambiguous power and her corruption of the chaste ideal of motherhood.[58] Maternal desires of all varieties are presented as uncontainable and dangerous forces with sexual connotations, highly disruptive and transmitted to the son via the powerful influence of the mother's position.

Beckford aligns the insatiable appetites of Vathek and his mother with sexuality but depicts the mother's to be a darker, more evil and destructive type that involves the control and manipulation of her son. Carathis is described as 'wicked, as woman could be' (p. 24), a woman 'passionately attached ... to the infernal powers' (p. 26). Vathek ensures that his mother's unrestrained appetite for experiments in the dark arts is sated when he is absent from the kingdom, telling her servant: '"Take care to supply whatever her experiments may demand"' (p. 31). He tries to appease her appetite by giving her a male substitute.[59] We are told that Carathis 'enjoyed most whatever filled others with dread' (p. 71). This description is similar to the words Calantha uses in Elizabeth Thomas's *Purity of Heart, or, The Ancient Costume* (1816) when she describes her potential for incestuous love: '"As if love is not twenty times more attractive, when it is forbidden, and sinful."'[60] Calantha's words, like the description of Carathis, are used to display the monstrous and dreadful appetites of these women for the transgressive. Carathis's manipulation of Vathek is demonstrated through her ability to reason with him when he is in a rage: 'her tears and caresses called off his attention' (p. 8). Her depiction as capable of soothing and controlling Vathek encompasses male and female gender ideologies; she possesses the seemingly nurturant ability to soothe her son's passions but does so to use him to attain a position of power.

Representations of rampant sexual or deviant appetites, evil or witch-like behaviour, manipulative and power-seeking desires are part of the myth established by a threatened patriarchy to denounce and destroy any non-conforming woman in a position of power. The rhetoric designating Carathis as aberrant is similar to that in the propaganda Lynn Hunt identifies that depicts Marie Antoinette as having monstrous sexual appetites leading to incest: 'a creature whose voracious sexuality knows no limits and no gender differentiation (or, for that matter, class differentiation)'.[61] Fincher describes Carathis as a mother who: 'connotes deviance and a dominant sexuality, traditionally associated with masculinity'.[62] All transgressive sexualities are united as dangerous in their non-heteronormative queerness. Fincher writes: 'Throughout the eighteenth century the term "monstrous" was used a constructive synonym for the bodies and desires of queer men', a point that strengthens the link between monstrous as descriptive of the transgressive nature of both mothers and queer men.[63] Homosexuality, much like voracious female sexuality, was linked to a dangerous blurring of gender, class, power and sex threatening to the patriarchy and found (re)articulation in the Gothic.

Carathis's appetites are portrayed in a deliberately ambiguous sexual/asexual light, affording her words and actions sexual and incestuous hints within a patently nonsexual framework. Part of this nonsexual framework is built upon descriptions of Carathis as 'chaste', although these foundations are destabilised by their conjunction with her deliberate self-insertion into her son's sex life.[64] In a scene rife with actions emblematic of the tearing of a hymen, Carathis enters a tented pavilion area where her son is bathing with his teenage lover. 'Carathis ... broke through the muslin awnings and veils of the pavilion ... Carathis, still seated on her camel, foamed with indignation, at the spectacle which obtruded itself on her chaste view' (p. 74). Carathis performs a traditionally male act as she not only penetrates the veils but then 'foams' with indignation on viewing her son and his lover together.[65] Fincher describes this scene as establishing Vathek's virility through a spectacle or performance but I contend that it is rather destructive to the ideas of masculinity and male virility.[66] The consummation is frustrated by the intrusion of the mother. It is her self-insertion that denies Vathek's insertion, rendering him impotent rather than virile and positions the mother as more masculine than the son. Much like the Countess in Walpole's play, Carathis's aggressive agency, usually only wielded by men, makes her monstrous.[67] This is not the first time Carathis has attempted to control or restrain Vathek's passions. When the evil Giaour restored Vathek's health, Vathek 'leaped upon the neck of the frightful Indian, and kissed his horrid mouth and hollow cheeks, as though they had been the coral lips and the lilies and roses of his most beautiful wives. Nor would these transports have ceased, had not the eloquence of Carathis repressed them' (p. 13). Here Carathis inserts herself between two men, cutting off a scene of potential same-sex desires. Carathis, the bad mother, acts as a barrier to a homoerotic experience, repressing her son's enthusiastic embrace of the Indian with her overflowing words.

Vathek sees Carathis's evil nature as the reason for his ultimate eternity in the hellish underworld, the Palace of Eblis. He ignores his own appetites, desires and actions that led him to commit acts of murder and torture, blaming his damnation on his mother. Carathis has driven him towards acts of violence much like the mother in Charlotte Dacre's *Zofloya* (1806), who, Haggerty concludes, has a murderous nature and is responsible for her daughter's inability to have a significant relationship.[68] Haggerty's reading locates the mother as a powerful figure who controls the sexual development of the child in her absence or presence, a notion Vathek subscribes to in his mother-blame.[69] Vathek claims that '"the principles by which Carathis perverted my youth, have been the sole cause of my perdition!"' (p. 91). He heaps further blame on his mother when Carathis is brought to Eblis's palace: '"execrable woman! ... cursed be the day thou givest me birth! ... [How] much I ought to abhor the impious knowledge thou hast taught me"' (p. 92). The knowledge imparted by the mother is impious and cursed; the mother who desires power inevitably fails as an educator because such knowledge from a woman is tainted by its non-conformity: she can provide only a perverted education. Carathis, unlike Vathek and Nouronihar, is undeterred by the terrible things she sees in the palace or the words of the condemned Soliman: 'nothing appalled her dauntless soul' (p. 93) and 'she even attempted to dethrone one of the Solimans, for the purpose of usurping his place' (p. 93). This final attempt to appropriate the ultimate male position of power is denied. Carathis, in spite of her lack of fear or penitence, turns into one of the countless wanderers of the palace, whose hearts are consumed by fire and in eternal agony. Again, comparisons to the paradigm of the voracious, monstrous mother of sociological understandings of incestuous mother–son relationships are easily drawn. As Landry argues, Carathis is 'the character whose excesses exceed even her son's ... the power behind the throne, this mother of all caliphs and sultans'.[70] Carathis seems the epitome of the conceptualisations of mothers whom McKinnon describes as displaying 'a sexual agency that is fully active and aggressive, one that does not display "proper" female reserve, control, and modesty'.[71] Much like Fincher's description of queer men who endanger 'the authenticity and stability of masculinity or femininity', Carathis's assumption of traditionally masculine qualities troubles such gender ideologies.[72]

This voracious mother is continually indicated as responsible, through her unmotherly urgings and non-maternal neglect, for her son's actions, sexual desires and appetites.[73] Vathek's insatiable desire for Nouronihar stems, in part, from his ability to view her as a mother substitute because of her relationship with her cousin/lover, Gulchenrouz, with whom she has an eroticised maternal bond. Gulchenrouz is described as a highly effeminate male who 'seemed to be more feminine than even herself [Nouronihar]' (p. 53). Positioned as a feminine child, Gulchenrouz treats Nouronihar as a mother: 'nestling, as usual, in the bosom of Nouronihar, [he] pouted out his vermillion little lips against the offer of Sutlememe; and would take it, only, from the hand of his cousin' (p. 55). Vathek angrily pronounces him an emasculated infant and asks Nouronihar's father: '"would you surrender this divine beauty to a husband more womanish than herself"' (p. 55) describing him further as '"a girl dressed up like a boy"' (p. 67). Gulchenrouz's childlike dependence on Nouronihar, who treats her lover as a son, causes Vathek to view her as the good mother he lacked. The Caliph's desire for her increases on seeing her maternal interactions with her cousin/lover as he wants both her maternal nurturance and desires her sexually.

The depictions of Nouronihar and Gulchenrouz are reimagined in Emily Brontë's *Wuthering Heights* (1847) in the relationship of the maternal Cathy and her effeminate, sickly, cousin/lover Linton, who is equally despised by the masculine and powerful Hareton. It is also possible to view Vathek's desire for Nouronihar as a substitute for his same-sex desire for the adolescent, childlike Gulchenrouz. We have already seen Vathek engaged in a scene with naked male youths when the Giaour demands the blood of fifty beautiful, noble-born children.[74] Vathek plots to feed them to the voracious Giaour by having a competition: 'the fifty competitors were soon stripped, and presented to the admiration of the spectators the suppleness and grace of their delicate limbs' (p. 22). He commands the crowd to let the boys come to him one by one as he has a gift for each, starting with his jewels and 'to the rest, each a part of my dress, even down to my slippers' (p. 22), giving away pieces of his attire to the naked and beautiful boys as he throws them (he believes) to the cannibalistic genie. Vathek's violence and transgressive sexuality are revealed to be the product of both his innate desires and his mother's demands and show his willingness to feed the monstrous, taboo appetites of individuals who command him to do so.

Ultimately, McKinnon's conclusion about the assumptions made regarding mother–son incest can be seen in Beckford's portrayal of the dominant and 'masculine' Carathis and the effects of this voracious mother on Vathek. 'Descriptions of maternal incest offenders often stress that these women ... are sexually compulsive, indiscriminate, and conspicuous. The sexuality of incestuous mothers is more "male" than "female".[75] Maternal incest is thus blamed on a non-traditional family structure: an overwhelming mother and a passive father who does not pose enough of a 'castrating fear' in his son; the father is condemned for his passivity, the mother for her agency, and maternal incest is understood as a consequence of 'unnatural' gender positions in the home. Carathis is delineated as the aggressive and powerful mother who has taken on the function of the absent father and disastrously miseducated her son, driving him to acts of violence with sexual undertones. Her deliberate and active presence in his sexual relationships causes incest by proxy. Beckford's mother–son relationship reveals impossible-to-resolve anxieties over the figure of the mother, her influence, power and control over her son's sexuality and education. This rearticulation of power dynamics results in a display of misplaced appetites and aggressions exposed as being as violent and voracious as those of the traditional structures. Carathis's assumption of the father's role and her control of her son's sexuality are reworked in Lewis's *The Monk*. Lewis employs Elvira, the chaste and ideal mother turned active protector of her daughter, and Matilda, the image of the Virgin Mother who corrupts and incites her 'son' to ever greater sexual depravities, to depict the two extremes available to the maternal role.

THE DANGER OF MOTHERS DENYING MALE PLEASURE

Matthew Lewis's novel *The Monk* traces the descent of the pious monk Ambrosio into evil, who, after being corrupted by the beautiful, gender-ambiguous Matilda/Rosario, murders his mother and rapes and murders his sister. Matilda, the image of the Madonna painting to which Ambrosio prays, epitomises both the chaste ideal of motherhood and the ultimate monstrous, evil mother in her sexual corruption of Ambrosio. Anolik's point about the effacement of women after marriage and motherhood in the Gothic is perhaps nowhere more apparent than when Ambrosio murders his mother in an attempt to remove her as an obstacle to his rape of her daughter.[76] Peter Brooks points to these scenes of rape and murder as culminating in 'disgust' and contextualises the novel's exposure of repression's consequences, illuminating the relevance of both feminist and queer readings of the text.[77] In finding her mother and restoring her in the family, Anolik argues that Radcliffe alters traditional eighteenth-century narratives positioning the mother as the daughter's enemy.[78] Lewis's removal of the mother inverts the Radcliffean model (itself a reversal) of locating and reuniting with the mother. In its representations of violence and sexual assault Lewis's use of incest resembles the violent usurpation of female wealth and title by uncles, wherein female positions of power are attacked by younger-brother uncles intent on acquiring the dominance denied them by social institutions.[79] Lewis's depictions of mothers reiterate the implicit violence of heteronormativity and the consequences of institutional demands for conformity.

Bersani's examination of political structures of oppression evidenced through the body in sadomasochism is seen in Ambrosio's sexually charged murder of his mother. In this scene bodily oppression is depicted via the suffocation of the mother, a literalisation of the political institution's oppression of female agency. The attack, a physical manifestation of the ideology of male dominance over female bodies, effaces the mother's textual presence. Elvira challenges the dominant hegemony by taking on the traditionally male role of protector and, in her defence of her daughter, denies her son's sexual desires. Ambrosio's violent aggression stems from his adherence to the ideology privileging male (sexual) power that we have seen, not only historically and within the Gothic, but also in the scholarly accounts that understand mother–son incest as monstrously unnatural. In this context, Ambrosio's actions are the consequence of heteronormative ideology. The murder Ambrosio commits in order to rape his sister is rife with erotic, incestuous undertones and sadomasochism.

> [W]ith one hand he grasped Elvira's throat so as to prevent her continuing her clamour, and with the other dashing her violently upon the ground, he dragged her towards the bed ... snatching the pillow from beneath her daughter's head, covering with it Elvira's face, and pressing his knee upon her stomach with all his strength, endeavoured to put an end to her existence ... [L]ong did the sufferer struggle to disengage herself; but in vain. The monk continued to kneel upon her breast, witnessed without mercy the convulsive trembling of her limbs beneath him, and sustained with inhuman firmness the spectacle of her agonies.[80]

The sexual allusions are ubiquitous in the description of the violent attack and Lewis blends the scenes of murder and attempted rape in a way that implies that the emotions experienced by the monk while suffocating his mother are akin to the desires he feels for his sister. Not only does the killing occur in a bedroom, but Ambrosio also uses a pillow from his sister's bed to smother his mother, symbolically uniting the murderous attack with the sexual one.[81] As his mother struggles beneath him, Ambrosio 'sustained with inhuman firmness' this spectacle; a description more suggestive of rape than murder. While the incestuous aspect of his crimes is yet unknown to Ambrosio, their existence causes Lewis's work to posit violent incest and matricide as the result of a patriarchal ideology. But in spite of the aggressive, sexually motivated attack, many scholarly accounts deliberately overlook the implicit incest here.[82]

Steven Blakemore mentions only that Ambrosio is 'the aggressive killer of his mother'[83] and nothing about the incestuous relevance of this scene, of the sexual connotations that position Ambrosio as more than just a killer. Blakemore is not alone in ignoring the incestuous subtext. In analysing the differences between Lewis's scenes of violence and Radcliffe's, Vartan P. Messier writes that 'in contrast to Radcliffe, Lewis is considerably more daring ... By making unprecedented use of transgressive elements, his strategy is one of unconcealed, unadulterated shock and horror.'[84] While Messier notes the connection between sex and violence in the scenes of Antonia's attempted rape and later rape and murder he concludes that Radcliffe: 'substituted Lewis' incest episode ... by having Schedoni spare Ellena when he realises she might be his daughter.'[85] Such critical comparisons of Lewis and Radcliffe overlook the incestuous implications in either one or both of these scenes. Messier's deliberate placement of Radcliffe's scene as outside the incestuous framework is meant to attest to its correspondence to a kinder, gentler (Female) Gothic novel than Lewis's. Of course, Radcliffe's representation of the evil Schedoni's very phallic knife that so nearly penetrates his niece's dress just as closely literalises sex and violent aggression as Lewis's novel does. In claiming that Lewis makes 'unprecedented use of transgressive elements' Messier ignores the spectacles of incest and violence in earlier Gothic novels by Radcliffe and others. Such a reading suggests that Radcliffe intended readers of her novel to infer that Schedoni's failure to rape and/or murder Ellena is due to his scruples regarding incest rather than a combination of his surprise at the discovery of kinship and greed when he realises how the familial bond could benefit him. Scholarly reproductions of the positioning of Radcliffe as writing a weak, feminine Gothic novel in comparison to Lewis's aggressive male version mirror the gender ideologies these writers strove to disrupt.

Images of disgust at female bodies dovetail remarkably neatly with Haggerty's understandings of male forms in peril. Haggerty's argument that 'abject, passive masculinity challenges the status quo with the "disgusting" proposition that some men are victims too ... expos[ing] the crack in normative masculinity'[86] illuminates how writers of the Gothic use the genre to explore the dangers of heteronormativity for men as well as women. After Ambrosio's murder of Elvira, her body becomes disgusting, a thing of repulsion to him: 'Ambrosio beheld before him that once noble and majestic form, now become a corpse – cold, senseless, and disgusting' (p. 264). He is similarly disgusted by the body of his sister, Antonia, once he has raped her, as he was repulsed by Matilda after having sex with her. Haggerty's treatment of the fetishised male allows us to see how these writers based the model for the fetishisation of the wounded or vulnerable male body on the figure of the effaced mother. The figure of the wounded, murdered, imprisoned and/or emaciated mother literalises the dangers of heteronormative society that dictates the legal and social subjugation of women.[87] Similarly, Haggerty finds Lewis's inversions fetishise male bodies, citing the emaciated and chained body of Reginald in Lewis's *The Castle Spectre* (1797) to argue: 'the lurid discovery here is the spectacle of pale, broken, and effectively castrated masculinity'.[88]

Haggerty argues that the spectacle 'exposes the vulnerable centre of heteronormativity itself',[89] just as Anolik's arguments point to this function of the imprisoned or absent mother. Anolik focuses on the mother's role in exposing the realities of legal and social conventions that cause the erasure of women, while Haggerty locates the violence implicit in such representations. Both arguments demonstrate the importance and ambivalence surrounding the figure of the mother. Using Joanna Baillie's *De Montfort* (1807) as an example, Haggerty argues that the play's homoerotics are eventually replaced with incest and establish Baillie's work's similarity to 'Walpole's fascination with similar tropes'.[90] These culturally inscribed representations of mother, incest and wounded male are merged in the Gothics written by Lewis, Beckford, Dacre, Baillie and Walpole to show the similar subjugation and vulnerability of or violence towards those outside of heteronormative culture. In this sense, the mother and the man who defies normative sexuality share many of the same qualities (the mother/whore dichotomy is similar to the masculine man/non-masculine way that Coleridge describes Walpole) and are subject to the same treatment. The queering of the Gothic becomes a crucial mode of theorising the role of the mother and understanding her placement in the genre, as well as allowing us to view depictions of similarly positioned men in a more complex way.

While some scholars understand *The Monk*'s conclusion and Ambrosio's death at the hands of the demon as Lewis's correction of a dangerous inversion, such a stance privileges the very gender ideologies that Lewis subverts. Blakemore concludes: 'writing ... when the French Revolution seemed to be inverting the "natural" order of things, Matthew Lewis, in the end, restores the natural order'.[91] The 'natural order', simultaneously upheld (through an aggressive male act of sexual violence) and inverted (through the eventual revelation of the transgression) via the incestuous murder of his mother and rape and murder of his sister, seems far from restored. It is at the novel's end that the first mention of incest is made when the virgin/whore mother turned gender-ambiguous demon says: '"That Antonia whom you violated, was your sister! That Elvira whom you murdered, gave you birth! Tremble, abandoned hypocrite, inhuman parricide, incestuous ravisher!"' (p. 361). Ambrosio ignores the disclosure, complicating how the revelation should be treated; he is uninterested in the incestuous aspect of his crimes and instead worries that he will be killed by the demon. His attitude toward his mother correlates to a line in Walpole's play in which Benedict says of the Countess: '"I cannot dupe, and therefore must destroy her"' (p. 222). The passage summarises the way Ambrosio comes to murder Elvira – she sees through his mask of piety – and the attitude of patriarchal institutions towards women who defy them: such women must be smothered, suppressed or effaced. Blakemore's conclusion points to Lewis's novel as ultimately upholding the dominant social institutions and ideologies that contributed to the incestuous rape and murders because it ignores the presence of mother–son incest. Yet Lewis's unifications of murderous and incestuous desires indicate that the novel is extremely critical of such institutions.

Ambrosio's discovery of his mother's identity reinforces his guilt for his destruction of the eroticised, subversive mother who held the key to his identity.[92] As we have repeatedly seen in the Gothic, the heroines' quests for their maternal origins are linked to their ultimate happiness. But in the case of Lewis and Polidori the heroine's quest is inverted into the villain/hero's discovery of the dead rather than of the living: knowledge only concretises these men's incapability of having a maternal figure. Polidori links the ghostly apparitions of Ernestus Berchtold's mother with the yearnings experienced by the titular character, uniting the sexual appetite to an immaterial presence with whom such physical desires are impossible to realise. The portrayal of Berchtold relating the appearance of his mother in ghost form suggests a breathless confusion at the tantalising vision: 'a figure; I cannot describe it to you. ... [H]er white drapery, breathed on by the wanton breeze, now betrayed the delicate form of her limbs, – now hid them from my sight' (p. 19). The 'wanton breeze' hints of Zephyrus, Greek god of the west wind who transports Psyche to her sexual union with Cupid and carries a wealth of associated images of marriage, death, birth and desires. These authors locate their male characters in the framework of incestuous mother–son relationships while denying the presence or realisation of desires to which the very structure of the relationships and depictions attests. Diana Wallace emphasises the importance of the mother to lineage and identity in the Female Gothic, if often as a ghost or haunting presence.[93] The further disruption of paternity through missing or dead fathers makes impossible the villains' ability to legitimise their desires through knowledge of their fathers; as demonstrated in *Vathek* and *The Mysterious Mother* it forces their development in relation to the unknowable mother. This type of inversion and reversal of the Radcliffean Gothic show the conjunction between what are viewed as two distinct modes of gendered Gothic writing. Rather than functioning as separate genres, the Gothic texts analysed in this chapter use similar methods to those explored in the rest of this book, one model relocating the missing mother to reclaim a matriarchal tradition and the other eliminating the mother in order to show the paradoxical inevitability and impossibility of queer desires in a heteronormative ideology.

Mother–son incest is unilaterally viewed by sociologists, geneticists and anthropologists as the most abhorred and unnatural incestuous relationship of all. But, as McKinnon points out, this most taboo of forbidden relationships seems to dominate the discourse on incest even while it remains the least practised. When Haggerty's observation that the 'disgusting' notions of male victims in the Gothic are assessed in conjunction with the horror of mother–son incest, a clearer picture emerges. Male victims of sexual assault or abuse are disgusting, particularly so at the hands of a woman who is meant to be a passive maternal ideal. The queerness of active, sexually aggressive mothers, like representations of chained and fetishised male bodies, disrupts conventional gender ideologies. The Gothic as written by Radcliffe, Parsons and Roche tends to locate the mother as the missing meaning of self rather than as a sexual aggressor. Concerned with exposing the dangers of patriarchy and heteronormativity to women, these texts have less need to use mother–daughter incest as a convention because society demands female victimisation through its ideology of legally and socially sanctioned violence against and domination of women. Gothic texts by authors such as Baillie, Dacre, Polidori, Beckford, Walpole and Lewis depict the mother as either the instigator or victim of incestuous sexual desires, employing mother–son incest to demonstrate the inability of heteronormative society to acknowledge male victims or permit the thwarting of male desires. These authors make spectacles of sexuality in which men are dominated or manipulated by the figure patriarchal society typically positions as the most passive, most invisible, least powerful and least capable of sexual agency of all: the mother. The figure of the mother, while seeming to fulfil irreconcilably different roles in what have been viewed by scholarship as the two types of Gothic, instead provides in both a subversion of the constraints imposed by heteronormative society and its gender and sexual ideologies that reveals the categories of Male and Female Gothic as ultimately reductive. Destabilising traditional power relationships, the figure of the incestuous mother is eventually recovered and it is at her mysterious, active hands that fetishised male bodies remain constant victims. Such a destabilisation remains paradoxical in its rearticulation of the power structures it disrupts, inverting the normative to stress heteronormative society's simultaneous and perpetual construction and destruction of queer sexualities.

NOTES

1 Joseph Shepher, *Incest: A Biosocial View* (New York: Academic Press, 1983), p. 97.
2 Karen Sanchez-Eppler, 'Temperance in the bed of a child: incest and social order in nineteenth-century America', *American Quarterly*, 47:1 (1995), 9.
3 Many scholars who study incest note that, while it is impossible to give clear numbers on rates of incest in society, estimates show boys are the victims in only 10 per cent of the cases. www.faqs.org/health/topics/68/incest/html [accessed 11 March 2011].
4 Shepher, p. 97.
5 Shepher, p. 113.
6 Judith Butler, 'Critically queer', *GLQ: A Journal of Lesbian and Gay Studies*, 1:1 (1993), 17–32. Butler examines 'the extent that homosexual attachments remain unacknowledged within normative heterosexuality' (25).

7 Leo Bersani, 'Foucault, Freud, Fantasy, and power', *GLQ: A Journal of Lesbian and Gay Studies*, 2:1/2 (1995), 18.
8 Bersani, 18.
9 That the Female Gothic is closely aligned to what is known as Male Gothic when it represents instances of uncle–niece incest, which rely on literalising the inherent violence in the power structures of this relationship, while in father–daughter, brother–sister and cousin relationships these heteronormative structures are eliminated, demonstrates the inherent instability of such gendered generic distinctions.
10 Bersani, 18–19.
11 Examples of mothers used as objects of sexual desire in the Gothic include Olivia in Ann Radcliffe's *The Italian* (1797), Louisa Bruyere in Eliza Parsons's *An Old Friend with a New Face* (1797), Lady Correlia in Sarah Sheriffe's *Correlia, or The Mystic Tomb* (1802) and Camilla in Elizabeth Thomas's *Purity of Heart, or The Ancient Costume* (1816).
12 Susan McKinnon, 'American Kinship/American Incest: Asymmetries in a Scientific Discourse', in Sylvia Yanagisako and Carol Delaney (eds), *Naturalizing Power: Essays in Feminist Cultural Analysis* (New York: Routledge, 1995), p. 42.
13 McKinnon, p. 37.
14 McKinnon, p. 37.
15 McKinnon, p. 37.
16 McKinnon, p. 40.
17 Sexually aggressive or promiscuous women in the genre often suffer disastrous consequences. Examples include Mrs Ashwood in Charlotte Smith's *Emmeline* (1788), Maria de Vellorno in Radcliffe's *A Sicilian Romance* (1790), Signora di Laurentini and Madame de Chenon in Radcliffe's *The Mysteries of Udolpho* (1794), The Bleeding Nun in Lewis's *The Monk* (1796) and the Countess of Dunreath in Maria Regina Roche's *The Children of the Abbey* (1796).
18 George E. Haggerty, *Queer Gothic* (Urbana: University of Illinois Press, 2006), pp. 32–7.
19 We see such 'unnatural' mothers in more peripheral positions or as stepmothers in Gothic novels such as in Radcliffe's *A Sicilian Romance*, *The Mysteries of Udolpho* and Sheriffe's *Correlia, or The Mystic Tomb*.
20 Ruth Bienstock Anolik, 'The missing mother: the meanings of maternal absence in the Gothic mode', *Modern Language Studies*, 33:1/2 (2003), 25–6.
21 For further analyses of the roles of mothers in eighteenth-century literature see Toni Bowers, *The Politics of Motherhood: British Writing and Culture, 1680–1760* (Cambridge: Cambridge University Press, 1996), Felicity A. Nussbaum, *Torrid Zones: Maternity, Sexuality and Empire in Eighteenth Century English Narrative* (Baltimore: Johns Hopkins University Press, 1995)

and Ruth Perry, *Novel Relations: The Transformation of Kinship in English Literature and Culture 1748–1818* (Cambridge: Cambridge University Press, 2004).

22 E. J. Clery, 'Horace Walpole's *The Mysterious Mother* and the Impossibility of Female Desire', in Fred Botting (ed.), *The Gothic: Essays and Studies* (Cambridge: D. S. Brewer, 2001), pp. 23–46.

23 Perry, p. 396.

24 See Max Fincher's *Queering Gothic in the Romantic Age: The Penetrating Eye* (Basingstoke: Palgrave Macmillan, 2007) and Haggerty's *Queer Gothic*.

25 Bersani, 11.

26 Bersani, 12–13.

27 David Punter and Glennis Byron, *The Gothic* (Oxford: Blackwell Publishing, 2004), pp. 169–70.

28 Robert Miles argues in *Gothic Writing, 1750–1820: A Genealogy* (London: Routledge, 1993) that 'the mother/son incest suggests the origin of this taboo is the nexus of father/church/state, the play's offended parties. As the Gothic aesthetic insists (through its idealisation of Romance) these taboos are rationally rooted in a providential nature, supporting political and familial legitimacy' (p. 119) while Clery finds the play resistant to its contemporaneous political hegemony.

29 Samuel Taylor Coleridge, *Specimens of the Table Talk of the Late Samuel Taylor Coleridge* (London, 1835), I, p. 154; reprinted in *Horace Walpole: The Critical Heritage*, ed. Peter Sabor (London: Routledge & Kegan Paul, 1987), p. 148; quoted in George E. Haggerty, 'Psychodrama: hypertheatricality and sexual excess on the Gothic stage', *Theatre Research International*, 28:1 (2003), 21.

30 Haggerty, 'Psychodrama', 21.

31 Haggerty, 'Psychodrama', 21.

32 Marcie Frank, 'Horace Walpole's family romances', *Modern Philology*, 100:3 (2003), 418. Frank argues that Walpole was aware of his play's themes being 'subsum[ed] under the rubric of sexual perversity and homosexuality'.

33 Horace Walpole, *The Mysterious Mother* in *The Castle of Otranto and The Mysterious Mother*, ed. Frederick S. Frank (Peterborough, Ontario: Broadview, 2011), p. 169. Subsequent references will be given in the text.

34 Jeffrey N. Cox, 'First Gothics: Walpole, Evans, Frank', *Papers on Language and Literature*, 46:2 (2010), 121–2.

35 John William Polidori, *Ernestus Berchtold; or, The Modern Oedipus. A Tale* (London: Longman, Hurst, Rees, Orme, and Brown, 1819). Subsequent references will be given in the text.

36 See Chapter 1.

37 Clery, p. 32. Clery defines incest tales as bourgeois conduct lessons and incest tragedy as representative of larger social chaos and attributable to no personal fault (p. 31).

38 Clery, p. 26.
39 Clery, p. 37.
40 Frank, 428.
41 Clery, p. 32. Similarly, Jill Campbell in her article '"I am no giant": Horace Walpole, heterosexual incest, and love among men', *The Eighteenth-Century: Theory and Interpretation*, 39:3 (1998) writes of the incestuous references in Walpole's letters and works that: 'their most surprising feature has to do with tone: these stories are consistently given comic or satiric rather than Gothic or high tragic treatment' (243).
42 Clery points to this crucial difference between Walpole's Countess, who lacks maternal feeling, and other mothers in incest tales who typically have strong maternal bonds with their sons prior to the incest (p. 36).
43 Cox, 133.
44 Mary Shelley's *Matilda* (1959) also employs the convention of similar physical characteristics between mother and daughter to presage the father's incestuous desires for his daughter as does Sheriffe's *Correlia, or The Mystic Tomb* (1802) while Emily Brontë uses cross-generational doppelgangers in *Wuthering Heights* (1847) partially to explain sexual attraction.
45 Clery, p. 36.
46 Clery cites 'conjugal passion' as responsible for the Countess's replacement of Edmund as his father's heir (p. 36).
47 Anolik, 26.
48 Frank makes a similar argument to Anolik, noting that 'incest blocks inheritance', pointing to incestuous behaviour as threatening to the proper means of transferring wealth and property (417).
49 Frank, 420.
50 Clery, p. 37.
51 Clery, pp. 30–2.
52 This is somewhat similar to Mary Robinson's Gothic novel *Vancenza; or, The Dangers of Credulity* (1792), in which the lovers discover they are siblings just before their wedding; the sister dies of a fever and the brother joins the army hoping to die in battle.
53 Rictor Norton, 'William Beckford: the fool of Fonthill', *Gay History and Literature*, updated 16 November 1999, www.rictornorton.co.uk/beckfor1.htm [accessed 21 March 2011]. Norton describes the autobiographical elements of *Vathek*, noting similarities between Carathis and Beckford's own mother.
54 Donna Landry, 'William Beckford's *Vathek* and the Uses of Oriental Re-enactment', in Saree Makdisi and Felicity A. Nussbaum (eds), *The Arabian Nights in Historical Context* (Oxford: Oxford University Press, 2009), p. 175.
55 Landry, p. 169. Landry also links the work with the Gothic: 'reliving in memory and imagination, the ruinous and doomed give Beckford's writing a certain affinity with the Gothic' (p. 169).

56 William Beckford, *Vathek*, ed Thomas Keymer (Oxford: Oxford University Press, 2013), pp. 3–4. Subsequent references will be given in the text.
57 D. S. Neff includes in his article 'Bitches, mollies, and tommies: Byron, masculinity, and the history of sexualities', *Journal of the History of Sexuality*, 11:3 (2002), 395–438 a useful bibliography on Beckford's homophilia, citing Eve Kosofsky Sedgwick's *Between Men: English Literature and Male Homosocial Desire* (New York: Columbia University Press, 1985) and Adam Potkay's 'Beckford's heaven of boys', *Raritan*, 13.1 (1994), 73–83.
58 Fincher, p. 85.
59 Marie Mulvey-Roberts offers an excellent treatment of Gothic women and the consequences of their 'excessive desire to know' in her chapter 'From Bluebeard's Bloody Chamber to Demonic Stigmatic', in Diana Wallace and Andrew Smith (eds), *The Female Gothic: New Directions* (Basingstoke: Palgrave Macmillan, 2009), p. 98. Mulvey-Roberts's analysis of forbidden knowledge makes use of Georges Bataille's assertion that transgression and taboo are inseparable, a notion readily applicable to Carathis's quest for knowledge. This appetite for forbidden knowledge is also discussed in Landry's chapter, in which she argues Carathis's 'quest for occult knowledge becomes itself a field sport' (p. 189).
60 Elizabeth Thomas, *Purity of Heart, or, The Ancient Costume, A Tale, In One Volume, Addressed to the Author of Glenarvon* (London: W. Simplin & R. Marshall, 1816), pp. 175–6.
61 Lynn Avery Hunt, *The Family Romance of the French Revolution* (Berkeley, CA: University of California Press, 1993), p. 115.
62 Fincher, p. 84.
63 Fincher, p. 69.
64 Landry points to Carathis's chasteness as an allusion to Diana, the huntress (p. 189).
65 See Chapter 2, p. xxx.
66 Fincher, p. 74.
67 Alethea Brereton Lewis's novel *Nuns of the Desert: or, The Woodland Witches* (1805) includes a similarly power-hungry and sexually voracious mother, Beatrice, who has affairs with young soldiers while she colludes with her husband's and son's plans to sexually assault her daughters' friends.
68 Haggerty, *Queer Gothic*, p. 74. Haggerty views Victoria's shortcomings as the ultimate consequence of having a mother who does not provide the bond that allows for female–female, non-heteronormative (and thus safe, non-sadomasochistic) desires to form.
69 Haggerty's use of this Freudian model to read Carathis requires a nurturing mother for healthy psychical development, a model of maternity that McKinnon assesses as based on a flawed ideology.
70 Landry, p. 188.

71 McKinnon, p. 40.
72 Fincher, p. 68.
73 Beckford's portrayal of Vathek shares similarities with scholarly readings of the heroine's psychosexual development in the Female Gothic as related to imagining bad fathers – see Diane Long Hoeveler, *Gothic Feminism: The Professionalization of Gender from Charlotte Smith to the Brontës* (Liverpool: Liverpool University Press, 1998), p. 56 – or relocating good mothers – see Haggerty, *Queer Gothic*, p. 31; Robert Miles, *The Great Enchantress* (Manchester: Manchester University Press, 1995), p. 106. This further troubles the Gothic's division into Male, Female or Queer categories.
74 Fincher argues that Vathek's interactions with the fifty children and with Gulchenrouz are metaphoric of sexual desires and penetration (pp. 73–6).
75 McKinnon, p. 40.
76 Anolik argues Elvira 'must be disposed of before the narrative can follow its course ... the author of the equally exciting and equally deviant Gothic text feels threatened by the presence of the normalizing and censoring mother' (27).
77 Peter Brooks, 'Virtue and terror: *The Monk*', *ELH*, 4:2 (1973), 259. Brooks analyses the novel as part of its contemporary movement in which authorial revelations of repression and its consequences underpinned many texts.
78 Anolik concludes that this causes the Gothic to be of ongoing use to writers desirous of subverting the patriarchy (32–40).
79 See Chapter 3 for an examination of representations of uncle–niece incest in the Gothic.
80 Matthew Lewis, *The Monk*, ed. D. L. MacDonald and Kathleen Scherf (Peterborough, Ontario: Broadview, 2004), p. 264. Subsequent references will be given in the text.
81 Ambrosio's smothering of his mother is equally a (sm)othering of his (m)other in that the murder renders his biological parent forever unknowable to him; he permanently others his other mother.
82 Likewise, scholars frequently overlook the incestuous threat in Radcliffe's reworking of this scene in *The Italian* (1797), discussed in Chapter 3.
83 Steven Blakemore, 'Matthew Lewis's black mass: sexual, religious inversion in *The Monk*', *Studies in the Novel*, 30:4 (1998), 528.
84 Vartan P. Messier, 'The conservative, the transgressive, and the reactionary: Ann Radcliffe's *The Italian* as a response to Matthew Lewis' *The Monk*', *Atenea*, 25:2 (2005), 39.
85 Messier, 41–2.
86 Haggerty, 'Psychodrama', 32.
87 Anolik, 23–46.
88 Haggerty, 'Psychodrama', 23.
89 Haggerty, 'Psychodrama', 23.

90 Haggerty, 'Psychodrama', 31.
91 Blakemore, 536.
92 Anolik points to the mother as subversive through her categorically dangerous position, being neither virgin nor whore (30). Similarly, Kelly A. Marsh argues that 'the mother's story is potentially subversive' in 'Jane Eyre and the pursuit of the mother's pleasure', *South Atlantic Review*, 69:3/4 (2004), 85.
93 Diana Wallace, '"The Haunting Idea": Female Gothic Metaphors and Feminist Theory', in Wallace and Smith, *The Female Gothic: New Directions*, pp. 26–41.

Coda: incest and beyond

> Like a malevolent virus, Gothic narratives have escaped the confines of literature and spread across disciplinary boundaries to infect all kinds of media ... Gothic texts deal with a variety of themes just as pertinent to contemporary culture as to the eighteenth and nineteenth centuries.
>
> Catherine Spooner, *Contemporary Gothic* (2006)[1]

This book has sought to bring to light the variety of incestuous configurations in the Gothic. In order to do this, I have relied not only on existing literary scholarship, but also on a broad methodological approach that includes anthropological, political, philosophical, legal and scientific insights. The interdisciplinary approach enables readings that expose the ways in which different incestuous relationships engage with eighteenth-century concerns over family, social obligation, individual rights, inheritance laws and desire. The fruits of this broad methodology are evidenced through recent works on the Gothic such as Diana Wallace and Andrew Smith's *The Female Gothic: New Directions* (2009). This collection of articles, all of which, to different ends, explore the Gothic while paying close attention to scholarship's traditional views on Gothic tropes and using a range of analytical tools, demonstrates how this approach is essential to rejuvenating Gothic studies and in bringing fresh perspectives to the foreground of the field.[2] Likewise, Lorna Piatti-Farnell and Donna Lee Brien's *New Directions in 21st Century Gothic: The Gothic Compass* (2015) is an exciting interdisciplinary collection of essays that examines the breadth of Gothic remouldings in various media and cultural products. I have sought, in a similar way, to illuminate the breadth of incestuous relationships and the issues with which they are united and also to open up new lines of enquiry for Gothic scholarship as a whole.

In examining the Gothic it becomes essential to recognise the genre as an unwieldy one that resists homogenising gestures of gendering either in its contemporary reception or in later scholarly readings. My desire is not to attempt to reject scholarship on the Gothic that uses the term the Female Gothic; the wealth of criticism on the Female Gothic has enabled the subversive potential of the genre to be reclaimed and evaluated in highly profitable ways. Scholarship on the Gothic was reinvigorated through its reclamation by feminist critics that helped to establish the genre's importance as an intervention into the contemporary debates of the eighteenth century. Nor do I wish to distance myself from the feminist perspective that has allowed incest to be understood as an abuse of power reflective of patriarchy's control over female bodies. Moving away from divisions of the genre can, nevertheless, provide new insights into the concerns and anxieties explored through generic conventions as common to writers of any gender and various political and religious beliefs, in such a way as to reveal that eighteenth-century explorations of natural rights and laws, female desire, inheritance, social and familial structures, egalitarian relationships and the distribution of power were not schematically determined by an author's gender or political or religious affiliations. By opening the genre up in such a way that gender and sexuality are not the primary categories of analysis, further paradigms of the incest convention – its complex configurations and their intersections with contemporary concerns – become visible.

Instead of attempting to assert a new narrative on incest in the Gothic, it seems more profitable to make use of a broad and flexible approach towards analysis that can in turn be applied to other generic conventions and the genre as a whole and avoids the danger of becoming entrenched within the sometimes claustrophobic narrative of Gothic criticism.[3] The Gothic's exploration of these issues through the convention of incest reveals a preoccupation with how institutions of power (be they political, legal, religious or patriarchal) deny freedom through systematic oppression and violence that is almost always sexualised. In what amounts to a prefiguring and disruption of Foucault's defence of s/m as a radical reimagining and sexualising of unequal power in society, the Gothic reveals that power relations inevitably sexualise the body of the subordinate.[4]

In forging new ground on which to conduct future examinations of the genre, it is important to understand and analyse, rather than to ignore and leave behind, previous modes of approaching the Gothic and the socio-historical conditions and events that gave rise to them. In so doing, the genealogy of Gothic scholarship – its different but related families, if you will – becomes itself a revealing method of examining the Gothic's literary and historical significance and its ongoing position as an object of fetishised scrutiny.

The Gothic's location as such has informed my discussion of representations of incest within the genre. Rather than consider the Gothic as preoccupied with deviant or aberrant sexuality, I seek instead to expose such labels as couched in the language of heteronormativity that the Gothic itself denied. In using a variety of incestuous relationships, Gothic writers reify the dual constraints exerted by family and society, the imbrication of power, desire and violence, the potential for egalitarian conjugality, denials of male victimisation and female desire and the exchange of women. Their concerns are embedded within incestuous desires and violations, underscoring how familial structures reproduce social rules and engaging with contemporary debates regarding the nature of kinship and individual rights. In these representations, writers resist the heteronormative demands that would deny any desires with the potential to subvert the economy of exchange necessary to patriarchy and the erotic aestheticisation of violence implicit in the control of those resistant to the normative. Gothic writers, often women or homosexual men, adopted a critical stance in relation to the heteronormative, patriarchal world and their work offers alternative models of sexualities, agencies and forms of desire that are as relevant to questions of gender and sexuality today as they were in the long eighteenth century.

Rather than offer a final word on the role of incest in the Gothic, or to look backward, I wish instead to look forward and to raise questions, to provoke discussion and debate and to propose further evaluation of Gothic texts – and conventions – beyond those studied here. There is a wealth of material that remains largely untouched by scholarship. Some novels upon which I could only touch within the remit of this book but that bear further scrutiny include Alethea Brereton Lewis's fascinating and odd novel *The Nuns of the Desert: or, The Woodland Witches* (1805); the many anonymous novels such as *Adeline; or the Orphan* (1790) or *Montrose, or The Gothic Ruin, A Novel* (1799); Sarah Sheriffe's interesting and at times bizarre *Correlia, or The Mystic Tomb, A Romance* (1802); and not at all least of these is the vast archive that comprises the Gothic fiction of the popular eighteenth- and nineteenth-century periodical the *Lady's Magazine* (1770–1832). The latter is a large body of primarily anonymous fiction that frequently takes up the conventions and concerns of the Gothic, yet the short stories and serialised novels remain almost entirely unstudied by scholarship, in part because they have been viewed, as the Gothic itself so long was, as unworthy of serious literary scrutiny. Much work thus remains to be done on the literature of the long eighteenth century and Romantic period, particularly on the enormous body of magazine fiction which so often contains surprising reworkings and unique treatments of Gothic conventions.

In moving forward, it is necessary to consider the ways in which representations of sexuality in the period examined in this book, the 1760s–1840s, shift, reappear and are exhumed in the genre's later cycles of popularity and in its various forms of cultural production. At key moments in the genre's development during the Victorian period, at the fin de siècle, in the mid-twentieth century Southern Gothic and in the current era's fixation on vampires and werewolves, while many aspects of the texts have metamorphosed the focus on desires and the forbidden has persisted. The very nature of the Gothic necessitates that this is so; the genre maintains a fundamental openness to alternative sexualities and relationships that begs consideration of the transgressive in its continual transformations. As Jerrold E. Hogle states, the genre's durability is due to the way 'it helps us address and disguise some of the most important desires, quandaries, and sources of anxiety, from the most internal and mental to the widely social and cultural, throughout the history of western culture since the eighteenth century'.[5] The argument regarding incest and its relation to sexuality and gender made in this book has implications for the convention's treatment in other works; how, for example, does sibling incest emerge in twentieth-century Gothic novels such as V. C. Andrews's *Flowers in the Attic* (1979)? With what set of concerns are depictions of cousin incest, aestheticised violence and abuses of power engaged in Joyce Carol Oates's *First Love: A Gothic Tale* (1996)? Can we reconcile Sarah Michelle Gellar in *Buffy the Vampire Slayer* with eighteenth-century heroines and what is at stake in doing so? The relationship between these modern representations and eighteenth-century portrayals of incest may be ambiguous, but considering their kinship expands the potential readings of not only the most recent Gothic revolutions, but also of their literary predecessors.

The early writers of the genre made use of the incest thematic to expose eighteenth-century inequalities such as the consequences of coverture and primogeniture, abuses of institutionalised power and women's subjugation within the state and home, often availing themselves of the period's philosophical rhetoric to do so. Pointing to these writers' preoccupation with political and social circumstances specific to the eighteenth century may seem an incongruous way of highlighting the genre's ongoing relevance. But whether we consider the Gothic in the form of an eighteenth-century novel or a twentieth-century television show, it is precisely the genre's mutability and ability to engage closely with contemporaneous issues that has such significant implications for our study of its history and future incarnations. In any society that seeks to marginalise, criminalise or efface those who would, like Calantha, 'love to step over every bound ... to run fearlessly forward, in spite of the maxims of the world',[6] the Gothic's inherent capacity for representations of the transgressive and marginalised is acute. This book has focused on the incest thematic to explore the Gothic's most omnipresent concern: that the extensive possibilities for human – and sexual – relations be more comprehensively understood. This is a concern that, I fear, is even more vital now than throughout the centuries of evolving Gothic fiction. I hope that this study urges further exploration of the various means, incest and beyond, through which the Gothic provides a safe space for its writers, readers and viewers to theorise and participate in alternative models and narratives of human existence.

NOTES

1 Catherine Spooner, *Contemporary Gothic* (London: Reaktion Books, 2006), p. 8. Spooner argues that 'we should be careful of assuming that Gothic simply reflects social anxieties in a straightforward manner' (p. 8).
2 Diana Wallace and Andrew Smith (eds), *The Female Gothic: New Directions* (Basingstoke: Palgrave Macmillan, 2009).
3 Lauren Fitzgerald points to the binary of male/female oppression found in Gothic plots as replicated through the conventions of feminist criticism that seeks to liberate the Female Gothic from its marginalisation by earlier male critics in 'Female Gothic and the Institutionalization of Gothic Studies', in Wallace and Smith, *The Female Gothic: New Directions*, pp. 13–25.
4 See Foucault's statements regarding s/m in 'An interview: sex, power, and the politics of identity', *The Advocate*, 400 (7 August 1984), 26–30, 58; and Leo Bersani's argument that the fundamental problem in Foucault's claim that

acting out sexualised reversals of dominant–subordinate power relations is a challenge to the social hierarchies of power is that such reproductions are themselves respectful of the 'dominance–submission dichotomy' without questioning fully the value of structures of power or the inherent eroticism therein, 'Foucault, Freud, fantasy, and power', *GLQ: A Journal of Lesbian and Gay Studies*, 2:1/2 (1995), 15–17.

5 Jerrold E. Hogle, 'Introduction', *The Cambridge Companion to Gothic Fiction*, ed. Jerrold E. Hogle (Cambridge: Cambridge University Press, 2002), p. 4.

6 Elizabeth Thomas, *Purity of Heart, or The Ancient Costume, A Tale, In One Volume, Addressed to the Author of Glenarvon* (London: W. Simplin and R. Marshall, 1816), p. 181.

Bibliography

PRIMARY SOURCES

Anon., *Adeline; or the Orphan*, 3 vols. London: W. Lane, 1790.

——, *Montrose, or The Gothic Ruin, A Novel*, 3 vols. London: R. Dutton, 1799.

——, Review of Eleanor Sleath, *The Orphan of the Rhine* [1798]. *The Critical Review, or, The Annals of Literature*, 27 (1799), 356.

——, Review of Eliza Parsons, *The Castle of Wolfenbach* [1793]. *The Critical Review, or, Annals of Literature*, 10 (1794), 49–52.

Ash, John, *The New and Complete Dictionary of the English Language*, 2 vols. London: Edward and Charles Dilly and R. Baldwin, 1775.

Austen, Jane, *Mansfield Park* [1814], ed. Margaret Drabble. New York: Signet, 1996.

——, *Northanger Abbey* [1817], ed. Deborah Rogers. New York: Signet, 1995.

——, *Sense and Sensibility* [1811], ed. Claudia L. Johnson. New York: W. W. Norton, 2002.

Barrington, George, *Eliza, or The Unhappy Nun: exemplifying the unlimited tyranny exercised by the abbots and abbesses over the ill-fated victims of their malice in the gloomy recesses of a convent. Including The adventures of Clementina, or The constant lovers, a true and affecting tale*. London: Tegg and Castleman, 1803.

Beckford, William, *Vathek* [1786], ed. Thomas Keymer. Oxford: Oxford University Press, 2013.

Behn, Aphra, *The Dumb Virgin; or, The Force of Imagination* [1688], in *The Works of Aphra Behn*, ed. Janet Todd, 7 vols. London: Pickering & Chatto, 1992, III.

Bennett, Anna Maria, *Anna; or, Memoirs of a Welch Heiress. Interspersed with Anecdotes of a Nabob*, 4 vols. London: The Minerva Press, 1785.

——, *Ellen, Countess of Castle Howel*, 4 vols. London: The Minerva Press, 1794.

Blackstone, William, *Commentaries on the Laws of England. Book the First. By William Blackstone, Esq. Vinerian Professor of Law, and Solicitor General to Her Majesty*, 4 vols. Oxford: Clarendon Press, 1765, I.

——, *Commentaries on the Laws of England. Book the Second. By William Blackstone, Esq. Vinerian Professor of Law, and Solicitor General to Her Majesty*, 4 vols. Oxford: Clarendon Press, 1768, II.

Brontë, Charlotte, *Jane Eyre* [1847], ed. Stevie Davies. London: Penguin Classics, 2006.

Brontë, Emily, *Wuthering Heights* [1847], ed. Pauline Nestor. London: Penguin, 2003.

Burney, Frances, *Diary and Letters of Madame D'Arblay, Author of "Evelina," "Cecilia," &c. Edited by Her Niece*, ed. Charlotte Barrett, 7 vols. London: Henry Colburn, 1842, III.

Byron, George Gordon Lord, *Manfred* [1816], in *The Complete Poetical Works*, ed. Jerome McGann, 7 vols. Oxford: Oxford University Press, 1986, IV.

Coleridge, Samuel Taylor, *Specimens of the Table Talk of Samuel Taylor Coleridge*, 2nd edn, ed. Henry N. Coleridge. London: John Murray, 1836.

Dacre, Charlotte, *Zofloya; or, The Moor: A Romance of the Fifteenth Century* [1806], ed. Adriana Craciun. Peterborough, Ontario: Broadview, 1997.

Davenport, Selina, *The Sons of the Viscount and the Daughters of the Earl: a Novel; Depicting Recent Scenes in Fashionable Life*, 4 vols. London: Henry Colburn, 1813.

Defoe, Daniel, *Moll Flanders* [1722], ed. Edward H. Kelly. New York: W. W. Norton, 1973.

Fielding, Henry, *The Welsh Opera: or, the Grey Mare the better Horse*. London: E. Rayner, 1731.

Fuller, Anne, *The Convent: Or, The History of Sophia Nelson*, 2 vols. London: T. Wilkins, 1786.

Haywood, Eliza Fowler, *The Force of Nature; or, The Lucky Disappointment* [1724], in *Secret Histories, Novels and Poems*, 2nd edn, 4 vols. London: Dan Browne and S. Chapman, 1725, IV.

Helme, Elizabeth, *Louisa; or, The Cottage on the Moor*, 2 vols. London: G. Kearsley, 1787.

Hervey, Elizabeth, *The Church of St. Siffrid*, 4 vols. London: G. G. and J. Robinson, 1797.

Holford, Margaret, *Warbeck of Wolfstein*, 3 vols. London: Rodwell and Martin, 1820.

Inchbald, Elizabeth, *A Simple Story*, 4 vols. London: G. G. and J. Robinson, 1791.

Jamieson, Frances, *The House of Ravenspur, A Romance*, 4 vols. London: G. and W. B. Whittaker, 1822.

Keats, John, *The Complete Works of John Keats*, vol. V, *Letters, 1819–1820*, ed. H. Buxton Forman. New York: Thomas Y. Crowell & Co., 1901.

Kelly, Isabella, *The Abbey of Saint Asaph*, 3 vols. London: The Minerva Press, 1795.

——, *Madeline; or, The Castle of Montgomery*, 3 vols. London: The Minerva Press, 1794.

——, *The Ruins of Avondale Priory*, 3 vols. London: The Minerva Press, 1796.

Ker, Anne, *Emmeline; or, The Happy Discovery; A Novel*, 2 vols. London: J. Bonsor, 1801.

——, *The Mysterious Count; or, Montville Castle. A Romance,* 3 vols. London: D. N. Shury, 1803.

Lamb, Lady Caroline, *Glenarvon,* 3 vols. London: Henry Colburn, 1816.

Lee, Sophia, *The Recess; or, A Tale of Other Times,* 3 vols. London: T. Cadell, 1785.

Lewis, Alethea Brereton, *The Nuns of the Desert: or, The Woodland Witches,* 2 vols. London: The Minerva Press, 1805.

Lewis, Matthew Gregory, *The Monk* [1796], ed. D. L. Macdonald and Kathleen Scherf. Peterborough, Ontario: Broadview, 2004.

Maturin, Charles Robert, *Melmoth the Wanderer* [1820], ed. Victor Sage. New York: Penguin, 2000.

Meeke, Mary, *Palmira and Ermance: A Novel,* 3 vols. London: The Minerva Press, 1797.

Millar, John, *Observations Concerning the Distinctions of Ranks in Society.* London: W. and J. Richardson for John Murray, 1771.

Moore, George, *Grasville Abbey, A Romance,* 3 vols. London: G. G. and J. Robinson, 1797; first published in the *Lady's Magazine* from 1793 to 1797 in instalments.

Parsons, Eliza, *The Castle of Wolfenbach* [1793], ed. Devendra P. Varma. London: The Folio Press, 1968.

——, *The Mysterious Warning, A German Tale* [1796], ed. Devendra P. Varma. London: The Folio Press, 1968.

——, *An Old Friend with a New Face: A Novel,* 3 vols. London: T. N. Longman, 1797.

——, *The Peasant of Ardenne Forest: A Novel,* 4 vols. Brentford: P. Norbury, 1801.

——, *The Valley of St. Gothard, A Novel,* 3 vols. Brentford: P. Norbury, 1799.

Polidori, John William, *Ernestus Berchtold; or, The Modern Oedipus. A Tale.* London: Longman, Hurst, Rees, Orme, and Brown, 1819.

Radcliffe, Ann Ward, *The Castles of Athlin and Dunbayne: A Highland Story.* London: T. Hookham, 1789.

——, *The Italian* [1797], ed. Deborah Rogers. New York: Penguin, 1995.

——, *The Mysteries of Udolpho* [1794], ed. Bonamy Dobrée. Oxford: Oxford University Press, 1998.

——, *The Romance of the Forest* [1791], ed. Chloe Chard. Oxford: Oxford University Press, 1986.

——, *A Sicilian Romance,* 2 vols. London: T. Hookham, 1790.

Reeve, Clara, *The Old English Baron* [1777]. Middlesex: The Echo Library, 2007.

Richardson, Samuel, *Clarissa, or, the History of a Young Lady* [1748], ed. Angus Ross. New York: Penguin, 1995.

——, *Pamela, or Virtue Rewarded* [1740], ed. Thomas Keymer and Alice Wakely. Oxford: Oxford University Press, 2008.

Robinson, Mary, *Vancenza; or, The Dangers of Credulity,* 3rd edn, 2 vols. London: the authoress, 1792.

Roche, Regina Maria, *The Children of the Abbey*, 4 vols. London: The Minerva Press, 1796.
——, *Clermont*, 4 vols. London: The Minerva Press, 1798.
——, *Nocturnal Visit: A Tale*, 3 vols. London: The Minerva Press, 1800.
Rousseau, Jean-Jacques, *Emile, or On Education* [1762], trans. Allan Bloom. New York: Basic Books, 1979.
——, *The Social Contract, or Principles of Political Right* [1762], trans. G. D. H. Cole. New York: Cosimo Inc., 2008.
Scott, Sarah, *A Description of Millenium Hall*. London: J. Newberry, 1762.
——, *The History of Cornelia*. London: A. Millar, 1750.
Scott, Walter and J. W. Lake, *The Poetical Works of Sir Walter Scott, With a Sketch of His Life*. Philadelphia: J. Crissy and Thomas, Cowperthwait & Co., 1838.
Sharp, Granville, *A Tract on the Law of Nature, And Principles of Action in Man*. London: B. White and E. and C. Dilly, 1777.
Shelley, Mary, *Frankenstein* [1818], ed. J. Paul Hunter. New York: W. W. Norton, 1995.
——, *Matilda* [(1820)/1959], ed. Janet Todd. Harmondsworth: Penguin, 1992.
Sheriffe, Sarah, *Correlia, or The Mystic Tomb. A Romance*, 4 vols. London: The Minerva Press, 1802.
——, *Humbert Castle, or The Romance of the Rhone. A Novel*, 4 vols. London: The Minerva Press, 1800.
Sleath, Eleanor, *The Orphan of the Rhine* [1798], ed. Devendra P. Varma. London: The Folio Press, 1968.
Smith, Charlotte, *Emmeline, The Orphan of the Castle*, 4 vols. London: T. Cadell, 1788.
Stuart, Augusta Amelia, *Cave of Toledo; or, The Gothic Princess. A Romance*, 5 vols. London: The Minerva Press, 1812.
Taylor, Sarah, *Glenalpin, or the Bandit's Cave*, 2 vols. London: Longman, Rees, Orme, Brown, and Green; Norwich: S. Wilkin, 1828.
Thomas, Elizabeth, *Purity of Heart, or The Ancient Costume, A Tale, In One Volume, Addressed to the Author of Glenarvon*. London: W. Simplin and R. Marshall, 1816.
Walpole, Horace, *The Castle of Otranto* [1764], ed. E. J. Clery and W. S. Walpole. Oxford: Oxford University Press, 1998.
——, *The Mysterious Mother* [1768], in *The Castle of Otranto and The Mysterious Mother*, ed. Frederick S. Frank. Peterborough, Ontario: Broadview, 2011.
Weston, Anna Maria, *Pleasure and Pain, or the Fate of Ellen; A Novel*, 3 vols. London: Thomas Tegg, 1814.
Wollstonecraft, Mary, *Maria, or the Wrongs of Woman* [1798], ed. Janet Todd. Harmondsworth: Penguin, 1992.
——, *A Vindication of the Rights of Woman* [1792], ed. Miriam Brody. Harmondsworth: Penguin, 1992.

SECONDARY SOURCES

Adler, Jerry, Anne Underwood and Marc Bain, 'Freud in our midst', *Newsweek* 147:13 (27 March 2006). http://search.ebscohost.com/login.aspx?direct=true&db=a9h&AN=20199528&site=ehost-live [accessed 20 May 2009].

Åkesson, Lynn, 'Bound by Blood? New Meanings of Kinship and Individuality in Discourses of Genetic Counseling', in *New Directions in Anthropological Kinship*, ed. Linda Stone. Oxford: Rowman & Littlefield, 2001, pp. 125–38.

Alexander, Richard D., *Darwinism and Human Affairs*. Seattle: University of Washington Press, 1979.

Anderson, Nancy Fix, 'Cousin marriage in Victorian England', *Journal of Family History*, 11:3 (1986), 285–301.

Anolik, Ruth Bienstock, 'The missing mother: the meanings of maternal absence in the Gothic mode', *Modern Language Studies*, 33:1/2 (2003), 24–43.

Ash, Angie, *Father–Daughter Sexual Abuse: The Abuse of Paternal Authority*. Bangor: University College of North Wales, 1984.

Backus, Margot Gayle, *The Gothic Family Romance: Heterosexuality, Child Sacrifice, and the Anglo-Irish Colonial Order*. Durham, NC: Duke University Press, 1999.

Bailey, Joanne, 'Review of Perry, Ruth, *Novel Relations: The Transformation of Kinship in English Literature and Culture 1748–1818*', H-Albion, H-Net Reviews (June 2006). www.h-net.org/reviews/showrev.php?id=11824 [accessed 30 March 2011].

——, *Unquiet Lives: Marriage and Marriage Breakdown in England, 1660–1800*. Cambridge: Cambridge University Press, 2003.

Baker, E. A., 'Introduction'. *The Monk*, by Matthew Gregory Lewis, ed. Tom Crawford. London: George Routledge & Sons Ltd., 1907; New York: Dover, repr. 2003.

Ballaster, Ros, *Fabulous Orients: Fictions of the East in England 1662–1785*. Oxford: Oxford University Press, 2007.

Barry, Kathleen, *Female Sexual Slavery*. New York: New York University Press, 1978.

Batchelor, Jennie, *Women's Work: Labour, Gender, Authorship, 1750–1830*. Manchester: Manchester University Press, 2010.

Bateson, Patrick and Peter Gluckman, *Plasticity, Robustness, Development and Evolution*. Cambridge: Cambridge University Press, 2011.

Battestin, Martin C., 'Henry Fielding, Sarah Fielding, and the "dreadful sin of incest"', *NOVEL: A Forum on Fiction*, 13:1 (1979), 6–18.

Beer, Gillian, '"Our unnatural no-voice": the heroic epistle, Pope, and women's Gothic', *Yearbook of English Studies*, 12 (1982), 125–51.

Bell, Vikki, *Interrogating Incest: Feminism, Foucault and the Law*. London: Routledge, 1993.

Bereczkei, Tamaz, Petra Gyuris and Glenn E. Weisfeld, 'Sexual imprinting in human mate choice', *Proceedings of the Royal Society B: Biological Sciences*, 271 (2004), 1129-34.
Bersani, Leo, 'Foucault, Freud, fantasy, and power', *GLQ: A Journal of Lesbian and Gay Studies*, 2:1/2 (1995), 11-33.
Bird, Benjamin, 'Treason and imagination: the anxiety of legitimacy in the subject of the 1760s', *Romanticism*, 12:3 (2006), 189-99.
Bittles, A. H., 'A background summary of consanguineous marriage', unpublished manuscript, Centre for Human Genetics. Perth: Edith Cowan University, 2001.
Blakemore, Steven, 'Matthew Lewis's black mass: sexual, religious inversion in *The Monk*', *Studies in the Novel*, 30:4 (1998), 521-39.
Botting, Fred, 'Introduction'. *The Gothic: Essays and Studies*, ed. Fred Botting. Cambridge: D. S. Brewer, 2001, pp. 1-6.
Botting, Fred, ed., *Gothic: The New Critical Idiom*. London: Routledge, 1996.
Botting, Fred and Dale Townshend, eds, *Gothic: Critical Concepts in Literary Cultural Studies*. London: Routledge, 2004.
Bower, Bruce, 'Oedipus wrecked: Freud's theory of frustrated incest goes on the defensive', *Science News*, 140:16 (1991), 248-51.
Bowers, Toni, *The Politics of Motherhood: British Writing and Culture, 1680-1760*. Cambridge: Cambridge University Press, 1996.
Brewer, William D., 'Unnationalized Englishmen in Mary Shelley's fiction', *Romanticism on the Net*, 11 (1998). http://users.ox.ac.uk/~scat0385/mwsfiction.html [accessed 12 May 2009].
Brickman, Julie, 'Female Lives, Feminist Deaths: The Relationship of the Montreal Massacre to Dissociation, Incest and Violence against Women', in *States of Rage: Emotional Eruption, Violence and Social Change*, ed. Renée R. Curry. New York: New York University Press, 1996, pp. 15-34.
——, 'Feminist, nonsexist, and traditional models of therapy: implications for working with incest', *Women and Therapy*, 3:1 (1984), 49-68.
Brooks, Peter, 'Virtue and terror: *The Monk*', *ELH*, 40:2 (1973), 249-63.
Brownstein, Rachel M., *Becoming a Heroine: Reading About Women in Novels*. New York: Columbia University Press, 1994.
Burriss, Eli Edward, 'The use and worship of fire among the Romans', *Classical Weekly*, 24:6 (1930), 43-5.
Butler, Judith, *Antigone's Claim: Kinship Between Life and Death*. New York: Columbia University Press, 2000.
——, 'Critically queer', *GLQ: A Journal of Lesbian and Gay Studies*, 1:1 (1993), 17-32.
——, *Gender Trouble: Feminism and the Subversion of Identity*. London: Routledge, 1990.

Buyske, Steven and Alex Walter, 'The Westermarck effect and early childhood co-socialization: sex differences in inbreeding-avoidance', *British Journal of Developmental Psychology*, 21:3 (2003), 353–65.

Campbell, Jill, '"I am no giant": Horace Walpole, heterosexual incest, and love among men', *The Eighteenth-Century: Theory and Interpretation*, 39:3 (1998), 238–60.

Castle, Terry, *The Female Thermometer: Eighteenth-Century Culture and the Invention of the Uncanny*. Oxford: Oxford University Press, 1995.

Cecil, Lord David, *Early Victorian Novelists*. London: Constable, 1934.

Chagnon, Napoleon, 'Male Yanamamo Manipulation of Kinship Classification of Female Kin for Reproductive Advantage', in *Human Reproductive Behaviour: A Darwinian Perspective*, ed. Laura Betzig, Monique Borgerhoff Mulder and Paul Turke. Cambridge: Cambridge University Press, 1988, pp. 23–48.

Chaplin, Sue, *The Gothic and the Rule of Law, 1764–1820*. Basingstoke and London: Palgrave Macmillan, 2007.

——, 'Spectres of law in *The Castle of Otranto*', *Romanticism*, 12:3 (2006), 177–88.

Chiu, Frances A., 'From nobodadies to noble daddies: writing political and paternal authority in English fiction of the 1780s and 1790s', *Eighteenth-Century Life*, 26:2 (2002), 1–22.

Chodorow, Nancy, *Feminism and Psychoanalytic Theory* [1989]. New Haven, CT: Yale University Press, repr. 1991.

Cleere, Eileen, 'Reinvesting nieces: *Mansfield Park* and the economics of endogamy', *NOVEL: A Forum on Fiction*, 28:2 (1995), 113–30.

Clery, E. J., 'Ann Radcliffe and D. A. F. de Sade: thoughts on heroinism', *Women's Writing*, 1:2 (1994), 203–14.

——, 'Horace Walpole's *The Mysterious Mother* and the impossibility of female Desire', in *The Gothic: Essays and Studies*, ed. Fred Botting. Cambridge: D. S. Brewer, 2001, pp. 23–46.

——, 'Introduction'. *The Castle of Otranto*, by Horace Walpole. Oxford: Oxford University Press, 1998.

——, *The Rise of Supernatural Fiction*. Cambridge: Cambridge University Press, 1995.

——, *Women's Gothic: From Clara Reeve to Mary Shelley*. Tavistock: Northcote House, 2000.

Colley, Linda, *Britons: Forging the Nation 1707–1837*. New Haven, CT: Yale University Press, 2009.

Conniff, Richard, 'Go ahead, kiss your cousin: heck, marry her if you want to', *Discover*, 24:8 (2003). http://discovermagazine.com/2003/aug/featkiss [accessed 20 March 2009].

Corbett, Mary Jean, *Family Likeness: Sex, Marriage and Incest from Jane Austen to Virginia Woolf*. Ithaca, NY: Cornell University Press, 2008.

Cossins, Anne, *Masculinities, Sexualities, and Child Sexual Abuse*. New York: Springer, 2000.

Cox, Jeffrey N., 'First Gothics: Walpole, Evans, Frank', *Papers on Language and Literature*, 46:2 (2010), 119–35.

Davidoff, Leonore and Catherine Hall, *Family Fortunes: Men and Women of the English Middle Class, 1780–1850* [1987]. London: Routledge, repr. 2002.

Davies, Stevie, 'Notes'. *Jane Eyre*, by Charlotte Brontë. London: Penguin Classics, 2006.

DeLamotte, Eugenia C., *Perils of the Night: A Feminist Study of Nineteenth-Century Gothic*. Oxford: Oxford University Press, 1990.

DeMause, Lloyd, 'The universality of incest', *Journal of Psychohistory*, 19:2 (1991), 123–64.

Dole, Carol M., 'Three tyrants in *The Castle of Otranto*', *English Language Notes*, 26:1 (1988), 26–35.

Dominelli, Lena, 'Betrayal of trust: a feminist analysis of power relationships in incest abuse and its relevance for social work practice', *British Journal of Social Work*, 19:1 (1989), 291–308.

——, 'Father–daughter incest: patriarchy's shameful secret', *Critical Social Policy's Special Feminist Issue*, 6:16 (1986), 8–22.

Durrant, David, 'Ann Radcliffe and the conservative Gothic', *Studies in English Literature, 1500–1900*, 22:3 (1982), 519–31.

Eagleton, Terry, *Ideology: An Introduction*. London: Verso, 1991.

Ellis, Kate Ferguson, 'Can You Forgive Her? The Gothic Heroine and Her Critics', in *A Companion to the Gothic*, ed. David Punter. Oxford: Blackwell Publishers, 2000, pp. 257–68.

——, *The Contested Castle: Gothic Novels and the Subversion of Domestic Ideology*. Urbana: University of Illinois Press, 1989.

English, Deirdre, Amber Hollibaugh and Gayle Rubin, 'Talking sex: a conversation on sexuality and feminism', *Feminist Review*, 11 (1982), 40–52.

Erickson, L., 'The economy of novel reading: Jane Austen and the circulating library', *Studies in English Literature, 1500–1900*, 30:4 (1990), 573–90.

Erickson, Mark T., 'Evolutionary Thought and the Current Clinical Understanding of Incest', in *Inbreeding, Incest and the Incest Taboo: The State of Knowledge at the Turn of the Century*, ed. Arthur P. Wolf and William H. Durham. Stanford: Stanford University Press, 2004, pp. 161–89.

Fawcett, Mary Laughlin, 'Udolpho's primal mystery', *Studies in English Literature, 1500–1900*, 23:3 (1983), 481–93.

Felski, Rita, *Literature after Feminism*. Chicago: University of Chicago Press, 2003.

Ferraro, Kenneth F., 'Women's fear of victimization: shadow of sexual assault', *Social Forces*, 75:2 (1996), 667–90.

Fincher, Max, *Queering Gothic in the Romantic Age: The Penetrating Eye*. Basingstoke: Palgrave Macmillan, 2007.

Finney, Gail, 'Self-reflexive siblings: incest as narcissism in Tieck, Wagner, and Thomas Mann', *German Quarterly*, 56:2 (1983), 243–56.

Fitzgerald, Lauren, 'Female Gothic and the Institutionalization of Gothic Studies', in *The Female Gothic: New Directions*, ed. Diana Wallace and Andrew Smith. Basingstoke: Palgrave Macmillan, 2009, pp. 13–25.

Fleenor, Juliann E., *The Female Gothic*. Montreal: Eden Press, 1983.

'Forbidden love: pull of attraction felt between adoptees, biological family members', *CBC News*, 7 May 2009. www.cbc.ca/canada/story/2009/05/06/f-gsa.html [accessed 5 June 2009].

Foucault, Michel, *Discipline and Punish: The Birth of the Prison*, trans. A. M. Sheridan-Smith. London: Penguin, 1979.

——, *The History of Sexuality Volume I: An Introduction*, trans. R. Hurley [1979]. Harmondsworth: Penguin, repr. 1981.

——, 'An interview: sex, power, and the politics of identity', *The Advocate*, 400 (7 August 1984), 26–30, 58.

——, *Power/Knowledge: Selected Interviews and Other Writings 1972–1977*, ed. Colin Gordon, trans. Colin Gordon, Leo Marshall, John Mepham and Kate Soper. Brighton: Harvester Press, 1980.

Frank, Frederick S., 'Introduction'. *The Castle of Otranto and The Mysterious Mother*, by Horace Walpole. Peterborough, Ontario: Broadview, 2003.

Frank, Marcie, 'Horace Walpole's family romances', *Modern Philology*, 100:3 (2003), 417–35.

Freud, Sigmund, *The Interpretation of Dreams*, ed. and trans. James Strachey [1953]. New York: Avon, 1980.

——, *Three Essays on the Theory of Sexuality*, ed. and trans. James Strachey [1953]. New York: Basic Books, 2000.

——, *Totem and Taboo*, trans. James Strachey [1950]. London: Routledge, repr. 1999.

Gallop, Jane, *The Daughter's Seduction: Feminism and Psychoanalysis*. Ithaca, NY: Cornell University Press, 1982.

Gamer, Michael, 'Gothic origins: new primary scholarship', *Eighteenth-Century Fiction*, 14:2 (2002), 215–22.

——, 'Introduction'. *The Castle of Otranto*, by Horace Walpole. Harmondsworth: Penguin, 2002.

——, *Romanticism and the Gothic: Genre, Reception, and Canon Formation*. Cambridge: Cambridge University Press, 2000.

Gilbert, Sandra M., 'Jane Eyre and the secrets of furious lovemaking', *NOVEL: A Forum on Fiction*, 31:3 (1998), 351–72.

Gilbert, Sandra M. and Susan Gubar, *The Madwoman in the Attic: The Woman Writer and the Nineteenth-Century Literary Imagination*. New Haven, CT: Yale University Press, 1984.

Gill, Pat, 'Pathetic passions: incestuous desire in the plays of Otway and Lee', *The Eighteenth Century: Theory and Interpretation*, 30:3 (1998), 192–208.

Goetz, William R., 'Genealogy and incest in Wuthering Heights', *Studies in the Novel*, 14:4 (1982), 359–76.

Gonda, Caroline, *Reading Daughters' Fictions 1709–1834: Novels and Society from Manley to Edgeworth*. Cambridge: Cambridge University Press, 1996.

Gramsci, Antonio, *The Prison Notebooks*, vol. I, ed. and trans. Joseph A. Buttigieg. New York: Columbia University Press, 1992.

——, *The Prison Notebooks*, vol. III, ed. and trans. Joseph A. Buttigieg. New York: Columbia University Press, 2010.

Greenberg, Maurice, 'Post-adoption reunion: are we entering uncharted territory?', Hilda Lewis Memorial Lecture, British Association for Adoption and Fostering, 5 October 1993, 1–22. www.geneticsexualattraction.com/AAPostAdoptionReunion.pdf [accessed 21 May 2009].

Greenberg, Maurice and Roland Littlewood, 'Post-adoption incest and phenotypic matching: experience, personal meanings and biosocial implications', *British Journal of Medical Psychology*, 68:1 (1995), 29–44.

Gubar, Susan, 'Representing pornography: feminism, criticism, and depictions of female violation', *Critical Inquiry*, 13:4 (1987), 712–41.

——, 'What ails feminist criticism?', *Critical Inquiry*, 24:4 (1998), 878–902.

Haggerty, George E., 'Literature and homosexuality in the late eighteenth century: Walpole, Beckford, and Lewis', *Studies in the Novel*, 18:4 (1986), 341–52.

——, 'Psychodrama: hypertheatricality and sexual excess on the Gothic stage', *Theatre Research International*, 28:1 (2003), 20–33.

——, *Queer Gothic*. Urbana: University of Illinois Press, 2006.

Haig, David, 'Asymmetric relations: internal conflicts and the horror of incest', *Evolution and Human Behaviour*, 20:2 (1999), 83–98.

Hallie, Philip, *The Paradox of Cruelty*. Middleton, CT: Wesleyan University Press, 1969.

Harpold, Terence, '"Did you get Mathilda from papa?" Seduction fantasy and the circulation of Mary Shelley's Mathilda', *Studies in Romanticism*, 28:1 (1989), 49–67.

Herman, Judith Lewis with Lisa Hirschman, *Father–Daughter Incest*. Cambridge, MA: Harvard University Press, 1981.

Hoeveler, Diane Long, *Gothic Feminism: The Professionalization of Gender from Charlotte Smith to the Brontës*. Liverpool: Liverpool University Press, 1998.

——, *The Gothic Ideology: Religious Hysteria and Anti-Catholicism in British Popular Fiction, 1780–1880*. Cardiff: University of Wales Press, 2014.

Hogle, Jerrold E., 'Introduction'. *The Cambridge Companion to Gothic Fiction*, ed. Jerrold E. Hogle. Cambridge: Cambridge University Press, 2002.

——, 'Recovering the Walpolean Gothic: *The Italian: Or, the Confessional of the Black Penitents* (1796-1797)', in *Ann Radcliffe, Romanticism and the Gothic*, ed. Dale Townshend and Angela Wright. Cambridge: Cambridge University Press, 2014, pp. 151-67.

Holcombe, Lee, *Wives and Property: Reform of the Married Women's Property Law in Nineteenth-Century England*. Toronto: University of Toronto Press, 1983.

Hunt, Lynn Avery, *The Family Romance of the French Revolution*. Berkeley, CA: University of California Press, 1993.

Irigaray, Luce, *This Sex Which is Not One* [1977], trans. Catherine Porter and Carolyn Burke. Ithaca, NY: Cornell University Press, 1985.

Jacobs, Janet Liebman, 'Reassessing mother blame in incest', *Signs*, 15:3 (1990), 500-14.

Jewel, Carolyn, 'Eleanor Sleath: a writer rediscovered', *Teach Me Tonight*, 25 March 2008. http://teachmetonight.blogspot.com/2008_03_01_archive.html [accessed 20 January 2010].

——, Interview with Megan Frampton, 'Friday with Carolyn Jewel!', *Risky Regencies: The Original, Riskiest, and Forever the Friskiest Regency Romance Blog*, 13 February 2009. http://riskyregencies.blogspot.com/2009/02/friday-with-carolyn-jewel.html [accessed 20 January 2010].

Johnson, Claudia L., *Equivocal Beings: Politics, Gender, and Sentimentality in the 1790s*. Chicago: University of Chicago Press, 1995.

Jones, Frederick L., ed., *Maria Gisborne and Edward E. Williams, Shelley's Friends, Their Journals and Letters*. Norman: University of Oklahoma Press, 1951.

Kaufman, Pamela, 'Burke, Freud and the Gothic', *Studies in Burke and His Time*, 13:3 (1972), 2179-92.

Kilgour, Maggie, *The Rise of the Gothic Novel*. London: Routledge, 1995.

Kilkenny, Beth, 'Representation of the repressed: women and the feminine in Eleanor Sleath's *The Orphan of the Rhine* and *The Nocturnal Minstrel*', *The Corvey Project at Sheffield Hallam University*, n.d. http://extra.shu.ac.uk/corvey/corinne/1%20Sleath/Sleath%20critical%20essay.htm [accessed 8 July 2009].

Kirsta, Alix, 'Genetic sexual attraction', *Guardian*, 17 May 2003. www.guardian.co.uk/theguardian/2003/may/17/weekend7.weekend2 [accessed 16 November 2009].

Klekar, Cynthia, 'The obligations of form: social practice in Charlotte Smith's *Emmeline*', *Philological Quarterly*, 86:3 (2007), 269-89.

Klekar, Cynthia and Linda Zionkowski, eds, *The Culture of the Gift in Eighteenth-Century England*. Basingstoke: Palgrave Macmillan, 2009.

Kuper, Adam, 'Changing the subject – about cousin marriage, among other things', *Journal of the Royal Anthropological Institute (NS)*, 14:4 (2008), 717-35.

——, *Incest and Influence*. Cambridge, MA: Harvard University Press, 2009.

——, 'Incest, cousin marriage, and the origin of the human sciences in nineteenth-century England', *Past and Present*, 174:1 (2002), 158–83.

Lacan, Jacques, *Écrits*, trans. Alan Sheridan [1977]. London: Routledge, repr. 2001.

Landry, Donna, 'William Beckford's *Vathek* and the Uses of Oriental Re-enactment', in *The Arabian Nights in Historical Context*, ed. Saree Makdisi and Felicity Nussbaum. Oxford: Oxford University Press, 2009, pp. 167–94.

Ledoux, Ellen Malenas, 'Defiant damsels: Gothic space and female agency in *Emmeline*, *The Mysteries of Udolpho* and *Secresy*', *Women's Writing*, 18:3 (2011), 331–47.

——, *Social Reform in Gothic Writing: Fantastic Forms of Change, 1764–1834* (Basingstoke: Palgrave Macmillan, 2013).

Lévi-Strauss, Claude, *The Elementary Structures of Kinship*. London: Taylor & Francis, 1969.

Littlewood, Roland, *Pathologies of the West: An Anthropology of Mental Illness in Europe and America*. London: Continuum, 2002.

London, April, *Women and Property in the Eighteenth-Century Novel*. Cambridge: Cambridge University Press, 1999.

Lonsdale, Roger, 'Introduction'. *Vathek*, by William Beckford. Oxford: Oxford University Press, 2008.

McKinnon, Susan, 'American Kinship/American Incest: Asymmetries in a Scientific Discourse', in *Naturalizing Power: Essays in Feminist Cultural Analysis*, ed. Sylvia Yanagisako and Carol Delaney. New York: Routledge, 1995, pp. 25–46.

Madden, William A., '*Wuthering Heights*: the binding of passion', *Nineteenth-Century Fiction*, 27:2 (1972), 127–54.

Malinowski, Bronislaw, 'Culture', in *Encyclopedia of the Social Sciences*, ed. Charles G. Seligman, 15 vols. New York: Macmillan: 1931, IV, pp. 621–46.

Marsh, Kelly A., '*Jane Eyre* and the pursuit of the mother's pleasure', *South Atlantic Review*, 69:3/4 (2004), 81–106.

Masse, Michelle A., 'Gothic repetition: husbands, horror, and things that go bump in the night', *Signs*, 15:4 (1990), 679–709.

——, *In the Name of Love: Women, Masochism and the Gothic*. Ithaca, NY: Cornell University Press, 1992.

Mauss, Marcel, *The Gift: The Form and Reason for Exchange in Archaic Societies* [1925], trans. W. D. Halls. London: Routledge, 1990.

Maynard, John, *Charlotte Brontë and Sexuality*, Cambridge: Cambridge University Press, 1984.

Mead, Margaret, *Male and Female* [1949]. New York: HarperCollins, 2001.

Mellor, Anne K., *Mary Shelley: Her Life, Her Fiction, Her Monsters*. London: Routledge, 1989.

Messier, Vartan P., 'The conservative, the transgressive, and the reactionary: Ann Radcliffe's *The Italian* as a response to Matthew Lewis' *The Monk*', *Atenea*, 25:2 (2005), 37–48.

Meyer, Susan, *Imperialism at Home: Race and Victorian Women's Fiction*. Ithaca, NY and London: Cornell University Press, 1996.

Miles, Robert, *Ann Radcliffe: The Great Enchantress*. Manchester: Manchester University Press, 1995.

——, *Gothic Writing, 1750–1820: A Genealogy*. London: Routledge, 1993.

——, '"Mother Radcliffe": Ann Radcliffe and the Female Gothic', in *The Female Gothic: New Directions*, ed. Diana Wallace and Andrew Smith. Basingstoke: Palgrave Macmillan, 2009, pp. 42–59.

Mitchell, Juliet, *Psychoanalysis and Feminism: Freud, Reich, Laing and Women* [1974]. Repr. as *Psychoanalysis and Feminism: A Radical Reassessment of Freudian Psychoanalysis*. New York: Basic Books, 2000.

Modleski, Tania, *Loving with a Vengeance: Mass-Produced Fantasies for Women* [1982]. New York: Routledge, repr. 2008.

Moers, Ellen, *Literary Women: The Great Writers* [1976]. Oxford: Oxford University Press, repr. 1985.

Moran, Leslie J., 'Law and the Gothic Imagination', in *The Gothic: Essays and Studies*, ed. Fred Botting. Cambridge: D. S. Brewer, 2001, pp. 87–109.

Morris, Polly, 'Incest or survival strategy? Plebeian marriage within the prohibited degrees in Somerset, 1730–1835', *Journal of the History of Sexuality*, 2:2 (1991), 235–65.

Moser, Thomas, 'What is the matter with Emily Jane? Conflicting impulses in *Wuthering Heights*', *Nineteenth-Century Fiction*, 17:1 (1962), 1–19.

Mulvey-Roberts, Marie, 'From Bluebeard's Bloody Chamber to Demonic Stigmatic', in *The Female Gothic: New Directions*, ed. Diana Wallace and Andrew Smith. Basingstoke: Palgrave Macmillan, 2009, pp. 98–114.

Neff, D. S., 'Bitches, mollies, and tommies: Byron, masculinity, and the history of sexualities', *Journal of the History of Sexuality*, 11:3 (2002), 395–438.

Nelson, T. G. A., 'The Ambivalence of Nature's Law: Representations of Incest in Dryden and His English Contemporaries', in *Incest and the Literary Imagination*, ed. Elizabeth Barnes. Gainesville, FL: University Press of Florida, 2002, pp. 117–37.

Nestor, Pauline, 'Introduction'. *Wuthering Heights*, by Emily Brontë. London: Penguin, 2003.

Norton, Rictor, *Gothic Readings: The First Wave, 1764–1840*. London: Leicester University Press, 2000.

——, 'William Beckford: the fool of Fonthill', *Gay History and Literature*, updated 16 November 1999. www.rictornorton.co.uk/beckfor1.htm [accessed 21 March 2011].

Novak, Maximillian E., 'Gothic fiction and the grotesque', *NOVEL: A Forum on Fiction*, 13:1 (1979), 50–67.

Nowak, Tenille, 'Regina Maria Roche's "horrid" novel: echoes of *Clermont* in Jane Austen's *Northanger Abbey*', *Persuasions*, 29 (2007), 184–93.

Nussbaum, Felicity A., *Torrid Zones: Maternity, Sexuality, and Empire in Eighteenth-Century English Narratives*. Baltimore: Johns Hopkins University Press, 1995.

O'Toole, Tess, 'Siblings and suitors in the narrative architecture of *The Tenant of Wildfell Hall*', *Studies in English Literature, 1500–1900*, 39:4 (1999), 715–31.

Ottenheimer, Martin, *Forbidden Relatives: The American Myth of Cousin Marriage*. Urbana: University of Illinois Press, 1996.

Otto, Peter, 'The Sadleir-Black collection', *Gothic Fiction*. www.adam-matthew-publications.co.uk/digital_guides/gothic_fiction/Introduction1.aspx [accessed 20 November 2009].

Park, Justin H., 'Is aversion to incest psychologically privileged? When sex and sociosexuality do not predict sexual willingness', *Personality and Individual Differences*, 45:7 (2008), 661–5.

Perry, Ruth, 'De-familiarizing the Family; or, Writing Family History from Literary Sources', in *Eighteenth-Century Literary History: An MLQ Reader*, ed. Marshall Brown. Durham, NC: Duke University Press, 1999, pp. 159–72.

——, *Novel Relations: The Transformation of Kinship in English Literature and Culture 1748–1818*. Cambridge: Cambridge University Press, 2004.

Piatti-Farnell, Lorna and Donna Lee Brien, eds, *New Directions in 21st Century Gothic: The Gothic Compass*. New York and Abingdon: Routledge, 2015.

Pinker, Steven, 'Strangled by roots: the genealogy craze in America', *New Republic*, 237:3 (2007), 32–5.

Pollak, Ellen, *Incest and the English Novel, 1684–1814*. Baltimore: Johns Hopkins University Press, 2003.

Potkay, Adam, 'Beckford's heaven of boys', *Raritan*, 13:1 (1994), 73–83.

Praz, Mario, *The Romantic Agony*, trans. Angus Davidson [1933]. Oxford: Oxford University Press, repr. 1970.

'Prohibited marriages: forbidden degrees of relationship'. www.weddingguideuk.com/articles/legal/prohibited.asp [accessed 24 June 2010].

Punter, David, *Gothic Pathologies: The Text, the Body and the Law*. Basingstoke: Macmillan Press, 1998.

Punter, David and Glennis Byron, *The Gothic*. Oxford: Blackwell Publishing, 2004.

Purves, Maria, *The Gothic and Catholicism: Religion, Cultural Exchange and the Popular Novel, 1785–1829*. Cardiff: University of Wales Press, 2009.

Quilligan, Maureen, *Incest and Agency in Elizabeth's England*. Philadelphia: University of Pennsylvania Press, 2005.

Radway, Janice, 'The utopian impulse in Gothic literature: Gothic romances and "feminist" protest', *American Quarterly*, 33:2 (1981), 140–62.

Railo, Eino, *The Haunted Castle: A Study of the Elements of English Romanticism* [1927]. New York: Humanities Press, repr. 1964.

Rajan, Tilottama, 'Mary Shelley's *Mathilda*: melancholy and the political economy of Romanticism', *Studies in the Novel*, 26:2 (Summer 1994), 43–68.

Renvoize, Jean, *Incest: A Family Pattern*. London: Routledge & Kegan Paul, 1982.

Richardson, Alan, 'The dangers of sympathy: sibling incest in English Romantic poetry', *Studies in Literature 1500–1900*, 25:4 (1985), 737–54.

——, 'Rethinking Romantic incest: human universals, literary representations, and the biology of mind', *New Literary History*, 31:3 (2000), 553–72.

Rivero, Albert, *The Plays of Henry Fielding: A Critical Study of His Dramatic Career*. Charlottesville, VA: University of Virginia Press, 1989.

Riviere, Joan, 'Womanliness as masquerade', *International Journal of Psychoanalysis*, 10 (1929), 303–13.

Rizzo, Betty, 'Renegotiating the Gothic', in *Revising Women: Eighteenth-Century "Women's Fiction" and Social Engagement*, ed. Paula R. Backscheider. Baltimore: Johns Hopkins University Press, 2000, pp. 58–103.

Rooney, Caroline, *Decolonising Gender: Literature and a Poetics of the Real*. New York: Routledge, 2007.

Rover, Constance, *Women's Suffrage and Party Politics in Britain, 1866–1914*. London: Routledge & Kegan Paul, 1967.

Rubin, Gayle, 'The Traffic in Women: Notes on the "Political Economy" of Sex', in *Toward an Anthropology of Women*, ed. Rayna R. Reiter. New York: Monthly Review Press, 1975, pp. 157–211.

Rush, Florence, *The Best Kept Secret: The Sexual Abuse of Children*. Englewood Cliffs, NJ: Prentice Hall, 1980.

Sanchez-Eppler, Karen, 'Temperance in the bed of a child: incest and social order in nineteenth-century America', *American Quarterly*, 47:1 (1995), 1–33.

Schmidgen, Wolfram, *Eighteenth-Century Fiction and the Law of Property*. Cambridge: Cambridge University Press, 2002.

Schmitt, Cannon, 'Techniques of terror, technologies of nationalities: Ann Radcliffe's *The Italian*', *ELH*, 61:4 (1994), 853–76.

Sedgwick, Eve Kosofsky, *The Coherence of Gothic Conventions*. New York: Arno Press, 1980.

——, 'Toward the Gothic: Terrorism and Homosexual Panic', in *Between Men: English Literature and Male Homosexual Desire*. New York: Columbia University Press, 1985, pp. 83–96.

Shaffer, Julie, 'Familial love, incest, and female desire in late eighteenth- and early nineteenth-century British women's novels', *Criticism: A Quarterly for Literature and the Arts*, 41:1 (1999), 67–99.

Shepher, Joseph, *Incest: A Biosocial View*. New York: Academic Press, 1983.

Shields, William, *Philopatry, Inbreeding and the Evolution of Sex*. Albany, NY: State University of New York Press, 1982.

Slipp, Samuel, *The Freudian Mystique: Freud, Women, and Feminism*. New York: New York University Press, 1993.

Smith, David Livingstone, 'Beyond Westermarck: can shared mothering or maternal phenotype matching account for incest avoidance?', *Evolutionary Psychology*, 5:1 (2007), 202-22.

Smith, John Maynard, *The Evolution of Sex*. Cambridge: Cambridge University Press, 1978.

Solomon, Eric, 'The incest theme in *Wuthering Heights*', *Nineteenth-Century Fiction*, 14:1 (1959), 80-3.

Spooner, Catherine, *Contemporary Gothic*. London: Reaktion Books, 2006.

Staves, Susan, *Married Women's Separate Property in England, 1660-1833*. Cambridge, MA: Harvard University Press, 1990.

Stelzig, Eugene, '"Though it were the deadliest sin to love as we have loved": the Romantic idealization of incest', *European Romantic Review*, 5:2 (1995), 230-51.

Stevenson, John Allen, '"Heathcliff is me!": *Wuthering Heights* and the question of likeness', *Nineteenth-Century Literature*, 43:1 (1988), 62-75.

Stone, Lawrence, *The Family, Sex and Marriage in England, 1500-1800*. London: Weidenfeld & Nicolson, 1977.

Tadmor, Naomi, *Family and Friends in Eighteenth-Century England*. Cambridge: Cambridge University Press, 2001.

Thompson, Wade, 'Infanticide and sadism in *Wuthering Heights*', *PMLA*, 78:1 (1963), 69-74.

Thormählen, Marianne, 'The lunatic and the devil's disciple: the "lovers" in *Wuthering Heights*', *Review of English Studies*, 48:190 (1997), 183-97.

Todd, Janet, 'Introduction'. *Matilda*, by Mary Shelley. London: Penguin, 1991.

Tolan, Fiona, 'Feminisms', in *Literary Theory and Criticism: An Oxford Guide*, ed. Patricia Waugh. Oxford: Oxford University Press, 2006, pp. 319-39.

Trumbach, Randolph, *The Rise of the Egalitarian Family: Aristocratic Kinship and Domestic Relations in Eighteenth-Century England*. New York: Academic Press, 1978.

Twitchell, James B., *Forbidden Partners: The Incest Taboo in Modern Culture*. New York: Columbia University Press, 1987.

Van den Berghe, Pierre L., *Human Family Systems: An Evolutionary View*. New York: Elsevier, 1979.

Varma, Devendra P., 'Introduction'. *The Orphan of the Rhine*, by Eleanor Sleath. London: The Folio Press, 1968.

Vaz da Silva, Francisco, 'Folklore into theory: Freud and Lévi-Strauss on incest and marriage', *Journal of Folklore Research*, 44:1 (2007), 1-19.

Von Sneidern, Maja-Lisa, '*Wuthering Heights* and the Liverpool slave trade', *ELH*, 62:1 (1995), 171-96.

Wall, Cynthia, '*The Castle of Otranto*: A Shakespearo-Politcal Satire?', in *Historical Boundaries, Narrative Forms: Essays on British Literature in the Long Eighteenth Century in Honor of Everett Zimmerman*, ed. Lorna Clymer and Robert Mayer. Newark: University of Delaware Press, 2007, pp. 184-98.

Wallace, Diana, '"The Haunting Idea": Female Gothic Metaphors and Feminist Theory', in *The Female Gothic: New Directions*, ed. Diana Wallace and Andrew Smith. Basingstoke: Palgrave Macmillan, 2009, pp. 26-41.

Wallace, Diana and Andrew Smith, 'Introduction'. *The Female Gothic: New Directions*, ed. Diana Wallace and Andrew Smith. Basingstoke: Palgrave Macmillan, 2009, pp. 1-12.

Warner, Michael, 'Introduction'. *Fear of a Queer Planet: Queer Politics and Social Theory*, ed. Michael Warner. Minneapolis: University of Minnesota Press, 1993.

Watt, James, *Contesting the Gothic*. Cambridge: Cambridge University Press, 1999.

——, 'Gothic', in *The Cambridge Companion to English Literature, 1740-1830*, ed. Thomas Keymer and Jon Mee. Cambridge: Cambridge University Press, 2004, pp. 119-38.

Wein, Toni, 'Gothic desire in Charlotte Brontë's *Villette*', *Studies in English Literature, 1500-1900*, 39:4 (1999), 733-46.

Westermarck, Edward, *The History of Human Marriage*. London: Macmillan and Co., 1903.

——, *A Short History of Human Marriage*. London: Macmillan, 1926.

White, Leslie, 'The definition and prohibition of incest', *American Anthropologist (NS)*, 50:3(1) (1948), 416-35.

Williams, Anne, *Art of Darkness: A Poetics of Gothic*. Chicago: University of Chicago Press, 1995.

Williams, Raymond, *The Long Revolution*. Peterborough, Ontario: Broadview, 2001.

Wolf, Arthur P., 'Westermarck redivivus', *Annual Review of Anthropology*, 22 (1993), 157-75.

Wolff, Cynthia Griffin, 'The Radcliffean Gothic model: a form for feminine sexuality', *Modern Language Studies*, 9:3 (1979), 98-113.

Wolstenholme, Susan, *Gothic (Re)Visions: Writing Women as Readers*. Albany, NY: State University of New York Press, 1993.

Wright, Angela, *Gothic Fiction: A Reader's Guide to Essential Criticism*. Basingstoke: Palgrave Macmillan, 2007.

Wyatt, Jean, 'A patriarch of one's own: *Jane Eyre* and Romantic love', *Tulsa Studies in Women's Literature*, 4:2 (1985), 199-216.

Ying-Chang, Chuang and Arthur P. Wolf, 'Marriage in Taiwan, 1881-1905: an example of regional diversity', *Journal of Asian Studies*, 54:3 (1995), 781-96.

Index

Note: 'n.' after a page reference indicates the number of a note on that page

Adeline or the Orphan 29n.73
Åkesson, Lynn 21, 30n.84
Anolik, Ruth Bienstock 19, 39, 78n.54, 145, 249, 257, 267–8, 275n.76, 276n.92
Ash, Angie 158–9
Austen, Jane 106–7
  Mansfield Park 156, 182n.28, 183n.41, 194, 201–2, 221
  Northanger Abbey 106–7, 134n.71, 204, 237n.50
  Sense and Sensibility 156–7
authority 85, 91, 135n.86, 146–9, 154, 159–64, 177, 184n.50, 201–2
  political 6, 77n.52, 251, 265
  see also family, obligation; paternal authority

Backus, Margot Gayle 15
Bailey, Joanne 14, 28n.63
Baillie, Joanna 270
  De Montfort 267
Batchelor, Jennie 182–3n.32, 236n.31
Beckford, William 7, 259, 267
  Vathek 251, 259–64, 269
Bell, Vikki 108, 136n.87
Bennett, Anna Maria 196
  Ellen, Countess of Castle Howel 16, 29n.75, 196, 208–12
Bersani, Leo 20, 247, 250, 265, 281n.4
Blackstone, William 19, 39, 72, 76n.27, 142
Blakemore, Steven 266, 268
Botting, Fred 10, 18, 23, 33n.112
Brewer, William D. 68
Brickman, Julie 9
Brontë, Charlotte

Jane Eyre 20, 80n.83, 196, 223–4, 229–33
Brontë, Emily
  Wuthering Heights 89, 117–28, 196, 210, 223–9, 273n.44
Brooks, Peter 264, 275n.77
brother–sister incest 85–138, 209–10, 265–6
Burney, Frances 1–2, 184n.50
  Evelina 77n.50
Butler, Judith 65, 113, 135n.86, 270n.6
Byron, Lord 83n.126, 128n.4, 213
  Manfred 32n.111

Campbell, Jill 273n.41
Catholicism 56, 80n.90, 81n.93
Chaplin, Sue 19, 42–3, 179n.2, 181n.13
childhood 64, 71, 107–9, 119–20, 126, 133n.49, 137n.112, 209–11, 222, 239n.63
Cleere, Eileen 201–2, 207, 237n.40–2
Clery, E. J. 7–8, 34, 44, 73n.2, 88, 93, 157, 170, 250, 255, 257–8, 272n.37, 273n.42
Coleridge, Samuel Taylor 2–3, 252–3, 267
  Osorio 137n.107
commodification of women 40–1, 57, 66, 81n.98, 95, 145, 155, 161, 165, 186–7n.79, 202, 219, 238n.56, 239n.60, 242n.94
  see also exchange of women; property, women as
convents 47, 49, 53, 56, 80n.90, 144, 152–4, 241n.82
courtship 218, 224
cousins 32n.102, 190–2, 210, 280
  incest between 125, 190–245, 235n.25

Cox, Jeffrey N. 253, 256
cross-dressing 215–16
customs *see* law, customs as

Dacre, Charlotte 248, 267
  Zofloya 262
Davenport, Selina
  Sons of the Viscount and the Daughters of the Earl: a Novel; Depicting Recent Scenes in Fashionable Life, The 21, 32n.103, 81n.97, 197, 217–23, 257
DeLamotte, Eugenia C. 12, 17, 140, 180n.4, 229–32
DeMause, Lloyd 68, 83n.123
demons 92, 264–8
desire *see* sexuality
discipline *see* punishment
Dominelli, Lena 9–10, 77n.51, 147
duty *see* family, obligation

Eagleton, Terry 6–7
Ellis, Kate Ferguson 8, 11–12, 39, 41, 92, 129n.6, 150
endogamy 58, 66, 89, 120, 126, 138n.131, 191, 198, 202, 207–8, 212, 219, 224–5
estates *see* property
exchange of women 10, 21, 35, 39–40, 46–51, 57–8, 64–73, 76n.30, 87n.97, 95, 99, 121, 127, 145–6, 152, 155, 179, 182n.25, 184n.48, 186–7n.79, 202, 207–8, 212, 219, 233, 238n.60, 239n.60, 240n.72
  see also commodification of women
exogamy 55–7, 89, 121, 146, 191, 202, 212, 233

family 147–9
  adoptive 152, 205, 208, 210
  affinal 80n.84, 191, 200, 205, 212, 234
  attraction to 54, 60, 79n.77, 87, 101, 130n.18, 136n.99, 138n.132, 144–6, 154, 196, 199, 204–5, 220, 225, 227
  authority 214–15, 223, 241n.82
  conjugal 28n.47, 229, 233
  consanguineal 15, 50, 125–6, 151, 154, 183n.45, 184n.46, 191–3, 197–8, 204–5, 212, 218, 229, 233
  nuclear 14–15, 37, 48, 63, 75n.19, 150, 218
  obligation 51, 56–7, 163, 198, 200–3, 208, 210–15, 221, 229, 234, 239n.64, 240n.72, 243n.100
  pride 98, 198–9, 219
  recognition *see* kinship, recognition
  resemblance 67, 125, 141, 201, 207, 218–19, 225, 230, 252, 256, 258
  reunions 65, 71, 89, 97, 101, 104, 113
  structure 189n.122, 191–2, 195–6, 202, 242n.94, 245n.134
father–daughter incest 11–12, 34–84, 158–9, 208, 246, 248, 253
Female Gothic 4, 7–12, 26n.29, 27n.38, 34, 91–4, 100, 130n.24, 140, 142, 149, 153, 177, 180n.4, 249, 266, 269, 271n.9, 275n.73, 278, 281n.3
Fincher, Max 250, 260–2
Finney, Gail 33n.116, 120, 122
Fitzgerald, Lauren 23, 27n.35, 93, 157, 281n.3
Foucault, Michel 20, 25n.21, 108, 135n.79, 145, 148, 184n.49, 247, 250, 278, 281n.4
Frank, Marcie 255, 257, 272n.32, 273n.48
French Revolution 195–6, 241n.85, 268
Freudian theory 4, 10–12, 18–19, 34–6, 63, 246, 255
  critiques of 18, 31n.87, 36–7, 74n.9, 74n.10, 74n.14, 75n.19, 75n.24
  see also Oedipus complex

Gallop, Jane 74n.13, 82n.110, 83n.130
Gamer, Michael 22, 33n.113, 41
genetic sexual attraction 21–2, 26n.75, 30n.84, 32n.108, 75n.26, 87–9, 99, 113–14, 118, 120, 207, 235n.5
  see also family, attraction to
genetics 21–2, 30n.84, 87–8, 113, 190–1, 210, 239n.63, 239n.67, 246
gift theory 32n.106, 151–2, 182–3n.32, 184n.47, 202–3, 211–12, 236n.31, 240n.72
Gilbert, Sandra and Susan Gubar 10, 18
Gill, Pat 16–17
Godwin, William 63–4, 68
Goetz, William R. 119, 123, 125
Gramsci, Antonio 6
Greenberg, Maurice 21, 89
GSA *see* genetic sexual attraction
guardian–ward 47, 49, 52, 54–5, 57–9, 144, 149, 158–60, 182n.32, 210

Haggerty, George 2, 12, 24n.6, 247, 249, 252–3, 262, 267, 269, 274n.68–9
Harpold, Terence 63–4

INDEX

Herman, Judith Lewis and Lisa Hirschman 4, 182n.28, 183n.40, 183n.45
heteronormativity 6–7, 23, 91, 108, 153, 178, 247–50, 261, 265–70, 279
Hoeveler, Diane Long 11–13, 17, 26n.24, 37–8, 54–5, 63–4, 68, 72, 80n.78, 180n.6, 201, 233
Hogle, Jerrold E. 131n.30, 185n.57, 280
Holcombe, Lee 161, 163, 186n.70
Hunt, Lynn Avery 260

ideology 6–7, 46, 91, 108, 141, 145, 148, 178, 216, 233, 242n.88, 247, 252, 262
illegitimacy 152, 196, 198–9, 208
imprisonments 11, 28n.51, 39, 53–5, 60–1, 72, 78n.60, 80n.90, 81n.104, 82n.104, 95–7, 100, 105, 108, 116, 136n.97, 141, 144, 150, 156, 162–8, 171, 175, 189n.113, 206, 208, 217, 230, 249, 267
  convents and 56, 80n.90, 171, 176, 206
incest see brother–sister incest; cousins, incest between; father–daughter incest; mother–son incest; uncle–niece incest
incest prohibition 15, 34–7, 65, 79n.71, 86, 89, 102, 108, 145, 181–2n.23, 216, 246–7
incest taboo see incest prohibition
individual choice and rights 133n.58, 142, 154, 163, 176–7, 186n.73, 195–8, 203–8, 212–15, 218, 223–4, 228–9, 234, 236n.30
  see also rights
inheritance 6–7, 13, 16–17, 20, 42–5, 62, 89, 95, 99, 109, 116, 121, 142–9, 153, 156–9, 163–5, 167–9, 174–9, 181n.13, 182n.25, 192–4, 201, 207, 222–3, 226–7, 230, 251, 257
  see also law, inheritance
Irigaray, Luce 10, 65–6, 184n.48, 239n.60, 242n.94, 247

Johnson, Claudia L. 94, 161, 176, 188n.96

Ker, Anne
  Mysterious Count; or, Montville Castle, The 28n.58
Kilgour, Maggie 11, 141–2, 149–50, 165, 169, 177
kinship 14–17, 22–3, 81–2n.103, 88, 123, 126, 190–200, 230, 232, 240–1n.78
  evidence of 110–12, 119, 171–2, 188n.94, 188n.95
  recognition 60, 67, 101, 129n.12, 133n.55, 135n.83, 136n.99, 170–1, 187n.89, 207, 238n.57, 256–7
  see also family, attraction to
Klekar, Cynthia 202–3, 211
  and Linda Zionkowski 21, 184n.47, 236n.31
Kuper, Adam 17, 29n.74, 30n.82, 199, 204, 235n.25, 239n.67, 242n.90

Lacan, Jacques 84n.133
Lamb, Lady Caroline 197
  Glenarvon 197, 212–13, 215–17
Landry, Donna 259, 262, 273n.54–5
law 19, 23–4, 109–11, 139–44, 155, 161, 175, 179n.2, 181n.13, 182n.25
  customs as 25n.9, 26n.23, 110–12, 145, 154, 216
  incest 19–20, 48–50, 79n.65, 108–11, 148, 193–4
  inheritance 19, 89, 163–4, 175–6, 205–6, 227
  marriage 23–4, 49, 79n.65, 193–4
  patriarchal 82n.110, 83–4n.130
  property 117, 139–41, 157–65, 186n.71, 188n.101, 188n.105, 205–6, 243n.109
Ledoux, Ellen Malenas 26n.25, 28n.52
Lévi-Strauss, Claude 4, 10, 21, 34–5, 39–40, 51, 86, 123, 191
Lewis, Alethea Brereton
  Nuns of the Desert: or, The Woodland Witches, The 240n.69, 241n.82, 274n.67
Lewis, Matthew 7, 130n.28
  Castle Spectre, The 267
  Monk, The 8, 19, 90–4, 115, 136n.93, 173–4, 251, 264–9
liberty see individual choice and rights; rights
London, April 163, 186n.73

Male Gothic 4–5, 8–9, 26n.29, 238n.58, 249, 270, 271n.9
marriage 39–40, 46–51, 66, 72, 95, 121, 142, 145, 148–54, 179n.2, 190–7, 204, 211, 218, 224, 229, 232–3
  forced 100, 107, 160, 168, 176, 188n.102, 226
  see also commodification of women; exchange of women
Masse, Michelle A. 18
Mauss, Marcel 21, 32n.104, 238n.60, 239n.62
Maynard, John 229, 232

McKinnon, Susan 248, 262–4, 269
Mellor, Anne K. 4–5
Messier, Vartan P. 8, 266
Miles, Robert 10–11, 99, 104, 153, 158, 173, 176, 272n.28
mistaken identity 51, 99, 101
Mitchell, Juliet 10, 180n.7
Moers, Ellen 7, 10, 157
mother–son incest 246–76
Mulvey-Roberts, Marie 274n.59
murder 11, 38, 44, 51, 59, 61, 78n.60, 83n.124, 95–6, 100, 116–17, 140–5, 155–6, 168–9, 172–4, 179, 180–1n.12, 208, 264–70

nation 215–16, 241n.85
Neff, D. S. 274n.57
Nestor, Pauline 224–5
Norton, Rictor 41, 273n.53

obligation *see* family, obligation; gift theory
Oedipus complex 10, 35, 64, 68, 101, 124
Orientalism 67–8, 83n.123, 83n.124, 83n.125, 83n.126, 259
orphans 61, 107, 111, 127, 133n.49, 144, 158, 211, 217

Parsons, Eliza 1–3, 7
 Castle of Wolfenbach, The 2–3, 5–7, 109, 143–57, 181n.17, 182n.28, 238n.56
 Old Friend with a New Face, An 271n.11
paternal authority 51, 55, 101, 104
 see also family, obligation; authority
Perry, Ruth 11, 14–15, 39, 54, 55n.84, 85, 104, 135n.83, 171, 173, 191–2, 198–9, 218, 221, 227, 239n.64, 240–1n.78, 250
Piatti-Farnell, Lorna and Donna Lee Brien 277
Polidori, John 251, 268
 Ernestus Berchtold; or, The Modern Oedipus: A Tale 251, 254, 268–70
Pollak, Ellen 17, 19–20, 57, 148, 193–5
pornography 146–7, 182n.31
primogeniture *see* inheritance; law, property; property
property 25n.9, 142–6, 156–9, 186n.70, 225–8
 women as 57, 98, 105, 143–5, 152, 158–64, 175, 179, 207, 215, 233, 240n.78
 see also inheritance; law, property
prostitution 165–6, 246
punishment 47, 108, 111–13, 116–17, 125, 135n.77, 136n.87, 162, 165

Punter, David and Glennis Byron 4–5, 252

queer theory 6–7, 247–51, 262–4, 266–8
 see also queer, sexuality
Quilligan, Maureen 16

Radcliffe, Ann 7–8, 27n.36, 37, 93, 130n.28, 132n.40, 157, 266, 269
 Castles of Athlin and Dunbayne, The 5, 29n.68, 94–100
 Italian, The 9, 12–13, 30n.80, 38, 131n.37, 143, 168–78, 266
 Mysteries of Udolpho, The 13, 30n.79, 96–7, 143, 157–68
 Romance of the Forest, The 40–1, 52–62, 96
 Sicilian Romance, A 5, 29n.68, 96, 100–6, 243n.97, 271n.17
Rajan, Tilottama 64
rape 51, 74n.9, 91, 94, 143–4, 153, 158, 164–6, 168, 170, 173–4, 180–1n.12, 187n.80, 208, 259, 264–8
Reform Act of 1832 223
revenge 95, 116
Richardson, Alan 32n.110, 92, 104, 106, 119, 133n.63
Richardson, Samuel 77n.50
 Clarissa 187n.82
 Pamela 77n.50, 132n.45
rights 133n.58, 142, 154, 163, 175, 178–9, 184n.47, 187n.84, 194–6, 223, 234, 236n.28, 243n.109
 see also individual choice and rights
Robinson, Mary 273
 Vancenza; or, The Dangers of Credulity 273n.52
Roche, Regina Maria 196
 Children of the Abbey, The 271n.17
 Clermont 20, 196, 203–8, 257
Romanticism 32n.110, 33n.112, 90
 incest and 22, 32n.111, 86–7, 90, 92, 106, 117–28, 130n.27, 133n.63, 134n.67, 137n.107, 138n.132, 146
Rooney, Caroline 85, 123, 128, 128n.4, 138n.123
Rousseau, Jean-Jacques 184n.47, 195, 237n.48, 240n.76
 Emile, or On Education 184n.47, 186n.68, 241n.80, 241n.83
 Social Contract, or Principles of Political Right, The 184n.47, 240n.76
Rubin, Gayle 10, 36, 39–40, 62

303

sadomasochism 247–8, 265, 274n.68, 278, 281n.4
Sanchez-Eppler, Karen 246
sentimental novels 22, 43–4, 76n.77, 77n.50, 87, 90, 129n.11, 184n.50, 196, 199, 208
servants 150, 166, 177, 183n.44, 199, 206, 224–5, 227–8, 238n.55, 252, 255
sexual abuse 91, 128n.2
  see also violence, sexual
sexual aversion 21, 210–11
  see also genetics; Westermarck effect
sexuality 35–7, 56, 67, 59, 83n.120, 94, 104, 109, 145, 175, 181n.22, 184n.49, 213–14, 229, 231–2, 247–8, 253–5
  constraints on 100, 112, 134n.65, 182n.28
  maternal 78n.56, 78n.61, 131n.37, 248–52, 255–6, 260–4
  queer 253–70
  transgressive 94, 134n.66, 178, 216–17, 224, 242n.88, 249–51, 255–9, 261–3
Shelley, Mary 63–4
  Frankenstein 32n.111
  Matilda 28n.58, 40–1, 63–73, 273n.44
Shepher, Joseph 4, 137n.112, 138n.132, 190–1, 246
Sheriffe, Sarah 15
  Correlia, or the Mystic Tomb 15, 78n.61, 86, 271n.11, 273n.44
siblings 22–3, 87–90, 99–101, 125, 201, 207, 209, 219–23, 230, 243n.97
  see also brother–sister incest
Sleath, Eleanor 106–7, 134n.70, 134n.73
  Orphan of the Rhine, The 5, 15, 106–17, 210
Smith, Charlotte 196
  Emmeline 78n.60, 79n.68, 196–203, 271n.17
Smith, David Livingstone 21–2, 108, 129n.10, 239n.63
Spooner, Catherine 277
Staves, Susan 139
stepmothers 100–1, 249, 271n.19
Stevenson, John Allen 120
Stone, Lawrence 14, 29n.64
suicide 30n.79, 69–70, 84n.130, 252, 258–9
sympathy 85–6, 171, 128, 136n.99, 171, 230

Tadmor, Naomi 14
Taylor, Jeremy 148–9
thefts *see* usurpations
Thomas, Elizabeth 196
  Purity of Heart, or, The Ancient Costume 20, 197, 212–17, 260
traffic in women *see* exchange of women

uncle–niece incest 3–5, 13, 20–1, 25n.9, 47, 60–2, 139–89, 203
usurpations 13, 17, 105, 139–45, 148, 153–4, 158, 163–5, 168–9, 173–9, 265

violence 4–5, 11, 16–17, 46, 54, 79n.73, 93, 100, 140, 145, 155, 172, 175, 179, 215, 258–9, 263–4, 267, 278–80
  sexual 4–5, 20, 57, 67, 91, 143–7, 157–61, 164–6, 170–3, 174–5, 187n.91, 243n.95, 248–9, 265–6
  see also rape
virtue 44, 54, 97, 147, 162, 183n.44, 187n.82, 213–16
von Sneidern, Maja-Lisa 120, 137n.110

Wallace, Diana 19, 39, 72, 142, 269
  and Andrew Smith 8, 275
Walpole, Horace 1–2, 19, 76n.36, 249, 253–4, 267
  Castle of Otranto, The 40–52, 140, 165, 173, 254–5
  Mysterious Mother, The 1–2, 5, 7, 131n.37, 251–9, 268–70
Warner, Michael 25n.8, 25n.20
Watt, James 8, 18–19, 42
weapons 28n.58, 51, 54, 155, 170, 172–3, 217, 241n.84, 258, 266
Westermarck, Edward 15
Westermarck effect 15–16, 38–9, 75n.24, 107–8, 133n.63, 239n.63, 240n.70
White, Leslie 86–7, 89
Williams, Anne 18
Williams, Raymond 6, 25n.19
Wollstonecraft, Mary 63, 187n.84, 195
  Vindication of the Rights of Woman, A 237n.48
wounded heroes 61, 96, 99, 103, 132n.44, 231–2, 242n.87, 244n.125
Wright, Angela 11, 141, 174

EU authorised representative for GPSR:
Easy Access System Europe, Mustamäe tee 50,
10621 Tallinn, Estonia
gpsr.requests@easproject.com

www.ingramcontent.com/pod-product-compliance
Ingram Content Group UK Ltd.
Pitfield, Milton Keynes, MK11 3LW, UK
UKHW021839140426
5217IPUK00022B/1520